BRITISH CINEMAS
AND THEIR AUDIENCES

This is a volume in the
Arno Press collection

ASPECTS OF FILM

Advisory Editor
Garth S. Jowett

See last pages of this volume
for a complete list of titles.

British
Cinemas
and their
Audiences

J. P. Mayer

With a New Introduction and Bibliography

ARNO PRESS
A New York Times Company
New York • 1978

Editorial Supervision: MARIA CASALE

———◆———

Reprint Edition 1978 by Arno Press Inc.

New Introduction and Bibliography
Copyright © 1978 by J. P. Mayer

Reprinted by permission of J. P. Mayer

ASPECTS OF FILM
ISBN for complete set: 0-405-11125-8
See last pages of this volume for titles.

Manufactured in the United States of America

———◆———

Library of Congress Cataloging in Publication Data

Mayer, Jacob Peter, 1903-
    British cinemas and their audiences.

    (Aspects of film)
    Reprint of the 1948 ed. published by D. Dobson,
London, which was issued in series: International
library of theatre and cinema.
    Bibliography: p.
    Includes index.
    1. Moving-picture audiences--Great Britain.
I. Title. II. Series. III. Series: Interna-
tional library of theatre and cinema.
PN1995.9.A8M25 1978   301.16'2   77-11387
ISBN 0-405-11141-X

FOREWORD

The present volume was published in 1948 by Dennis Dobson of London as a sequel to my *Sociology of Film*, which had been published two years earlier by Faber and Faber, also in London. The latter book was included in the film series published by the Arno Press in 1972, to which I have added a *Retrospect* (pp. xv-1viii). I have re-examined my findings and the methods applied and drawn some general conclusions, not only in respect of film influence, but also with regard to the effects of television on our contemporary audiences. An extensive, but by no means complete, bibliography was also attached to these pages. It is gratifying to know that my earlier volume has until now been issued in four impressions.

I am, consequently, not too surprised that the Arno Press has now decided to reprint also the sequel to *Sociology of Film* and invited me to add a few additional observations. Again I have added to my retrospective remarks a bibliography which ought to be used in conjunction with that of the earlier volume.

I recently had the opportunity of investigating some 200 children of the age groups 5-8 at our primary school in Stoke Poges, in respect of their television viewing. A questionnaire was submitted which was filled in under the guidance of the teaching personnel and some 20-30% of the children were kept awake, or showed fright and shock phenomena after watching television programmes. Further investigation is imperative, particularly individual interviews. I hope to publish the results of this investigation in full at a later date.

In the meantime I would like to express my gratitude to the Headmistress of the school, Mrs. Eve O'Sullivan, for giving me facilities to undertake this investigation. I also wish to express my profound gratitude to my Secretary, Mrs. Valerie Andrews, for her devoted, constructive and efficient help.

August 1977
J.P.Mayer
Tocqueville Research Centre
University of Reading
England

INTRODUCTION

1

I must begin these observations with an autocritical reflection. When I wrote this volume, I attempted to describe the film experience following Lévy-Bruhl with the concept: *participation mystique*. However, when I wrote my *Retrospect* to *Sociology of Film* in 1970, I abandoned this term and replaced it, again following Lévy-Bruhl's thought during the last phase of his life, by the term *participation mythique*. I permit myself to refer the reader to the closer argument in my *Retrospect* which it is perhaps superfluous to repeat here. Mythical conceptions persist in human nature. One needs only to think of the contemporary interest in witchcraft or astrology to prove this point. (When I had sent my friend David Riesman the new edition of *Sociology of Film*, he wrote to me: "I agree with what you say about the contemporary interest in witchcraft, except my students want *to be* witches!") Perhaps late phases of civilisation like ours, stressed and strained by over-bureaucratisation and sophisticated technology, cause this eruption of irrational and mythical forces which have been dormant or subterranean. Perhaps, too, these factors explain the inclination of our contemporaries towards visualisation. All these points are more fully explained and documented in the *Retrospect* to our previous volume.

Yet I do not think that these auto-critical remarks prejudice the two main studies which the present volume puts before the reader. The first study attempts to relate the film experience to the patterns of life. I believe the personal documents which we have obtained speak for themselves. Here I refer only to two short paragraphs: many of the horror, terror or fright examples, we read on page 147 of the present volume, deserve the closest study (see for instance documents 24, 46, 26). These experiences are of such intensity and persistence that they must raise the question whether the mental health of the community is not seriously endangered by their uncontrolled continuance.... Play, play with shock, the love of adventure, thrill, excitement, suspense are indispensable elements of human nature. There can be no objection that films should to a certain extent appeal to those instincts or emotional attitudes. But it is an immense problem to what extent the degree of suspense, thrill, etc. is healthy or when it becomes harmful. We believe our documents, which are in fact self-confessions, may provide material to solve this problem.

We believe it is poslsible to study the psychological mechanisms of suspense, thrill, fright and similar phenomena in relation to their social effects. Once these phenomena are adequately studied, it might be possible to say where, in principle, their use by the visual media of cinema and television may have a destructive or positive result.

I conclude this first study of *British Cinemas and their Audiences* with a remarkable document by one of our contributors, who was at the time he wrote his film biography 25 years old (see our document 60). Indeed in this document films appear as the dominating educational influence on human life. The author of this fine piece of self-analysis is indeed movie-made. It seems essential to quote our author himself: ''...the films had built a conception of life, which life itself, tended to contradict, my ideals made through films, not being realized in true-life. But instead of making me disbelieve in and dislike film-life, it made me bitter towards real life. Films taught all the things I should like to associate with life. Crime does not pay, the wrong-doer getting his just deserts; kindness pays; love-thy-neighbour; plumping for the 'small' man 'flaying' the rich; making the best of life; 'true' love wins in marriage; decency; the mild and honest man triumping over the immoral, unscrupulous one; all the ideals worthy of life, which we would all like to see, or would we? At least, one would presume so. It is oft-remarked that films should be more like life. If they were, people would be disgusted to 'see' how they lived and would protest strongly; in fact, of course, such a film would never get past the censor. So, I maintain, as that course is impossible, that, as has also been said, that life should be more like the films. I try to live my life as films would have us believe, and they have helped me to get a great deal out of life, though it is 'tough' going'' (pp. 151-2). I feel I have nothing to add to the few lines evaluating the confession of our film-made author which I wrote at that time: "One might well ponder over these sentences and put them into the context of European ethical reflection. (But it would require a whole book to trace the process of how our value patterns have become increasingly empty and meaningless. Perhaps, one day, I shall write this book.) It is a long and depressive journey from Aristotle's *Nicomachean Ethics* to this document, but it may well be that our young author who so sincerely strives to formulate his *Weltanschauung* is not less representative for our contemporary moral conception of life than the great Greek philosopher was for his age" (p. 152).

Many of our documents have found their way, not always with my consent, into other publications on film problems.

2

Our second study is concerned with film preferences (pp. 153-288). Here again the answers to our questionnaire speak for themselves. The short interpretation of them (pp. 239-244) underlines the salient points. "(1) In what state is the present mass taste with regard to films? (2) Is the film industry right when it says: 'we provide the entertainment the public wants'? Both questions are, we believe, firmly answered for the careful student of our documents. These answers are by no means encouraging in the light of a general diagnosis of our contemporary scene. We take the second question first, because it is the easier one to answer. However depressing the standards of film taste may be, it is certain from the perusal of our documents that the British film exhibiters do *not* provide the entertainment the public wants. Almost the whole so-called second feature output is rejected by a majority of our contributors...; the cheap detective or murder films are unmistakeably disliked. Nor are the 'stupendous' American musicals liked by all. These definite and sometimes even refreshingly abusive criticisms by our contributors are the more remarkable as most of them are not 'highbrows'. (Some who think they are highbrows suffer from lack of self-analysis.) They are all ordinary average English, Scottish, Welsh or Irish people. We quote for example a wonderful passage from document 37A: 'Murder and mystery films: I dislike those with a corpse in every reel, secret panels and rooms, hooded fiends and other childish devices. Usually the villain is either perfectly obvious or else the plot is so complex that you end up by wondering if you yourself did the horrors you have seen.' It seems obvious that the majority of our writers have a definitely different taste from the American film goer in Middle Town for whom Hollywood mainly caters'' (p. 239).

At the end of this second study we venture to formulate some further conclusions. ''The documents show that most contributors have only seen American or British films. Those who have seen Russian, French or German films regret that they cannot see more of them. This, clearly, reflects on the commercial practice of the big exhibitor circuits whose managers alone must be blamed for the serious and potentially dangerous lack of internationalism in the film tastes of our contemporary masses.

We believe that the questions which were put at the beginning of this interpretation have been answered implicitly. One can say that in spite of the dictatorship in taste with all its serious repercussions on our value patterns, as it is exercised by the circuit monopolists, the hope of raising film taste is not entirely forlorn—yet.

The forefathers of British audiences once listened to Shakespeare. It was their response which made the Elizabethan theatre possible.

Our material—we must stress it again—defies any easy attempt at typification; either of a sociological or psychological nature. Of course there are affinities between class stratum and film preferences (see for example Document 15A). Moreover there are relations between temperamental structure and film taste (Document 42A), but we did not feel justified in drawing general conclusions in this respect. It is quite possible that further research might usefully start where we left off.

It is also true to say that many of our documents show little discrimination. They accept what is put before them, they do not select.

The ultimate choice between a further levelling down or a constructive use of those positive norms which lie open to everyone who has read our documents responsibly is a decision of cultural leadership which was a self-evident truth in the Athens of Euripides as in the Paris of Louis XIV.

A democratic State, fully aware of its task, requires a leading and responsible *elite* not only in the sphere of politics but also in the realm of culture" (pp. 243-4).

Perhaps our conclusions of 1948 should be somewhat qualified now. The dramatic decline in cinema audiences in Europe and in America and the corresponding increase of television audiences, to which I have referred in my *Retrospect*, have forced the film distributors and our television managers to show greater internationalism. No doubt we see now more French, Japanese, Swedish and Italian films than we saw at that time.

3

We must now ask ourselves: is it justified to republish a book which analysed film influences and film tastes nearly 30 years ago? I have pointed out in my *Retrospect* in *Sociology of Film* that cinema audiences have dramatically decreased since 1943, when the social survey report about cinema audiences, appended to this volume, was undertaken. Thus I wrote in 1970: "For the last 10 years cinema audiences have decreased in number by more than half. While, 10 years ago, the cinema goer went to the cinema 23 times a year, he now goes less than 10 times." This development has, since then, continued.

However, as many of the films which have been discussed in *British Cinemas and their Audiences* are now being shown on television, it seemed to us important to remind the present generation of television viewers what their parents have felt and thought 30 years ago when they saw the same films. No doubt the average film-ware shown on television shows a higher degree of 'sophistication'. Crime, sex and violence are not any more simple and straightforward, they have become complex and not rarely vicious.

Consequently I am convinced that the main trends of our findings have only been strengthened. As television viewing has dramatically increased, our children, as my own recent investigations reveal, spend some 30 hours per week before the television screen. This does not only apply to British, but also American, children and no pious or palliative suggestions by the Annan Report will change this fact.

Children from 5-8 years see on television films which frighten them, keep them awake and encourage them to imitate their heroes, like *Starsky and Hutch* or the invincible *Six Million Dollar Man*, not to mention *Dr. Who*.

Nor should we omit that sexual 'permissiveness' begins now at the age of 13 upwards, with boys and girls, which is certainly to a large extent due to the lack of content control, not only by the authors but also by the film exhibitors and, of course, the parents. A film like *Last Tango in Paris* must certainly have introduced hundreds of thousands of youngsters into varied sexual practices, not to mention other films. Perhaps in another few years such films will be shown on the television!

Having almost concluded this paragraph on a rather pessimistic note, I feel I should mention a film entitled *A Touch of Love* which I have seen a few days ago on British television. In it a young woman is expecting a baby, after a rather furtive love affair during one night. She insists on having her baby and bringing it up herself against all reasonable advice of her elders and the friends of her own generation. Against the background of the mass age and its negative "permissiveness" the young woman perseveres. By chance she meets the man, a tender and sensitive television announcer, who, for one night, has broken out of his loneliness, apparently assuming that a young woman is "on the pill" if she spends the night with a man.... At another chance meeting, perhaps 3 years later, the man meets his one-night companion again, but she doesn't reveal to him that he is the father of her child. They part from each other, not light-heartedly, but separated by misreading the language of their souls. Perhaps the young man is less aware of the inner life of the girl than she is of his; it is easy to give in the bodily drives, but it is difficult to harmonise soul and body. The film's message is simple but significant: a new life can grow out of such an occasional encounter. A mother's love is perennial. Here is a film which has depth, tension, a film which is critical of our time but not despairing. One must congratulate the B.B.C. for having shown this film at 9:25 p.m. and one can only hope that many thousands of young people have seen it and taken in its profound message. But, alas, one swallow does not make a summer.

I have suggested in my *Retrospect* various measures as would seem to me necessary steps in cultural planning, which has always seemed to me more vital than economic planning. I am suggesting the introduction of television and film appreciation in all schools from primary schools upwards and also teacher-training to enable teachers to give critical appreciations of film and television material. Finally, one would have to create a greater interest within universities to study the effects of film and television.

4

Some final conclusions of these observations seem obvious:
1. The visual experience has a stronger impact on human beings than reason, particularly on the young. The image overpowers, as it were, reason and has brought about a dangerous disequilibrium of the human being. Our contemporary human being is to a large extent visually oriented. Read for example the following extract from the *Slough Evening Mail*, 17 May 1977: "The sight of three Mafia gangsters chasing a hero across the television screen was too much for a South African viewer, who pulled out his gun and put a bullet through the screen. Mannie Saldsman, a television repair shop owner, said in Johannesburg today a customer in the store was watching the latest episode of Rich Man, Poor Man. In the sequence 'Poor Man' Tom Jordache was being chased across the stage of a New York cinema by the gangsters. The excited customer leaped to his feet, yelled 'I'll get them'—and shot a gangster in the back." This example is telling as far as the psychological mechanisms are concerned. Of course, we would have to know much more about the person who used the gun.
2. Perhaps the concept "mythical participation" needs some further explanation. Myth does not replace reality, but it has

a reality of its own. The mythical object has for the viewer an immediate identity and is not in need of later logical reflection. In fact myth has a logic of its own.[1]

3. I am fully aware that my studies are qualitative and not quantitative. Many of my critics who have accepted my findings, questioned my qualitative approach to these problems. Though I am convinced that some compromise between quantitative and qualitative studies of subjects under discussion might be possible, if the financial means were to be made available, I still maintain that only a qualitative approach towards the phenomena of film and television influences can be constructive.

I have quoted in my *Retrospect*, Goethe, and I quote him here again:

Was ist das Allgemeine?	What is the general?
Der einzelne Fall	The individual case
Was ist das Besondere?	What is the particular?
Millionen Faelle	Millions of cases

I concluded *British Cinemas and their Audiences* with a passage from Seneca. This new introduction I wish to close also with a quotation from Seneca, which I take the liberty of borrowing from Professor Michael Grant's admirable book on *The Gladiators*, to which I have drawn attention in my bibliography. "Man is a thing which is scared to mankind. But nowadays he is killed in play, for fun! It was once a sin to teach him how to inflict wounds or receive them. But now he is led out naked and defenceless and provides a sufficient show by his death." I assure my readers that this frightening Roman parallel is not far-fetched: I have recently seen on television on a Sunday afternoon after 2:00 p.m. a film entitled *Demetrius and the Gladiators*, an apt illustration to Professor Grant's book. You saw a kind of pudding consisting of a portion of sex and 'love', cruelty, the gladiator's sadism, with a little mixture of Christianity—all apt to introduce hundreds of thousands of children into the nauseating and frightening decadence of the late Roman Empire.

---

[1] Cf. Ernst Cassirer, *Wesen und Wirkung des Symbolsbegriffs*, Darmstadt, 1956.

BIBLIOGRAPHY

METHOD—GENERAL

Baudrillard, J. *La Societe de Consommation*. Préface de J.P. Mayer, Paris, 1970. Fundamental.

Cazeneuve, J., and Victoroff, D. *La Sociologie. Les Idees—Les Oeuvres—Les Hommes*, Paris, 1970. Informative.

Cazeneuve, J. *Dix Grandes Notions de Sociologie*, Paris, 1976. Suggestive.

Dumazedier, J. *Sociologie empirique du Loisir: Critique et Contre-Critique de la Civilisation du Loisir,* Paris, 1974.

Duvignaud, J., ed. *La Sociologie: Guide alphabetique,* Paris, 1972. Useful.

Gadamer, H.G., and Vogler, P. *Neue Anthropologie*, 6 vols., Munich, 1972. Encyclopaedic and fundamental.

Gans, H.J. *Popular Culture and High Culture*, New York, 1974.

Hirst, I.R.C., and Reckie, W.D., ed. *The Consumer Society*, London, 1977. Suggestive.

Klages, H. *Die unruhige Gesellschaft: Untersuchungen uber Grenzen und Probleme sozialer Stabilitat*, Munich, 1975.

Krüll, M. *Schizophrenie und Gesellschaft*, Munich, 1977.

Leff, G. *The Dissolution of the Medieval Outlook: An Essay on the Intellectual and Spiritual Change in Fourteenth Century*, New York, 1976.

Makkreel, R.A. *Dilthey: Philosopher of Human Studies*, Princeton, 1975.

Malraux, A. *L'Homme precaire et La Litterature*, Paris, 1977.

Montagu, A. *The Nature of Human Aggression*, New York, 1976. Important.

O'Higgins, P. *Censorship in Britain*, London, 1972.

Radzinowicz, Sir Leon, and King, J. *The Growth of Crime: The International Experience*, New York, 1977. Fundamental.

Scheler, M. *Spate Schriften*, Bern, 1976. A classic.

Thibault-Laulan, A.-M. *Le Langage de L'Image*, Paris, 1971.

Thibault-Laulan, A.-M. *L'Image dans la Societe contemporaine*, Paris, 1971. Fundamental.

PSYCHOLOGY

Davie, R., and others, *From Birth to Seven: A Report of the National Child Development Study*, London, 1972.

Fromm, E. *The Crisis of Psychoanalysis: Essays on Freud, Marx and Social Psychology*, Penguin, 1970.

Hofstätter, P. *Psychologie*, Frankfurt am Main, 1957.
Jung, C.G. *Dialectique de L'Inconscient*, Paris, 1973.
Jung, C.G. *Un Mythe moderne*, Paris, 1974.
MacLeod, R.B. *The Persistent Problems of Psychology*, Pittsburgh, 1975. Very suggestive.
Piaget, J. *The Origin of Intelligence in the Child*, Penguin, 1977.
Rothacker, E. *Die Schichten der Personlichkeit*, Bonn, 1965.
Wallon, H., ed. *La Vie mentale: Encyclopedie francaise*, vol. VIII, Paris, 1938. Indispensable.

ETHICS

Bourke, V.J. *History of Ethics: A Comprehensive Survey of the History of Ethics from the Early Greeks to the Present Time*, New York, 1968.
Höffe, O. and others, ed. *Lexikon der Ethik*, Munich, 1977.
Holbrook, D. *Sex and Dehumanization*, London, 1972.
Longford, Lord, *Pornography Report*, London, 1972.

HISTORY—HISTORY OF AUDIENCES

Dubuy, G. *Le Temps des Cathedrales: L'Art et La Societe, 968-1420*. Paris, 1976. A classic.
Grant, M. *The World of Rome*, London, 1974. Outstanding.
Grant, M. *The Gladiators*, Penguin, 1971. Fundamental.
Heer, F. *The Medieval World: Europe from 1100 to 1350*, London, 1974.
Lough, J. *Paris Theatre Audiences in the Seventeenth and Eighteenth Centuries*, Oxford, 1972.
Moore, R.W. *The Roman Commonwealth*, London, 1943.
Ray-Flaude, H. *Le Cercle Magique: Essai sur le Theatre en rond a la Fin du Moyen Age*, Paris, 1973.
Walcot, P. *Greek Drama in its Theatrical and Social Context*, Cardiff, 1976. Valuable.

MASS MEDIA—GENERAL

Annan, Lord, *Report of the Committee on the Future of Broadcasting*, London, 1977.
Appia, H., and Cassen, B. *Presse, Radio et Television en Grande Bretagne*, Paris, 1969.

Balle, F. *Institutions et Publics des Moyens d'Information: Presse-Radiodiffusion-Television*, Paris, 1973. Very useful.

Bertrand, J.-C. *Les Mass Media aux Etats-Unis*, Paris, 1974.

Burgelin, O. *La Communication de Masse*, Paris, 1970.

Cazeneuve, J. *La Societe de L'Ubiquite: Communication et Diffusion*, Paris, 1972.

Cohen, St., and Young, J. *The Manufacture of News: Deviance, Social Problems and the Mass Media*, London, 1976.

Devol, K.S., ed. *Mass Media and the Supreme Court: The Legacy of the Warren Years*, New York, 1971.

Feldmann, E. *Neue Studien zur Theorie der Massenmedien*, Munich, 1969.

Golding, P. *The Mass Media*, London, 1974.

Graham, H.D., and Gurr, T.R. *Violence in America: Historical and Comparative Perspectives*, New York, 1969.

Howitt, D. and Cumberbatch, G. *Mass Media Violence and Society*, London, 1975.

Kato, H. *Japanese Research on Mass Communication: Selected Abstracts*, Honolulu, 1974.

Larsen, O.N., ed. *Violence and the Mass Media*, New York, 1968. Fundamental and immensely suggestive.

McQuail, D., ed. *Sociology of Mass Communications*, Penguin, 1972.

Read, W.H. *America's Massmedia Merchants*, Baltimore, 1976.

Seymour-Ure, C. *The Political Impact of Mass Media*, London, 1974.

Turnstall, J. *The Media Are American: Anglo-American Media in the World*, London, 1977. Important.

CINEMA—FILM

Bergman, I. *Face a Face*, Paris, 1976.

Brenderson, A.F. *Critical Approaches to Federico Fellini's "8½"*, New York, 1974.

Cohen, L.H. *The Cultural-Political Tradition and Developments of the Soviet Cinema, 1917-1972*, New York, 1974.

Higham, C. *The Art of the American Film*, Anchor, 1974.

Jacob, L. *The Rise of the American Film*, New York, 1969.

Karpf, S.L. *The Gangster Film: Emergence, Variation and Decay of a Genre*, New York, 1973.

Keilhacker, M. and others. *Filmische Darstellungsformen im Erleben des Kindes*, Munich, 1967.

Kracauer, S. *Nature of Film: The Redemption of Physical Reality*. London, 1961.

Morin, E. *Les Stars*, Paris, 1972.

Noguez, D. *Presentation, Cinema, Theorie, Lectures*, Paris, 1973.

Rimberg, J.D. *The Motion Picture in the Soviet-Union: 1918-1952. A Sociological Analysis*, New York, 1973.

Stephenson, R. and Detrix, J.R. *The Cinema as Art,* Pelican, 1972.
Tudie, A. *Image and Influence: Studies in the Sociology of Film,* London, 1974.
UNESCO. *The Influence of the Cinema on Children and Adolescents: An Annotated International Bibliography,* Paris, 1961. Useful; see Nos. 104 and 142.

TELEVISION

BBC. *Children as Viewers and Listeners: A Study by the BBC for its General Advisory Council,* London, 1974.
Brown, R., ed. *Children and Television,* London, 1976.
Elliott, P. *The Making of a Television Series: A Case Study in the Sociology of Culture,* London, 1972.
Goodhardt, G.J., and others. *The Television Audience: Patterns of Viewing,* Saxon House, 1975.
Glucksmann, A. *Violence on the Screen,* London, 1971.
Hagemann, M. *Fernsehen im Leben der Kinder,* Bern, 1972.
Noble, G. *Children in Front of the Small Screen,* London, 1975.
Shulman, M. *The Ravenous Eye: The Impact of the Fifth Factor,* London, 1971. Important.
Smith, A. *The Shadow in the Cave: The Broadcaster, the Audience and the State,* London, 1976.
Whitehouse, M. *"Who Does She Think She Is?"* London, 1971.

ASTROLOGY—WITCHCRAFT

Boll, F., and Bezold, C. *Sternglaube und Sterndeutung: Die Geschichte und das Wesen der Astrologie,* Leipsic, 1931.
Davies, R.T. *Four Centuries of Witch Belief,* London, 1947.
Eisler, R. *The Royal Art of Astrology,* London, 1946.
Mandrou, R. *Magistrats et Sorciers au XVIIIe Siecle: Une Analyse de Psychologie politique,* Paris, 1968.
Marwick, M., ed. *Witchcraft and Sorcery,* Pelican, 1970.
Palou, J. *La Sorcellerie,* Paris, 1960.

INTERNATIONAL THEATRE AND CINEMA

EDITED BY HERBERT MARSHALL

British Cinemas and their Audiences

Sociological Studies

From *Ivan the Terrible* (see Introduction page 9)

British Cinemas and their Audiences

Sociological Studies

by J. P. Mayer

London DENNIS DOBSON LTD

First published in Great Britain in 1948 by Dennis Dobson
Ltd., 12 Park Place, St. James's, London, S.W.1. All rights
reserved. Printed in Great Britain by Whitehill (Printers)
Ltd., Birmingham
141/R

CONTENTS

LIST OF ILLUSTRATIONS

'It has always been with me a test of the sense and candour of any one belonging to the opposite party, whether he allowed Burke to be a great man . . . The simple clue to all his reasonings on politics is, I think, as follows. He did not agree with some writers that that mode of government is necessarily the best which is the cheapest. He saw in the construction of society other principles at work, and other capacities of fulfilling the desires, and perfecting the nature of man, besides those of securing the equal enjoyment of the means of animal life, and doing this at as little expense as possible. He thought that the wants and happiness of men were not to be provided for, as we provided for those of a herd of cattle, merely by attending to their physical necessities. He thought more nobly of his fellows. He knew that man had affections and passions and powers of imagination, as well as hunger and thirst, and the sense of heat and cold. He took his idea of political society from the pattern of private life, wishing, as he himself expresses it, to incorporate the domestic charities with the orders of the state, and to blend them together. He strove to establish an analogy between the compact which binds together the community at large, and that which binds together the several families that compose it. He knew that the [rules that form the basis of private morality are not founded in reason, that is, in the abstract properties of those things which are the subjects of them, but in the nature of man, and his capacity of being affected by certain things from habit, from imagination, and sentiment, as well as from reason.'

WILLIAM HAZLITT, *On the Character of Burke.*

To B——

PREFACE

THE FOLLOWING STUDIES AND documents implement my *Sociology of Film*, published earlier by Faber & Faber. Yet the present volume does not presuppose the reading of the previous book.

From the author's point of view the present work is more mature, less groping with a new and difficult subject-matter. When I began these studies, more than three years ago, the method and scope of a sociology of film had first to be developed, defined and tested. Thus the first book was to some extent a personal experiment in sociology, whereas the present volume ventures to present its problems more objectively. It treats the cinema as one of the most powerful social institutions of our time.

The Introduction (Chapter I) sketches the cultural and historical framework within which films and audiences must be understood. The ensuing studies are complementary to each other and form, as I hope, an organic unity; they attempt to define and to illustrate the social and psychological influence films have on our lives. Chapter II shows how films may influence the individual—from the cradle to the grave, as it were; Chapter III raises the difficult problem of film preferences against the background of the two preceding studies. 'Retrospect' (Chapter IV) defines the basic assumptions of a constructive film policy in a modern mass state.

It is for the reader to judge whether the author has fulfilled his earlier promise to outline the field for a sociological investigation of the film phenomenon; he sincerely hopes that other and more competent investigators will correct his findings and carry them further.

While working on this material, I have received the most gratifying support without which this book would be less complete. I have to thank the Central Office of Information for allowing me to print the pioneer report on 'The Cinema Audience' of *The Social Survey*, so admirably worked out by Mr Louis Moss and Miss Kathleen Box. I am also deeply indebted to the kindness of Mr Maurice Cowan, the Editor of *Picturegoer*, without whose encouraging and generous help this volume could never have been written.

The material, obtained through the good offices of *Picturegoer*, was primarily selected and transcribed by Miss Drusilla Bursill. I am most grateful to her for her enthusiasm and cool judgment.

To my friend Miss Marjorie Nicholson fell the heavy burden of preparing and rearranging the first draft of this volume for print. I had underestimated the time and strength the completion of an investigation of this nature would require. Moreover, older literary obligations could not any longer be postponed. Thus Miss Nicholson took over with a fresh mind and gave these pages their final shape. As we have worked together for years in the WEA movement, our approach towards the problems of a sociology of film was based on agreement on fundamentals. Without her help, I doubt whether I would have had enough stamina to see this enterprise through, for the hundreds of bad and worse films I had to see throughout these years began to affect sight and soul. I am profoundly obliged to Miss Nicholson.

For some of my prospective reviewers I should like to add a few words on *method*. It is easy to reject the findings of the following pages by saying that there exist 25 to 30 million weekly filmgoers in this country and that this book is based only on some 110 documents though they were selected from about 400. Moreover, all my reaction material is based on many hundreds of minute case studies in addition to those which have gone into this book and which served as corroboration of the documents submitted. Against such criticism one might perhaps observe that before some qualitative structures of film reactions are firmly established, any purely quantitative conclusions are bound to remain vague. Appendix I may show how our case documents could make the figures of *The Social Survey* report concrete and telling. I did not want to burden this book with methodological reflections, as it is, according to R. H. Tawney, 'a commonplace that the characteristic virtue of Englishmen is their power of sustained practical activity, and their characteristic vice a reluctance to test the quality of that activity by reference to principles'. A full exposition of the 'principles' which are implied in this book with regard to the justification of the case-method can be found in Professor Allport's study: *The Use of Personal Documents in Psychological Science*, New York 1942, to which anyone who has doubts about the validity of the case-method should refer.

I take the liberty of referring to this admirable study in my Preface as reference to this book has been overlooked by some of the reviewers of my previous *Sociology of Film*. Perhaps it is not too much to hope that if one draws attention to a source-book in one's Preface, reviewers will take notice of it.

London, June 20th, 1947   J. P. M.

I. INTRODUCTION

THE INADEQUATE ATTENTION THE social and cultural
implications of the cinema have hitherto received can perhaps
be explained by the departmentalization of our contemporary
civilization.

The break-up of the world conception of the Middle Ages
was followed by modern Rationalism which attempted to
reduce all spheres and activities of the human being to reason.
The attempt failed. Burke, the German Romantic Movement,
later Kierkegaard, Nietzsche and Georges Sorel finally exposed
the misleading optimism of the movement of Enlightenment.

But we are still very far from a new and synthetic conception
of the human world. Religions have become institutionalized
and as institutions have lost their hold on our souls. Political
parties or Trades Unions have lost their character as social
movements; they are firmly in the hands of their own bureau-
cracies. Natural sciences are divorced from social sciences,
philosophy from theology, art from life, economics is still predominantly guided by the narrow profit motive of *laissez-faire*.
The planning centres of the State appear to think more in
terms of social mechanics than in terms of a belief which needs
reintegration, reformulation. For we lack a unifying belief, a
new purpose for a society devoted to peace. It is easy to have a
belief, if we have an enemy.

All these 'spheres' of human activity are largely divorced
from each other; they are departmentalized.

Against such a background the eminent existentialist philosopher, Karl Jaspers wrote his book *Man in the Modern Age*[1]
from which I quote: 'The venturesome doings of individuals
show forth what is unattainable by the masses, but what the
masses admire as heroism and feel they would themselves like
to do, if they could. Such individuals stake their lives as moun-
tain climbers, swimmers, aviators, and boxers. These, too, are
victims, at the sight of whose achievements the masses react,
alarmed, and gratified, being inspired all the while with the
secret hope that they themselves, perhaps, may become enabled
to do extraordinary things.

A contributing factor in promoting a delight in sport may,
however, be that which, in classical Rome, unquestionably

[1] Karl Jaspers, *Man in the Modern Age*, London, 1933, pp. 70, 59.

3

helped to attract crowds to the gladiatorial shows, namely the pleasure that is felt in witnessing the danger and destruction of persons remote from the spectator's own lot. In like manner the savagery of the crowd is also manifested in a fondness for reading detective stories, a feverish interest in the report of criminal trials, an inclination towards the absurd, the primitive, and the obscure. In the clarity of rational thought, where everything is known or unquestionably knowable, where destiny has ceased to prevail and only chance remains, where despite all activity, the whole becomes insufferably tedious and absolutely stripped of mystery—there stirs among those who no longer believe themselves to have a destiny establishing ties between themselves and the darkness, the human urge towards the alluring contemplation of excentric possibilities. The apparatus sees to it that this urge shall be gratified.'

The cinema is a part, probably the most significant part, of this apparatus. The majority of our modern masses, including ourselves, do not go to the cinema only because they have no homes, or because their homes are less comfortable than the picture houses, nor do they go only because the cinema is cheaper or more within reach than theatre or concert; they form those interminable queues in our big cities because they feel lost and empty without participating in this magic world of the screen. There is no lack of cheap (good and bad) books today; and it may also be doubted whether loving couples form the majority of cinema audiences, though many of them, we admit, enjoy the protective semi-darkness of the cinema. No; there exists a fundamental urge within us, the urge for diversion, amusement (*divertissement, Zerstreuung*).

It was probably Pascal who in his *Pensées* discovered the phenomenon of our fundamental urge for diversion for the first time in modern history. To the reader of Seneca (See Appendix II) it is rather a rediscovery, a sociological parallelism, arising from the similarity of problems between the later Roman society and the modern mass age. 'J'ai découvert', writes Pascal, 'que tout le malheur des hommes vient d'une seule chose, qui est de ne pas savoir demeurer en repos, dans une chambre.'[2]

More than three hundred years later the great Swiss historian, Jacob Burckhardt, expresses the same despairing thought in one of his letters to a friend: 'Vollends nun eine Kindermassenversammlung, wie unsere dummen Basler-Kollossal-Kinder-

---

[2] *Pensées*, Brunschvicg edition, No. 139. ('I have found that the whole trouble with people comes from one thing, that is the inability to live in peace, in one room.')

feste! Wer doch als Kind nur hie und da wahre Freude empfun-
den hat, weiss, dass dieselbe im grossen Haufen nicht gedeihen
kann. Aber es ist, wie Sie sagen: man will die Leute beizeiten
zu Massenversammlungen erziehen. Es wird dahin kommen
mit den Menschen, dass sie anfangen zu heulen, wenn ihrer
nicht wenigstens hundert beisammen sind'.[3] It is extremely
doubtful whether Burckhardt would have changed his view, had
he been able to witness Mr Rank's Children's Cinema Clubs.
Nor should we fail to add an English voice to this small band
of lonely warners. R. G. Collingwood in his *Principles of Art* has
given us a suggestive outline of the history of European amusement art, at the end of which the cinema finds its adequate
place: 'A history of amusement in Europe would fall into two
chapters. The first, entitled *panem et circenses*, would deal with
amusement in the decadent world of antiquity, the shows of
the Roman theatre and amphitheatre, taking over their
material from the religious drama and games of the archaic
Greek period; the second, called *Le monde où l'on s'amuse*, would
describe amusement in the Renaissance and modern ages, at
first aristocratic, furnished by princely artists to princely patrons, then transformed by degrees through the democratization
of society into the journalism and cinema today . . . '[4]
To Collingwood film is identical with amusement art. 'Then
came the cinema and the wireless; and the poor, throughout
the country, went amusement mad. But another event was
happening at the same time. Increased production combined
with the breakdown of economic organization led to the
appearance of an unemployed class, forced unwillingly into a
parasitic condition, deprived of the magical arts in which their
grandfathers took their pleasures fifty years ago, left functionless
and aimless in the community, living only to accept *panem et
circenses*, the dole and the films.' Collingwood is obviously wrong
when he explains the mass attendance of the cinemas by the
phenomenon of unemployment. The mechanization of the
economic process is not a breakdown, but this fallacious economic analysis need not concern us here; what Collingwood sees
correctly is the fact that the cinema stands at the end of a long,
historic process.

[3] *Jacob Burckhardt's Briefe an seinan Friedrich von Preen*, Stuttgart, 1922,
p. 130. ('Now to our mass childrens' meetings like our silly colossal childrens'
festivities in Basle. Whosoever as a child has felt now and then true joy, knows
that the latter cannot be felt in the presence of crowds. But it is as you say;
people are educated in good time for mass meetings, but one day it will come
about that men will weep, when there are not at least a hundred of them, crowded
together.')
[4] *The Principles of Art*, p. 97.

Must the fate of our civilization be similar to that of the Roman Empire? 'The parallel', writes the eminent historian and philosopher, 'so far as it has yet developed, is alarmingly close.'

Yet Collingwood's book is chiefly concerned with art, though he realizes that we can neither close the cinemas nor can the masses of cinemagoers 'be elevated by offering them, instead of these democratic amusements, the aristocratic amusements of a past age'. It appears that Collingwood fails to see that the cinema is not only amusement art: Chaplin, Disney, René Clair, André Malraux, Eisenstein have proved that film can be made into a new art medium.

It is essential to grasp the new though largely still potential grammar of this new art medium. Louis Mumford, the alert American sociologist, has outlined its meaning against the background of the older arts.

'One must distinguish', writes Mumford, 'between the motion picture as an indifferent reproductive device less satisfactory in most ways than direct production on the stage, and the motion picture as an art in its own right . . . Not plot in the old dramatic sense, but historic and geographic sequences are the key to the arrangement of these new kinetic compositions: the passage of objects, organisms, dream-images through time and space. It is an unfortunate social accident . . . that this art should have been grossly diverted from its proper function by the commercial necessity for creating sentimental shows for an emotionally empty metropolitanized population, living vicariously on the kisses and cocktails and crimes and orgies and murders of their shadow idols. For the motion picture symbolizes and expresses . . . our modern world picture in the essential conceptions of time and space which are already part of the unformulated experience of millions of people, to whom Einstein or Bohr . . . are scarcely even names.' These sentences are taken from Mumford's book *Technics and Civilization* which he published in 1934. There are only six years between Mumford and Collingwood, yet while the latter shows a distinctly contemplative attitude towards the problems of our time, the former is a participant. He interprets the world in order to change it.

Nor does Mumford fail to relate the structurally new language of the cinema to previous epochs of Western civilization. For he continues: 'In Gothic painting . . . time and space were successive and unrelated: the immediate and the eternal, the near and the far, were confused: the faithful time-ordering of the medieval chroniclers is marred by the jumble of events presented and by the impossibility of distinguishing hearsay from observation and fact from conjecture. In the Renaissance space and time were co-ordinated within a single system: but the axis of these events remained fixed . . . within a single frame established at a set distance from the observer, whose existence with reference to the system was innocently taken for granted.'

Against the medieval and the Renaissance type of visualization, Mumford sets the modern visualization as typified by the motion picture: 'Today, in the motion picture, which symbolizes our actual perceptions and feelings, time and space are not merely co-ordinated on their axis, but in relation to an observer who himself, by his position, partly determines the picture, and who is no longer fixed, but is likewise capable of motion. The moving picture, with its close-ups and its synoptic views, with its shifting events and its ever present camera eye, with its spatial forms always shown through time, with its capacity for representing objects that interpenetrate, and for placing distant environments in immediate juxtaposition—as happens in instantaneous communication—with its ability, finally, to represent subjective elements, distortions, hallucinations, is today the only art that can represent with any degree of concreteness the emergent world view that differentiates our culture from every preceding one.'[5]

Mumford's analysis is significant as a document of our contemporary passion for pure visualization, but it may be doubted whether our world view is really as much fuller as the American sociologist would have us believe.

Mumford's 'concreteness' lacks the subtle, inter-related, intangible character of the historic process. *Individuum est ineffabile*. We are part of the historic process and only through history do we understand ourselves. The human being is above all *animal rationale*; the concreteness of the film medium is above all visual, in spite of 'sound'. Moreover the human being has developed speech, *logos*, as an instrument of self- and world-understanding. Animals see, too, but they see differently.

Film is hardly a means for a better orientation and organization of our perceptual world. Great novels like Tolstoi's *War and Peace* or Goethe's *Wilhelm Meister* may be to a lesser degree expressions of the 'emergent contemporary world-picture', but they interpret the mysterious meaning of our lives more adequately than film.

Moreover, the scientific work of men like Einstein and Bohr is intimately linked up with the long and tragic history of

[5] Lewis Mumford, *Technics and Civilization*, pp. 341, sqq.

European rationalism. The world for which these men stand is nearer to the philosophy and fate of Empedocles than to our modern superficiality. Never perhaps in the history of science has it been so far removed from the concreteness of visualization as today.

That the visual element is over-emphasized in the world conception of film can perhaps be illustrated by another consideration. In the Athens of the fifth century B.C., or during the Middle Ages, and again in Molière's or Shakespeare's age, theatre and festivals were part of a heightened life. In these periods audiences were organic, whereas modern audiences are atomized—in spite of their mass character. In Athens as in the Elizabethan theatre speech and image were harmoniously adjusted to each other. Measurement and balance, an ordered hierarchy, characterized play and audience.

Yet if we read the classical witnesses of Roman decadence, for instance Seneca or Petronius, we find the same traits which mark the contemporary cinema. Circus, pantomime, feast, spectacle, public baths had in Rome probably the same social function as films of today like *Gilda, Madonna of the Seven Moons, Scarlet Street, The Wicked Lady*, and many others. What was then realistically shown in the arena is shown today on the screen. Like the Romans, we have become spectators.

Mumford blames the commercial cinema for this development. We should rather blame State and society, which tolerate the usurpation of a realm of culture which under contemporary circumstances should never be left to the law of *laissez-faire*.

We can still use the brake of new legislation. The Roman parallel is drawn here as a warning, as a possible tendency. We must rediscover the healthy balance of speech and image, before it is too late.

Hope may perhaps be justified. Aldous Huxley's *Brave New World* is not quite a social reality—yet. For we are still sons of mothers and fathers, and moon and stars still shine on our tormented cities:

O das Neue, Freunde, ist nicht dies,
dass Maschinen uns die Hand verdrängen.
Lasst euch nicht beirrn von Uebergängen,
bald wird schweigen, wer das 'Neue' pries.
Denn das Ganze ist unendlich neuer,
als ein Kabel und ein hohes Haus.
Seht, die Sterne sind ein altes Feuer,
und die neuern Feuer löschen aus.[6]

[6] Rilke, *Der Ausgewaehlten Gedichte Anderer Teil*, Leipsic s. a., p. 62.

The table on which I write is not explained by a complicated formula of vector analysis, if it ever can be explained by such a formula, it is the table on which I have played chess with a friend. The table has a history which the mathematical formula cannot express. We are part of this history. Indeed we make this history. The street you walk is not a street half a mile long and sixty feet wide, it is the street you walked with your girl friend and you looked together with her towards the stars. Where may she be now? Perhaps the medieval artist, who paints the angel's hand which holds the millstone larger than perspective would justify, is nearer to concreteness than any of our modern realists;

Glaubt nicht, dass die längsten Transmissionen
schon des Künftigen Räder drehn.
Denn Aeonen reden mit Aeonen.
Mehr, als wir erfuhren, ist geschehn.
Und die Zukunft fasst das Allerfernste
Ganz in Eins mit unserm innern Ernste.[7]

The poet is the better sociologist.

What Jaspers, Burckhardt, Collingwood, and Mumford have in common is a somewhat contemptuous attitude towards the masses. The four thinkers—together they represent the European-American civilization—give some indication of the cultural and social problems with which the cinema presents us. Their attitudes and views reflect to some extent the national societies and social systems which nourished their thought. For this reason they had to become part of these pages.[8]

They lack humility, the heritage of Christianity. They see the dangers which confront us, they warn but they have no remedy, because they do not indentify themselves with those to whom their warnings are addressed.

[7] *Ibid*, p. 62.

[8] This introduction (like this book) is predominantly concerned with the sociological problems of the cinema as they arise in England today: a country where the mass society finds itself in the transitional stage from *laissez-faire* to a planned society. We have refrained from an analysis of the situation of the cinema in Soviet Russia, as the political and ideological presuppositions of Soviet Russia are structurally different from the English ones. They would also then be *different* if we had a completely State-planned society in England.
A film like *Ivan the Terrible* (Part I) shows superbly as a work of art the potential possibilities of film which were discussed above: complete harmony between word and image, though this harmony appears to place the film among the heroic sagas, like for instance *The Song of the Nibelungs*. It is poetry, not ordinary conversation which is co-ordinated to images. At the same time *Ivan the Terrible* appears to bear the message of the Soviet State: the Caesaro-Papism of Ivan and his bodyguard stand (perhaps?) for the leader of the Soviet State and the Communist party. Thus this film projects a mythical past into a mythical present. *Our* world is too historical for the acceptance of such a myth.

Pascal is not of this company. He was a Christian thinker. While he accepted the social conformity of the society in which he lived, his Christian conscience united him with all the orders of this society: high and low. Perhaps nowhere has he expressed his social philosophy more powerfully than in his *Trois Discours sur la condition des grands*.[9] Speaking to a Duke, he says: 'Si vous êtes duc et honnête homme, je rendrais ce que je dois à l'une et à l'autre de ces qualités. Je ne vous refuserai point les cérémonies que mérite votre qualité de duc, ni l'estime que mérite celle d'honnête homme. Mais si vous étiez duc sans être honnête homme je vous ferais encore justice: car en vous rendant les devoirs extérieurs que l'ordre des hommes a attachés à votre naissance, je ne manquerait pas d'avoir pour vous le mépris intérieur que mériterait la basesse de votre esprit.' Pascal does not divorce intellectual or social superiority from the basic spiritual equality between men. 'Il faut mépriser' he says in the third speech, 'la concupiscence et son royaume, et aspirer à ce royaume de charité ou tout les sujets (including dukes, philosophers and sociologists) ne respirent que la charité, et ne désirent que les biens de la charité'.[10] It is important to remember that Pascal was a great scientist. In full possession of the latest achievements of science in his century, he profoundly felt the need for a new science of the human being which would explain 'the order of the heart' (*l'ordre du coeur*). The stress is significantly on order. He did not find many followers, but just because he remained a lonely pioneer and prophet, it was thought useful to remind ourselves of the ultimate aims of his thought.

We are small wheels within a big machine. We are tools which others handle. We serve machines, we perform routine duties without grasping the meaning of the whole. The complex rationality of the world of which we are part, is torn from our instincts and sentiments. Beliefs—we no longer have.

Our evenings find us tired, empty, bored. It takes too much of an effort to read a book or even to talk. So we go to the cinemas where we can be passive, and yet participate in some-

[9] Pascal, *Pensées et Opuscules* (Brunschvicg minor), p.236, sq. ('If you were a duke and a good man, I would treat you according to both of these qualities. I would not refuse you any of the ceremonies due to you as a duke, nor the esteem due to a good man. But if you should be a duke, without being a worthy man, I would do you justice just the same: for in paying you the outward respect which the social order attaches to your birth, I would nevertheless inwardly hold you in the contempt your base nature would deserve.')

[10] *Ibid*, p. 238. ('One must despise the lust for worldly goods and its kingdom and aspire to that kingdom of love in which all subjects breathe nothing but goodwill, and desire only the wealth of charity.')

thing to which our sleeping souls respond. Thus we forget ourselves.

It seemed important to get a glimpse of the part films play in our lives, the lives of people who can no longer stay alone in one room. Hence the attempt to relate the film experience to the life curve of our contemporaries. Nor could we halt there, for the question arose: what films do the masses prefer? Is it correct to say that our own age is following the path of the late Roman Empire? Hence the long study of film preferences. Furthermore we could not leave out the statistical inquiry which we were allowed to incorporate into our own studies. It was essential to know what the social composition of our cinema audiences is like.

Our anonymous contributors speak for twenty million or more. They speak for many classes, for many age-groups, for men and women. It was felt that they should speak, for once, for themselves. Not through a critic who 'knows better'. Nor through the mouth of the 'superior' intellectual who by chance or choice went to a better school, to university to become a planner who then directs 'masses' according to the questions he thinks fit to ask and the answers he receives from mass polls. They are mostly his own answers.

The temptation to make these chapters into a smooth, slick story was considerable. It was resisted because we felt that through such unedited documents alone future students of the social influence of film might profit.

If it is true, as Pascal taught us, that all human unhappiness results from one thing: that we can no longer come to rest in one room, it seemed imperative to ask those who seek diversion, why they seek it, and what they derive from it.

We cannot go back to our lonely rooms, because history moves forward, though not necessarily progressively.

II. FILMS AND THE PATTERN OF LIFE

'What is it on which our attention is focused? If the nature of social structures as created by and as fulfilling man's needs and purposes, then we are sociologists. If the nature of mind as revealed in the structures which they have built, then we are psychologists. It is a difference of attitude in regard to a common material.'

—R. M. MacIver.

1. PRELIMINARY

THE FOLLOWING SIXTY DOCUMENTS represent only an instalment of some two hundred motion picture autobiographies which were obtained through a competition in *Picturegoer*.

Our first competition (see *Sociology of Film*, pp. 181 sqq.) was guided by two questions: 1. Have films ever influenced you with regard to personal decisions or behaviour? and 2. Have films ever appeared in your dreams? Some of the following documents cover again the answers to these two questions, but the second competition was intended to do much more than this. Though there is no doubt that the result of the first competition gave us a first glimpse of the complexity of the film experience, it was felt that the experiment should be repeated in such a way as to give the contributors a chance to adapt their answers more intimately to the experience of their individual lives, showing the effect of films on their whole development rather than on only one or two aspects of their lives.

This method is in no way new. Charlotte Buehler applied it in her study *Der menschliche Lebenslauf als Problem* (1933) and Herbert Blumer based his study on *Movies and Conduct* (see *Sociology of Film* pp. 145 sqq.) partly on motion picture autobiographies. Actually, the very phrasing of our guidance-sheet as it was published in *Picturegoer*, is a condensation from Blumer's somewhat more elaborate one. This is the text to which our documents responded:

Your Help Needed Again

Some weeks ago our readers were good enough to take part in a competition on audience reactions, and supplied a University lecturer with valuable material.

He has suggested another competition. Readers are asked to write their motion picture autobiographies. You are asked to

13

be truthful and frank, and not to feel any restraint in writing fully about your intimate personal experiences. Naturally, your anonymity will be kept. State your name, age, sex, occupation, parents' occupation, nationality. Here are some notes as guidance given by the lecturer:

1. Trace the history of your interest in films. How you first became interested. What films you liked at first? What kind you liked next? Age at each stage. With whom did you go as a child, and how often? How did films influence your play and other activities? Were you ever frightened by a film? Describe the scene of the picture. Do you find it hard to control the emotions aroused by films?

2. What have you imitated from films in mannerisms, dress? Did you ever fall in love with your screen idol? Have films made you more receptive to love-making?

3. Describe fully any temptations or ambitions due to films. Did you yearn to travel or want to leave home? Did they make you dissatisfied with your way of life or your neighbourhood?

Did films give you vocational ambitions, to become a soldier, lawyer, nurse, etc.

Four prizes will be awarded for the best answers: £3 3s. od. for the first, £1 1s. od. for the second, and two of 10s. 6d.

Yet there is a deeper methodological reason which induced us to link up an inquiry into the psychological and sociological structures which determine the film experience of our contemporary masses with the experience of life generally. Dilthey in one of his grandiose fragments writes, 'Only life understands life',[11] a maxim which ought to guide all human studies. Ultimately the biographer alone is a true and reliable social scientist. Our contemporary psychologies and sociologies are so vague and so full of empty generalizations because they are not sufficiently related to the experiences and self-interpretations of the individual. Through the individual we understand his group, his class, his generation, his people, the institutions and ideas, the techniques etc. which shape him. The cinema is today one of the most important social institutions. Its impact on the lives of our contemporary masses must be inter-

11 *Nur Leben versteht Leben.* Cf. Dilthey, *Ges. Schriften*, Vols. VI and VII. Apart from Dilthey, there is much to be learnt from the wisdom and wealth of experience which went into Sidney and Beatrice Webb's *Methods of Social Study*, London, 1932.

preted through the medium of the individual filmgoer. Only through him, so it appeared to us, can the social function of the cinema be adequately described.

It is not our intention to drive home a specific point. What we hope to show through our documents is the impact of the cinema on the *development* of the individuals who responded to our competition. That is why the documents are practically unedited. They are published as we received them. Had it been possible to follow them up with interviews, we might have been able to fill numerous gaps. But even in their present form our documents provide ample material for a *qualitative* appreciation of the film experience. It is regrettable that all the two hundred could not be published at once, owing to limitations of space. What we offer is an instalment, not a selection.

There remain two questions to be asked: (1) Have the writers of the documents answered sincerely, or have they yielded to the temptation to exaggerate their own experiences and to glamourize themselves in doing so? (2) Can the writers be taken as a representative sample of our population? The answer to the second question we leave to the analysis following the documents. The first can be answered, in the last resort, only by a psychologist who checks up on each individual case. Yet it is our impression that their sincerity is striking, with one or two exceptions. Many contributors seemed to welcome the opportunity of expressing themselves, and while, no doubt, it provided an emotional outlet for some, this does not necessarily detract from the validity of what they say. We hope that the documents will be treated with the respect that they deserve and will not become a vehicle for demonstrations of the cleverness of certain kinds of pressmen whose publicity sense so frequently obscures their humility.

2. DOCUMENTS

Nearly all the documents are contributed by people who went, or were taken, to the cinema before they were of secondary school age. The largest group certainly went before they were ten, and it is likely that many actually visited cinemas even before the age which they give as being the age at which the first impression of the cinema was made on them. The earliest recorded visit is given in Document No. 1.

No. 1

AGE: 25.   FATHER'S OCCUPATION:
SEX: M.   ELECTRICIAN
OCCUPATION: CLERK.   MOTHER'S OCCUPATION: ——
NATIONALITY: ENGLISH   MAY 27, 1945.

At the age of twenty-five, I have literally gone to the cinema all my life. I first entered a cinema (in my mother's arms) at the age of one month. I have therefore been going to the cinema for exactly a quarter of a century. Even in this movie-minded era, I fancy that must be a rather unusual record for one of my age.

Apart from that, my life so far has been commonplace and dull enough. My parents are working class (my father is a works electrician). I am a clerk in a printing office, but my interests are literary—books, the drama and more especially, the movies. My nationality is English, with, possibly, a touch of Irish and Welsh.

Last, but not least, I am a bachelor, and have every intention of remaining in that happy state. I have never yearned for the company of the opposite sex (or even my own sex; I am not a good mixer). I have never experienced anything in the nature of romance or sexual love.

To return to my childhood: Admittedly, in those early days cinema-going was largely a habit. A family party of us (I had one brother three years my senior) would go to the local Grand Electric Theatre every Monday and Friday (there being a mid-week change of programme).

My early cinema-going being such an indiscriminate family affair, concentrated on one cinema, it was inevitable that many big films passed us by, much to my regret in later years. Nevertheless, from my earliest days I took a genuine interest in what came my way.

I have vivid recollections of such events of the early 'twenties as *Metropolis*, the silent *Beau Geste* and *Seventh Heaven*, *The Kid*, *The Iron Horse*, Lon Chaney's *Hunchback of Notre Dame*, Clara Bow in *It*, and Rudolph Valentino, besides other, obscurer films, some of them even farther back.

This is a mixed bag, you will notice. While Mother would not have gone herself to see any blatantly immoral or irreligious film (we missed *King of Kings* because it offended family susceptibilities), she believed that anything fit for her to see would do us no harm, if we were brought up on right lines.

I think she was right. At any rate, I never suffered from any censorship of my films or reading matter; yet today I am as clean-living, decent-minded, and law-abiding young man as anyone I know.

In those days all films came alike to me. Of course, I liked Westerns and exciting sword-and-cloak pictures; but at the same time I could sit through sentimentalities and love scenes without becoming bored—and I have many happy recollections of Francis

Marion Jnr.'s rib-tickling, sometimes subtle sub-titles. Oddly enough, what I had least taste for was, typically juvenile fare, slapstick comedy—Our Gang, the early Chaplin, and the like.

Up to now, I have probably given the impression of a peculiarly precocious, emotionally-stable youngster. To balance this picture a little, therefore, let me place on record that invariably, after seeing a particularly exciting movie, I would re-enact the screen hero's exploits. Thus, as Fred Thompson or Tom Mix, I would make a hundred 'indians' bite the dust; or as Captain Blood (Warren Kerrigan's version, not Erroll Flynn's), I would perform miraculous piratical exploits with a toy pistol and a wooden sword.

But as far as *harmful*, unhealthy emotions were concerned, arising from screen passion, or crime, or horror, I never experienced any such, though I must have seen some 'hot' love scenes, and did see (at the age of eleven) *Dracula* and *Frankenstein*. When I hear of children being frightened or emotionally excited by the cinema, I attribute it to faulty parental training. From my earliest years, I was concious that screen characters were merely actors playing a part, and I realized that what one saw portrayed was not always 'the thing'.

Perhaps at this point, it might be well to jump ahead, and say that to this day my emotional re-actions have not radically altered. Being unemotional and not romantically inclined, I have never felt myself in love with leading ladies. (I admire their art, which is another matter). Of course, my approach is maturer now than when I was a boy, and I am more interested in the technical aspects of the cinema.

During all this early period of my life, I invariably went with my family. I never went to children's matinées, either alone or with friends. I would be about twelve when I first entered a cinema on my own, and it was a year or so later before I began to do so as a regular habit. (I still do not go with friends, of either sex. I go to the cinema, not for companionship, but to enjoy the films. For that reason, when I do not go by myself, I go with my mother—for the simple reason that my mother is the only person I have met whose tastes coincide with mine.)

My breaking away from the family party was the real beginning of my cinema-going career. It was now that movies became a hobby instead of a habit. I began to read film journals avidly and to develop a more critical, discriminating approach. From that, it was a natural step that I should start going to other cinemas, in order to follow all the big films. While I had always taken an intelligent interest in the players, it was now that I began to follow the fortunes of individual stars. In short, I had become a fan.

From then on, over the last ten years or so, the cinema has become my one absorbing interest, and I might reasonably claim to have as great a store of movie knowledge, past and present, as any moviegoer in the country.

At this point I take the liberty of introducing the enclosed letter of mine from *Picturegoer* (by a coincidence, the same issue as this questionnaire was announced in), because I think it has some bearing on the subject.

The Waaf referred to was about my own age, yet by her obvious ignorance of Ruth Chatterton, who retired only a few years ago, she made me feel like a cinema veteran. I think the explanation is that girls, especially, may be given occasional treats to the cinema, but do not begin to go regularly or seriously until they start work, and have money and friends of their own—whereas I was, as it were, brought up in the cinema.

It is perhaps inevitable that my interest in the cinema should go deeper than that of most mortals. Of course, there are plenty of patrons, like me, who have developed a critical faculty, and who are also interested in the technique of film-making. But in my case, that feeling has developed into a dual ambition—perhaps wishful thinking would be a truer description—one, that I might some day be in the movie business, and two, to live in America.

As for the first of these, I have unlimited enthusiasm, and that was all the movie pioneers had. I sincerely believe that if I had the chance to get practical experience in a studio, I could find a place in the industry—not as an actor, certainly. Perhaps as a scenario-writer. I have literary ambitions and have already had some stories published.

My desire to go to the States had its origin in American films, but I am not fool enough to think that American life is just like Hollywood. What I do know is that everything American has an indescribable appeal to me. I like the American people, their idiom and way of life. I can tell by audience re-actions that mine is not the normal British standpoint. Everybody likes American films, but with me, things British often irritate me, whereas for anything American I feel an unreasoned, impassioned loyalty such as one is usually supposed to have for the land of one's birth.

Whether I ever realize these ambitions or not—the odds seem against it—the cinema has unquestionably shaped my life as it would otherwise never have been, and with a little luck—and much perseverance—it may yet open the door to a new existence.

The following letter was enclosed:

So Soon Forgotten

I greatly appreciated Mooring's article on James Dunn, especially his comments on the fickleness of Hollywood fame. I have just come across an example of that.

I went to see the re-issue of *Dodsworth*. The cinema announcements gave the stars as David Niven, Paul Lukas, and Walter Huston. Yes, in that order. No mention at all of Ruth Chatterton,

whose brilliant portrayal of Fran Dodsworth was in the nature of a
swansong to a distinguished career.

To add to the irony of the situation, a young Waaf (though not
so very much younger than I) remarked to her companion: 'She's
good, isn't she? I wonder who she is. Mary Pickford or somebody.'
Yes—somebody, indeed. In an era that knew George Arliss as the
'first Gentleman of the Screen', Ruth Chatterton was surely its
'First Lady'. Her retirement left a gap that has never quite been
filled.

The second document contains a reference to the earliest age
at which any of our contributors recorded that an impression
was left by a film—the age of two. The writer is one of the few
who sees that films may come to influence her life in undesirable
ways:

'Without films I am miserable. Sometimes I think they have
become a habit, almost a drug: but I can still criticize films and
while I can I am in no danger of becoming a film drug addict.'

No. 2

AGE: 18.   PARENTS' OCCUPATIONS: ——
SEX: F.
OCCUPATION: ——
NATIONALITY: BRITISH (probably). JULY 18, 1945.

The first picture I ever saw was *Woopee* in 1929. I was two.
I liked it.

I first became interested in films because I was taken to see them.
At first I liked every film I was taken to (although I preferred the
legitimate theatre) save for a few slapstick and Laurel and Hardy
efforts where physical discomfort was the cause of laughter. Now I
can look at somebody being bopped on the head without wincing,
although such scenes do not produce the appropiate "belly laugh"
but merely a slight cracking of the face where I am concerned.

Colossal musicals I liked best, at first; then kid pictures: at eight
or nine I began to like gangsters, at fourteen, sophisticated comedies,
then films featuring adolescents. Now I look for originality and/or
perfection, in any type of picture, with special favourites thrillers
(non-mystic) plus comedy, and pure dialogue comedy, with perhaps
some music. Two good examples of these were *Farewell my Lovely* and
Road to Zanzibar. I am eighteen years old now.

As a child, I went to the pictures with my family; father, mother
and younger brother. As far as I remember we went about once a
month, whenever there was 'something good on'. At ten I began
going regularly once a week with a girl friend.

The question of films influencing my 'play and other activities'
does not arise in the former case. I can't remember 'playing' as

such, after the age of three: before that age I was not influenced to a great extent by anything more than my immediate surroundings, home. My sort of 'playing' was to act out real life, either with my brother or with imaginary characters. I still talk to myself, and films have undoubtedly influenced me here because I always talk to myself in an American accent, and often think that way too. Most of the films I have seen were American because American films are the best. Another aspect of the influence of films on my life has been the fact that, from the age of four, I have wanted more than anything else to be a film star.

I have often been frightened by a film. In particular, I remember one scene, in a film whose title I forget and whose actors I can't remember. I think it was British. A medieval King, alone in his bed-chamber; bare stone and shadows; thunder and lightning outside; inside, the King was uneasy. He picked up a mirror and looked at himself. Then he writhed and passed out. Somebody had painted a ghoulish face with blood streaks over it, onto the face of the mirror. The scene was badly acted, badly directed and badly staged, and yet it gave me one of my worst moments in the cinema.

The only emotion aroused by films which I find it hard to control is the emotion of wanting to be a film star.

In other ways the films have had very definite influences on me. Murder mysteries etc. have made me cautious. When I am alone in a house I always see to it that I sit in an advantageous position for dealing with prowlers, murderers, ghosts and other intruders: facing a door, or mirror, with some sort of weapon handy, such as a poker. When entering a room I am careful about exposing myself in a light; I push the door back as far as it will go, before I venture in, in case somebody is lurking there to surprise me. Detective stories have probably played their part in influencing me in this way, but the screen being visual is always more compelling.

After every film I see I find myself conciously or unconciously copying the voice, walk, dress or mannerisms of some star, male or female, but this usually doesn't last, unless in such a small degree that I am unaware of it. I just stated that I 'copied' the dresses of the stars, but this is not quite true; I merely 'noted' the styles and formed my ideas on dress from the good (and bad) points of the stars' dresses.

Have I ever fallen in love with my screen idol—what is love? I don't know. My 'favourite' at the moment is Bing Crosby. He is my favourite actor, crooner, singer, comedian, radio artist, human being, everything. I think of him constantly: I wonder what his reactions are to certain news items; I try to imagine what he is doing at different times during the day; I plan various films for him, and think up ideas for his radio show. I wonder how his wife and kids are, and I wish I could meet him some day before he gets any older.

I listen to people's conversation about him, read every news item about him, study the daily newspapers to see what times he is broadcasting, and plan my day as far as possible not to interfere with my listening. When two programmes, which might possibly feature Bing, are broadcast simultaneously, on different wave-lengths, I wear out the dial on the radio switching from one programme to another, in case I should miss any 'Bing time'.

I worry over his publicity, note whether he gets top billing etc. I would rather hear Bing sing not too well, than hear anybody else sing superlatively. I enjoy a Crosby musical flop better than anybody else's hit. I love the sound of his speaking voice.

When I read that Mr Crosby is standoffish to press-men I defend him; some call him lazy but I applaud his unwillingness to be pushed around. In the same way that Sinatra causes 'teen-age 'bobby-socks' to swoon, so Bing produces a comparable although less drastic effect on me. I don't pass out, but I feel completely limp when I hear him; relaxed and soothed. His voice makes me happy so that I smile and feel I want to laugh out loud. When I see Bing on the screen my heart thumps and I want desparately for everybody to like him.

Whether all that is love I don't know. To me it seems more like hero worship, and in spite of this fanaticism I have never written to Bing, asked for his autograph or collected his newspaper clippings, all because, I fear, I am too lazy.

My pre-Bing screen favourite (Crosby has always been my favourite singer) was Mickey Rooney. Whether I outgrew him, or whether he outgrew his screen roles, I don't know. I do know that I am no longer 'mad about the boy' although I still like to see his pictures. My reasons for liking him less were not caused by his marriages either. The stars' private lives make no difference to their performance on the screen.

Apart from Bing shining in all his glory at the top, my list of film favourites is long and varied. Each time I see a picture with one of my favourites I think I like him better than any other, until I see the next film.

Unlike so many critics I like adolescent and child actors on the screen. There are few poor artists among them and they can usually be relied upon to outshine the adults.

As yet films have not influenced my love life. I haven't had one. Perhaps screen idols make me critical of the boys I meet, but none of them has even interested me sufficiently to make me love him. I like to see love scenes on the films however, not historical, or Charles Boyer romances, but ordinary boy and girl loves, for these teach like nothing but first hand experience what love means.

Every single film I see brings on that old yearning to be a film star, but films like *Keys of the Kingdom* or the Dr Gillespie films make me feel ashamed of my selfishness and make me want to help suffering humanity, but these self-sacrificing ambitions fade quickly to give way to my more selfish desires.

I do yearn to travel; but whether this is the influence of films or whether it is the result of my parents always talking of their travels

I do not know. No film has ever made me want to leave home, in fact some films have tended to make me feel home is the only place for me in the cruel and wicked world. By 'home' I mean my family, for the house in which I live and the village where I was born, my friends and the people I know are nothing to me.

As for temptations, films have I think dissuaded me from yielding to them, for in almost every movie virtue triumphs. At the moment I have a tendency to cheat the London Bus Company out of their fares but I cannot blame films for this. It is really a kind of suppressed anti-capitalism in me I think; and of course a useless way of trying to revenge myself on rude 'bus-conductors.

Films have not exactly made me dissatisfied with my way of life. Often, films like *A Tree Grows in Brooklyn* have made me humble and greatful for what I have; but every time I leave the cinema I come out more and more determined to succeed and better myself.

Now I go to the pictures every week. Every week I find something to like in the pictures I see. Without films I am miserable. Sometimes I think they have become a habit, almost a drug; but I can still criticize films and while I can I am in no danger of becoming a film drug addict. Meanwhile films continue to give me more pleasure than anything else in life.

An even more definite impression was made by the first film seen by the writer of Document No. 3. She did not 'like' her first film, but she will 'always remember' it. This 'rather sordid' film she saw at the age of 3½ years.

No. 3

AGE: 16½
SEX: F.
OCCUPATION:
  APPRENTICE TO HAIRDRESSING
NATIONALITY: BRITISH

FATHER'S OCCUPATION:
HEADMASTER
MOTHER'S OCCUPATION:
HOUSEWIFE

The first visit to the cinema was one which I shall always remember. It was a rather sordid film and fortunately I didn't understand it very well, for it was the film of *The Wandering Jew* with Conrad Veidt in the heading part. I couldn't have been more than three and a half at the time and yet remnants of that picture still stand out vividly in my mind. Perhaps that was why the cinema entrigued me, and after that I went to nearly every Saturday matinee. I soon found out that I enjoyed the historical films best although I believe that the lovely costumes had a great deal to do with it, for I can often remember the times when I would come home and dream that I was the lovely heroine in a beautiful blue crinoline with a feather in my hair. I used to pray so hard for that crinoline, but later on it changed to a spotted muslin party dress like Shirley Temple used to wear. At first I used to go to the pictures with my two sisters—one being five years older than me and the other being eight years older—but often they didn't want to drag a 'baby' around, and so when Saturdays came, I would clutch my fourpence in my rather sticky hand, and make one dash for the pictures where I could sit enthralled on my throne in the very front seat, I liked going by myself better than with anybody, and always did this, until I was getting on for twelve, when one afternoon I went to see a film called *The Tower of Terror* with Wilfred Lawson in the main role. Looking back on things I cannot make out why that film—that one particular film—upset me so—, for I had been to murder films *Scarlet Pimpernel* films and even torture films, and sat there enjoying them with childish bloodthirstiness,—but right from the beginning of this film I sat trembling with fear in my seat, and when the part came where he dug up his dead wife I just gave one cry and made a mad dash for the cloakroom where I was violently sick.

I confided this with my 'middle' sister who immediately began to take a motherly interest in me, and after that, we always went together. Both of us had and still have exceptionally good memories for learning, lines, prose, etc. and often—especially in the winter evenings—we could come home, criticize the film which we had just seen, and then, remembering the parts, act it to suit ourselves. I had always wanted to be an actress and had put up with the good natured teasings of my family, with the firm belief that one day I would be one, and although time gradually went by, never once did I believe I would be anything else but that. The queer thing was though, I never actually imitated the actors or actresses, I just wanted to know them, to know about their private lives, who they were married to, etc. The only 'screen idol' with whom I ever fell in love was Leslie Howard, but later on I went in for, and won a competition where my 'idol' was to give the prizes, and then I realised that although he was very nice and charming, he wasn't as nice as Tony (my poor boy friend who had patiently waited for my infatuation to pass off).— And that is really about all of my motion picture autobiography— probably just an ordinary, every day tale, and although Tony and I still go regularly to the cinema, we are never influenced by the films or their meanings, for although we enjoy nearly every programme, *we* are more interested in what really happens than in fictional stories.

This last sentence is echoed by Number 4, whose first film also made a definite impression on her. It is noteworthy that this first impression, one of fright, is also her last—'Once I get outside a cinema I return to real life, and though I may have enjoyed a film immensely, it does not, and never has affected my everyday existence, with the exception of the shoes *and the impressions* of fear which I have experienced'. This woman saw her first film when four years old.

NO. 4

AGE: 39
SEX: F.
OCCUPATION: PRIVATE SECRETARY
NATIONALITY: BRITISH:
  SCOTCH ON MOTHER'S SIDE

I was four years old when I saw my first film. It was given in a tent at a Vicarage fête and to me its principal feature was a train. When a close-up was shewn of the engine, I piped: 'I hope it doesn't come out of the picture' and was rather frightened, but only momentarily.

My two brothers, both senior to me, were film-fans, although the word had not then been invented. They occasionally took me to the pictures and we sat, for 4d. each on wooden benches. Most of the films were Westerns, with a Roman-nosed hero called, I think, Broncho Billy. These early films did not thrill me very much—I was at that time between 4 and 6. I used to get hungry and want to go home, but there is no doubt that my early initiation made me a lover of the cinema.

After I was 6 I became more interested and preferred exciting serial films and 'comics', especially Charlie Chaplin, but thought Roscoe Arbuckle was repulsive and not in the least funny.

From 12 to 16 was the romantic and morbid period.

From 16 onwards my taste began to mature and I became more discriminating. Even when I began to visit the cinema with boys and later, with men friends, I went with the strict intention of seeing the film and no other.

My father died when I was 17 and before that he had retired from business. Apart from his intellectual hobbies, he made the cinema a means of relaxation and I used to go with him, about once a week. This began when I was about 11 years old and although I never remember the unfitness of certain films being discussed before me, I cannot remember seeing anything unsuitable when I went with him.

When I was 12, I used to love seeing films with a strong love interest and I enjoyed being made to cry. I cannot remember the chronological order of the films I saw between the ages of 12 and 16, but I was intensely affected by such films as *Smilin' Through* (with Norma Talmadge) *Peter Ibbetson* (Wallace Reid) *Beau Geste* (Ronald Colman) and so on.

I greatly admired Norma Talmadge, Mary Pickford and Nazimova and used to think about them a lot, but never wished to be like them or tried to copy them in any way. It was the romantic atmosphere which I enjoyed. I fell in love with Ronald Colman at this early age and he is the only film actor who has ever stirred me to romantic speculations. I think, possibly, because he was a 'gentleman'. I was a bit of a snob when I was young.

Rudolf Valentino, about whom my contemporaries raved madly, did not stir me an atom.

I was very frightened on several occasions.

During the 12 to 16 period I saw a serial film featuring Harry Houdini and dominated by a being in a sort of diver's suit called *The Automaton*. This creature crashed through walls like a tank and seemed to recognize no human limitations to its activities. I was very afraid of this and it haunted me for quite a year afterwards.

I have always been very afraid of the supernatural and although I am more reasonable now I still dare not read ghost stories, or see horror films. (I could not even make myself see the Belsen news-reel).

On another occasion I was very frightened by the apparition of the Four Horsemen of the Apocalypse and on yet another by a creature shrouded in a black cloak (in *The Gaucho*, with Douglas Fairbanks Sr.) whose appearance every time was heralded by two terrifying notes in a minor key.

Incidentally, within the last 10 years I have seen one horror film and that was seen accidentally. It featured Boris Karloff and was called, I think, *The Black Room*. The latter was a sort of oubliette down which Karloff hurled the bodies of his victims. Even now, the recollection of this film makes me shudder.

The films had no external influence on me whatever. Outside the cinema was my customary environment, a good one, reinforced by a training from early childhood in the appreciation of good literature, good music, good pictures and the hearing of intelligent conversation. I was conscious of the fact that the world of the cinema was a fairy world and had no resemblance to real life. This did not prevent my thinking about the films I saw and sometimes reconstructing their plots to my own satisfaction. I loved the beauty and smart clothes of the heroines, but never attempted to copy them, with a single exception.

When I was 17 I saw a star (I forget her name) about whom the boy I was with said: 'She has the most lovely little feet and her shoes are always beautiful'. I had nice feet and made a vow that the same should be said of me. I don't know whether it ever was, but I always bought the nicest shoes and stockings I could afford and shoes are still my pet luxury, even in these days of coupons.

The only emotion I found hard to control (this from 12 years onwards) was weeping. I would sit and cry copiously at a sad scene, but remain untouched by a sentimental one. The only film which made a permanent impression on me in this way was *The Way of All Flesh* with Emil Jannings. I can still recall the acute misery which this film caused.

I ought to add that I have been a facile tear-shedder all my life, although I have a cheerful disposition, so that the films are not entirely to blame.

I cannot say that films have made me more receptive to love-making. I never really believed that film heroes were much like real men and my experience of men, which is adequate, has reinforced this theory.

(In fact I have only once in my life been deeply moved by a love scene and that was on the stage and was simply overwhelming. The actor was Matheson Lang in *The Wandering Jew*, about 12 years ago. I apologize for this digression).

All this is not to say that I have not been interested and sympathetic, (although extreme and artificial love-making amuses me) and a really well acted love scene can make me and always has made me feel sentimental. I have often thought—when seeing him, but not otherwise—that I should like to be kissed by Ronald Colman. I still think so.

I have never suffered any temptation from seeing films, felt dissatisfied with my way of living or experienced any vocational ambitions.

Certain films have reinforced my desire to travel but not inspired it.

To sum up: Since the age of 12 I have been a regular cinema-goer and have enjoyed myself thoroughly while seeing and hearing the films, but once I get outside the cinema I return to real life, and although I may have enjoyed a film intensely, it does not, and never has affected my everyday existence with the exception of the shoes and the impressions of fear which I have experienced.

The same impression of her first film, also seen at the age of four, is recorded by a married woman of 27. Her 'memory of a scene' in it 'is still vivid because of the terror' she experienced at the time.

NO. 5

AGE: 27	FATHER'S OCCUPATION:
SEX: F.	RAILWAYMAN
OCCUPATION:	MOTHER'S OCCUPATION:
TYPIST, BUT MARRIED, WITH HOME	FACTORY WORKER
NATIONALITY: BRITISH	

MY MOTION PICTURE AUTOBIOGRAPHY

My interest in films began at the age of four. Now almost twenty-eight, the memory of a scene in the first film I ever saw is still vivid because of the terror I experienced at the time.

My mother and grandmother, both ardent film fans of the Valentino era, always went to the cinema together; Listening to them talking about the things they had seen my curiosity knew no bounds and I begged to go with them to see such wonders. My plea was granted.

All went well, until that scene I remember so clearly of the hero and heroine trapped by an explosion in a disused mine; their being seperated—he fumbling his way along one dark tunnel, she another. They were lost in the pitch darkness. My heart bled for them and I wept noisily.

Grannie, desperate to soothe my distress, told me I was a silly little girl, that it was 'only a picture', that the two would escape from the dark tunnel, I had only to wait and see, how. Escape, however, was long arriving and during that time I was heartbroken by their sufferings and in utter misery continued to sniffle in the darkness.

At last, poor Grannie, obviously gripped by the film and loth to leave to take me home, as Mother was, declared that a little boy behind, was laughing at me.

Such shame! A little boy laughing at me! I had exposed my cowardice and was now an object for derision!

Surreptitious glances to the row behind revealed no little boy, but if Grannie had said so, he was there, all right, somewhere further back, I supposed.

That early experience left me with a horror of darkness and loneliness. For many months afterwards, Mother was burdened with the task of soothing my attacks of night terrors. After dreaming I was lost in a dark tunnel, with a roof so low I was compelled to crawl on my stomach, the darkness suffocating me, I would awake screaming.

Periodically, these attacks persisted in adult life but while the screaming fortunately disappeared, the dominant sensation was always that of suffocating accompanied by a frantic struggle to reach air and light. My doctor called it a 'phobia', treated me, and for three years I have not experienced an attack.

I did not visit the cinema again, until I was eight, and then it was always in the company of other children. We went Tuesdays and Thursdays. Hoot Gibson, Tom Mix, Tom Tyler and His Pals were my delight. How I admired these 'he-men' of the great open spaces! They were strong and brave, I was weak and cowardly—the little boy's derision had given me an inferiority complex—but in these film stories the strong protected the weak, jeering villains were given good hidings, and noble deeds were done in defence of the weak and helpless.

This adoration of the 'Buffalo Bill' type of hero remained until I was about fourteen. Somewhere about that time I saw *Trader Horn* and then it was the fearless explorer type which won my fervent admiration and awakened a yearning for travel—knowledge about things strange and wonderful. I had read books on travel but no narrative, however brilliantly written, had captured my imagination as did this film. After that, all the subsequent jungle pictures were favourites, the *Tarzan* stories, *The Lost World;* the Mr and Mrs Martin Johnson films.

Something of an introvert, due to the inferiority complex before mentioned, the adoration of the 'tough guy' has a curious slant in my case. Introverts, being as a rule studious, from fourteen until eighteen, four evenings a week were spent at night school after the day's work. Consequently, dances and other youthful pursuits were cut out of my existence, voluntarily, in favour of the make-believe world, which, nurtured by much film-going, was infinitely more fascinating.

The screen 'tough guy' became my ideal, not so much in a physical sense for in him I saw mainly *protection*.

Lounge lizards, smooth-mannered men of the world seemed to represent, en masse, that little boy who derided me as a weakling. Tough guys did not deride, but to my mind, kept undesirable elements at bay by sheer animal strength. Put less crudely, it was perhaps the subconscious need for someone strong and fearless to believe in me, discover I was the superior being I longed to become and so instil confidence by sheer worship.

Some time ago, believing such emotions had passed, I was astonished to find this chord was struck while watching the film *Butch Minds The Baby*.

Brod Crawford's part as 'Butch', the rough diamond with a heart of gold but too shy and clumsy to declare his love to Virginia Bruce (the superior being) provided a strange, emotional satisfaction to me.

The films made up my mind for me regarding the choice of a husband. If I married it would be to a 'he-man'—no-one else would do. Of course, if he were handsome, so much the better!

Nevertheless, it was a bit of a jolt when I did find him—perfect in every detail—and a fine boxer in the bargain, that lots of other girls found him terribly attractive, too! The snag was, that these other girls had attended to their personal appearance ready for reality when it came—my shoulders were stooped with crouching over books, I had ruined my eyes and now wore spectacles.

It was around 1937, when the craze to be 'different' began. One point was in my favour. My rivals, in their attempts to look 'different' merely succeeded in all looking alike—stamped with the same stamp as it were. Anyway, be that as it may, I married my 'tough guy' a year later.

From my own experience, I would say there is a definite emotional thrill in watching screen lovers kiss, but in my case the thrill is only momentary and does nothing more towards the stimulating of desire.

Among horror films, one scene stands out in my mind. In *White Zombie*, when the corpses, acting under the villain's influence, worked the sugar(?) presses with horrible, mechanical apathy, their dead eyes staring ahead glassily, the shuffling of their feet and the creaking of the press as their bodies leaned against it to push it round, a sound like a moan of distress followed by a pathetic whimper. Neither the much-boosted *Dracula* nor *Frankenstein* conjured up such horror as did this scene. My blood ran cold.

I have achieved spiritual satisfaction by watching some films—I say satisfaction—because I am easily moved by spiritual themes which arouse the desire to weep, not in sadness but in a form of ecstasy difficult to explain. *Song of Bernadette* did this for me, as did certain scenes in *A Canterbury Tale*.

Yet I cannot recall experiencing it in *The Sign of the Cross* many years ago. I am looking forward to seeing it again.

Although I would not go so far as to say films have given me any ambition—save that of the urge to travel—they have definitely *stimulated* it. *Jack London* definitely gave me courage. When I saw him burn his early MSS I went straight home and in one fell swoop destroyed all mine, making a fresh start as he had done. *Seeing* him do it made all the difference. Getting rid of the whole mass of rubbish produced from the creaking machinery of the beginner writer's mind was like casting off a burden. Since then I have written and destroyed many thousands of words, but each time, having sifted the wheat from the chaff, my work has improved and I made progress.

Furthermore, films give me ideas, nowadays. Not in the same street as plagiarism, mark you, but watching how twists come into screen plots, how characters react in various situations.

'Tough guys' are still my favourites. Having the devotion and loyalty of one of my own has gradually destroyed the inferiority complex which once threatened to hold me back both in social life and ambition. I have films to thank for showing me the type of man I needed for a life partner. I no longer fear slim, smooth-mannered lounge lizards, for I know if any of them tried any monkey business my 'tough guy' would without wasting words, knock them flat!

No such lifelong influence is recorded by No. 6, but the 'horror' impression is again vivid in her story. She even records an 'inclination' towards horror films. She is also a good example of the 'escapist' approach to films, and states that they had on her an effect which (judging by our documents) is unusual: 'The only other effect films had on me was a desire to have several boy friends and to be serious with none.'

NO. 6

AGE: 30   PARENTS: DECEASED
SEX: F.
OCCUPATION: HOUSEWIFE, MOTHER WITH 2 CHILDREN
NATIONALITY: BRITISH

I started my film going at the early age of 5, and I took a great interest in films from the start. I used to go to a penny matinee every Saturday, with my sister, 4 years my senior, and our two friends also sisters. Between the ages 5 to 9, I saw a variety of films, the titles of which I just don't know. There was always a serial and a travelogue, very different from the ones we see today. I know that this was the only part of the programme which bored us. The serial was popular, and the films we liked best were the open air type, with plenty of cowboys, Indians, and shooting. I remember my mother taking me to see *The Sheikh* when I was about 7, and I was very thrilled with it, but films like *East Lynne* and *The Old Curiosity Shop* were far too depressing for me at that time. Films didn't influence us to any extent in those days. I can remember my sister and her friend were always discussing the stars, and of course there were games of cowboys and Indians with the boys.

From the age of 9 I lived in a city, and still continued with the weekly matinee, which now cost 2d. or 2½d.! I gradually found myself inclining towards the tender romantic type of film, such as *Seventh Heaven*, *The White Sister*, *Garden of Allah* and *Annie Laurie*. Spectacular films were always a draw, for instance, I saw *Moon of Israel*, *Last Days of Pompeii* (with Victor Varconi the handsome hero, a far cry from the 'Hitler Gang'.) Then *The Deluge*, *Ben Hur*, *King of Kings*, and *The Sign of the Cross*. I have always liked costume films.

When first talkies appeared, I had a passion for the big musicals such as *The Broadway Melody* series, and the Jessie Matthews' successes, but after 2 or 3 years they began to pall. I had a sudden inclination to horror films, and when I was about 18 I started seeing all Boris Karloff's films. *The Mummy* was the one which gripped me most, and I think the only film in which I have covered my eyes. This was during the scene in which the Mummy comes to life and walks out of the mummy case, takes the parchment from the young scientist's hand, and walks out with it. I think this was the most ghastly scene I ever saw, and I had a nightmare after that film! After seeing *The Blue Room* I felt I couldn't see another horror, and I haven't seen one since.

Then in 1937, (I was 22) Jeannette Macdonald and Nelson Eddy became my top-line favourites, after seeing them in *Rose Marie*. I made a point of seeing all their films. At 16 I fell for Ramon Novarro, Ronald Colman and others, but Nelson Eddy is the only star who can thrill me now, and it is the effect of his lovely singing voice that does it.

Costume films are my favourites, and if I can see a costume film with music, I ask for nothing better. Sophisticated comedies come next in popularity with me, and I think Norma Shearer was one of the best stars in this type of film. I was 16 when I saw *Private Lives* and others.

Since 1939 I have not been able to go to the cinema so often, but when I do I find I am more critical of the Actors and the plots. Apart from *Mrs Miniver* I haven't seen any war films. I have tried to get away from it on my few visits to the cinema, and have seen such films as *Pride and Prejudice*, *Gone with the Wind*, *Random Harvest*, *Elizabeth and Essex*, *Frenchman's Creek*, etc.

I find it easier to control my emotions than in my younger days. I get a lump in my throat during a sad scene, but I can remember sobbing bitterly over a film when I was about 10 years old. I also used to scream with laughter at the antics of such comedians as Laurel and Hardy, (much to the disgust of my friends). I don't remember ever acting scenes from films, but I think I did try to copy mannerisms and expressions of popular stars at the time when I had just started work. (16). I can remember making a copy of a dress worn by Janet Gaynor, for myself, when I was 18. The only other effect films had on me was a desire to have several boy friends and be serious with none. I found it didn't work! I always found that real life romance fell far short of the ideal romance on the screen, with all its glamour.

Although I often dreamed how lovely it would be to be a famous star in films, I never went to any lengths to study Dramatics or Elocution, or anything that might have helped. I certainly think that films make you dissatisfied with your own way of life. The average working girl never has in real life, such a lovely home or apartment, or the clothes and boy friends (plus car) that the screen girl is shown to have. Of course, there is another way of looking at it, which is that we go to films to see a more glamourous and luxurious way of life, a life we should like to live ourselves. I definitely go to the cinema to be taken out of myself, and to forget the cares of housework, rationing, and washing baby's nappies! Carry me into the past with Laurence Olivier, Nelson Eddy, Greta Garbo, and the others and I'm happy!!

Five years was also the starting age for the writers of Documents Nos. 7-10. They record definite impressions of their earliest visits, after which attendance at the cinema became habitual.

No. 7

OCCUPATION: I LEAVE SCHOOL IN OCTOBER (1945)
PARENTS' OCCUPATION (MOTHER): HOUSE-WIFE. (DAD) WELDER
SEX: MALE
NATIONALITY: ENGLISH

I can well remember the first time I ever went to the pictures, at the age of five. I went with some boys older than myself, and we had to stand in a big queue they got their tickets first and they left me to get my own. When at last I did get it they had gone inside without me. All at once I ran out of the pictures up the street and started to cry. As I was half way up the street a policeman called me and asked me what I was crying for I told him and showed him my ticket and he took me in. That was my first experience. I first became interested in flims because every Saturday afternoon my pals went somewhere and when I asked them they promised to take me. I used to go every Friday night to the pictures with my parents. This went on till I was about eight and then I started to go with my pals. Mostly we went to see cowboy pictures and when the programme was ended we would dash up the road and betend we where cowboys. We would make masks and lots of other things. Robin Hood pictures. From the age of 5 to seven, I used to be mad on cowboy pictures. From seven to 9 I used to be mad on serial pictures. and flying pictures such as Flash Gordon and a trip to mars and those short comidies. From 9 to 11 I liked to see a good mystry or boxing pictures. At this stage also I liked a syntimental picture. I confess I used to cry at a lot of pictures. From 11 to 12 I used to spend a lot of money and travell a long way to see no particular picture at that. At this time from 11 to 12 no particular flim took my fancey exsept jungle pictures (*Tarzan*) or pictures about the war. From 13 till now I like to see a longer and more sober picture such as *The Story of Doctor Wassel* or *The song of Bernadette*. but besides these flims I like to see a good comedy team play in a long picture (Abbot & Costello) and those little pictures about Hobbies. From the age of 11 to 12 I used to pay any amount of money to see a picture and some times I had to wait a very long time before I could get anybody to take me in and sometimes nobody would take me in at all. When I was young the one thing I used to go for besides seeing the pictures was to het some ice-cream. I go to the pictures 3 or 4 times a week. Now I come to the idols of my flim career. When I was a child my Idol was Shirley Temple. Now I am older my Idol is Betty Grable and although some people say shes common I do not agree with them. The man I like best is Bing Crosby and I am sure I shall always like him.

Flims do influence my play and other activities because I can pick my words better and I can put more feeling into my plays at school and I may add when I come home I try to describe the flims to my parents trying to put the actions in also.

I have only once been frightened of a flim *The Gollywog* or some thing like this is the sceen that terrified me. It was a dark lane in the country the wind was blowing very hard making a errie sort of noise. All the trees were blowing about. It was pouring down with rain and the the night was pitch black. A woman was coming along the lane and as she reached a tall bush a hand reached out and got her round the neck. Next there was a shrill screem. When I came home I had a night-mare all about this flim and this particular sceen and it frightend me so much that I would not go out on a dark night without someone for a long time. I do find it hard to controle my imotions aroused by flims, for instance if I see a good flim I tell everybody to go and see it but if its a bad flim I tell them it a waste of money to go and see it. I used to have a lot of auguments with my school-pals about this subject and I have lost quite a few pals this way.

In Flims I have imitated lots of things in my manner. For instance science I have been going to the pictures I always touch my hat when I meet anybody. I always greet every body with a smile. When I bump into anybody I always say I am sorry. If I pass in front of anybody I always say excuse-me. I have also learned to become better mannered at the dinner table.

In dress I always have a creace in my trousers. I always put grease on my hair and have a parting in it. I always keep my clothes clean and I do not have any pins in them. I always strip to the waist when I wash. I clean my teeth every morning. All these things I have imitated from the flims. Flims have also made me very observant. Flims have given me knowledge and a lot more ideas in love making. I have got one ambition due to flims and that is to become a flim star myself. Wehn I tell anybody they just laugh but I think to myself you'll see. Another ambition due to flims. When I see what beautiful houses the flim stars live in then my ambition is to live in one of these houses and have a private swimming pool in my garden. Yes I certainly do yearn to travel and I should not mind leaving home to go any where as long as I could take my mother and father with me or keep in close contact with them.

I cannot say that flims have ever made me dissatisfied with life but I can safely say flims do make me dissatisfied with my neighbourhood and towns. From what I have seen they are not modern for instance there are no drug stors on the corner of the stree where you can take your girl friend and have some ice-creem or a milk-shake. In our town there are no sky-scrappers or realy high buildings and there are not half as many buildings which are lit up as those on the flims are such as Broadway. Flims have given me one vocational ambition and that is to become a flim-star.

It was not untill about 6 months ago that I took to flims seriously. I then heard that you could send for flim star photographs So I started to collect their adresses and send up for their photos. I now send up for about 3 a week. So far I have had only had 3 come back. Next I heard that a fortnightly book came out called the picturegoer came out and only cost 3d. So now I have this fortnightly book with my comics.

Well in the future I am looking forward to see some even more better pictures and I do hope in the future that there will be more flims in technicolour. As I think coloured flims are better to watch than black and white ones. I shall also be looking forward in the future to see some fresh faces on the screen.

I am
Yours Trully
....
No. 8

AGE: 23
SEX: M.
OCCUPATION: SHOP ASSISTANT
NATIONALITY: BR.
FATHER: ACCOUNTANT

Naturally, I first became interested in films as a youngster. What kiddy is there that does not like to see a picture show?

I remember going to them soon after starting school (5 yrs. old), seeing the antics of a baby called Snookums, who had quite a big curl, also seeing Topsy and Eve in *Uncle Tom's Cabin,* I believe.

Later on I saw Tom Mix, Tim McCoy, the cowboys; also comics like Charlie Chaplin, Harold Lloyd, Buster Keaton and Keystone Cops, etc. These would be between 5 and 10 yrs. old.

I remember the silent films and the words flashed on, well after the action had happened.

I loved the cowboy pictures and the serials. How exciting it seemed to be when one episode ended with a terrific climax and the notice 'To be continued next week' flashed on. How I waited impatiently, for that next week, to know the solution. There were mystery serials too!

Laurel and Hardy were favourites too.

Around 11 yrs. of age I cared for any type of film, I thought I was getting a big lad and I could fathom 'all that was taking place'.

There were more comedies those days, they catered to make you laugh more!

The pictures were not lavish or super colossal efforts but what was attempted, was thoroughly digested and enjoyed by the audiences. No fabulous prices were paid for stars and stories and it was real entertainment, now although some very good films are made these days, it's more of a *money making* proposition.

My father mostly took me to see any picture and sometimes my brother, but I was equally confident to go on my own or with my small mates; (we could often ask for an adult to take us in for half, offering them the cash, of course).

I saw many of these earlier shorts etc., though, when I went to Saturday matinees.

I have always gone to the films at least three of four times a week.

I led up to films, first seeing short comedies, etc., cowboys, then murder and mysteries, then naturally at about the age of four-teen as love crept into my heart, I was apt to see love stories and romances.

Films have influenced me, I've imagined myself in the roles of Cowboys, Indians and Bad men, and as a hero.

I-ve been a little frightened of terror films but later on I've realized they were only celluloid characters and my common-sense soon adjusted matters. I often get a lump in my throat during a sad scene.

I detest cruelty to any pet or animal during a scene and I would hiss the villain, as they did in the olden days. I try and take tips in love affairs and romance pictures, one never knows that one day it may provide me with an ever lasting sweetheart of my own.

I do try to imitate one or two stars and come away with the feeling I am good etc., but it wears off; after all they are only folks like you and I, really.

I fell in love with plenty of actresses but when I think of the make-up and grease paint I look around and see equally good, if not better everyday girls that are more beautiful and graceful.

I've yearned to go on films etc. but I know the futility of it all, I suppose it must be born in one. Maybe the 'big lights and large pay' tempted me.

I've wanted to go abroad, particularly America, but after hearing my pals' versions of the States and other countries (trained as air-crews) I think of my own country and my own neighbourhood and I am quite satisfied.

No matter what one is, I believe pictures give no inspirations and ideals. I'm only a shop assistant, started at 17 yrs. age till 20 yrs old, when I joined, but I was greatly inspired by 'Kipps'.

It proves that with hard work and will-power we can attain what we desire!

Hoping this will help you, I've written it rather hurriedly and not so much in detail as I would have liked but there you are.

No. 9

AGE: 15.   FATHER: ARMY SERGEANT.

SEX: F.   NAT: RUSSIAN

OCCUPATION: AT SCHOOL.   MOTHER: CLERK. NAT: ENGLISH.

I used to go to the cinema when I was about five with Mummy. Mummy says we went—always in the cheapest seats—because as we were so poor (my father did not live with us and seldom gave us any money) that she wanted to escape from the reality of bills, summonses and how to get money.

At first I liked Disney, Shirley Temple and the Astaire-Rogers films best. I seldom understood the plot.

The next that I liked were gangster films, plenty of 'blood and thunder' and smart jokes in them. I used to build up imaginative stories around them.

One film I remember very clearly although I saw it when I was seven (eight and a half years ago) was *The Good Earth*. It was my favourite for a long time.

The films that terrified me most was *King Kong*. I saw it with my brother when I was about seven. I still have an impression of the hopelessness of the hero and heroine when they were fleeing; of the Lockness Monsters chasing them through inky seas and of the land disintegrating all around them. Quite often I dream of it. Recently I dreamt of the inky seas engulfing me. Usually I can glide into more pleasant dreams.

I have always made up stories (with myself as heroine) round the film stories and heroes that I have liked. *Robin Hood* was a favourite for a long time.

After *Waterloo Rd.* I liked Stewart Granger very much—I have a 'soft spot' for villans, not of the Gestapo variety—but when a friend who works in the office at one of the film studios divulged to me that Mr Granger was cross-eyed and swore horribly . . .!

During the war Gestapo pictures have thrilled me, maybe it's a cruel streak in me. Goodness knows I don't take pleasure in cruelty outside the cinema.

The last film I saw with my brother before he died in hospital in February was *A Guy Named Joe*. Although he enjoyed a good picture, he found them on the whole a waste of time. He did not show it but I could see the film impressed him. I cant think why I did not see what was coming when I saw that film.

Mummy and I felt 'at home' in a cinema, I suppose that is why it was only two weeks after his death and my grand-mother's (my grand-mother died the day after my brother) that we again went to the cinema. We saw *Wilson*. The death of Mrs Wilson made me cry a little, though I dont usually.

I thoroughly enjoyed *Blithe Spirit*, but Mummy felt a little upset after it.

Last week we saw *A Tree Grows in Brooklyn* and that nearly broke our hearts, some of the incidents were so like what happened to us when we were very poor. The deaths were very heart-rending. We saw it on Friday and the atmosphere stuck with us for some time.

I find that after a film that I have enjoyed very much, that has many beautiful glamour girls in it I feel irritable and want something better out of life—I try not to be irritable.

Films *have* made me want to travel, to think and to waste much time that I should have spent on homework, but they are a great comfort.

No. 10

AGE: 12.   SEX: M.

I am righting the Answers out of your help needed again.

I first became interested in films when I was five. I am now 12 years of age. I first became interested in films was at school, I heard some boys talking, about a film about cowboys. And then my favourit film became cowboys, Gangsters, my favourit film stars were Buck Jones, James Cagney, Marea Montez, Songa Henei, I was then eight. I then became interested in murder, Tarzans, I was now ten, untill I was eight I went with my Mother and father twice a week. I was often playing at Cowboys and Soldiers. I was never frightened by a film and I do not find it hard to control my emotions aroused by films I imatated a American Slang from films with the 'Dead End Kids' in I never fell in love with my film idol and films never made me any better at love making. I sometimes thought I would like to travell and work on a ranch. they never made me dissatisfied with my way of life or my neighbourhood. Although I marvelled at the things they had that we had not got it never made me want to be a soldier etc. only some times to live on ranch in the wilds of Canada. Dear Sir I hope I have done it Good enough to win at least 10s. 6d. as I am saving up to by a bike.

It is clear from the documents that, even at the early ages so far recorded, the children were seeing films made for adults, No. 11 writes of her 'weekly excursion', at the age of five, 'to the local picture palace where all the kids from the surrounding districts would wend their way every Saturday afternoon to see weekly serials'. Her 'enthusiasm' for these shows was 'infectious', but of the first 'adult' film that she saw, she remembers 'nothing except the fact that just as the hero kissed the heroine' she commenced to suck her 'orange'. Yet she went to another adult show six months later, and saw a film with a 'horror' scene which gave her nightmares. It is not clear from her letter whether she was then barred from children's as well as from adults' film shows, but it should be noted that the next film she records is *Robin Hood*. We assume that there was, therefore, a gap until the age of eight. Nevertheless, the effect of the films was still profound, to such an extent that 'gradually as' she 'grew older', she 'realized the hold the cinema was getting . . . The days between one film and the next became obscure'.

No. 11

AGE: 18.　　FATHER'S OCCUPATION: IN ROYAL NAVY
SEX: F.　　MOTHER'S OCCUPATION: HOUSEWIFE.
OCCUPATION: SHORTHAND-TYPIST.
NATIONALITY: BRITISH.

'Sara! Sara! Are you ready?' came a call from next door. In No: 9 all was confusion, a small girl of five dived madly from her chair grabbed her tammy, her money from the sideboard and her bag of aniseed balls from the mantlepiece and flew for the back door.

Yes, it was me, off for my weekly excursion to the local picture palace where all the kids from the surrounding districts would wend their way every Saturday afternoon to see Buck Jones, Mickey Mouse, The Dead End Kids, etc. in weekly serials. This was my first introduction into the magic world of movies; and it was looked forward to with immense anticipation, so great in fact that the only punishment that could really upset me was to stay home on a Saturday afternoon.

My enthusiasm became so infectious that my parents decided to take me to an adult show, and so with many warnings about being quiet and threats that I'd get a pasting if I wasn't, we sallied forth equiped with a bag of bullseyes and an extremely large and juicy orange.

Of that first adult film I remember nothing except the fact that just as the hero kissed the heroine I commenced to suck my orange. Never again vowed my parents, and so back I went to my weekly twopenny rush.

Six months later I was again taken to an adult show by a very indulgent aunt who didn't realise what she was letting herself in for. Unfortunately the film had an element of horror in it and one scene from the film haunts me still. It showed a young girl who owned a mill and who was surrounded by enemies. I can remember distinctly how one night as she lay in bed, a figure dressed all in black, crept over the rope bridge which separated the mill from the living quarters, sidled up the stairs and very slowly opened the bedroom door. I can still hear the squeak of the hinges as the door moved and the heroine's scream. I'm afraid this gave me nightmares, and once again I was barred from the cinema.

At the age of eight I again ventured into the cinema world and became ensnared by the characters I saw. After every performance I would move around in a dream, drifting along acting the parts of all the stars.

Then I went to see *The Adventures of Robin Hood* and I promptly fell in love with Errol Flynn and rushed to see his every film. I still have a number of the photos I collected in the first flush of my crush on him.

Gradually as I grew older I realised the hold the cinema was getting on me. The days between one film and the next became obscure all I lived for was Saturday.

After seeing technicoulor musicals I became dissatisfied, picking fault with my parents, my friends, and worst of all my country. Luckily my common sense came to my rescue and I interested myself in the stars. Rita Hayworth, Betty Grable, and Alice Faye adorned my bedroom walls, pushing out Errol Flynn and William Powell.

Maria Montez and Jon Hall in their fairy tale films filled me with a wild desire to travel, to see for myself, even though my inner self told me that the Baghdad I was seeing was constructed by carpenters under the direction of a director, who saw everything through rose tinted glasses. This fact was brought home to me in *Four Jills and a Jeep*. How distorted is the American idea of Britain. We don't all hunt the fox and talk county.

War films became the vogue round about my fourteenth birthday and I went absolutely mad on them. I was never one of the people who hated war films, I adored them, in my mind the brutality of the Germans became even clearer and my hate for them more strong; in my imagination, I became a nurse, a spy, an underground worker caught by the Germans, undergoing torture but for ever remaining silent.

The best war films in my opinion were those depicting a handful of Americans against a horde of Japs, i.e. *Bataan, Guadalcanal Diary* and such films as these. I came out of the cinema exhausted because I had been fighting their battle for them.

My attention wandered once again, to films such as *Jane Eyre, Rebecca* and *Frenchman's Creek*, which films I must state have made me a Joan Fontain fan for life. *The Constant Nymph* left me with a feeling of loss, and added Charles Boyer to my list of exceptionals.

My heart-throbs have changed as I have got older, first they were dashing like Errol Flynn, then charming like Pierre Aubert, debonair like William Powell, audacious like Arturo de Cadova and now quiet and insulting like Alan Ladd (of *And Now Tomorrow* fame). Each in their turn have made a great impression on me, and have influenced me in my daily life, to the extent that I have always been on the lookout for men like them.

Films have done a lot for me, developed dress and colour sense, and a wild desire to see the world; to be a somebody, not just a someone in the daily pattern of life. Who knows where this desire may lead us; but wherever it does, good or bad, Filmland will have definitely started it.

Another broken record is outlined by a schoolboy of 15½. He also was 'thrilled' by his first visit, at the age of 'five or six', but his visits remained infrequent until he was ten. Nevertheless, he records visits to special children's matinees when he was 'seven or eight', together with the usual 'horror' experiences. 'The films shown at these special shows were for the most part totally unsuitable to my mind.'

NO. 12

AGE: 15½   FATHER'S OCCUPATION:
SEX: M.   TRANSPORT MANAGER
OCCUPATION: SCHOOLBOY
NATIONALITY: BRITISH

I have been attracted to the cinema now for nearly ten years. I have always been fascinated by the phenomenon of moving pictures. If I find the film I am watching is exceptionally good, I forget that what I am watching is really a string of transparent photographs and I join in the situations with the characters. The film, to my eyes, takes a third dimension. That is one reason why I like the cinema so much, providing the films are good, the situations become realistic to me. I feel like shouting advice to a character in moments of peril, to Quote an example, I recently saw a film called the *Woman in the Window*, in which a timid professor killed another man in self-defence. The woman in whose flat the murder took place and the professor, dispose of the body and all evidence to safeguard the man's reputation. Together, they rolled up the body in a blanket and carried down a dark stairway into the road below to a waiting car. They seemed to take an infinitely long time to do this. The suspense was really cleverly produced. My nerves were really on edge during this sequence.

My interest in films started when I was taken about ten years ago to the cinema by an aunt. I remember being thrillled by this visit. My mother tells me I used to sit on the stairs for hours, pretending I was at the pictures. I was then five or six. I hardly went at all for at least two years. When I was seven or eight, I visited special childrens' matinee at the local cinema. The films shown at these special shows were for the most part totally unsuitable to my mind. One film, presented in serial form, was about the efforts of a criminal gang to obtain a secret ray lamp. I was particularly frightened by views of the criminals, dressed in a hideous disguise chasing silently down dark passages under London. A policeman was strangled by a pair of hands which came out of a shadow behind him. I was afraid to look at the screen during many of the scenes. The films I liked most at this time were cowboy films and cartoons.

My visits at the time were still very infrequent and remained so until about 1940.

When I was nine my parents took me about once a month. One result of going to the cinema more was that I became more critical; I formed certain likes and dislikes. I hated and still hate pictures with jazz bands which were introduced every other minute to make a din. I like films which make some effort to introduce good music. Much to my pleasure, there have been many such pictures later.

I hardly visited the cinema at all in 1941 because of the 'blitz'. But during 1942 I went at least 40 times and saw a great variety of films; then, I liked crime, thrillers and murder films although I did *not* want to do anything criminal afterwards or to imitate the bad doings of the gangsters. I was not easily scared by this kind of film then.

I went many times during 1943. I added to my 'likes' more sophisticated comedy. I especially enjoyed films poking fun at the well-to-do English family, although I have always held them in respect. Two comedies of this type that I thoroughly enjoyed were *Turkey Time* and *Don't Take it to Heart*. I like films depicting the future, like H. G. Wells' *Things to Come*. That brings my picture autobiography almost up to date.

I saw a picture about a year ago that really frightened me. It was called *The Phantom of the Opera*. It concerned a musician who was embittered with rage when a music publisher stole his life's work, a piano concerto. He strangles the thief in the presence of a secretary who throws a bath of acid into his face. He wandered, disfigured in the sewers under the Paris Opera House. In the end an opera singer with who he is infatuated pulls away his mask, and in a blaze of colour the audience saw the man's disfigured face with deep acid wounds on the right side. I remember keeping at a safe distance away from the acid bottles in the school chemistry laboratory for quite a while afterwards.

It is mainly through the influence of travel films that I want to travel when I am older. Foreign lands always look so beautiful when seen through the lenses of a technicolour camera.

It is probably through the influence of American films that I sometimes write without thinking the American spelling of such words as colour, theatre, and honour. I have so often seen these words spelt on American film titles etc.

In a film called the *Glass Keys* a man cleans his teeth by the ingenious method of applying the paste directly to his teeth and then brushing afterwards. I use this method when I am in a hurry. It is quite a good method.

I do hope the *true* facts will help you in your research.

Jean-Louis Barrault in *Les Enfants du Paradis*

From *Les Enfants du Paradis* : An embrace as an inner experience . .

P.S. I have only fallen in love with one screen actress. She is Phyliss Calvert. I admire her for her sweetness and pure English diction.

It is difficult to place the first 'effective' visits of the writers of the next three documents. No. 13 records an 'interest' in films 'as early as I can remember', but started to go weekly to children's matinées at the age of six. No. 14's first visit occurred at the age of two, but the child seems to have taken no interest in the film then shown. Her next stage, or, in her own words, 'bad habit', did not begin until 'about six or seven'. The writer of No. 15 was taken to the cinema when she was six weeks old, and states that subsequently she was taken 'quite often' because she could be relied upon to remain fairly quiet. Her first actual recollection was at five, and she 'can very well remember' *City Lights*, but she records the third 'milestone' at the age of seven.

NO. 13

AGE: 19 YEARS 10 MONTHS
STEP-FATHER: WOOD LAG DRILLER
MOTHER: HOUSEWIFE

My first interest in films began as early as I can remember, I was about six years when I started going weekly, but the films I saw were usually the kind shown at children's matinees, for the most part serials.

The ones I remember that interested me first were the cowboy serials starring John Wayne and I used to get very excited and could hardly wait until the following Saturday afternoon when I could see another episode with John Wayne in some tight spot.

I used to go with my sister who is three years older than myself and we have always taken a keen interest in films, every picture of stars or film extracts etc. we used to cut out and paste in a large scrap book to show to our friends.

One of our games would be to have an audience of two or three school-friends and my sister and I would 'act' a small part from a film, impersonating the stars and having our friends try to guess the film.

I dont remember my first experience of being frightened by a film but quite recently I covered my face at the sight of Spencer Tracy 'changing' in two or three scenes from *Doctor Jekyll and Mr. Hyde*.

My usual reaction to an exciting film was to clench my hands and dig my nails into the palms, I still do react that way but when I used to go to the matinees and got excited I used to jump up and down in my seat and it wasn't an unusual thing to hear all the other children shouting out to their particular hero in the film that someone was coming up behind them in an exciting part of the serial.

I have always taken a very keen interest in Deanna Durbin's films and I used to copy her hair styles and note the styles of her clothes, mine were never exactly the same but accessories were an easier matter and I nearly always took much more interest in Deanna's wardrobe than that of any other star.

When I became interested in boys I enjoyed Deanna's first love affair with Robert Stack in *Her First Love* and used to tell my 'boy-friend of the moment' to note the way Robert Stack held Deanna in his arms and kissed her.

The settings of the love-scenes always held my interest and I've always noted little tricks (which I've put into practice) such as curling my boy-friend's hair in my fingers or stroking his face exactly as I've seen my screen favourites do in their love scenes, one of the first things I noticed was that an actress always closes her eyes when being kissed and I dont need to add that I copied that too.

My ambition for a number of years was to become a film actress, although I took up dancing I only got as far as travelling in a Pantomime as a chorus girl with a very small speaking part until I finally started work at the age of fourteen as an office girl which put a stop to my ambitious ideas.

When I've been to a film (especially one in Technicolour) I always walk home feeling disgusted with the drab town I live in, the paint-work of doors etc. seem awfully dull and dresses look plain after seeing the glorious scenery and stylish clothes in the film.

As an ardent film fan and a regular reader of *Picturegoer* I have enjoyed writing these notes and I hope they are of some use in your research work.

NO. 14

AGE: 23   PARENT'S OCCUPATION:
OCCUPATION: SHORTHAND-TYPIST   STOREKEEPER
NATIONALITY: BRITISH

Seems I must have been a born film fan, if my childhood recollections are anything to go by. I still remember shedding tears at *Sorrell & Son,* and laughing at the antics of Charlie Chaplin.

I was first taken to the Cinema at the ripe old age of two, and so I am informed, the film was *Carnival* starring Matheson Lang; needless to say, my father now tells me that he had a 'carnival' with me too. First I stood up on his knee and waved to the man in the seat behind; then I suddenly realized that the woman in front had rather a tantalizing feather in her hat and made a grab at it. After a few caressing words from my fond parents, with perhaps a smack or two on the legs, and a handful of chocolate stuffed in my mouth, I then settled down for a while. Mother says heaven help them if sweet rationing had been in force then.

The next stage in my Cinema life, or should I say the next bad habit, was at the age of about six or seven and concerned those rip-roaring 'Westerns' so popular years ago. During the inevitable runaway stagecoach scene, with outlaws and whatnot in the chase, I would suddenly rise from my seat, push my way into the gangway and slowly walk towards the screen shouting 'Go on, they've nearly got you'. My mother, in much disgust, would then have the pleasure of running after me, yanking me back into my seat, amid cries from the back of 'Keep that child quiet', 'Put some gum on her pants', and other less-delicate remarks. After one or two of these 'happenings', Westerns were definitely taboo in our house. I eventually outgrew this habit, but guess it must have had a bad effect on my film tastes, as I now loathe 'Westerns'. Maybe I'm still scared of their hypnotic power.

At the age of about ten, *Sorrell & Son* was the film which really stirred the sentimental side of my nature. I went with my mother to see this, and think I'm quite truthful in saying that both of us wept from start to finish, and our conversation afterwards must have sounded something like this—'Wasn't it a good sniff film, Muriel, sniff'. 'Oh yes mother sniff sniff', 'We must get your Dad sniff to come and see it sniff sniff'. Finally, not only poor Father, but Mother and I, went to see the wretched picture again—with more weeping from the female members of the party. The old gag 'It was a marvellous film, I cried all the time' certainly applied in this instance.

As time went by and I left school, I had a craze to be a Chorus Girl, so naturally my film tastes turned to Musicals, and I think my feet literally tapped as I watched the then-raving-beauties dance their way across the screen. This ambition did'nt last for very long, and from then onwards I began to take films seriously.

I learned to appreciate the acting of individual stars, the technique of certain producers, sound effects, etc., etc., in fact everything which goes to make a good film.

I will not comment upon my vocational ambitions taken from films, as these have been so varied that I'm afraid it would take a good-sized book in which to relate them all. However, such films as *Madame Curie, Story of Louis Pasteur, First of the Few, Nurse Cavell, Song to Remember*, etc. certainly do much to inspire and to bring about the realization that, although oneself may never do anything to warrant a statue, there have been and always will be men and women whose names will be handed down in history, and films are a sure way to keep these names evergreen in the minds of the community. (I might mention Hollywood are always up-to-the-moment in this respect).

Regarding fashion, I myself have taken dozens of clothes and hair styles from films, and will continue to do so, as I believe that this is a sure way of keeping in step with the fashions. It is certainly far better to take a style from a character in a film than from a picture in a magazine, where only one angle is usually shown. This applies particularly to clothes, as in films we are shown both close-ups and distance shots, and one gets a better impression in this way than by studying fashion magazines. I remember copying a very alluring style from a dress worn by Myrna Loy in one of the 'Thin Man' series, and felt quite 'Hollywood' in it, and incidentally this same style appeared in one of our own fashion books, months later. The Americans are so much more in front of us with accessories too, and films give one a good idea of how to put these to good use.

I think my emotions are more quickly aroused by 'background' music in films than by anything else, e.g. *Now Voyager*, *Casablanca*, *The Common Touch*, *Great Lie*, etc. If the same scenes were played, minus this background music, I feel certain I would remain unmoved, but the simple addition of softly-played music does much, I consider, to improve the sincerity of the acting. However, as music has always held a very soft spot in my heart, maybe I'm prejudiced.

One film which greatly affected me was *Song of Bernadette*; I'm not a religious fanatic by any means, but after seeing this film I really felt that I would faithfully go to Church every Sunday from then on. Many stirring films have been made in the past, but this is the only one which I have thought about for weeks afterwards. *Bernardette*, in my opinion, is a landmark in the film industry, and should be left as such and not copied by all & sundry in an effort to better it. There can never be two *Song of Bernardette* films.

I think the foregoing just about constitutes my film experiences in the past, which I trust will prove interesting.

NO. 15

AGE: 23   PARENT'S OCCUPATION:
OCCUPATION: LABORATORY ASSISTANT   MINER
NATIONALITY: BRITISH

MOTION PICTURE AUTOBIOGRAPHY

Not many can claim, as I do, the distinction of having been a filmgoer all their lives, but I can and do claim that distinction. From my earliest days, I have been actively interested in films, those who act in them, and those who make them. Because of this, films have influenced me and given me ideas, in more ways than one, throughout my life.

I cannot recall my first visit to the cinema, as I was taken there by my parents when I was only six weeks old. This occurred in 1922. I am told I rendered that occasion remarkable, by trying to remove the headgear of the lady who was seated in front. After this, I was taken quite often to the cinema by my parents, because I could be relied upon to remain fairly quiet.

My first personal recollection of a visit to the cinema comes when I was five years old. In those days, my family resided at . . . , Co. Durham, and they used to take me to the Queen's there. I can remember, quite clearly, being seated in the circle on my mother's knee. We must have been seated in the first row, because I can remember trying to peer into the black pit below, being much more fascinated by the moving lights, as people came and went, than by anything showing on the screen, of which I have only a vague recollection.

My next motion picture mile-stone came in 1929. My family had come to live at N., a small village six miles west of Newcastle-on-Tyne. I had often been taken to the small cinema there, to see silent films—I can very well remember *City Lights* with Charles Chaplin. However, to Newcastle came the first 'All Talking, All Singing and All Dancing' film—*The Singing Fool* with Al Jolson. My parents took me to Newcastle to see this film, and we had to wait for a long time in a queue outside the Stoll Theatre, where it was being shown. Eventually, we gained admittance and how bitter was my disappointment, when I discovered that I couldn't understand a word that the actors were saying. On top of that, the harsh and raucous voices frightened me. My father, who had only just returned from America and Canada, informed me, that it was only because I was unfamiliar with the American accent, that I was unable to understand the dialogue. He was right because, after one or two further visits to the 'Talkies', I could understand the dialogue perfectly.

For a time, our little local cinema exhibited part 'Talkie' and part 'Silent' films, but eventually the silent films were squeezed out. From being seven years old until I was ten or eleven years old, I can remember seeing such films as *The Blue Angel* (From which I have a much clearer recollection of Emil Jannings than of Marlene Dietrich); *Hell's Angels* with Jean Harlow, Ben Lyon and James Hall; *Red Dust* with Jean Harlow and Clark Gable. At this time, I used to love to see Jack Holt and Ralph Graves in such films as *Dirigible*. I think that these two must have been my first film favourites. It has always been a peculiar trait of mine, that, in most cases, I admire film actors and actresses in pairs.

At this time, I used to be taken to the cinema, by either my parents, my grandmother, or my cousin Raymond, who was seven years older than myself. Soon, I conceived the notion of keeping a Scrap-Book of my favourite stars, in fact, anyone connected with films at all, had their likeness pasted into my book.

A new interest presented itself shortly, in the form of the early musicals, such as *Broadway Melody*, *Sunny Side Up*, etc. I was taking piano-playing lessons myself, just then, and the effect of these musical films with their catchy tunes, sung by such stars as Bessie Love, caused me to be very discontented with my Daisy Waltzes etc., that I was learning to play. My mother, however, promised me that if I should practise very hard at my scales and waltzes, she would buy me some music from the films. I now have about 2,000 copies of songs, most of them from films, among my music. I can still recall how wonderful I thought the song '*If I had a talking picture of You*', to be. I have not only collected songs from the films, but also, I have often fallen in love with pieces of good music by various composers. Films like *Blossom Time, Dangerous Moonlight; Love Story, A Song to Remember; Song of Russia,* have all added to my repertoire, their quota of lovely music. To hear music played superbly on the films is a grand incentive to play music superbly oneself and to seek as near perfection as possible.

Two new stars captured my imagination in the 1929-1933 era, namely Janet Gaynor and Charles Farrell. How I revelled in watching winsome, sweet Janet Gaynor and manly Charles Farrell and how bitterly I was disappointed to discover that these two were not married in private life, but worse still, were each married to someone else. I simply couldn't see how two such wonderful people could not be in love with each other.

1933 marked another mile-stone in my film-going career with the advent of *Gold-Diggers of Broadway* in glorious Technicolour. I had long since discovered my ability to draw, but when I saw this film my artistic desires burst into flame. Were there ever such wonderful dresses seen before on earth? I suppose that if I were to see this film now, I would think it crude, too highly coloured, and the dresses old fashioned. But I thought it was wonderful then and for weeks afterwards, I sketched designs for dresses, all over my books, and nothing suits me better after seeing a good musical, than to knock off a few sketches of the various dresses or costumes worn and to improve and alter them to suit my own taste. At the same time, to encourage my artistic abilities, my mother ordered *Picturegoer* to be sent to our house each week and I have been a regular reader since then, never having missed one copy.

My first introduction to a horror film, was at the age of eleven or twelve, when my cousin took me to see *King Kong*. I was absolutely fascinated, but not really frightened. Only one film has ever frightened me. It wouldn't scare me now, of course, but I was only twelve, when I saw it. The film in question was *The Mystery of the Wax Museum*. Although I only saw this film once, I have an indelible impression of it on my mind. The scene which struck me with horror, was that in which the girl destined to be 'Marie Antoinette' slapped the face of the villain of the piece and broke his wax mask. I can never forget how I was paralysed with horror. For quite a while after that, I looked behind me at the slightest noise and didn't care to enter dark rooms alone. However, I soon conquered this feeling and since then, I have seen most of the Frankenstein's & Draculas, without being frightened, but with a pleasurable thrill.

When I was eleven years old, I started to attend the local secondary school and had my first experience of what were known as 'pashes' or 'crushes' on various film-stars. Everyone had a favourite, with Bing Crosby well in the lead. Bing's photographes were very scarce, because of the great demand. I had no particular favourite, until one night, I saw *Queen Christina*. From then on, I was a Garbo fan. I followed her career with great interest and made a point of seeing her films, until *Two Faced Woman*, and after that, I bothered no more about her. *Queen Christina* had well and truly fired my imagination—I felt tragic for weeks after.

My school pals and I made a habit of visiting the cinema on a Friday night—Friday being the only night that we could safely leave our homework until the next day. On one of these occasions, we saw Fred Astaire and Ginger Rogers in *Flying Down to Rio* and that brought on a dancing craze. We saw every Rogers-Astaire film that was ever made and during lunch-hour breaks at school, the changing-room rang with the strains of the 'Carioca' etc. I learned to dance and became very proficient and I can hold my own with anyone on a ballroom floor. I wonder how many people have been induced to take up dancing through watching the twinkling toes of Fred Astaire.

From the age of twelve to fifteen, I attended the cinema regularly, true to my usual fashion, I once more became fascinated by a pair of stars—this time, Nelson Eddy and Jeanette Macdonald. I first saw Nelson Eddy in *Naughty Marrietta* and he at once struck me as being different, although his voice was an added attraction to my musical ear. *Rose Marie* further captivated me and I saw every film that these two made. I bought the selections of music from each of their films and for quite a while I had a musical comedy craze. I went to see other musical films at this time, such as *One Night of Love* and *Tell Me To-night* and of course, the films made by Deanna Durbin.

While still at school, I became interested in French films. At that time, I was studying French fairly intensively and besides that, I was corresponding with a French family. We used to exchange papers and magazines and I used to send *Picturegoer* to my friends in France and they sent French film literature to me. I was never able to see many French films, as they are scarcely ever shown in N——.

I left school when I was nearly seventeen, and started to work in a laboratory. At this time, I became much more serious minded with regard to films and instead of seeing anything and everything, I began to choose the films that I wished to see. Just after leaving school, I began to collect books, and books and films became intermingled. I often went to see a film after reading the book, although often I was disappointed in the film. In this way, I came to see *Gone With the Wind*, *Pride & Prejudice*, *The Stars Look Down*, *Rebecca*, *The Rains Came* and many others. Similarly, I often bought the book after seeing the film, for example, *The Grapes of Wrath*, *Jamaica Inn*, *My Son, My Son*.

I soon started to value stars for their acting ability and not for their, more or less, pretty faces. Such actors as Spencer Tracy and Laurence Olivier always win my admiration, as do such actresses as Greer Garson and Vivien Leigh, when compared with the ephemeral charms of a Betty Grable.

Came the war and film-going had to be relegated to second place in favour of A.R.P. duties. I still managed to see a lot of films, however. I have never liked to see war pictures, especially the American type, which are usually far from reality, with too many heroics and too much bombast. I don't mind a decent war film of the British 'In which we Serve' type. I discovered about this time, a rather peculiar trait of mine, I cannot bear to see pictures of great suffering or of concentration camps or doctors performing operations etc. I always feel faint in such cases. I suppose this must be due to the fact that I have a very vivid imagination. A prime example of a film that affected me in this way, is *Hatter's Castle*.

I cannot say that films have very influenced me to take up another career nor can I say that I have ever fallen in love with a film idol, except for schoolgirl 'crazes'. I have often wished to travel after seeing a 'Travelogue' especially as my father has travelled fairly extensively. Films have given me many hobbies, though, and have influenced me to seek greater perfection in things like music and drawing. On top of that, films have given me a great deal of pleasure in more ways than one and I hope they will continue to do so. I hope that the motion picture industry will progress for art's sake and not for the more mundane sake of box-office returns.

Document No. 16 is another which lacks clarity on the point of the actual age at which cinema-attendance began. The writer's interest clearly dates, however, from the age of seven. In this case, it is quite impossible even to attempt to isolate the effect on the writer of his attendance at the cinema and the effect of other circumstances.

NO. 16

AGE: 15	OCCUPATION OF STEPFATHER:
SEX: M.	AERO INSTRUCTOR
OCCUPATION: SCHOOLBOY	OCCUPATION OF MOTHER
NATIONALITY: BRITISH	BEAUTY EXPERT

My interest in films really woke up when I saw *Strange Cargoe*, Clark Gable-Joan Crawford. I was then about seven. The first film I saw was a dancing film and I remember very much trying to dance with my younger sister after seeing it. Later on I saw *Snowwhite* but was simply terrified by the old witch. At about 10 I saw the *Wizard of Oz* which I enjoyed very much. At about 11 I enjoyed love films very much; I still do. I have never really enjoyed war films like most boys. The films that stand out mostly in my mind are *Strange Cargoe*, *Snowwhite*, *Wizard of Oz*, *Robin Hood*, *Dawn Patrol*, *Gone with the Wind*, *My Friend Flicka* and *Dragon Seed*. When I was small I usually went with my Grandfather about once a month. I now go twice in one day sometimes.

The scene in *Snow White* which terrified me was when the witch came to Snow Whites cottage in the woods and sold her the apples. For months afterwards I would hate going to bed in the dark and always sing very loudly when dressing to frighten the witch away.

I have imitated many things from the films but mostly my hair has suffered. Yes suffered. I used to Bleach it when in the bathroom. I copied smoking from the films. I started at nine and am still going strong. When courting at school I used to put flowers in my sweethearts desk.

My film idol is Errol Flynn and I fell madly in love with him after seeing *Dawn Patrol*. I think about him at nights, pretend I am with him and dream about him. I have never felt about a film actress in this way.

I would not know much about love making. Although I may say that most love making goes on in the pictures.

The only ambition that I have had from the films is to become a film star. I have often tried to run away from home. When I was evacuated I was unhappy and tried it.

The films taught me to tell lies and to become sly and to steal.

They have also taught me a great deal about sex. At the age of twelve the average child knows a lot more than parents would think.

On the whole English films rather than American teach me things. *Fanny By Gaslight* is a good example. I could almost guarantee that every child over fourteen knew what had been going on when the maid picked up the cuff links from under her mistresses bed.

The films have always made me want to go to America.

I have always been dissatisfied with home. I want a terrific house with tennis courts and swimming baths. I want plenty of servants but I should always want to make my own bed.

It has also taught me to look down upon neighbours and I think them ugly, fat and ignorant. I go to school in the country and despise country people.

On the whole I would say that films have not done me any good. My mother has forbidden me to go to the pictures during school time at all. She says they distract me.

I hope my letter will help you in your most interesting work.

Documents Nos. 17, 18 and 19 also record the beginning of attendance at the age of seven, attendance being generally at children's films. Like the preceding documents, they demonstrate very clearly the effect of serial films in forming a *habit* of attendance which, in the case of many of our contributors, has become fixed.

NO. 17

AGE: 18 YRS. 8 MONTHS   FATHER:
SEX: F.   MECHANICAL ENGINEER
OCCUPATION: MOTHER:
    CIVIL SERVICE CLERK   HOUSEWIFE
    P.O. TELEPHONES
NATIONALITY: BRITISH

It was at the tender age of seven, when I first embarked upon the exciting and mysterious adventure of a visit to the cinema, under the supervision of Mother and Father; and ever since then, almost as far back as I can remember, I have had a deep interest in the film world and all concerned with it, an interest which increased in intensity as I grew older. The first film I saw was a silent one, and I remember leaving the cinema feeling rather excited and a wee bit sorry for some poor man, who had fallen head first into a barrel of flower.

Time passed and I became more friendly with the other children in my street, and the excursions to the cinema became frequent and exciting—exciting because I began to understand the actors and actresses, and the stories woven around them, which gave us young-sters our regular Saturday afternoon entertainment. To miss even one of these shows with my little playmates was a heart-rending dis-appointment, because I knew I should miss the next episode in the film serial. The latter was always my firm favourite, whatever the story. I hero-worshipped Larry Crabbe in *Flash Gordon's Trip to Mars.* At this time I would be about nine years old, and even then I was quite jealous if anyone else had a photograph of Mr. Crabbe.

Films affected our play very much. Our second favourite was a good Western film, with plenty of shooting, fighting and fast riding. After becoming thoroughly worked up about Buck Jones or Ken Maynard, we would enact these films, in versions all our own, after school each day the following week.

Donald Duck and Mickey Mouse followed closely on my list in third place. I adored Walt Disney cartoons, and, if I may be so bold as to admit it—I still do!

I disliked animal pictures intensely, because they all made me weep. They might not have been sad, but still I choked up when one was showing. I think it may be as well to add here that in all these months of picturegoing I was never frightened by any film, indeed every film was such a new thrill and experience that I don't think I ever thought of fear.

During this time, too, new words crept into my vocabulary, and I remember clearly that my parents were quite shocked when I first used the word 'scram' before them! I liked to copy expressions used by my favourite actors, and use them often. One of the latter was Shirley Temple, and I liked to think that I could give a very good impression of her singing 'Animal Crackers'. She was a firm favourite of mine and my friends.

At the age of thirteen, when I was enjoying second year at high school, and when the Saturday trips to the local cinema had ceased, I was experiencing varied emotions as a result of picture-going. It was then that I first began to pick out the films I wanted to see, and to go not just out of habit or for the sake of going, but because I knew just what it was I had a desire to see. Passionate schoolgirl 'crushes' followed each other as new and handsome men made their appearances on the screen. Many were the nights I cried myself to sleep because John Howard, Preston Foster or Robert Taylor was so far away. One glimpse of any of them would have sufficed and I felt I would have been the happiest girl in the world. Possessing a vivid imagination, I had wonderful dreams of being discovered by a Hollywood talent-scout, of visiting Hollywood and perhaps even playing opposite one of my favourite movie stars.

But inevitably I had to put these preoccupations in the background because lessons and homework needed concentration; at the age of sixteen I matriculated, and a little later left school to earn my own living.

An important load off my mind, I was again free to think more and spend more time upon what had once been a cherished hobby. I found I had lost none of the former interest; indeed, I indulged in a little wishful dreaming, and the one temptation was to run away from home and become an actress like Jane Withers. This I knew could never materialise, circumstances would not permit, so I had to be content with regular film-going and collecting pictures and magazines.

Then I once remember having a desperate desire to become a nurse, when I saw Rosamund John act so wonderfully well in *The Lamp Still Burns;* but it was a mere whim because I liked the film so much, and passed away in a matter of days.

So to the present day. The cinema is my main source of entertainment, and I am not really difficult to please as far as films are concerned. I like most kinds of productions but my favourites are flying epics, such as *A Guy Named Joe* and *Thirty Seconds Over Tokyo*, and straight dramatic stories, of the kind that *Old Acquaintance* represents. I have a deep admiration for Van Johnson, Irene Dunne, Bette Davis and Spencer Tracy; I envy them because their kind of life is so far beyond my reach, because the work they do is so hard and so very interesting, a job after my own heart.

Films have a great influence upon me. I find myself trying to be original in my method of attire, and copy Hollywood beauty 'tips' when using make-up: I find it hard to control the emotions aroused by a touching or very dramatic scene, and I cry very easily. The desire to become an actress is still prevalent and my interest in drama has increased. Thus I have become rather dissatisfied with my present existence and with the neighbourhood in which I live, but I love home life and, until the world is at peace again and our loved ones are safely restored to us, I am content to remain as I am, and just to

plan and dream about a long awaited trip to that intriguing city of
Hollywood, to see for myself everything and everyone that contri-
butes to the making of the entertainment I love so much.

NO. 18

AGE: 26   OCCUPATION: HOUSEWIFE
SEX: F.   PARENTS: DECEASED
NATIONALITY: BRITISH

I have, I think, been an ardent movie-goer since I was seven. I was
a 'dreamer' and highly imaginative, and the films were an escape
from the ordinary, sordid, everyday world. I lived in a land of make-
believe. In those far-off days, I belonged to the local 'gang' of youngsters and many hours were spent re-enacting the latest film we had
seen. Westerns were top favourite then, and later it was the *Tarzan*
series. Strangely enough, while most of my young companions idol-
ised the 'dashing hero', I always admired the 'villain of the piece',
and many a tear have I shed when the scoundrel has been killed or
caught. Even now, my tastes haven't changed. Stewart Granger,
Clark Gable or Robert Taylor leave me cold. But show me a film
with George Sanders, Lon Chaney or Raymond Massey, and my
nerves tingle with excitement and admiration for their cunning and
villainy. I have always maintained that it takes a *good* actor to be a
scoundrel. I have never been frightened by even the most horror-
fying film. The 'fairy-tale' type of picture has always drawn me. Such
as *Cobra Woman*, and *Arabian Nights*. Fantastic and colourful, yet
strangely beautiful, such films have aroused inside me such depths of
longing, such bitterness, such hatred against Fate that forces me to
live in a drab, hum-drum world. It's the sort of feeling that I get
when I listen to those exquisite dances from *Prince Igor*, by Borodin.
It's something that I cannot explain, even to myself. Perhaps I
haven't quite grown out of that age of 'Prince Charmings and lovely
beggar-maids'.

Only once have I fallen in love with a screen-star. And that was
Conrad Veidt. The magnetism, the compelling personality of him
'got me'. His voice, his mannerisms fascinated me. I hated him,
feared him, loved him. When he died, it seemed as if some vital spark
went out of my 'imagination' and dream-world; like a child who suddenly learns that there is no Santa Claus and that bold, handsome
knights are just unreal things. I had that same sort of agonised
feeling.

To me, the screen has always meant a peep into another world.
How I have longed to cast off the dulled shackles of today and step,
free and proud and ecstatic, into that misty dream-world. Alas for
my dreams!

Throughout the years of 'film-going' I have never found an actress
who appealed to me. Good though many of them are, not one lives
up to my expectations. Too exotic or too 'pretty-pretty'. Where is the
exquisite, dainty, fairy-like creature of my dreams? Not having been

an ardent film-fan of any actress, naturally I have never tried to imitate any one of them.

Do films make me dissatisfied? Definitely they do! I find myself comparing my home, my clothes, even my husband. I get extremely restless and have a longing to explore uncharted lands.

Sometimes, after seeing such films as *Sanders of the River* or *King Solomon's Mines*, I have a feeling—a savage, exultant feeling and I want to dance to the beat of native drums. The thud-thud of tom-toms always shakes me to the depths. Such is the effect of films on me. I have never gone to a film just because it happened to be a 'good' one. *Wilson, Mrs. Parkington* etc. bore me. So drab is my real life that my screen world must be colourful and exciting—something to stir the emotions and to lift one to a mad, unholy heaven! Always it has been thus—Always it will be thus with me. The screen is to me a God.

NO. 19

AGE: 21 OCCUPATION:
SEX: M. AUDIT CLERK (SOLDIER)
NATIONALITY: BRITISH FATHER: BUS CONDUCTOR
MOTHER: HOUSEWIFE

My first introduction to films was at the age of seven, when my parents who had been taking turns at going out, decided that I was big enough to go with them took me about once a fortnight to one of the local cinemas. I hadn't very much interest in what I saw, as quite naturally, the films were of more interest to adults. My two older brothers created my first real interest by taking me to what was then known as the 'Tuppenny Rush' on Saturday afternoons. Here was entertainment for juveniles, cowboys, bandits and the intriguing serials which kept us guessing from one week to the next.

The effect on our play was fairly simple, cowboys and Indians was favourite with the participants adopting such names as Tom Mix and Buck Jones.

My visits to the cinema at this time were at the most once per week. Outstanding amongst my recollections of early 'talkies' was *The Sign of the Cross* and later *Whoopee*.

The first time that I was really frightened by what I saw on the screen was in a film called *Murder by the Clock* which really did scare me. The most outstanding scene that I have never forgotten, was the one where the family concerned were sat at dinner and the crazy son, a youth of about 20, sits with a horrible demoniacal look on his face and handles his knife in a most horrifying manner, as if it were a dagger, and all the while the clock can be heard ticking monotonously in the background. I had difficulty in sleeping for quite a few nights.

On account of my age I was unable to see such films as *Dracula* and *Frankenstein*, and when I did see them later, I regarded them as extremely funny and absurd.

From the age of twelve onwards I gradually increased my visits and interest in films, at twelve I was content with nearly anything, though some films such as *Mutiny on the Bounty* I found to be exceptionally good. I've always had a preference for films of historic interest and films of the classic books, such as *Henry VIII* and *David Copperfield*. I enjoy and am moved by real life films such as *Love on the Dole*, *The Citadel*, *The Stars Look Down* and others that come in a similar category. American films, apart from musicals, I deplore, as I cannot understand their way of life nor can I comprehend how such a 'mélange' of races manages to live together at all. I prefer British films because I regard them as more sincere and satisfying.

I honestly believe that I have not assimilated any of the customs or habits shown on the screen, though I think females, especially young ones, are more likely to do this.

Since I started taking a real interest in films, when I could pick out the good from the bad, I've always fancied myself as a bit of a talent spotter. That is I've sometimes seen an actress (being a male I was more interested in them than actors) playing a small, insignificant role and I've decided that some day she'd be up at the top as a real leading lady. One of these is the British star Sally Gray, whom I first saw in *Mr. Reeder in Room 13*. I was definitely impressed and decided to watch out for her next film. I made a point of seeing her in *Lambeth Walk*, *The Saint in London*, *A Window in London*, *The Saints Vacation*, all of which made me more certain that here was an actress who would be Britain's best.

Up to late 1940 it had just been a case of seeing her name in the cast of a film and going along to see it. Then one day, on my way to work I happened to see a copy of the *Picturegoer* Xmas number, with a photograph of Miss Gray on the cover. I bought it, and that was the start. Since then, I've accumulated files of cuttings and data about this one actress. I started a collection of stills from her films and put them in albums. I wrote to her and obtained an autographed photograph, which I had framed and hung on the wall of my bedroom, where it still is.

From my data I found her birthdate and sent her a birthday present, which she acknowledged, later I sent other and more valuable gifts, and at the time—I decided to join up I was saving, to be able to send a gift for Xmas. The reason for this heroine worship was brought about, I think, by a lack of interest in life which was caused by all my companions having left for the services, and it certainly did fill the void. A psychologist would be able to define it more clearly. Apart from giving me a desire to see this actress in person on the West End stage, which is still alive, the films I have seen have never made me ambitious or want to travel. I was always sceptical of films depicting foreign lands. During this war I have travelled a great deal in the Mediterranean area, North Africa and Italy and I am still very sceptical of the travel films which I see.

Films have never made me dissatisfied with my lot, and through what I saw of conditions abroad, it will take a great deal to make me discontented. I have never had any hallucinations about my capabilities, and films have not influenced my decision as to a career.

The high standard of comfort of the modern cinema as against the theatre, and the difference in price of admission, is I think, the main factor why I visit the cinema more than the theatre.

While films are my chief means of recreation, I am not such a great connoisseur as to be able to tell if a film is badly directed or well produced, all I can say about any film is whether it is good or bad. I have a great weakness for visiting cinemas in strange towns, and look on it as a form of adventure. The cinema is not quite a habit with me, I have to know a film is good before I go to see it, and when there is a glut of second raters I sometimes don't visit a cinema for months.

Whilst I have been in the Army I have become less interested in films as many other distractions claim so much of my leisure time. Though I would still make a big effort to see a film in which my favourite actress is acting.

This narrative is, I am afraid, very incomplete, though I have honestly tried my best to give you any helpful information. Should there be any queries, I shall be only too pleased to answer them to the best of my ability.

The next group consists of documents which specify no particular age, but record, in every case, regular attendance at 'children's' shows. 'It was the usual thing for a child, in my district at any rate', writes No. 20, 'to go to the cinema, and *what we were really interested in was the "following up"*.' No. 21 is also interesting, for although she thinks of the screen world as a 'dreamworld' and is therefore not made dissatisfied with her way of life, she cites a film which has affected several contributors, *The Lamp Still Burns*. This film 'was mainly responsible for my taking up student nursing at this hospital and I can only thank all the people concerned in the production for their moving portrayal of the characters, which so greatly influenced my decision'.

NO. 20

AGE: 17   OCCUPATION: TYPIST
SEX: F.   NO PARENTS

I can't remember that at first I had any interest in films. The Cinema was just a place you went to on a Saturday afternoon. It was the usual thing for a child, in my district at any rate, to go to the cinema and what we were really interested in was the 'following up'. *Rin Tin Tin* was a great favourite and another kind that generally went down well was the 'White People versus Indians' kind of thing. It was a favourite game, after we came home from the picture house, to play at what we had just seen and we girls had to submit to being tied up, shot at and very thoroughly given a rough time. My age at this time I don't quite know but I think I was about four years old. I went with the rest of my playmates and we numbered about 10. At this time I was also an ardent fan of Shirley Temple and Jane Withers although I liked Shirley the best. I remember seeing *The Little Colonel* and another film when she sang 'Baby take a Bow' about this time.

Then I must have been a little older because I remember liking Jean Harlow and I am sure I was young because I am still teased about an incident that happened one Saturday afternoon. I wanted to go to the cinema very early and said that I couldn't stop to have lunch as I would be late. My Grandmother was rather bewildered as it was about 12 noon and the cinema didn't open until 1 p.m. and asked me why I couldn't wait and I very solemnly replied that I wanted to see Jean Harlow going into the cinema. Well I was allowed to go early alright but I'm afraid I never saw anyone entering and I was first in that day. I can remember the film a little but it's rather hazy, although I think that she co-starred with William Powell. About this time instead of playing at Cowboys and Indians we played at keeping house and dressed ourselves up in old evening dresses and high-heeled shoes and tried to copy the manner of our favourite film star. I saw another film of J. Harlow with Robert Taylor and on the same programme was a Crime Does Not Pay and I remember being a little surprised when I saw Robert Taylor in the part of the crook. It must have been a very early film of his. It always stuck in my memory as rather odd seeing him in such a small part and on the same programme in a film where he was the leading man.

I saw *King Kong* and although I was rather scared at the time it did not make me so afraid as a film of Boris Karloff's I saw. The film was *The Black Room* or something like that and I never went back to see one of his again until, not very long ago, I saw *The Climax*. I enjoyed that alright but for weeks after I saw the first one I was afraid to go to sleep as I used to dread dreaming about it. I can't tell you what scene it was that was the worst as the whole picture terrified me.

Always, after seeing a Dr. Kildare film, I have had ambitions to be a nurse but I am afraid they were short-lived although I had them quite often as I never missed one of the series. Dr. Kildare was my conception of a doctor and even though there was so much talk about him I never lost faith and I believe that, for all the talk, he has done more than some of the stars who joined up of their own accord and were back in Hollywood again after receiving an honourable discharge. I never dreamed so many stars had bad stomachs.

When the war started I was eleven years old and my screen idol was Ty Power but since then I have changed a great deal. I still like Ty Power but he doesn't seem to be the same as he was when I saw him in *Suez*, he is not as good and at that time I thought he was the most wonderful man in the world. My greatest thrill was seeing a picture with him in it and where he starred with Linda Darnell. I

From the Film *La Belle et la Bete*. Perhaps the most important film experiment in recent years. (cf. Jean Cocteau's fascinating book *Diary of a Film*, Dobson.)

From the Film *The Last Chance* A Swiss film with an international team and a message of hope.

think Linda Darnell is one of the most beautiful girls in Hollywood and I have liked her ever since I saw her first film *Hotel for Women*. I still think there is no one like her. I am older now and have changed a good deal in what I like and do not like in a film. I go all out for a good actor now. I have two favourites and they are very different from one another. No. 1 is James Mason, who I think is very attractive. I like his voice and his appearance and I think he is a wonderful actor, also I think he is good-looking. I don't know why I like him but there is no one to beat him except perhaps No. 2. He is Van Johnstone and before I go any further I do not want you to think that I am a bobby-sock fan or whatever it is they call them. I think there is nothing more idiotic and lothsome than swooning over anyone. I read enough about that sort of thing when Frank Sinatra was the 'latest thing'. In the case of my liking Van Johnstone its the same as my liking James Mason. I do not know what attracts me or how it attracts me, all I know is that although not exactly good-looking, he is no Ty Power, he has a nice face and there is something about him that makes you like him. Though it cannot work with everyone as my chum can't stand him. She admits he is a good actor but thats all. He just doesn't exist to her.

Yes, I think I have fallen in love with a star but I am not saying with whom or why as I think that comes under the heading of P.P. even though I do not know him.

When I saw *Marriage is a Private Affair* I certainly came under the heading 'Did you ever imitate a star'. I put my hair in the page-bob like Lana Turner and kept it like that until I saw *Thirty Seconds Over Tokio* when I changed it to the way Phyllis Thaxter had hers. I am afraid films have made me very dissatisfied with the way I live and of the manners of people. I love the way everyone when acting knows just how to behave with perfect grace. When with a woman they remember all the little things so many men seem to forget. Above every thing films have made me discontented with being poor, and I am not ashamed to say so because it is the truth and you asked for that. I have always had ambitions to play the piano, perhaps this doesn't amount to much but I haven't been able to realize this ambition just as I haven't been able to realize so many others.

I could go on for ever and I have said so much already that I had better stop. Thank you for giving me this opportunity.

NO. 21

AGE: 19   FATHER: HEAD CLERK
SEX: F.   SOLICITORS MANAGING CLERK
OCCUPATION: STUDENT NURSE
NATIONALITY: BRITISH

I have been considering answering your request for a motion picture autobiography ever since the May 26th *Picturegoer* fell into my grasping hands a week ago, until I could not resist the urge this morning and refused to be tempted by the thoughts of a luxury lay-in or even 'mon petit déjeuner', so please spare me the cruel information that you are accepting no more contributions as I could not bear the thought of so much wasted energy.

My interest in films was first awakened, when I was expected to accompany my elder brothers and sisters to the nearest cinema perched on a hill some two miles distant, so that my parents were free to choose their particular choice of entertainment on Saturday afternoons. We were 'treated' to the front stalls but even on Saturday pennies did not always provide sufficient odd cash to travel in style so the hike not only enforced an early start, but also a delayed return.

My superiors would converse very learnedly on the way about the respective merits of the film we were about to see and it always used to puzzle me how they knew so much about it when they had not even seen it. Tarzan was a great favourite of mine in those days although even then my fellow hero-worshippers were inclined to be slightly cynical as well as highly intrigued by his magnificent feats.

I must have reached the imposing age of eight years or thereabouts when I considered *Alice in Wonderland* a film worthy of a three hours' wait in the pouring rain at the aforementioned cinema partly because I had had visions beforehand of myself playing the part of the heroine. These were inspired by my mother's insistence that I was the image of the 'real Alice' for whom the studio was searching, but my photo only resulted in a letter of thanks, the news that the part had been allotted to Charlotte Henry and the rapid subsidence of my dreams of fame.

These have never returned to the same extent since I have realised that magnificent swimming pools, publicity and glamour do not necessarily make for happiness, although there are times when I envy the stars the projection of their personalities on the world at large.

There is a spark of vanity in most of us which is encouraged by being the centre of attraction in some sphere however small and it must be wonderful to know that strangers too are aware of that irrepressible charm.

The disadvantage however is that people are apt to think of their screen heroes and heroines only in terms of their screen personalities instead of men and women with the ordinary trials of life plus those of their unreal environment to face.

It is mainly because of this that I am satisfied with my obscurity in the work I have chosen and have no great desire to change places with the hard working people in the entertainment world.

I always used to imagine that Hollywood hair styles, clothes and make-up were well out of my reach, but since the advent of natural beauty has arrived, it has become apparent to me that the rest are only appendages to produce the desired effect.

Ingrid Bergman is far more truly glamourous than Ginger Rogers in all her films, in *Lady in the Dark* while Ginger herself has no need to rely on the artificial props.

Studios tend to bring out a sparkling new star and rely on his or her talents from the start, but then gradually fit those same distinguishing features into the old pattern, thus forming an entirely new, less exciting personality.

The screen world always appeared as a dream world and although it has given me the desire to travel it has not made me feel dissatisfied with my way of life.

Travel films, pictorial, nature study, documentaries all interest me as they have something to teach, while films made from books encourage my love of literature.

My time is obviously running short with the result that my reply is conforming to the conventional pattern set by the lecturer for 'guidance' only, which may have prevented many irrelevancies if they had been consulted earlier and provided more of the required information. Nevertheless I intend to conclude this autobiography which more rightly belongs to the readers column, with the information that films have given me vocational ambitions to become a soldier, lawyer or nurse etc: to be more precise *The Lamp Still Burns* was mainly responsible for my taking up student nursing at this hospital and I can only thank all the people concerned in the production for their moving portrayal of the characters, which so greatly influenced my decision.

NO. 22

AGE: 39
SEX: M.
NATIONALITY: BRITISH
PARENTS: DECEASED

OCCUPATION:
CHECKER AND INSPECTOR OF CASTINGS

My initial interest in films was aroused entirely by serials, such as *The Clutching Hand*, *The Adventures of Elaine*, *Singaree*, *The Iron Man* and the immortal story of *The Broken Coin*. Each episode contrived to end in a particularly thrilling climax which, I confess, stimulated the desire to see the following chapter, yet, for my own part, I do not believe that entirely created the stimulus, which demanded a continuation of visits to the pictures, sometimes extending over a period of twenty weeks.

As I try to bridge the years and recapture the impressions of boyhood, I am convinced that the story value of these serials, (despite the incredible incidents strewn along the whole series of episodes) were largely responsible for my early enrolment as a 'Film Fan'.

These films were for the most part seen in company of my elder brother, or occasionally a school friend, these films largely influenced our choice of games, generally we took turns being the intrepid hero or the villain, who seldom had one single redeeming feature, as near as I can say my age when these pictures were the vogue would be between eight and twelve.

When I was about thirteen or fourteen I remember as clearly as yesterday, the duelling scene in the picturisation of *Rupert of Dentzau*.

An unending panorama of names and personalities flit across my mind, Charlie Chaplin's genius in the days of *The Tramp*, *The Champ*, *Easy Street*, and *The Gold Rush*. The late Douglas Fairbanks in his most outstanding roles as D'Artagnan, in the immortal Dumas Classics, Lord Sterling, Chester Bonklin, Rex Turpin, inextricably mixed up with motor cars, fire hoses, ladders, whitewash and custard pies, the pioneers of slapstick *The Keystone Bobbies*, Harold Lloyd the creator of *Lonesome Bike* with Bebe Daniels as his excellent foil, the late Larry Simon who invariably fell at least once in all his pictures, with equal indifference from skyscrapers and cliffs, stony faced Buster Keaton the human punch bag who took all they gave without batting an eye. To balance the illustrious array of males, I remember the stirrings of chivalry initiated by Pearl White, Barbara La Mar, Corrine Griffith, these idealistic ladies inspired a yearning for romance, whilst I was still a youthful adolescent, yet the standard they set was a very high one which perhaps, accounts for my being happily married. Greta Garbo held my affection for years, yet I confess, one viewing of Gerda Maurua, in *The Spy* captivated me to the exclusion of all previous convictions.

Despite all these impressive personalities not one influenced me one iota except emotionally, the honour of awakening ambition goes unconditionally to Deanna Durbin, who not only inspires both young and old with the melody of her voice, but also has the power to stimulate and sustain me, in my belated efforts to make use of my talent for drawing, how often have I been tempted to let sleeping dogs lie, yet always am I urged on hoping that I can at least learn how to draw professionally, so that should the need arise I can make use of a gift which so far I have completely neglected, when Deanna sings she seems to sing to me alone, that, I well know, is merely illusion, but I would dearly love to make it come true.

I am conscious of leaving many gaps in my film autobiography, yet to record it fully would take a full sized book.

NO. 23

AGE: 37   OCCUPATION: HOUSEWIFE
SEX: F.   NATIONALITY: BRITISH

Films have been my hobby for years, I'm now 37.

The first film I can remember clearly was one of which the comedian Pimple made as a Scotch Soldier leading others, I know it was very funny to me at the time. We used to pay a 1d. Saturday afternoons and as we came out we were given a bag of sweets.

Then a few years after, I can remember Jack Mulhall in light comedian roles in which he was perfect, I still catch glances of him in small parts now at the movies. Then I was in the flapper age when Rudolph Valintino was the hero, and when his picture was on *The Shiek*. I know we girls had to stand to get in and we were saying 'Isn't he marvellous', 'I wish I was Agnes Ayers'. I bought every photo I could possibly get of him, and my bedroom was surrounded with him, so you see there were pin-up-boys in those times too.

Even now when I see old pictures of him in your magazine I still get a little romantic feeling, silly isn't it how a picture does effect you of anyone.

His picture *The Four Horsemen* was one of his greatest, but when I went to see that, it was dark when I came out and being young, I was terrified all the way home. 'The Horsemen' were following me all the way. I ran as hard as I could. I think the silent pictures effected people more than the talkies, as I think hearing them talk makes it less creepy. I know 'Lon Chaneys' always upset me.

Sometimes I wish they would show one of the old silent ones occasionly as I'm sure the children of today don't realize the wonder of the film worlds progress through the years. I still go very often to the pictures in fact I'd like to go more often. I like to go on my own and get carried away by the acting especially when it is an actor you have a little warm spot for, for I'm sure youngsters aren't the only ones who go because they like the ways and actions and little mannerisms of their favourite actors.

I like Ralph Bellamy because he reminds me of someone years ago.

NO. 24

AGE: 43   OCCUPATION: HOUSEWIFE
SEX: F.   HUSBAND: MERCHANT SEAMAN
NATIONALITY: BRITISH   FATHER: CABINET MAKER

I suspect this competition is for young people, but as you don't say so I am embarking on my favourite subject, picturegoing.

I have gone to pictures and theatres from infancy. As a child, I waited all the week, for a Saturday Matinee. About ten years of age I always went twice a week with my mother. She is still an ardent film fan. Her first words, arriving here on holiday last year, 'I see you have *Murder in Thornton Square* down the road, let's go, I do enjoy a good murder'.

The kind of films I like are, all films. My earliest recollection is of keystone comedies, cowboy pictures, Max Linda, Roscoe Arckbuckle, Mary Miles Minter, Mary Pickford, Lazimova Pauline Frederick. Those were the days. Then the serial pictures, *What Happened to Mary?*, *Tiger Face* etc. When life was unbearable until the next episode was shown. I was about fourteen then. I wanted to be a stenographer, so I took a post as usherette in a new cinema in our town, going to a commercial school during the day, and the cinema at night.

Yes, I think the films did influence my play. At school I used to get my playmates together, and stage plays, I didn't act myself, but made all the dresses and rehearsed them, turning the cupboards at home into dressing rooms. Purloining the bedspreads for stage curtains. It was during the great war, and quite often I had two shillings to give the teacher on Monday, proceeds from Amateur theatricals, to buy cigs for the soldiers.

Frightened by films, yes many times and still am at times. I thought Snowhite a most terrifying film. I have seen it four times to try and overcome my fear, but in my mind it still remains sinister. I liked *Trader Horn* the first time I saw it, it made a shocking hole in my manners. The black men, were swinging across the river on branches, whilst crocodiles snapped at their legs. As one of these men was taking off, I suddenly swung myself out of my seat into the lap of the person, an entire stranger, next to me. I held my feet as high as I could in the air, so as not to be bitten. Ye Gods, what a commotion, it was many moons before I had sufficient courage to go back to the Empire Leicester Square.

The acting was excellent in *Gone With the Wind*. I heard a very strange noise and I discovered two girls in the row in front, arms round one another actually sobbing. Yes I think most people regardless of sex or age find it difficult to control their emotions when the acting is good.

I am most interested in dress and mannerisms and speech of actors and actresses, but wouldn't want to copy them. Although if impressed by a picture I pick out the part I should like to play, and rehearse parts of it, because I have a conviction, I can act as well as most people.

Films would never make me more receptive to love making, quite the opposite. I consider most love scenes, sickening and some even obscene. Taking into account the re-action of most audiences the tutting and shuffling about, I think many people feel the same. Its the type of emotion I don't wish to see depicted, it brings it down to a cheap level.

I haven't suffered any temptations or ambitions through film going. I like travel, but find that the excellent travel pictures we get, satisfy that longing. No they do not make me dissatisfied with my life. I wish we had more news theatres, we haven't one in this city at all. You would think someone would recognise the possibilities. Any building could be used, in my native town, we have one cinema, made out of a disused stable, and another one out of a church, we sit in pews. I was staying at a remote village, the films are shown once a week in the church hall, all seats a shilling each. Carry your seat any part of the hall you wish.

NO. 25

AGE: 17½   OCCUPATION: SHORTHAND-
SEX: F.   TYPIST
NATIONALITY: BRITISH

My first contact with the screen was when I went, together with my elder sisters, to the 'Mickey Mouse Club'. There, for the admission fee of 2d per week, we saw one full length film, one cartoon and the serial film. The full length film was usually a western, packed with thrills which made all and sundry enter into the spirit of what was going on, and even I, at the early age of five could understand enought to cheer the hero and 'Boo' the villain. The cartoon always brought laughter, and the serial suspense. The show would end with the hero jumping from a plane; or riding to the rescue of his lady, then would appear a notice saying, 'Will Bob Blane live after his daredevil jump to freedom?'; or 'Will Tom Faraday succeed in rescuing Betty from the hands of Black Hawk?'—Come next week and find out. And you can guess we did all we could to help Mother so that we should be allowed to go the following week.

It wasn't until I was about ten years old that I went to the 'grown-ups' cinema, other than on special occasions. Then I started going every Saturday afternoon. There were five cinemas in the town where I lived and it was certainly hard to make up my mind which one to go to. I usually chose one with child film stars in: Freddie Bartholomew, Mickey Rooney and Shirley Temple being my favourites. The Dead End Kids invariably brought a visit from me. Their daring escapades and fights intrigued me more than those of the cowboys and Indians at the Mickey Mouse Club.

At the age of fourteen I really became a film-fan in earnest. By this time I had obtained a part-time job which gave me more pocket-money than my parents could afford to give me, and I went to the cinema at least twice, and sometimes three or four times a week. My parents said that going so often would interfere with my education because I wasn't giving enough time to my homework, but they were wrong, because I managed to obtain first position in class every term. Some films definitely helped me with my examinations with regard to history and literature.

Well by this time the types of films I was chiefly interested in were musicals, romances, and dramas. My film favourites then were, and still for the most part are, Vivien Leigh, James Mason, Bing Crosby, Bob Hope, Robert Taylor and Clark Gable. I never have, and I don't think I ever shall, really and truly idolise a film-star. I admire Bing Crosby's singing; I think Bob Hope is the best comedian on the screen or radio; Robert Taylor and Clark Gable make handsome heroes; Vivien Leigh's acting as Scarlet O'Hara in *Gone With The Wind* was brilliant; and James Mason is an actor in the highest sense of the word.

I made a point of not going to see films which were alleged to be frightening. My main reason was because after seeing *Dr. Jekyll and Mr. Hyde* I had a nightmare. While I was actually seeing the film I barely turned a hair, but after seeing the same thing in my dreams I was thoroughly frightened and I was even crying when I woke up. And even now, after about two years, the mention of *Jekyll and Hyde* sends cold shivers through me.

As a general rule I enter into the spirit of the film, and during the filming I really do become part of it. I very seldom try to suppress my emotions in a cinema. If I want to laugh, I laugh (even if nobody else seems to think it funny), and if I want to cry, well, I just go ahead and cry. Of course, I feel rather silly sometimes, but then, there are probably others sharing my feelings.

With regard to imitating from films, I have often tried new hair styles but usually without success. I have certainly envied Rosalind Russell's and other film-stars' clothes, but under present day conditions I have never yet managed to get new material, or felt justified in altering something else in order to copy.

Films about European countries always have a special interest for me, especially those about Switzerland and France, the former for skating, ski-ing and climbing, and France for a gay life, and I hope that when final peace comes and everything gets back to normal, I shall have the opportunity of seeing these countries myself.

At the present time, owing to the evacuation of my office, I am only able to see a film once a week, because the nearest cinema is ten miles away and transport is not available at convenient times. However, I manage to keep informed about films from the *Picturegoer* and *Picture Show* and although I have not seen very many films recently, I know I have not lost, nor ever shall lose, my enthusiasm for the screen.

NO. 26

AGE: 19	MOTHER'S OCCUPATION:
SEX: F.	HOUSEWIFE
OCCUPATION: TYPIST	FATHER'S OCCUPATION:
NATIONALITY: BRITISH	MINER

Almost the only thing I can remember of my very early film-going experiences, is seeing a band of horses thunder across the screen, and burying my head in my mother's arm with a yell because I thought we were going to be trampled to death.

I used to go to the cinema fairly often when I was a child—once a week on Saturday night. Whether it had any ill-effect on my moral outlook or warped childish brain, I don't know, but during the week I waited eagerly for Saturday, probably because I didn't have to go to school on Saturday anyway. I don't know why this visit to the cinema every week gave me so much happiness. It was only a poky little cinema about a hundred yards from my home and my contemporaries vowed that the place was infested with rats—two at least—and one could easily pick up a few unwelcome visitors! I used to go with my three cousins and our Grandmother, and we sat in the back row of the cheapest seats which cost only fourpence.

The amount of pleasure we got for fourpence was amazing. We arrived promptly at 6.30 when the doors opened, and claimed our usual seats. Then, after taking off our coats and hats, we would bring out all kinds of sticky concoctions and chew noisily. When we had become acclimatised, we would read what we considered to be the very best literature—namely the *Wizard*, *Chips*, *Schoolgirls' Own* and *Film Fun*. The show started at 7.0 and as soon as the lights dimmed, we settled down and hardly spoke a word, except to ask Gran what the butler meant when he said, 'Indubitably', and whether the man with the pimple on his nose would come back and murder the heroine.

Cowboy films were my favourite at that time—I was about nine or ten. I think we all liked them. We would cheer and boo energetically and my boy cousin would jump up and down with exitement when the hero chased the villain at the end of the film and handed him over to the Law. I used to like Hoot Gibson best of all because he would walk nonchalantly down the street chewing gum, while the villain's gang lay in wait for him on roofs and in barrels. Then, when everyone in the audience was thinking his end had come, he would whip out his pistols and knock off the gang one by one, put the pistols back in his holsters and continue his stroll—nonchalantly.

When I was twelve our numbers had decreased from four to three. My eldest cousin started working at a local Printer's and was, therefore, too important to go with us to the cinema. At that time one cousin . . . and I developed a craze for those musicals starring Dick Powell, Ruby Keeler and Ginger Rogers. (Incidently we developed a craze for Dick Powell, too). We used to hum 'I'll string along with you', 'Honeymoon Hotel' and such, and execute what we fondly hoped to be intricate tap-dancing steps. We would dress up, I remember, and pretend to be glamourous lovelies with scores of good-looking admirers simply swooning at our feet if we so much as gave them a glance. (She was Ginger Rogers and I was Ruby Keeler). Of course, it was rather awkward to prevent ourselves tripping over our evening dresses, but as they were only coats tied round our waists with the sleeves, it really didn't matter.

My eldest cousin's brother died when I was almost thirteen, and my cousin went to live in another district, so I was rather lonely. After a while I went to the cinema with a friend from school—on Tuesdays and Saturdays. I remember seeing a film in the *Frankenstein* series that almost scared me to death. The scene which drightened me most was when the heroine was alone in her room getting ready for her wedding, and the Monster stood looking in at the open window. She was entirely unaware that he was there, and he came through the window—nearer and nearer. I was so nervous that night when I had switched off the light and got into bed that I kept turning round quickly, trying to peer into the darkest corners of the room to see if he were there. After a few minutes, I got up and dashed downstairs! Not long afterwards I went to see both *Dracula* and *Frankenstein* at the same performance. ('We dare you', said the advertisment). I was hardly scared at all. Probably each film counter-acted the other.

When I was about fifteen, I used to like romantic films but I would never admit it to anyone. The film heroes, quite understandably, were so much more gentlemanly and dashing than the callow youths I knew, who, at a dance would stroll up, say 'Come on', and then look round nervously, in case someone heard them. I fell in and out of love with practically the whole of Hollywood's manhood. I used to like the boyish, open-air type best, but even then some of their love-making on the screen made me feel silly and embarrassed.

During the past few years films have made me want to be smart and glamorous. After seeing beautiful creatures displaying the latest and most expensive creations all evening, I go home, gaze at myself in the mirror and give up all hope. I have often thought, like many other silly adolescents that it would be marvellous if some famous producer from Hollywood, or even Elstree, would discover me—as if I had ever been lost! Seeing films has made me want to go to America and see for myself how the Americans live—probably half the population live in penthouses, and the rest wallow in dirt in filthy tenements.

Most of all, I think, films have made me dissatisfied with my life. I know that all the stories are not true, and the characters merely exist on celluloid—I have told myself that hundreds of times—but somehow my brain refuses to accept it and I am more dissatisfied than ever. Films are like a drug—the more one has the more one wants, and yet, after seeing a film there is no satisfaction. Everything seems flat and dull when the last scene flickers out, and knowing that—I still go.

NO. 27

AGE: 21 YEARS 11 MONTHS   FATHER DECEASED
OCCUPATION: WEAVER   MOTHER'S OCCUPATION:
IRISH BORN   CANTEEN ASSISTANT

My first visit to a cinema was a little unusual. One of my sisters showed us that by going in at the back entrance we would not have to pay. Everything went well and we enjoyed the film: *She Learned About Sailors* with Lew Ayres and Alice Faye,—so well in fact, that we decided to repeat the experiment next day. Unfortunately, however, we were not so lucky the second time, for the manager caught us and gave me a good talking to, my other sister having left me in the lurch, when she saw what was happening. For ages after that little episode I could not pass that cinema without shivering. I did not go to a film again for over two years as I now knew that it cost money to do so and money was something that I never had. By running messages I was able to earn enough money to pay for a children's matinee, nearly every Saturday afternoon. As can be expected, it was always a Western plus a very exciting serial film. I enjoyed them very much and as soon as the show was finished, I was already looking forward to the next week's film. When I was about thirteen Mother took us all to see *Rose Marie* and after that Nelson Eddy and Jeanette McDonald were our favourite stars, that was until Deanna Durbin, Mickey Rooney and Judy Garland appeared on the screen. Then I was at the age when college pictures, showing life on the campus, graduation etc. interested me mostly. Then came the Betty Grable musicolours, which I still enjoy when I see them, but I have since learned to appreciate such films as *Random Harvest*, *Mrs. Miniver* and recently *Since You Went Away*.

The most frightening scene on the films, as far as I can remember was in *Her Jungle Love*, when a white man, bound up like a mummy with only his eyes showing, was thrown to the crocodiles. I was imagining what that man must have felt like, not being able to move a muscle or shout even, all he could do was just to lie there, watching the crocodiles come closer and closer and realise his own helplessness.

I'm afraid I don't find it hard to control my emotions, for instance while watching the film *Since You Went Away* I glanced around me and discovered that I was the only female that I could see who was not sniffing into a handkerchief. I found *Dragon Seed* much more moving, even then I did not weep. I was however very excited over the fight between John Mills and Stewart Granger in *Waterloo Road*, it was so different from the usual Hollywood faked fights.

It would be very hard to imitate any dress styles from the films. Even in the so-called Hollywood 'Fashions' shops there is nothing like the cut or even the colours seen on the screen. The only mannerism I can think of that we have imitated are the wise-cracks and the jive talk. Such as 'Don't strain the brain Jane' and 'Cut the steam Dream', etc. Did we ever fall for our screen idols? I guess most of us have, I know Dennis Morgan has been my favourite for a number of years now and I'm pretty sure he will be for a long time yet.

I don't see how anyone who has seen those beautiful 'Traveltalk' films can help but yearn to travel. They certainly make me yearn alright. Films do make you dissatisfied with your way of life, after all watching the screen your interest is held because something is happening all the time, something that is different and doesn't—speaking generally—happen to us. Once outside the cinema, all that is changed, I know exactly what to to expect the next day and the day after and so on, so that we often feel a little discontented with our way of living.

To conclude, and I'm glad to have got this off my chest, so to speak.—To conclude, I must admit that films have not given me any vocational ambitions as to nursing etc. No, but it has made me wish that I had lots of money to travel, spend and enjoy myself and go to the pictures, well of course!

Numbers 28, 29 and 30 state no actual age, but attendance began early. In these cases, however, the films seen were not children's films. These writers went with their parents and saw, presumably, the type of film which the parents wished to see themselves. Although there was no serial to arouse the desire to 'follow up', the writer of No. 28 states that from about seven to thirteen the cinema was 'a passion' with her—'I could not go too frequently to satisfy me, and when thwarted in my desire I created scenes as some children do over toys'. The habit was allowed by the parents to persist, although 'One of my earliest recollections is hearing my mother saying that she would have to cease taking me to the cinema if I continued to have violent dreams about them'. No. 30, who was taken by her parents once or twice a week 'at a very early age', took little interest in the films she saw, but was frightened into a nightmare by *The Hunchback of Notre Dame.*

NO. 28

AGE: 19   FATHER: ELECTRICAL ENGINEER
SEX: F.   MOTHER: HOUSEWIFE
OCCUPATION: CLERK
NATIONALITY: BRITISH

Since I am only nineteen this film autobiography is necessarily limited. However, I have been a constant film-goer as long as I can remember, commencing at a very early age when I was taken by my parents once or twice every week. From the age of about seven to thirteen the cinema was a passion with me—I could not go too frequently to satisfy me and when thwarted in my desire I created scenes as some children do over toys, sweets etcetera. I realize now that the films were to me an escape from a dull, uneventful, very ordinary childhood. They represented excitement, adventure, romance and new ideas which I had never met before.

One of my earliest recollections is hearing my mother saying that she would have to cease taking me to the cinema if I continued to have violent dreams about them. Concerning the dreams I remember nothing, but I know that I resolved then never again to mention my reactions to a film, or opinion of one, otherwise I should be forbidden to go to what was rapidly becoming to me a veritable fairy-land. This resolve, by the way, undoubtedly made me secretive and I rarely told my parents what I thought about anything.

But the films were merely an escape. In those days, the idea never occurred to me that the places and the men and women characterised in films had any connection to reality. The life which the film heroes and heroines lived, in no matter what type of film I saw, 'high society' or 'slum', was too utterly alien from the world in which I lived.

From the age of seven to fourteen I do not think that I had any preference as to which type of film I most desired to see. Any film was acceptable. Although I think that I was most impressed by any film, be it a lavish Hollywood musical of an historical impossibility, which contained beautiful extravagant costumes, rich in colour and spectacle. But I was never seized by a desire to possess such lovely clothes, nor did I sigh with envy at the synthetic beauty of 'stars', or their magnificent houses and trains of servants,—simply, I think, because I did not connect these things with reality. The cinema was merely a form of fairy tales and as such I do not think that it did me any harm.

In my opnion it is only when children try to apply movie-life to actual life that juvenile delinquency results, otherwise if it is impressed upon them that it is merely an imaginary world at which they are gazing they will only be the happier for a few hours entertainment. But, naturally, I realize that this applies only to a child of limited intelligence and imagination as I was at the time. I accepted my parents' explanation that 'it was all made up' whereas a more sensitive and imaginative child would not have done so. But such a child should not be allowed to go to the cinema at an early age.

After I had reached the age of fourteen however, I began to accept the cinema merely as a method of entertainment. I attached no importance to it, I merely went if I was in the right mood and if I thought there was a good film showing. I no longer went to satisfy a passion for escape, other interests filled my time more satisfactorily. My school-life broadened my horizon—literature and the theatre brought more content than the bizarre, unreal cinema could ever do.

My tastes in films had definitely crystallised. I still like historical films but now for their history, not their costumes, although my interest in history had often made me wonder why film-makers must always introduce inaccuracies—nearly in every case, unnecessarily. Why make Queen Elizabeth a sloppy, emotional woman when the quality for which she was noted was that her supreme love was England and she was a Queen more than a woman. But in *Elizabeth and Essex* she was pictured as deeply in love with Essex— the one love of her life—and finally she made the supreme sacrifice for England with great emotion—nonsense! Elizabeth loved only herself, she may have liked lovers to satisfy her vanity but she would have sacrificed everything she loved without a second's thought for the throne and power.

This love of inaccuracy in historical films is the more puzzling as the truth would invariably make better films. In the *Prime Minister* if Hollywood simply must ignore all the political side of Disraeli's life except the sensational moments of victory and defeat, and concentrate on his romantic life, why misrepresent it? The beauty of the fact that Disraeli could say that Mary Anne was the perfect wife lay not in the fact that she was a frivolous, flirtatious, romantic young girl but that she was almost fifty and twelve years older than he was.

Catherine the Great, however, was the supreme example of twaddle. Anyone who knew but the bare facts of Catherine's life and her marriage with Peter must either have blushed or giggled hysterically at such a ridiculous film.

In my judgement of films too, I deplore the fact that ninty-nine per cent of every film issued can be typed. Thus it became my ambition to pick out the other one per cent of films to see—the film that did not fall into a definite category. I was tired of typed movies —Westerns; snobbishness in high society; the depths of degradation;

country life—local boy makes good; detective story—police baffled—
dapper amateur triumphant; love story—impossible situations—
misunderstandings which two minutes sensible conversation could
have cleared up—naturally with a happy ending; and so on, many
other so familiar types.

By now of course I had linked up films with reality, and I dis-
pised the futile attempts to portray life, so showily, gaudily, and
synthetically. But in the last few wartime years I have encountered
with delight good British films, with solid British humour, no gags
or cracks as the Americans put it, but definite British wit. Their
portrayal of village life, where everyone knows his neighbour's
affairs as well as his own, are truly delightful and they get the right
atmosphere. British films about Britain are now, in my opinion, the
best films to see.

In my search for an original film I eventually found *Citizen Kane*.
I was intensely interested. It was the first time I had seen a film
which did not tell the audience what to think but made them think
for themselves. One of the many reasons why I think the theatre is
superior to the cinema is that one can use one's brains occasionally
at the theatre but never at the cinema. The uniqueness of *Citizen Kane*
delighted me. Except for clumsy surprise endings which annoy one
because they are obviously there for no other reason but to surprise
the audience, one can really always foretell the ending of the film
and indeed the whole story from its type. But in *Citizen Kane* the
whole story was original, it was not a type, it possessed atmosphere,
a good plot, (which is often considered unimportant by film-makers),
unusual photography and excellent acting by unknowns and not
stars who depend on a good pair of legs to see them through every
film.

I am painfully aware that my opinion in this matter is not shared
by many. *Citizen Kane* was not a popular box-office success, audiences
prefer not to think, they like types.

I was not influenced by the films at an early age because I felt
they had no bearing on this life and later when I saw that they were
supposed to represent sections of people's lives their failure produced
only an amused contempt. I was never frightened by the conventional thrillers, grotesque make-up or the villain about to kill the
hero because I knew that there would be a happy ending—films
were not related to life and crime did not pay. One film however
which I saw when I was about eight did have a frightening effect
upon me because it presented a new idea to me—mental torture. I
now cannot remember the title or what it was about clearly. I think
that Sara Haden and Basil Rathbone were in it and that the latter
had forced himself into this lady's house and was trying to drive her
insane in order to procure her money. The acting was very good
and I was haunted for weeks and still now, I retain the impression
of fear at seeing this lady becoming more frightened and convinced
that she was insane. The film was not *Gaslight* or *Thornton Square*

versions which, considering they had the same theme I thought amateurish in comparison. I vividly remember Sara Haden's large expressive eyes dilated with fear as Basil Rathbone bent over her with a jewelled cigarette-case in his hand. I do not remember anything else about it—I suppose it ended according to type.

With true femininity I enjoy a good love-story and if it is the sorrowful type which ostentatiously does not end happily ever after, such as *Now Voyager*, I can give myself up entirely to the luxury of the moment and indulge my emotions, weeping at the touching scene before me. It never lasts however and immediately the film ends, sometimes before, I can analyse the ridiculous and unlikely situations quite coldly as if I had not been moved at all.

I have never imitated films in anything. I go to the cinema for entertainment—not example. At about fifteen I fell in love with Conrad Veidt. At the time he represented my idea of a perfect man—handsome, distinguished, cultured, intelligent, an attractive foreign accent, a perfect lover—all the most desirable qualities. Moreover he was nearly always the villain who I think is usually much more attractive than the insipid hero. This infatuation died with him, although I still like to see re-issues of his films—that is when I can persuade myself to forget that the type he represented— the rather dated, courtly perfect lover is exaggerated and rather trying.

The question 'Have films made you more receptive to love-makng' I cannot answer since I like the intellectual company of men only, much prefer women friends and contrary to many girls of my own age I cling to the old-fashioned belief that nineteen is too young for boy-friends and love-making in which, anyway, I have no interest.

How can I answer the questions concerning temptations, ambitions, dissatisfactions arising from films since I have never let any film influence my life. The films I have seen are always too much interested in the hero's and heroine's private affairs to make me interested in the vocation in which they are engaged—but only, it seems to me, as a background, a nurse, an actress, member of the services or other professions.

Books and the theatre have influenced me but not films and I think this is because it is largely a question of one's own will how one is influenced and I never believed that the films were a good influence. Undoubtedly they make some children dissatisfied with their life, they drive some to crime in imitations of 'gangsters', they cause unhappy marriages because boys and girls especially the latter, conceive a too romantic idea of love and marriage from the screen. I think a Children's Cinema is most desirable; specially made films could influence children in the right direction.

As to adults of the present generation most of them go to the cinema from habit and lack of any other occupation, and they delight in nudging their neighbour and pointing to a Hollywood lovely and saying 'She's just been divorced for the fourth time', and people will doubtless go on seeing films for precisely the same reasons.

NO. 29

AGE: 21½   FATHER: AIRCRAFT WORKER
SEX: F.   MOTHER: HOUSEWIFE
OCCUPATION: FACTORY WORKER
NATIONALITY: BRITISH

For many years now I have been interested in films. They are my chief hobby and I glean every bit of information I possibly can about the film world. While I was a child, even though I was interested, the films I saw are very vague in my memory. But one in particular stands out. It is *Mutiny on the Bounty*. My father took me to see it. Usually I went alone. I never went more than once a week. Now I go about four times, providing of course the film is good. It wasn't until I was about fourteen that my real interest began. Dramatic films are my favourite type, films such as Bette Davis would star in. But I always enjoy a musical or a comedy. Horror films hold a kind of fascination for me. Even though the events sometimes frighten me, and I want to hide my face until it is over, it seems to draw me lide a magnet and I have to watch. I once had a bad scare. It was in the film *The Uninvited*, starring Ray Milland. Towards the end a door suddenly flew open. The unexpectedness of it made it worse. I thought all the ghostly happenings were over. I was so scared I screamed loudly. I am very emotional especially if a film is sad. Before I realise it the tears are springing into my eyes. Films such as *All This and Heaven Too, Blossoms in the Dust, Dark Victory* and many others drew forth lots of tears. I feel as if I can place myself in the circumstances of those who are playing the part.

When I see a film I like to notice the way an actress carries herself. The way she talks when in company. I think this is useful especially if one is apt to have an inferiority complex. I notice also the way of speaking. Of course in the latter case I give more attention to our own English stars. Some of them are very beautiful speakers. Often I have copied film stars' clothes. In films about modern times such lovely clothes are worn and I have a flair for smart clothes. So if I see something I like I make a mental note to copy it.

I have never actually fallen in love with my screen idol but I have sometimes had a silly notion that he would make a nice husband.

Films have never given me any temptations but sometimes I have been fired with the ambition to be a good dramatic actress and to be able to have it said of me that I was such. But this is the result of vivid imagination of which I have a lot. I have always longed to travel all round the world and see everything of interest. Travel broadens the mind. As for leaving home I never wanted to, but I do now. I should be quite willing to make my own way in life because I am very independent. I can never say films have made me dissatisfied with my way of life. Indeed after seeing some films I prefer my own way of living.

Concerning vocational ambitions, I have often thought I should like to become a nurse but my parents always dissuaded me saying the work was too hard. But I saw the film *The Lamp Still Burns* and I thought this a very fine example of life as a nurse. Anyone who was thinking of becoming a nurse ought to have seen it to give them an idea of the strict routine of this noble career.

To sum up I will say I have seen many films, some of them not so good, others very good, and not only have I been entertained, but I have increased my knowledge of life and its ways.

NO. 30

AGE: 18
SEX: F.
NATIONALITY: BRITISH
OCCUPATION: BANK CLERK

FATHER: IN ARMY

My Mother and Father were and are interested in films, therefore, I naturally started filmgoing at an early age. Being so young, I did not take much interest in the films, and I have a very hazy recollection of ever seeing them. A few scenes of the *Hunchback of Notre Dame* with Lon Chaney in the title role, stick in my mind; partly because it is the only film that has frightened and given me a nightmare. The scene to which I refer was the one where the young girl Esmeralda was about to be taken by the soldiers and the Hunchback, when he saw what was happening, jumped up and down on the narrow parapet of the Cathedral, seething with rage, and that night I dreamt that he was jumping up and down on my bedrail.

When I was about eleven, I was very fond of musicals, cowboy and Walt Disney pictures and was bored with serious films of any kind, but after being evacuated for about a year, I changed. I no longer liked musicals and funnies, I thought they were a waste of time and money, my interest was now aroused by films such as *Rebecca* and *Gone With the Wind*. I simply revelled in seeing bold bad men, and I was extremely annoyed when Rhett Butler softened with his baby daughter Bonny. I still like that type of man best and I think the two men who play that role best are Alan Ladd and James Mason. The only kind of film I have never had time for were slushy love films, especially with Charles Boyer, he appears to me to be a repulsive man.

Since I returned home from Cornwall and seen its impressive coastline and countryside, I naturally wanted to see films about that and other parts of the country as in *Frenchman's Creek* and *Canterbury Tale*, the latter having given me a peace of mind which I had not know for some time, and a longing to go to Canterbury.

Through seeing so many films I have, unconsciously adopted various mannerisms from the stars, and I am now trying hard to drop these ways, as I am tired of people telling me about it.

Films have done two things to me. The first is to show me that the best mode of dress is the simple one, as it is neat and at the same time gives a finished appearance. The second point is that it has made me despise the boys of about my age, with whom I have been out with. After seeing the polished lover on the screen it is rather disillusioning to be kissed by a clumsy inexperienced boy. I have tried not to feel like that about them, but I still find that I would rather go out with a girl-friend or an older man than a young boy.

The screen has deepened my yearning to travel to other countries and see them for myself, instead of reading books and seeing films about them. Although it is not as easy as it sounds, because of the expense, so I have made up my mind to train as a draughtswomen in an aeroplane factory and earn as much as I possibly can.

It is all very well seeing marvellous houses and apartments on the screen, but how do you think we feel when we see our own home? I personally look at my home, in a semi-detached flat, with disgust, and I don't invite my friends home because I don't want them to see the place where I live. I know that it is shortage of houses that has forced us to take a flat, but I find that, rather than explain the situation to them, I would not invite them there. A film I saw last week did comfort me a little, and that was *Give me the Stars*, but would all my friends be as understanding as Emrys Jones was in that film?

I find that films are very influential and play a great part in the lives of regular picturegoers who study the films.

Seven is definitely stated as the age of 'initiation' by Nos. 31 and 32, both of whom record fear-impressions.

NO. 31

AGE: 16   FATHER: WELDER
SEX: F.
OCCUPATION: KEEPS HOUSE WITH MOTHER
NATIONALITY: BRITISH

I first became interested in films when I was seven.

Micky Mouse and other colourful films where my chief interests up to the age of ten.

It was then that I began to like Musical Comedies, Detection, and adventure films. Then I was about twelve I saw *Dangerous Moonlight* and in this I first heard the *Warsaw Concherto* which has been my faverite since then.

I viseted the cinema once a week with my parents.

Films never realy affected my play but we did sometimes dress up and make believe we were film stars or play cowboys.

I was once frightened by a ghost film, but I dont remember being frightened since, becouse I always knew it was just acting and not real.

I never find it hard to control my emotions at a film.

When I was young some films would make me wont to become an actress. I am still interested in acting but I shouldn't wont to act now. Travel films often make me wish I could visit some of the places shown for a holiday, but I have never had any wish to leave home.

The films I like best now at sixteen are periodical and others such as *Wuthering Hights*, *They Came to a City*, *Dene Parodise*, *Henry V*, etc.

I like technicolour if it is made naturally as it was in *This Happy Bread*.

My favourite films-stars are, Penelope Ward, Lawrence Olivier, and Anton Wallbrook.

NO. 32

AGE: 20   FATHER: CRANE DRIVER
SEX: M.   MOTHER: HOUSEWIFE
OCCUPATION: FACTORY HAND IN PLASTICS FIRM
NATIONALITY: BRITISH

I were going to the Cinemas with an elderly girl friend when I were around 7 yrs. old, seeing Nelson Eddy and Jeanette McDonald films, but weren't so keen then, so when I found myself a boy pal, we used to go to the pictures twice per week. Was then I became very interested in films. My favourite pictures used to be 'Westerns' and those weeping films of Shirley Temple's during the 1930's. When I saw *Frankenstein* and *Dracula* posted outside a cinema I was wanting to see them that week. Believe me, although I was only twelve and in shorts, I was able to get in, with an elderly stranger of course. Inside, we parted which made me very lonely, *Frankenstein* the last reel was on, where you see Monster up on the windmill with the Doctor and village people seeking him. Through the whole programme I was not a bit scared, till it was all finished and it happened to be dark outside plus a long walk, but I couldn't do that, I practically flew. Frightened out of my wits, in case I should have met Boris Karloff. Boy was I glad I got home safe. Now I understand why children under sixteen are unable to get in a cinema when by themselves.

Well since then at the age of twelve up to now I make 'Horror' films come second liking to the films which I'm deeply interested in which are the Detective type. Where same star appears in each Series. Such as *The Falcon*, *Michael Shayne*, *Charlie Chan*, *Saint*, *The Thin Man* and *Sherlock Holmes*. The more I see them, the easier and quicker I can spot the murderer.

The third best pictures are the Tough Guy kind, with Humphrey Bogart heading first then Alan Ladd and James Cagney. Those type of films have not made me big or swell-headed at all, but, they certainly have brought me out of a dream. Seeing Scrapping and Boxing has got me that way. To make things clearer I'm able to stand up to anyone as long as they are not more than two stone heavier than I. Being as I myself weighs only a 'Featherweight', 8 st. 7 lb.

To change the subject to Love, I'm not very keen on seeing those films, I happen to use my own according Love on girls, and no film star imitating. When I was 18, I were planning to be a Detective, as the type I saw on the films. But now I don't think much more about it, as I'm sure I would be a failure.

My moment ambition is Engineering, and my pass away time is free hand drawing, have been at it for years. I'm wishing for a new ambition, to go on films myself. I've not known myself to think I'd be a flop. Being I've acted in a few plays when I was at school. Should I be lucky enough to have a chance at it, I most likely would keep my fingers cross, hoping to appear in a Drama.

To get back to love, when I saw *Rosalie* in which Eleanor Powell co-starred in I must confess I loved her in my mind. Then I saw all her latest films after that, and since then I've loved her with my heart. I even wrote to her asking for a photograph, after I saw her in *Rosalie*. And I got the photo O.K. There's another two, I love so much on the screen, Paulette Goddard and Barbara Stanwyck. Pity I pick on elderly girls, to take a liking to, on the Screen. Films have not made me dissatisfied with my way of living in my life, only the wanting to become an actor is the jealously I have. But I may have hope and luck yet.

Johnnie (Tarzan) Weissmuller jungle films come fourth best. That would be the type I'd like, if drama failed. I'm physically fit and I'd be gladly to stare a lion out. Being I have as much courage as I have strength. I'm also light and quick on my feet as well as the eyes. But I couldn't stand for a snake. They're too quick sometimes.

I should immagine that, in present Drama rough and tough films they're should be little of Love, less killing, not too much fighting, but most of all plenty of fast action. Superman stuff, so-called crooks knock over cliffs, or smacked clean through a few storey Building window. Its all fake I know, I have studdied films myself, the human eye tells the truth, I've picked out many of mistakes from all kinds of pictures in these scenes. I didn't wish to write up about it, not on a case it might make the Studio small, but in case it may mean someone to lose their job.

You see, I wouldn't like anyone to try and get me out of work. So you see then how I see things. And besides everyone practically makes mistakes every day.

Hope you will excuse writing and mistakes, and I hope you will find I haven't left anything out. So I'll say here's hoping for the best. Keep them rolling. The Show must go on. And keep the world happier.

Three more contributors record their first visits to the cinema at the age of seven, but in these cases they do not appear to have attended regular children's matinees, and the impressions are not stated to have been very deep until a later date. No. 33 'was not one of those children who were allowed to visit the cinema unaccompanied, at an early age'. She has 'but dim recollections' of her first film, and the one scene which she remembers was not, as in so many cases, one of horror. After this, she went only very rarely for a few years. One is struck by the fact that although the habit of filmgoing nevertheless did develop and the impressions made by the films were strong, the writer has many other pleasures: 'the countryside, the garden, music at the turn of a knob'. 'Films are a most pleasing form of relaxation . . . but for myself, I rarely regret the return to earth'.

No. 33

AGE: 22
SEX: F.
OCCUPATION:
   MOTHER AND HOUSEWIFE (FORMERLY BOOK-KEEPER)
NATIONALITY: BRITISH

June 1, 1945

Being young, my auto-biography as a filmgoer and the effects that this amiable passtime have had upon me will, necessarily be reliant upon films of recent years.

However, to start at the beginning :—

I was not one of those children who were allowed to visit the cinema unaccompanied, at an early age. My introduction to the magic world of make believe came when I was aged seven years though I have but dim recollections of the film.

Indeed I remember merely one scene where a curly haired child, clutching a little dog, ran down some wide stone steps after having rescued her pet from, I think, an auctioneer. For a few years after that I went to the cinema only very rarely and my next distinct impression is of *Choo Chin Chow*.

Perhaps this particular film remains in my memory so clearly as I have always been rather sensitive to the pain of others and the sight of the slaves straining against their ropes to turn the great wheel in the entrance of the robbers cave, filled my heart with pity.

After this came a few Shirley Temple films which left no lasting impressions and then I became a Ginger Rogers fan.

I was about eleven years old at the time for I remember I had just started High School and the increase in my pocket money enabled me to buy more film books from which I extracted all the Ginger Rogers before cutting out various other photographs to be used as 'swops'.

Ginger Rogers—I dreamed of her at night, thought of her all day, filled my scrap books with hundreds of photographs of her, hummed her songs, fluffed my hair out in daring imitation, locked myself into my bedroom and *was* Ginger Rogers.

I could imagine nothing more wonderful than to be able to dance and to sing and I even began to take my music lessons more seriously.

When the storm of this passion subsided I do not know but at fourteen I had turned my affections elsewhere and the object of my schoolgirl adoration was Spencer Tracy.

At this time of my life I think I was becoming more interested in the male sex generally and I liked my heroes strong and rugged.

Mr. Tracy has the doubtful honour of being the first screen hero for whom I shed tears. I cried my way through *Test Pilot, Captains Courageous, Boys Town* and many more.

After a while, as with Miss Rogers the storm gradually blew itself out and I was left with many beautiful memories, two autographed photographs, and no regrets.

As I furthered my education my tastes were developing. I was becoming fond of classical music, good literature and art.

It was at this stage that I turned more to British films. I admire greatly British humour, Shaw's plays and English scenery. None of these are ever exploited as fully as they might be.

Leslie Howard, Hugh Sinclair, Ralph Richardson, David Niven, I liked them all but what most appealed to me were their voices. Clear, true, cultured English voices. Yes, I could close my eyes even now and listen to the music of beautiful words well spoken and for this one reason shall always prefer good British films.

Though I do not consider myself unduly sensitive horror films have a most terrifying and lasting effect upon me.

Once, in a fit of bravado I went to see one of the *Frankenstein* series and remember the after effects even more clearly than the actual film. For several weeks I was literally terrified of going out in the dark, would not venture upstairs alone and imagined that huge, awful creature was always behind me.

Most decidely my first 'horror' film was also to be my last. I have often since seen eerie scenes in films and even though I know them to be ridiculously unreal and far fetched, yet these are the scenes my thoughts dwell upon long after I leave the theatre.

However it is not only frightening scenes that I remember for a long time.

From *Wings of the Morning* I remember the gay gypsy encampment. From *Mans Castle*, the squalid shack homes. The death scene from *Wuthering Heights*, the classroom scene from *French Without Tears*, the beautiful ending to *The First of the Few* with Spitfires flying away into the sunset. Scenes both bright and sordid come to my mind and there seems to be no connecting link, no reason why these images find a place in my memory.

In recent years my picture going has been both regular and frequent but I find that of all the hundreds of films that I must have seen only a very few have had any great emotional effect upon me.

Lassie Come Home was one of these. It could not fail in its appeal to a dog lover. *How Green was my Valley* was delightfully human with no attempts made at glamourisation. It was most touching yet had not the depressing qualities of *Grapes of Wrath* for instance.

Recently I have been most impressed with *Keys of the Kingdom* and *A Song to Remember*. The first found its appeal in its religous sincerity and left me with that beautiful uplifted feeling one experiences after attending a church service.

The second I enjoyed mainly for the music and after such a strong dose of Chopin I walked home with my feet treading air and my head in the clouds. A grand-to-be-alive spirit enveloped me and I was quite unable to talk for hours after I had seen this film. I was so full of the sheer beauty of it.

I would like to see films more true to the lives of great composers and artists. There are a wealth of such biographies so far untouched by the film script writers. Many of the lesser known works of classical writers could be made into film material and would, I am sure, have a universal appeal.

In all my years of filmgoing no film that I have seen has made me return dissatisfied to my own home. If I gaze enraptured at the gilt palaces of the movie queens my envy is merely momentary. To me, it seems an unreal world and I do not yearn for a closer inspection.

There is too much beauty around me, the country side, the garden, music at the turn of a knob. No! I can live without exquisite clothes and streamlined cars.

Films are most delightful to watch, a most pleasing form of relaxation. There are always times, especially during these war years, when one welcomes the brightness of a good musical film, the crazy patter and antics of a good comedian, but for myself, I rarely regret the return to earth.

How good it has been to sit and unload all my facts and theories and how delightfully personal one can be on paper. Not for a fortune would I have admitted my faults and failings aloud. It is satisfying to sit back now safe in the knowledge that I shall probably never come face to face with the reader of this letter.

Vivid recollections are recorded in Documents 34 and 35, but there is none of the impression of early overwhelming impressions created by some of those previously quoted. It should be noted that No. 34 was taken to the cinema despite parental disapproval, while No. 35 states 'I did not go very often in my childhood, and what films I did see were carefully picked out by a wise Mother'. No. 35 has nevertheless been deeply impressed by the films, and appears to be as great an 'addict' as some of the writers who have recorded constant attendance from an earlier age. She is well aware of the effect of the infatuations for film 'heroes' which she has experienced—'the attentions of the local boy irritated me. I was contemptuous of his rather dull dates, and felt that his perfectly ordinary advances were childish and inexperienced . . . Perhaps one day the right boy will scatter this fruitless idealism, imprinted so strongly by the films. *I hope so*'.

NO. 34

AGE: 21   FATHER'S OCCUPATION
SEX: F.   TRAVELLER
OCCUPATION: CHEMIST'S ASSISTANT   MOTHER'S OCCUPATION:
    AND HOUSEKEEPER   HOUSEWIFE
NATIONALITY: BRITISH

At the age of seven I went to see Charlie Chaplin in *Gold Rush*. This was my first experience of Movie Pictures. I was greatly impressed and talked of nothing else for weeks. It is rather a long while ago but I think I have remembered the right title.

My parents, being somewhat narrow-minded, didn't approve of me going to the movies so young, but my youngest aunt rescued me from a somewhat restricted future and often called for me, with the intention of taking me to see a movie.

I must have seen dozens of films but none impressed me until I saw Shirley Temple in *Bright Eyes*. I was a little older than her at the time and was baffled to think that any child could be so pretty and act so well. This film made me dissatisfied with myself, I was plain and had straight hair, not to mention freckles on my nose. I was ashamed to think that anyone could do so much while I was a plain little nobody. *Bright Eyes* reduced me to a shower of tears and my parents vowed they would never let me go again. After this I didn't have the chance to go very often, as my Aunt left town.

When I was nearly eleven I was asked to take my young brother to the movies. This made me very annoyed but I was forced to do this or stay at home. The result was that I didn't see much of the films, I was too busy keeping him quiet.

I think 'Cowboy' films were the only ones we ever imitated as we lived on the outskirts of the town and were near to fields and spinneys. This made our games quite as exciting as films.

I have never been frightened by any film but several have left unpleasant memories. I think Boris Karloff is the only actor to whom I have taken a great disliking.

Very few films have emotionally effected me but those which have are as follow. *Love Story*, *A Song to Remember* and *Phantom of the Opera*. I think the latter had a great effect upon me. I went to see it five times. Musical films of a more serious nature are my favourites and are often the cause of my decisions. At the time I saw *Phantom of the Opera*, I was very worried about a personal matter, but the music and the atmosphere rested my mind and after a long walk home I was able to give my reply without any further worry. After seeing a film of this nature I like to go for a good long walk alone and to go over my past life to review my present life. I think so much more can be expressed by music than by a lot of talking and although I can't read a note of music I never miss listening to classic music. I never miss listening to such music in films. That was my reason for seeing the life of Chopin, *A Song to Remember*. I am one of those unaccomplished individuals who can't sing, dance or act, but I have a great urge to write. Often after seeing a film I go over several parts and although I can't remember the exact wording, I fill in my own words in the way I know the actor or actress has spoken.

After seeing *Old Acquaintance* with Bette Davies I was told that I could have taken her part, because in real life I act as she acted then and mine isn't acting. I enjoyed this film and went home and started to write my life story up to date. Maybe one day I'll finish it but I think I would need to see that film again before I could get the inspiration to finish it.

My dress allowance has never been large enough to copy any film dresses and I think I can honestly admit that no dresses have ever attracted me as much as those worn in *Love Story* by Margaret Lockwood. They were very simple but were of the type that most young girls could wear and afford.

No, I have never fallen in love with any screen idol. What would be the use of it. Life is far too serious at present, to go around falling for someone who isn't aware of your existence and to whom you are as much as a speck of dust. No! I don't intend lavishing any love or affections on any film star. I like and admire many of them and they give me many happy hours. I think some are marvellous actors and actresses but who wouldn't be with their salary. Anyone with the right chance and with a bit of 'go' in them would go all out for that rate of pay. In our own way we are all actors and actresses but our rates of pay are somewhat out of proportion. I think many films will tend to make the young set more receptive to love making but if they have any sense they will pinch themselves because it gives a false impression of their own lives. The lives of ordinary working people are not meant to be influenced by films because their surroundings are not suitable, it only tends to make them dissatisfied with life.

Films have made me long to travel especially those about the sea. My biggest regret is that I wasn't a man, otherwise I'd have gone to sea.

I think most films have wonderful scenery and I imagine climbing hills and mountains and sailing on lakes until someone beside me says: 'All that is made of cardboard and paper'. I wish folks would keep their thoughts to themselves, because it so often spoils the atmosphere caused by the films.

When I saw *Love Story* I heard a loud voice say, 'That isn't Margaret Lockwood playing so and so'. I was so annoyed I got up and found another seat but heard this remark again.

Films make me yearn to write. I always answer any letters after a really good film I find it is the only time that I can go straight ahead with them with perfect ease.

Speaking as one of many millions of ordinary people I am quite certain that films make all of us dissatisfied with our own surroundings but there are very few who ever get any further than being just dissatisfied for the rest of their lives. Others who are more ambitious get ideas from films and it is often through films that people travel. I personally know of someone who was quite content with their own humdrum life until they were inspired by a film. Now I'm told this person is overseas in the NAAFI. She had the chance to travel overseas and went. I hear that she has never regretted travelling and at one time she told me the sea was terrible and nothing would induce her to go abroad. This proves that films make us curious and envious of countries and peoples across the many waters.

I would like to travel and when I see cliffs and the sea combined with the country I wish I could visit every coast in the world. Maybe travelling would inspire me to write more but I think a musical back-ground would be needed too.

In my opinion the world is half asleep. In films there is usually a musical background where one is needed but in life we have to rely on odd musical programmes on the radio. Life would be so much happier and cheerful if there were more music in everyone's heart and soul. This may sound sentimental but I'm the last person in the world to be sentimental about anything.

Music, films and writing are the only things in life which really transfer me to a brighter and happier world. Reading makes me more serious and thoughtful but also helps me to get away from the toils and worries of the world today. Life is so dull and ordinary that I intend getting all I can out of films and all they have to offer. I don't envy folks who don't like films, they must find life too dull for *words*.

The above is now completed and I hope it will help you to see just what my part of the world thinks about the movies. I have spoken to many people since I started this and they all seem to be of the same opinion as I am, but none of them are sporting enough to write it all down. To me they are missing such a lot, there is so much of one self that can be revealed and relieved by writing. I shall look forward to any other competitions which may come along. Why don't you ask the film admirers to submit their own experiences? Some of them may be worth it in fact my own life has had more incident than most films I've ever seen. Some would be somewhat sordid but life is sordid at some time or other. None of us live model lives and you would get a great deal of laughs out of many of the workers lives. I could write a book on my past experiences. Little do people realise that the world just isn't as they see it on the movies. It is probably as well they don't.

NO. 35

AGE: 22
SEX: F.
OCCUPATION: CLERK
NATIONALITY: BRITISH

PARENT'S OCCUPATION
CLERK

I am not quite sure just how much films have influenced my life—or whether certain dreams and ambitions were born in me. But on looking back over several years of film-going, I can honestly say that many of my ways of thinking and some actions which are going, I hope, to have a great bearing on my future, have been directly influenced by films.

The first picture that I can remember with any distinctness was *The Desert Song* with John Boles. I suppose I must have been about six or seven, a very excited little girl, escorted by my Mother. I can recall, not so much any definite scene or personality, as a feeling that here was a different world from my own—a strange, pretty world. And so was born a longing, later to grow into an obsession, to see this different world. I suppose the seeds of this ambition must have been already in me, and were only awaiting some tangible pressure to start growing, because at that tender age surely no single moving picture could have so affected me.

My subsequent cinema-going is a little hazy after that. I did not go very often in my childhood, and what films I did see were carefully picked out by a wise Mother. But my next vivid recollection was of gangster films. In my early teens I would see any and every crime picture, however inferior, and I often found myself longing to be a part of these stories, to take part in the most blood-curdling adventures, a very natural hankering for adventure, I believe. And about this time, I started indulging in the very common practice of keeping a film diary and scrap-book.

It was also about then that I first saw Deanna Durbin in *Three Smart Girls*. It was Deanna whom I have to thank for initiating me into my first attempt at curling my hair, and breaking away from the previous straight school-girl bob. Of course, my Mother had to be consulted, but she agreed with me that if it was all right for Deanna, then it should be all right for me, so there I was with a centre parting, and curly hair! Another direct influence of films on my life.

As I gradually grew up, my hair styles changed according to the latest screen fashions, often to the vast amusement of my friends. But there the influence of the latest glamorous fashions had to stay. My Mother's slender purse could not stretch to new dresses as they took my eye. And I doubt very much if it would have done so had it been possible! I think, however, that the stars kept me aware that neatness and smart, tailored clothes were the keynote of attraction, even if they did have to last a long time. I felt that there was a certain standard to be lived up to. And I sometimes experienced a real exaltation when various friends told me that I resembled such and such a film star! Until commonsense told me that each of my so-called 'likenesses'—and there were about four or five of them in all—were totally different, both in features and mannerisms, which must have made me a real mongrel! But at least I knew moments of ecstacy. Even the following douche of cold reasoning couldn't kill their memory.

It was in my early teens that I first fell in love—and that was with Jan Kiepura, whom I had seen in *Tell Me Tonight*. Love? Infatuation you would say! And I suppose you are right. But it was heartbreak-

ingly real to me. I was assured by adults that I would soon grow out
of that phase. But no! All through my teens I continued falling in
love, with one film star after another. And each time was sheer
torture—a desperate longing to be made love to by them all. Sometimes it would last for days, sometimes for weeks or even months,
awakened anew each time I saw them. Nobody knew just how
miserable I felt. Certainly not my Mother, who would probably have
given me a good spanking had she known how deeply I adored them
all. To her, it was just a plain case of 'school-girl infatuation'. I sincerely hope that other youngsters don't go through such hell.

And yet, looking back, it was all so real to me that I don't think I
would otherwise have known such complete and utter happiness as
when I used to dream that one day I could meet those people. I
believe it must have been the effect of these desperate infatuations
that has altered my outlook on love—whether for good or bad, time
alone will tell. I soon found out that the attentions of the local boy
irritated me. I was contemptuous of his rather dull dates, and felt
that his perfectly ordinary advances were childish and inexperienced.
They lacked something that I felt I wanted. But what it was I never
could discover. And so it went on, from one mundane friendship to
another—always dull and prosaic. And yet I have finished some
really very pleasant friendships because of this intangible longing for
something different: something based, I suppose, on my very early
idea of love. How it will end, I don't know. Perhaps one day the
right boy will scatter this fruitless idealism, imprinted so strongly by
the films. I hope so.

But this screen influence has, I think, been mostly for my own
good. For a long time, my longing to see the countries shown so
enticingly in pictures had been growing steadily, and I had decided
that my future must lie in travelling. I had done nothing concrete,
however, to fulfill this ambition. Pictures like John Carroll's *Hi
Gaucho* had made me interested in South America, and anything
Spanish. But it was the Tyrone Power version of *The Mark of Zorro*
that sent me out the next day to buy a Spanish grammar book. And
from that day I have never looked back. I was keenly interested in
the language, and the growing knowledge of that made me take up
other subjects which have now pretty well secured for me, with the
advantage of a few certificates, the career which will fulfill my
travelling ambition.

But there have been many pictures, mostly historical, such as *The
Charge of the Light Brigade, Lives of a Bengal Lancer, Sixty Glorious Years*,
etc., which have always been kept apart from those which I could
feel were making some sort of an impression on me which would
probably be for worse instead of better. These films gave me an
exultant pride in my own country, and her achievements. A pride
which has, I believe, helped to steady a rather impressionable and
emotional nature. And such films, together with many like *Rebecca,
The Man in Grey, Captains Courageous, Fury* have made me appreciate

acting, and instilled in me a sense of criticism which must have partly counteracted the effects of emotion rather than admiration which haunted my teen years, and which will still break out if not kept under control.

I have been told that all these film influences (or those about which my friends know) have made me discontented with my monotonous suburban life, and have led to periods of unhappiness and depression. But I am glad. For they have given me ambition, ideals, something to work hard for, something to set my head above the boredom of routine. I am wondering whether films will have any more influence of my future life. I doubt it, because I think I have met all the stages of impressions now!

Nos. 36 and 37 began regular attendance at the cinema at the age of eight, on moving from the country into a town. No. 36 went some weeks 'as often as five times', and usually 'at least twice a week'. No. 37 from the age of eight has 'averaged three times per week, occasionally four'. She says that she criticizes the films she sees more than her associates.

NO. 36

AGE: 22
SEX: F.
OCCUPATION: MEDICAL STUDENT
NATIONALITY: BRITISH

FATHER'S OCCUPATION:
FOREMAN IN PETROL
DEPOT

Up to the age of eight, I lived with my mother, father & sister 10 years older than myself, in the small country town of . . . , Aberdeenshire. Of course, there were no pictures there. On trades holidays, we always went into Aberdeen, wh. was a great treat to me, & it was on one of these occasions I saw my first film. I can't remember my exact age, probably it was 5 or 6 yrs. I can still remember odd unimportant scenes from it, but I would not be able to tell you the name unless I had heard my parents talk about it. It was *The Singing Fool*. I was too young to really understand what it was about. I remember I did sometimes think about the film & the scenes in it afterwards, but I do not think it made a greater impression than the first time of anything does.

I did not see any more films until we moved to . . . There I found that it was a recognised thing for all the children I played with to go to the pictures often. They knew the names of all the film stars & their latest films. They went whenever they could get anybody to take them, & they always went together to a children's matinee on a Saturday afternoon.

My parents started to go to the pictures more often & I went with them every time I was allowed. They themselves were rather particular that it was only the 'good' films they went to see, so they did not often have to deny me on the grounds of the film being unfit for children. Just at this stage, about 8-12 years, my appetite for the pictures was insatiable. I would go to anything & everything, & had no pronounced likes or dislikes, except that I thought all love scenes silly & the purely love film, which had nothing much in it but one love scene after another, bored me beyond words. But even if I thought the big picture was like that, I still did not refuse to go, as I was always hopeful that the second feature or something in the rest of the programme, would make up for it.

I usually went to the pictures with my father, mother or sister . . . But we had not been in . . . long before we made friends with the people who lived next door—a widower some years older than my father, & his daughter, a few years older than . . . This girl was of a very restless type & could not bear to spend any evening sitting quietly at home. She went in for golf & other sports, but during the winter especially her chief form of entertainment was the pictures. Like myself, she did not care what she went to, & she usually saw every film that was being shown in the 4 picture houses during the week, unless it was physically impossible. She did not like going alone, & would often come in & ask one of us to go with her. As my mother or sister did not care to go unless it was a film they really wanted to see, it usually fell to me to go, & I was never unwilling. Some weeks I went as often as 5 times, usually at least twice a week.

I think it is important to say that from the very earliest, . . . had talked to me about films, & acting, etc. & I realised just exactly what they were from the beginning. I never had any notions that they pictured a real world—except the newsreels, which I always enjoyed very much for the simple reason that they were the only true-to-life things in the programmes. I knew that to thousands of people in Hollywood & London, making films was just a job, & a job without much glamour attached to it in most cases. (Although I would not understand what 'glamour' was, in the beginning!) My sister used to like to buy the film books, & from looking at the pictures I came on to reading them. So I gradually came to begin to criticize the films & the acting, & to form my own standards of good & bad.

Despite the fact that I knew the films were all only make-believe, I did get carried away by them to some extent. This is illustrated in connexion with the only time I was really scared by a film. My mother & I were at the picture-house called the Cinerama. I would be about 9 or 10 years old. We had seen the big picture (I do not remember the name of it, but I remember the other details most vividly) & were seeing a comical short feature called *Gambolling Lambs*, with a pun on the 'gambolling' as it was about a sophisticated men's club in New York where the chief pursuit was gambling. The story was about a girl who had to dress as a man & enter this place for some purpose. I remember her getting sick after she had had to accept a cigar. Then there was an interval of comedy, where two funny men were capering, one being a drunkard lying over a bar, the other the bartender. I was enjoying it in high glee, when the bartender bent down behind the bar, no doubt to reappear with something very funny. I was expectantly watching, when he came up with a horried, grotesque mask or his head. I got a dreadful shock & looked away from the picture instantly. Mother told me she would tell me when to look again. Even when she said it was all right, I remember only daring to look up for a second or two, as I was frightened that a sudden flash of that man in the mask might come on again, & I did not want to see it. As soon as that film was over, I felt better, but for some little time after that the vision of that mask would suddenly flash into my mind. I wished to goodness I had never seen it. It used to come particularly just as I was going to sleep at nights. But gradually, the fear of it disappeared, and strange to say, it did not prevent me going to the pictures. Although from then on, if it looked as though there would be anything frightening in the film I would tell whoever was with me 'to tell me when to look again'. The funny thing is that although I remember all those other details, the thing which impressed itself so much on my mind at the time—the mask—now entirely escapes recollection. I know it was horrible to look at, but I have no clear idea what form it took. I think it was rather like an over-sized human head with staring eyes. I have often thought I would like to see that film again, just to see what the thing was really like that scared me so.

After that, I absolutely refused to go to any film which was an out-and-out horror film—*Frankenstein*, *Dracula* or any creepy murder story. I remember when *King-Kong* came to . . . , all my chums raved about it, but I refused to go as I thought I would be frightened. Later on, when I was about 13, I took my courage into both hands & went to see a Charlie Chan film with my father. I was delighted with myself, because instead of being scared I honestly enjoyed the film, & from then on 'Charlie Chan' was a great favourite of mine. But even to-day, I will not go to a horror film.

Another rather queer incident in connexion with the films occurred about this time. When I was ten I returned alone to . . . for a visit to friends. . . . now had the films in the town hall twice a week. The people I stayed with had hardly been at all, but of course I was so film conscious that I prevailed on . . . , a girl about my sisters age, to take me one night. Again it was a supporting picture which upset me, but this time it was one shown before the big picture. It was a comedy, rather on the Edgar Kennedy style, about a man who was very well-meaning, but every time he tried to do anything it turned out wrong. I don't know whether this has any connexion with my feelings or not, but it seemed to me I was like that, too. I was never a good child, & was continually getting rows from someone, usually my mother, for the things I did. Often, admittedly, the rows were well-deserved, but sometimes I did things with very good intent, & they went wrong, & so used were my parents to my naughtiness that I never got any credit for good intentions. So when

I saw the man in the film being treated badly for trying to do good, I felt intensely sorry for him, & I was most annoyed at all the people in the hall laughing. I felt what he needed was sympathy, & the people were cruel to laugh at him. Every time a new incident occurred, my feelings mounted. The climax came when the man was mending a ladder for a friend. He laid it along the pavement. When he had finished it & had gone to fetch the friend to see it, some silly person came along & never noticed the ladder & walked on it & broke every rung. Of course, the friend, on seeing it, was most annoyed at being made a fool of, & having his ladder broken worse than before. I felt all the emotion of misinterpreted motives just as if I had been the man, & was nearly crying with vexation. Although . . . would be very angry at leaving before we had seen the big picture, I asked her to take me out. She said, 'Don't be silly. It's only in fun'. That did not help me much, but I watched the man mending the ladder again. Then the same thing happened again. This was too much for me altogether, & I insisted on . . . taking me out. Once outside, my excitement disappeared, & I was again not prevented from returning to the films at the next opportunity. At other times, I do not ever remember my emotions being difficult to control. I never cried at sad films as a child, although I do sometimes now.

I never liked going to the children's matinées with my friends. I can only remember going about two or three times, not any more. I did not like it for several reasons—first, I somehow never felt stable enough in watching a picture unless I was with an adult. Then, at these matinees the younger children were so noisy you could never enjoy it properly. Also, a large part of the programme was always devoted to a serial adventure story. Usually, it was a ridiculous thing about somebody's adventures on the moor & I hated that sort of thing.

It is interesting, also, to record a child's reactions to child stars. Shirley Temple was a little younger than I was, but I always detested her films. She was always so good, seeing her on the films was a continual reproach to me about my own naughtiness. My parents did not fail to point out what an example she was & that made it worse. When I saw Jane Withers as the bad girl in *Bright Eyes*, I liked her instantly. This was no stuffed Ninny, this was someone after my own heart. Every film in which Jane was naughty, I thoroughly enjoyed.

Between my 12th & 13th years, a great change came over my attitude to films. I do not remember how it began, but I eventually reached a stage where I refused to go to any picture at all. I used to sneer at the pictures & say there was no fun there, sitting in a picture house. Whereas I had formerly known every film being shown in the town & the names of the stars in them, & all the details about the future attractions, I now took no interest whatsoever, stopped reading film books & considered that films were entirely a thing of the past for me. Even when mother & . . . tried to persuade me to go,

From *La Belle et la Bete.* The beast of the fairy tale, not the film monster
devised to thrill and to shock . . .

From the Film *The Mummy's Curse*. A contrast to the previous illustration.

I refused & used to stay in the house alone, perfectly content with my own way of passing the time (reading, chiefly, I think) & never regretting not having gone with them. I know this stage lasted a good few months, but whether it was as much as a year I do not remember.

Gradually, I started going back to films. But now I was very particular what I went to, & often refused the next-door neighbour's invitations. I had developed, from nowhere, well marked likes & dislikes. I did not like Western films, nor any musicals, even those which played modern music were 'out'. I preferred the film to be a well-known one which had scored a success in London, & objected to going to obscure or second-rate films. I still thought long-drawn-out love scenes silly, & was embarrassed by them, but I was not so ready now to condemn out of hand all love as being silly. I still had no emotional reactions to a love scene, though, nor to any male hero. In fact, the only emotion I remember feeling at this stage was when I saw a girl being ill-treated by men. I remember vividly a scene in Laurel & Hardy's *The Bohemian Girl* where the gypsy girl was being dragged out to be whipped. She was stripped & lashed to a post. Of course, she was saved at the last minute. That scene stimulated me a great deal, & I would enact over & over again in the privacy of my own bedroom any scenes like that, with me playing the heroine, of course I usually altered it so that I was not saved so promptly. My saviour was never the film hero, but the particular boy in my class at school that my imagination had fastened on for the time being. This effect of being excited by a scene of a girl being badly treated went on for a long time, until I was 16, at least, I am sure. It gradually faded, but it can be still be reactivated occasionally.

I have never had any reactions to a love scene, & never fallen in love with any film star. I still feel irritated if a love scene is very intimate & long drawn out, but I quite enjoy the more everyday love scenes, without feeling in any way excited by them. Perhaps I had better add that my 'private life' is quite normal. I have been engaged since I was 20, my fiancé being overseas most of the time. Even his absence & the terrific longings I get to have him back, fail to stir me to any adoration or substitution of a male star. There are those I like more than others, even those I admit it might be quite nice to have making love to me, but there is no adoration in it.

When I was 14, I had more or less recovered from my period of abstinence from the films, except in regard to musicals. I was never musical myself, I had never learnt to play the piano, & at school I was the standing joke of the singing class, for I could sing on only one low note. In particular, I hated anything 'classical', which mother & . . . liked a lot & would often have on the wireless. The very worst of all was opera—a lot of screeching women, I used to say. Then Deanna Durbin's film, *Three Smart Girls* came to . . . I had read in the film books about this 14-year old girl who was such a startling success. My immediate reaction was—here is another Shirley Temple, a goody-goody. When I read that she was a singer, too, I was absolutely repelled & decided I would never go to one of her films. During the week it was in the town, we heard glowing reports. At the end of the week, mother & . . . were going, & as I had a certain amount of curiosity about what this star was really like, I went too, but protesting that of course it was not the kind of thing I liked, & I would be sure to be bored to tears.

I had never enjoyed a film so much before. When we came out, mother asked me triumphantly, 'Now, wasn't it good?' I had to admit it was. There was something so natural & vital about Deanna, that she fairly caught my imagination.

She became my first & only screen idol. I collected pictures of her, & articles about her & spent hours sticking them in scrapbooks. I would pay any price within the range of my pocket money for a book, if it had a new picture, however tiny, of her in it. I adored her & my adoration influenced my life a great deal. I wanted to be as much like her as possible, both in my manners & clothes. Whenever I was to get a new dress, I would find from my collection a particularly nice picture of Deanna & ask for a dress like she was wearing. I did my hair as much like her as I could manage. If I found myself in any annoying or aggravating situation, which I previously dealt with by an outburst of temper, I found myself wondering what Deanna would do, & modified my own reactions accordingly. She had far more influence on me than any amount of lectures or rows from parents would have had. I went to all her films, & as often I could, too. In my 14th year, the family left . . . for . . . , another small town, 17 miles from . . . When one of Deanna's pictures was in . . . , I would go in specially to see it & sit enraptured through at least two performances. Then I always went again later when it came to the picture house in . . . Once, I remember, re-issue of *Three Smart Girls* was showing at another town about 12 miles across country from . . . & very awkward to get at. I was anxious to go & wanted to cycle across, but mother would not let me, & was rather against my going alone, even by bus. But I was allowed to go in the end & thoroughly enjoyed myself watching 'my Deanna', as I called her.

I bought all the records she made & played them over & over again. My interest began to extend beyond Deanna. At first, I had just put up with the singing as a necessary adjunct to her charming personality. Then I came to admit the songs were lovely, yes, even the operatic ones, when she sang them. Then I realised they were lovely songs when any good singer sang them. Then I realised there were a lot of lovely songs that Deanna never sang. I began to go to other musical films, such as Jeanette Macdonald's & Nelson Eddy's.

I stoutly maintained Jeanette's voice was not nearly as clear or as pure as Deanna's, but I enjoyed her singing very much. In order to be able to discuss & appraise the merits of various singers, I had to know a little about music. My interest in the subject grew & grew & now I am a keen opera fan. I also cherish an ambition, which

many of my friends find incomprehensible, to become a musical performer myself in the only way open to me—as a pianist. I do not
mean I want to become a professional pianist, but I would dearly
love to be able to play the piano myself, so that whenever I was in
the mood I could sit down & play any piece I liked.

I still never miss a new Deanna Durbin film, but once is quite
enough to see them these days. They totally fail to stir any emotion
in me, although if I go to a re-issue of one of my early favourites,
I experience a faint re-echo of the old joy.

Films had nothing whatever to do with my final choice of profession, although I had several hare-brained ideas based on films—
such as newspaperwoman—before deciding. But besides my musical
leanings they left another profound mark on me. This is in reference
to travel. My father is Irish & he had told us from earliest days about
his home on the west coast, so my ambitions always included travelling there. Geography at school & any books I read about foreign
countries made my ambitions wider. Films broadened this, & more
than that, made me feel I did not want to stay in this country when
I grew up. My choice of country to live in was America. Even now,
although I realise the picture of America & the American people
given us by the films is rather distorted, I still think it would be the
most interesting & pleasantest country in the world to live in, &
would like to emigrate there if I ever got an opportunity.

NO. 37

AGE: 20   FATHER'S OCCUPATION:
SEX: F.   SECURITY WATCH
OCCUPATION: M.O.W.T.
 CIVIL SERVANT—INLAND REVENUE
NATIONALITY: BRITISH

I first became interested in films at the age of 8 yrs. when the
family moved into the town from the country. I was really fascinated
by them & wanted to go every day, instead of school, gradually I
settled down to town life and went as often as my pocket money
would allow. In my early years of 'film-going' I enjoyed Westerns
Murders, & Mysteries etc. When I was 10 yrs. old I went to a Secondary School and though I still had a liking for those stated above I
began to like a good story and good acting. By the time I was 14 yrs.
old I still enjoyed visiting the cinema but was now getting hard to
please in the type of film I liked. After turning 15 yrs. and to this
present day I prefer an original story & get a little tired of these
continual films where one can guess the plot after the first few scenes.
I seem to be able to spot the shots which are 'faked' or have a different background very easily and this tends to make me very critical.
I now enjoy any kind of film where the actors give a good performance whether it is a musical, mystery or straight play. I like comedies in the hands of Bob Hope. Rosalind Russell & Abbott &
Costello.—

Joan Davis, mysteries with an unusual twist in the plot & any film with actresses like Phyllis Calvert, Greer Garson, & Bette Davis. To quote examples of the types—

1. *My Favourite Blonde. My Sister Eileen. Rookies. Kansas City. Kitty.*
2. *Laura. Farewell My Lovely.*
3. *Madonna of the Seven Moons. Blossoms in the Dust. Dark Victory.*

Although I used to avoid British films, it is now my aim to see everyone I can that comes to the local cinemas. It is very seldom that one finds faked scenes obviously filmed & the stories are extremely good, also the best point the acting is magnificent & nothing Hollywood can produce will convince me that we have not the finest actors & actresses in the world. Some of the recent British films I have enjoyed were *This Happy Breed. The Way Ahead. Waterloo Road. Twilight Hour. Halfway House* & others too numerous to mention.

My friends say that I pull a film to pieces too much to enjoy it, but when I am watching the film I cannot help automatically noting errors in the plot, photography etc. and even if there are many faults, I usually enjoy the film. I enjoy a film most that has a real story with real people in it, and action that could happen in everyday life. I also like a film such as *The Wizard of Oz*, because of its absolute removal from everyday affairs, and I think Walt Disney has achieved great art in his full length cartoons.

Ever since I was eight I have averaged three times per week, occasionally four. From eight years to ten years old I always went with my brother who is three years older than I. From ten years to sixteen years old, always with one or another of my various school friends. From sixteen years, to date I have usually visited with friends from the office, my mother & mostly by myself, when I enjoy it most, because then there is no one to chatter & distract my attention.

As far as I know films did not influence my play or activities in any way. I played all the usual sports at school and my hobbies are drawing & painting water colours. I suppose though that as a youngster our games were based on westerns we had seen.

I have only once been frightened by a film, that was *The Invisible Man* with Claude Rains. The scene that remains persistently in my memory showed Claude Rains unwinding some bandages from about his head & gradually it became apparent that there was nothing underneath. I have never dreamt about films but that one scene sticks in my mind & I remember being badly frightened & turning to my mother for comfort & safety. Nowadays nothing ever affects me that I see on the screen.

I find that if it is a really good film that holds my attention my emotions are moved according to the action of the story. For instance I laugh heartily at Bob Hope & weep silently with Bette Davis, but the moment the film ends I give an involuntary sigh & almost immediately my emotions are under control. Sometimes nothing moves me, I saw *Arsenic and Old Lace* a little while ago & could hardly refrain from yawning, yet quite a number of people were nearly bursting with laughter. I felt that none of the characters were real, only being acted for the film, and the plot utterly ridiculous, therefore I was unable to become interested. When I saw *The Constant Nymph* I felt quite angry with Alexis Smith for not understanding Joan Fontaine and there were tears in my eyes at the final scene when she dies after hearing Charles Boyer's music. I could quote many other instances but you would not have time to read them, I am trying to illustrate that if the players act well & convince me that their emotions and experiences are real then I become oblivious to the surroundings & become completely immersed in the enjoyment of the film.

I often adopt phrases used in films when joining in office chatter, in fact it is quite the vogue to be able to quote actual speeches from films these days. I am not sure if this is a mannerism, but to illustrate my previous remark, Bette Davis in *Old Acquaintance* uses the phrase 'There are some things a woman does not do!' & you will realise that this remark can be used quite frequently either as a joking reply or to stress a definite refusal. Sometimes by quoting such a remark I have been given praise for a quick wit and often find that conversation can be enlivened by appropriate use of such phrases. I find that by seeing so many films my vocabulary has increased and I can hold my own in conversation by sometimes unconsiously copying the attitudes & inflexion of the voice of some of the better stars, Phyllis Calvert being my first choice of a correct diction.

I have never fallen in love with a screen idol because I have never had one. I have several favourite male stars, Robert Donat, Laurence Olivier and Cornel Wilde being first three, but could not imagine falling in love with any of them, besides they are all usually married. I have never been out with a boy friend so would not know what effect films have had on my feelings towards love-making. I often feel that some of the love scenes are absolutely ridiculous and spoil the film, but to quote the example of Greer Garson & Walter Pidgeon in my mind, is the best example of love making on the screen.

My travel ambition caused by films is to travel to Hollywood & the British Studios to see exactly how they make the motion pictures. I am keenly interested in the technical side of motion photography & would be delighted to know all the inside 'dope' on the different methods of filming special sequences, such as underwater scenes, the use of miniatures for long shots. I have no ambition to become an actress, but would give anything to have a job in a large motion picture studio. After seeing some of the Travel Talks of Mr. J. Fitzpatrick I feel envious of the rich people being able to afford to go and see these beautiful show places of the world in reality, and would be tempted to throw away a steady job & see the world if my good sense would not interfere and point out that security counts so much these days. I am content therefore to see the wonders of the world depicted through the eye of the camera, but would jump at the chance to travel if the opportunity came my way.

Films have never made me dissatisfied with my life as, even though we are not rich, just ordinary working class people, we are happy and live in quite a nice suburban part of town. I have always wanted a modern detached house in the country not too far from town but do not think this desire has been prompted by any film I have seen.

My only vocational ambition is to become an Established Civil Servant and rise to the top by means of promotion. I have never seen a film about our branch of the service, so I can safely say that I have not been influenced by films at all in my decision.

NO. 38

AGE: 21   FATHER'S OCCUPATION:
SEX: M.   SCHOOLTEACHER
OCCUPATION: MOTHER'S OCCUPATION:
    R.A.F.(BANK CLERK, PRE-WAR)   DRESS DESIGNER
NATIONALITY: BRITISH

My interest in films has been life-long, that is to say as far back as I can remember anyhow; probably to when I was about 8 years old.

Strangely enough my taste has altered little throughout the years, I have always had a passion for Western films, films with plenty of adventure and action in them, and of course a romantic interest thrown in. On the other side I have a weakness for satirical humour and sarcasm, and polished dialogue. Monty Wooley being my favourite exponent of the latter. I attribute much of the mild success I have attained to the influence of the films. They have taught me to be careful with money, meticulous in dress, good-mannered, even-tempered, to try and view things from the other person's point of view, and last but not least—hard work pays dividends.

I have never felt dissatisfied with my home or surroundings, rather have I learnt to appreciate them more when I see how badly off I might be. I never really thought of the sacrifices my parents made until it was brought home to me by one or two films.

I freely admit that I have learned a lot on the technique of love-making from the films. Probably all I know in fact.

So you see from my point of view, films are a good thing.

NO. 39

AGE: 20   FATHER: DECEASED
SEX: M.   MOTHER'S OCCUPATION:
OCCUPATION: SOLDIER   WAR WORKER
NATIONALITY: IRISH-WELSH

To write on such a subject as this proves to be a fascinating pastime. Its a subject on which so many views have been expressed that its easily seen that as entertainment or a subject for argument, films and all attached to the name, hold a very prominent place.

Years ago, when I was at the tender age of eight, my evenings were spent in gathering coke to help out the fuel at home. Money at that was very scarce owing to a world wide slump in industry and

my little effort helped. Films, to me, were just a figment of imagination, to be seen only through the eyes of luckier people who had
actually had the amazing experience of going to a cinema.

One eventful evening while I was carrying on my little job, my
twin sister flew down in a flurry of skirts with the exalting news that,
my mother having won a little money in a raffle, we were to be
treated to a seat at the cinema.

Oh! what joys I knew at that moment. I have never before or
since moved so fast in such a good cause. Breathless, but still clinging
to my little flour sack of coke, my sister and I hurried home. My
mother made me go through the to me, quite severe, routine of
washing and for once I was so determined to go to see the film that
I actually washed my neck without being sent back to do it.

My mother decided that, since it was a summer's evening, we
should go to the cinema just us two kids alone. Away we went. It's
queer really to think that altho I remember the thrill of going, I
have only the vaguest idea of the actual film. I only remember that
it featured Gracie Fields and she rode on a lorry full of oranges in
one scene.

Shortly after I began to go quite regularly to Saturday matinées.
I took no notice of the main film then but was keenly interested in
the serials, to which I looked forward very much.

Then I came down to earth with a jolt, at a slightly later date,
when I saw Fred Astaire-Ginger Rogers in *Life of Vernon and Irene
Castle*. I quickly became filled with a decided ambition to be a
famous dancer and started to try out there and then. Even today,
I still tap dance as much as possible in our own concert parties,
tho I still am only a poor amateur.

Next thing I remember of films was after a blank period of years.
I saw one day a particularly vivid poster outside our local cinema
advertising the latest of a new star 'The Brazilian Bombshell'. I
determined to see if she was as good as she was boasted to be and
was not disappointed tho she was not at the time, the star of that
particular film (I think it was *Down Argentina Way*).

I then had the pleasure of seeing Bette Davies for the first time in
Dark Victory. Our film shows are often three years old or more before
we see them in our village, and you just take what comes, when it
comes, hence the fact that I was so late seeing *Dark Victory*. I
remember the fact that Bette gave a high class performance and
resolved there and then to follow her carreer in the film world. I
have done so by the simple method of seeing all her films or as near
as possible, including old ones that were screened before I was
interested and by reading *Picturegoer* and the critics reviews in the
papers. I am still of the opinion that she is definitely, even after her
long career, still the best dramatic star in Hollywood.

Stangely enough films have never given me any ambition beside
the one of dancing. Nor have they made any influence on my play
except in one case. That is, that since light reading is my hobby, I

always try first, to read books that have been made into films to see how much they differ and also to see how many books I would like filmed. An absorbing game is to get a book full of characters and try to cast the stars as the characters to form a film that has not too many names, yet will hold your interest. In a lull in my fighting last year, I tried this, spent quite a while arguing as to the cast I'd choose for the film *Ten Little Niggers* (by Agatha Christie). I have never been actually frightened by a film tho I did get quite an eerie feeling when watching the film *The Unvited*.

In dress I have not been swayed by any star, since man's choice of dress is far more limited than a girl's. My sister, who is tall and dark does tend to dress like Heddy Lamarr. Love making to me is, as yet, a subject not broached very freely. Luckily enough, my girl friend is also a keen film fan and she, like myself, has a hearty dislike for most love scenes, especially those of Char. Boyer. So I need no technique but my own and should I try to imitate a star, she'd know at once and I'd be in the soup. I've not fallen in love with any screen idol, since Bette, as she herself would, I'm sure admit is not the type to fall in love with.

For Bette Davies, I feel an admiration that words can't express. How a woman can go on a screen, knowing that she is only acting, and act like she does, is amazing. I myself have been lucky enough to see one of her latest films *Mr. Skeffington* in Paris and she fully deserved the Academy Award for her performance in that.

Two girls only have even made me feel that I'd like to fall for them. They are Judy Garland, and Mitz in *Mayfair*. All the other stars, for the purpose of falling in love, leave me cold.

Today, at the age of twenty, I am one of the keenest film fans one can imagine and I am a glutton for film news. In any discussion or arguments on films in our billets I am usually called in to settle the point. Unless the films are too far gone to be remembered I'm quite well versed in their stars etc.

I go to day to see a film, not only for the relaxation offered by it, but also to criticise or compliment the stars, on screen, script or costumes. I always regard films as my opinion in view of those offered by the critics who write in daily papers.

I think that the cinema is an institution which is world famous and will remain so, and I wish it every success. I intend to remain a film fan for many years to come!

Yours faithfully,
'Soldier Boy.'

No. 40 also began filmgoing at the age of eight, attending regularly with her grandmother until, at the age of twelve, she played truant from school to see the kind of film which she had never been allowed to see. Her contribution is one of the most striking documents amongst the sixty.

AGE: 30   FATHER'S OCCUPATION:
SEX: F.   COMMERCIAL TRAVELLER
OCCUPATION: CLERK   MOTHER'S OCCUPATION:
NATIONALITY: BRITISH   HOUSEWIFE

I started film-going at the early age of eight—and adored Bebe
Daniels from then, until now; custard pies, Keystone Police, and—
most of all, the Western films of silent days! I went always with my
Grandmother, and, although we could afford the better seats,
always had—on account of her sight, to sit well to the front among
the whistling stamping orange-eating patrons—a thing which has
made me dislike and despise the smelly poor for all time. I adored
the noisy out of tune piano, and always tried to emulate the noisy
thumping that passed as musical accompaniment, never having
patience to practice scales and my 'show-piece' Mignosiette(?) as I
should have done—so to this day I only play by ear. I fell in love
with Ken Maynard—a dark rather saturnine man who rode a
beautiful white horse, and collected everything I could find printed
about him, begged his show posters, and treasured every picture I
found of him anywhere. At twelve I wondered *what* sort of films
they were that I was never allowed to see, and played truant from
school one afternoon—with another small and curious-minded
friend—to see my first 'sex' film. It was of the trials and temptations
of a rather blowsy continental actress, and puzzled us for weeks,
setting us wondering about things we had never before bothered
about. *Did* men kiss women like that, and *did* babies come unwanted,
from such episodes and behaviour? So my curiosity aroused, from
Ken Maynard at eight I sneaked off at twelve—now unescorted—
to see all the extravagant and unreal epics of sex and high living I
could find. Did it do me any harm? Yes—I'm afraid so. Children
should never be allowed to see at such an early age, the ugly side of
life and I have only myself to blame. When I am asked to 'take me
in lady, its an "A" film' my refusal is always firm. Now boys
seemed tame who couldn't hug and kiss like the exaggerated figures
on the screen, and being silent films, I always imagined the dialogue
to be more fiery than any the censor would pass. *The Hunchback
of Notre Dame* frightened me to death and to this day I hate the
shudder that passes through me at the sight of an ugly or deformed
person. *Frankenstein* kept me awake at night and gave me nerves.
The fresh notes Al Jolson sang filled me with wonder, and with
these musicals—the morbid faded from my film-going entertainment, both horror and sex. There wasn't time to think about exotic
love-making or blood-drinking vampires when you could hear
clever people singing—see dancing more wonderful than you ever
imagined, and above all listen to all these wonderful people *talking*!
Yes, talkies and above all—musicals, cleared the air for me! Films
with a story were now clever and interesting, and what if I did try

to look like Joan Crawford—I tried to look like Norma Shearer too—so it all balanced itself out. Anyway I was often better dressed than before (I am now in my teens), and my hair looked more cared for and more attractively arranged. Films definitely *did* make me more receptive to love-making *and* I expected it to be a more experienced job than I would have done had I not seen—on the films—how love should be made! Leslie Howard made love kindly, Clark Gable was tough and a go-getter, Cary Grant gay but rather dangerous, Ronald Colman ministerial, Errol Flynn impossibly venturesome and Bob Montgomery the *ideal* gentleman etc. etc. etc. I looked for all these qualities in my friends and measured them up by it. Once I fell in love desperately with a man who was the absolute double of Cary Grant. He wanted me to elope—and although everyone warned me against him—I nearly did so—blinded with the glamour of his likeness to the screen star. Luckily my father found out a week before they arrested him as an embezzler so that was that! Films where the heroine is poor but beautiful, have come by wealth and adventure by choosing the primrose path in life have always—in a submerged urge sort of way—tempted and fascinated me. The situation has *never* risen in my life—but the outlook on it is there. I have always had great ambition—fed by films—to be a journalist. I don't suppose that it is much like its prototype in N. York or the idea we get of it on the screen, but how I'd love to find out. I've wanted to travel, yes, but not so much the world as to cross America from N. York to the Pacific Coast, in one of those stream-lined buses, seeing the towns and villages en route and meeting the people who live in them. I'd like to see Honolulu too, even though they tell me most of the natives have tuberculosis. This all reads as if films have made me very pro-American, and I'm afraid that *is* so. I am not dissatisfied with home life or environment, one meets the same class of people in every station of life, in any country. Suburban life here is dull, but so would it be in New England, as in London or New York one would find a more mixed and bohemian crowd. By saying that I mean I have no urge to roam, through film-going, and to travel the world is, more or less, the ambition of everyone who uses the brains they were endowed with. British films have never in all my life, made the *slightest* impression on me. They are dull, ugly and uninspired—generally a stage success filmed because it was that or a poorly produced musical. There are very few real British film stars, and those stars of the stage who grace the screen at intervals are too old to photograph well, poor dears. The inanities of George Formby leave me cold, the American sense of humour I adore. I once studied Christian Science because Mary Pickford believed in it, I truly believe in the survival of souls, since I saw *Topper takes a trip*. Bing Crosby singing 'Holy Night' gives me more religious uplift than all the dull sermons of our snobbish Vicar, and I'd rather hear Jimmy Durante's croak than Barbara Mullens silly little squeaking whisper. The greatest thing that has come out of my film-going was the ability it gave me to understand and see the viewpoint of the men from America who came here to fight with us. It also gave me an earlier understanding of the facts of life than I would have had, and made me dissatisfied and impatient with the inferior in entertainment. Not—at thirty—I choose my film going carefully, *never* just 'go to the pictures'—and whether it is Carmen Miranda or Bette Davis, Micky Rooney or Humphrey Bogart, Walter Disney or Shakespeare. I am a discriminating picturegoer. From custard pies to Orson Welles is a long way, but it has been a happy and worth-while journey.

The last document in the eight-year-old age group is No. 41. The writer did not attend films regularly until she was ten, but her first visit, at the age of eight, made a lasting impression on her. She did not go because she wanted to do so, and 'was hardly introduced to films in the best way', beginning with a Boris Karloff film which haunted her dreams for two years. Though she regards films 'as an enjoyable pastime—nothing else', her record shows that they continued to make a very deep impression upon her.

NO. 41

AGE: 17	FATHER'S OCCUPATION:
SEX: F.	COMMERCIAL TRAVELLER
OCCUPATION:	MOTHER'S OCCUPATION:
CLERK IN THE INLAND REVENUE	HEAD OF OFFICE DEPT.
NATIONALITY: BRITISH	OF A GOWN FACTORY

MY MOTION PICTURE AUTOBIOGRAPHY

My name is . . . ; I am 17 years of age; was at school until 4 months ago and since then have commenced work as a clerk in the Inland Revenue.

Both my parents are English—and so far as I am able to trace there is no other nationality prevalent in my family for at least four generations.

My father is a commercial traveller and, since the beginning of the war, my mother has been the head of the office department of a gown factory.

As my essays have never been very orderly, I hope you will not mind if I follow the outline depicted in the *Picturegoer*.

In the first place I am asked to trace the history of my interest in films. To begin with I did not go to the pictures because I was *interested*—but because my *parents* wanted to go, and I could not be left at home. In my opinion I was hardly introduced to films in the best way; for, at the age of eight my grandmother took me to see a Boris Karloff 'Horror' Film!—I still remember parts of it now:—of course, I don't feel any fear of it now,—but I remember how, for about two years afterwards, every night I'd dream through that film again as if the actions and happenings were part of my life. At the present time, I dimly recall a hidden passage under the stair, from whence Karloff emerged to commit his murders. My parents still joke to me about how I never would go upstairs by myself—for to me then, there were no 'bogies' of the 'horned' type but only *one*—a man with a black handkerchief over the lower part of his face—who came steadily nearer and nearer . . . until he was right beside me and then I'd wake up screaming. Perhaps an odd occurrence which may originate from this experience, is the fact that even now I sometimes moan in my sleep; and queerly enough, when I am told I have been doing this, I have no recollection of any dream or nightmare. In fact, I feel as though I've had an untroubled night's sleep.

As you can probably guess, I could not be induced to go to the pictures for sometime afterwards. But at the age of 10, I went to see a Ginger Rogers—Fred Astaire musical in which, oddly enough, dream sequences were portrayed throughout the film. Miss Rogers was supposed to be suffering from nightmares and in the end she was satisfactorily cured by Fred Astaire. She was not the only one to be cured of bad dreams—after seeing this I ceased to have nightmares about Karloff—But instead, I had pleasant dreams in which each night I danced, had fun, I wore lovely clothes, I was in the company of a handsome man who,—and this was—and still is—important to me—was clever and well-known.

Until I was 12, I only went to see musical films. I have rather an impressionable temperament, and after the 'Karloff' episode, my parents wisely decided to introduce me gradually to the more serious type of films. I surprised them! One day I came home and announced that I had been to see a murder film—and what was more that I had overcome my fears and had thoroughly enjoyed it. The crowning achievement of this venture was that for the first time after seeing a film I did not dream, and since then I have never dreamed about a film again. Musicals still remained my favourites but a close second was the *Raffles* and *Saint* series of films. These pleased me mostly becasue of their witty dialogue to-day I cannot possibly enjoy a film which has poor dialogue.

At the age of 15, I began to be more critical of films than I had hitherto been. I began a film diary—not because I have a bad memory!—but because I wanted to see if I could put into words my feelings and emotions concerning a film. At 15, I saw more dramatic pictures than I had done in the past 3 yrs. About a third of these films were war films. These, I'm afraid, left very little impression on me as regards patriotism, especially American war-films which seemed to be made solely in order to impart to people the knowledge of how wonderfull they are, and so, in consequence, the average person seeing them does not bother to exert himself further.

As regards my taste at the present moment, I will go and see any musical in technicolour—even though it has a poor story—any well acted film—provided it does not concern the war, and any costume films for which I have a tremendous weakness.

In answer to the question of finding it hard to control any emotions aroused by films, I must confess that, in the last year or two, my emotions have never been aroused to any great extent. However, before this, I was frequently reduced to tears by films and this made a depression in my spirits for the rest of the day. Any emotions that arise from a film nowadays, are not aroused by the story or happenings in the film but by the sight of the film. For instance I was disgusted by the film *Somewhere I'll find you* where Clark Gable just continued to make love to Lana Turner for something to do—in fact in order to make the film. The other emotions caused by films are envy and jealousy—but these do not remain long once I am out of the cinema.

I have never bothered to imitate *clothes* from film stars, though I frequently copy accessories and copy the ways of matching styles—practically every three days I can walk into the office and someone will say—'Heavens! She's changed her hair again!' I was not *aware* I adopted mannerisms from film stars, but, as I wanted this to be an authentic report, I asked my friends & to my surprise they said I definitely did! They said I keep up a certain mannerism for several weeks and then I drop it for another, only the previous ones occasionally come up again too! For example I am told I used to curl my lip at one corner, and then I had a habit of brushing my hair up with the *back* of my hand and now I seem to be in the habit of slightly raising my left eyebrow when I'm annoyed. In fact, I seem to *unconciously* adopt mannerisms from stars.

I have never fallen *desperately* in love with my screen isol because I have so many and because each time I go to the cinema the star of the film automatically becomes my idol until I see the next film.

Films definitely have made me more receptive to love-making and they have made me regard love-making as more of a technique than as an outcome of emotions. I am told that as regards love-making I am like—to use an Americanism—an ice-cube; probably this is caused by seeing so many love scenes on the films that the sight or participation in them has ceased to effect my emotions.

I am asked to describe fully any temptations or ambitions due to films, but I'm afraid I can't remember any—this does not mean that I haven't had any because I have them frequently, but because they remain with me so little time that I forget them almost immediately.

The remaining questions can be answered 'en masse'. I have yearned to travel, wanted to leave home, been dissatisfied with my way of life and neighbourhood, and been given ambitions, *but* these feelings have soon disappeared because I have come to regard films as dreams or day-dreams commercialized; and I have taken pleasure in them, found educational knowledge in some of them, and reality in others; but I have walked out of the cinema into my everyday life and background and regarded the films as an enjoyable pastime—nothing else.

The nine-year-old group contains four documents, Nos. 42, 43, 44 and 45. No. 42 does not state precisely when her visits to the cinema started, but records her first great impression, one of fright, at the age of nine. The writer of Document No. 43 has no recollection earlier than at nine, when he saw an adult film and then began to attend children's serial performances regularly each week. Despite this comparatively late start, he writes, 'my lust for films has increased and my interest deepened with each new phase of movie progress until I now eagerly await each new production'. Similarly, No. 44 records somewhat irregular attendance after the age of nine, but now, at 20, speaks of 'what has become in the last eight or so years an almost 100 per cent interest in good human dramas'. No. 45 records distinct impressions from the age of eight or nine, then a break from eleven to thirteen. Although films still make a powerful impression on her, they have not crowded out other interests.

NO. 42

AGE: 16 YEARS 3 MONTHS
SEX: FEMALE
OCCUPATION: OFFICE CLERK (JUNIOR)
NATIONALITY: ENGLISH

PARENTS' OCCUPATION:
FATHER—CHAUFFEUR
MOTHER—HOUSEWIFE

I was too young to remember at what age I started going to the pictures, but I can vaguely remember seeing one silent film, the memory is very hazy. I suppose I became interested because I saw something different from everyday life, saw Americans with their glamorous clothes and heard their different way of speaking, saw so many things that I had not the chance of ever seeing. In some ways I think some films are very educational, they are so explicit, regarding films that are sometimes given about English country trees and farms and how our industries compare with other countries. It is so easy to understand with the diagrams that are shown. It was very rare that I went to the pictures with anyone else but my mother, so my tastes were naturally nearly always the same as hers, which were mostly funny films with George Formby and Will Hay and other stars similar to these two.

A scene from a film called *The Fire of Chicago* with Tyrone Power will always remain in my mind, I don't think I have felt so scared in my life, I clung to my mother's arm and turned as white as a sheet.

Even now after seven years I can remember that vivid scene—of all the people in Chicago fleeing from the blood red flames that were gradually enveloping the whole city, seeing some people who were old and could not get along very fast just swept down by the mad rush of everyone trying to reach the river to safety with all the belongings they could muster in the short time before the flames were greedily licking their homes, and hearing the screams of agony and pain of people who were being burnt to death.

Then as I grew older I started going by myself, and liking American films better than English ones because they had more kick in them and were not so stodgy, I am not running all English films down as I myself have seen quite a few good ones. Sometimes I went once a week but more often once a fortnight, it depended if there was a good film on that I wanted to see, I never went just for the sake of going. But now at 16 my ideas have altered in many respects regarding films, I am a great fan of swing and jive and love any films with Bing Crosby, Bob Hope, Betty Hutton and Esther Williams, I could mention many more stars but it would take too long. These films appeal to me so much more than English films because for example Bob Hope is so witty and you only have to look at him and you want to laugh. I don't think there is an English star who is equal to him, and he and Bing Crosby make a good team. By mentioning those few stars you can gather more or less what type of film I like best. Technicolour films with sparkle in them come second with me especially with all the beautiful colours there are in films like *Bathing Beauty* and some of the previous Betty Grable pictures.

I cannot say I have imitated anything from films, except maybe a bit of slang much to the disgust of my family. As for falling in love with my screen idol I certainly have not, but many times have been and in some cases still am infatuated with them, also films have definitely not made me more receptive to love-making. Naturally not many films are complete without a little love, but when they just go endlessly on with the stars being silly over each other all the time I squirm about in my seat and wish to goodness that it would stop.

Seeing a lot of Sonja Henie's and Belita's film have made me want to be able to go to Switzerland and learn to ice skate, and go to America and be taught how to be a good dancer and how to jitter-bug, this dance (if you can call it a dance) fascinates me tremendously.

Sometimes I feel dissatisfied with my way of life in the neighbourhood, I often wish I could live near a big town like London and see more of the fun and jollity of youth but I don't doubt I would miss many of the things in the country that I have always been used too.

I forgot to mention in Question 1 about my emotions in regarding films. In the picture *Lassie Come Home* when Lassie was making her long journey home from Scotland to Yorkshire, and all the hardships she was enduring I felt that I just wanted to have a good howl, and for days after whenever I thought about her I felt all weepy, but this was mainly due to the fact that I am very fond of animals and cannot bear to see anything pitiful happen to them even in a film. There are other types of films that affect this way too, and others just bring a lump into my throat. *A Guy named Joe* affected me deeply and also 30 *Seconds over Tokoyo* and then some films that are supposed to sad are just like any other ordinary film to me and I do not feel anything at all.

NO. 43

AGE: 22   FATHER'S OCCUPATION:
SEX: MALE   RAILWAY INSPECTOR
OCCUPATION: CLERK
NATIONALITY: BRITISH

At about the age of nine I distinctly recollect seeing the first 'Ramona' picture and as far as I can remember that was the first motion picture impression I had. Later on I joined a Children's Club at a local cinema where I used to see various serial films each Saturday morning. On these special occasions I would organize a meeting at a secluded street corner where a clique of us reproduced certain thrilling scenes from the exciting cowboy and adventure plots just seen. Also I remember on one occasion sneaking to see a horror film against my parents' wishes and returning home so impressed by it that I finished up with a nightmare and a caning in the bargain. I definitely used to be emotionally aroused by such films and still am. In fact my lust for films has increased and my interest deepened with each new phase of movie progress until I now eagerly await each new production.

I have never been the least bit affected by love making on the screen and have always considered it a normal action here as it is in real life. My particular screen idol is Bette Davis who is adept at mannerisms and noted for her particular style of acting. I've often caught myself using her mode of speech during a conversation using clipped phrases and highly dramatic movements. Yes. I'm sure this actress has influenced my way of thinking and doing things in every-day life. I have seen most of her films four times over and when she is billed at a local cinema it's a certainty that's where I'll be found most evenings that week. Needless to say I'm of a very imaginative nature and after seeing an exceptionally dramatic movie I have it on my mind for days and revisualise each scene until I could now tell one the plot almost word for word re: dress, camera work and maybe certain phrases in the script. Yes. I most certainly am movie mad.

Films have given me no temptations or ambitions except *the ambition* to become somehow connected with the stage or screen. I've never wanted to leave my home, but have often times faced the fact that this would be necessary if ever I attempted to fulfill my ambition. As to travel I have often wanted to do so and films have multiplied this yearning. In a way this longing has made me dis-satisfied many times with my way of life not because I feel greater than it, but because I have ambition in me and know that 'no-one

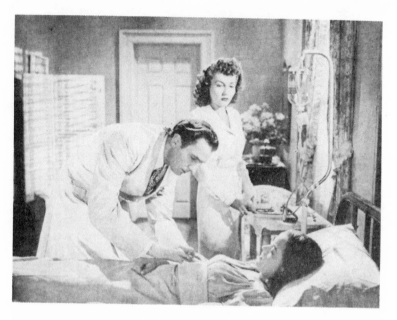

From the Film *Shock*. If you want to be in fear of your doctor, go and see this film and take your children with you.

From the Film *Dr. Renault's Secret*. An 'A' Film which should have been certified 'H'.

Story: A young American, Dr. Forbes (John Shepperd), arrives in France to claim his fiancee, niece of a scientist, Dr. Renault (George Zucco).
Forbes is met at an inn, where he is to spend the night, by a strange character named Noel (J. Carrol Naish), a native of Java, who is to escort him to the chateau next day. The scientist's gardener, Rogell, an ex-convict, also is at the inn. A drunken American, Austin, goes to sleep in Forbes' room by mistake and is strangled.
Next day, Forbes goes to the chateau, where he is met by his fiancee, Madeline Renault (Lynne Roberts). A Great Dane wanders into the garden and Madeline adopts him until his owner shall have been found. That night, before dinner, the dog attacks Noel for no reason. Because the police figure the murder of Austin was a mistake and that Dr. Forbes was the intended victim, the dog is permitted to run loose in the grounds, but that night the dog is strangled with a heavy chain.
Next day, Bastille Day, a celebration is being held in the village. Noel, who idolises Madeline because she befriended him, is ridiculed by two villagers, the bartender and the barber, because he dances so clumsily. Later that night, Noel is seen swinging from a tree to the roof of the inn. He kills the bartender by hurling him out of the window. Then he kills the barber with a razor. At the scene of the murder of the barber, Dr. Forbes finds a clue to Noel's guilt.
He goes back to the chateau with Madeline, and sends her to her room. In the laboratory he discovers Renault's records of his experiments with Noel. Renault wanted to prove the descent of man from ape. He had been able to make one, Noel, talk and act like a man, but had been unable to give it a human conscience.

(from the Trade Circular synopsis)

gets something for nothing' and consequently I realise I shall have to break away from my present surroundings in order to really make good.

Apart from interest in films I have always felt keenly towards a doctor's career, but here the matter of finance has prevented further thought on this subject. This desire has often been stimulated by such films as *Sorrell and Son*, *The Lamp Still Burns*, and more recently that fine production on the life of *Mme. Curie*.

I'm also a lover of music, my tastes varying from Beethoven to Benny Goodman although I must say I do prefer the classical side. Consequently I have often been thrilled by such musically saturated films as *Unfinished Symphony*, *Song of Russia*, and more so with that beautiful picture *A Song to Remember* which contained such liberal lashings of Chopin.

Being so very keen on movies I beg, buy and steal any information in the way of cuttings and magazines I can. I have a fair collection of such things and have spent many a happy hour saving and scanning these.

I am truly thankful to the film industry and the organization behind it for the great pleasure I have derived from its film productions.

No. 44

AGE: 20 YEARS 6 MONTHS   FATHERS' OCCUPATION:
SEX: M.   BUILDERS LABOURER
OCCUPATION: 2ND CINEMA OPERATOR
NATIONALITY: ENGLISH

The first nine years of my life were marred by an almost continuous illness. This naturally prevented me from seeing many films during that period. If there is any truth in the opinion of some people that young children are only interested in Cowboys and Indians or gangster films, then perhaps the reason I never enjoy such films is because I had very little oportunity of seeing them. However, I still have vague and somewhat pleasant memories of Buck Jones and Tom Mix, etc.

Until I was 14 yrs. old I was always accompanied by my parents when going to see a film. Sometimes I went to children's matinees with my brother and sister. The fact that my father was often unemployed somewhat delayed cinema going as a serious hobby for me. Going to the pictures with my sister at about the age of 13 yrs. could I think, be credited with what has become in the last eight or so years an almost 100 per cent interest in good human dramas. I can't say what film of this type I saw first but I can say that such films as *The Human Story* with James Stewart and *The Magnificient Obsession* with Robert Taylor and Irene Dunne were among the first films I thoroughly enjoyed. These two films definitely proved that I was by no means immune from tear shedding during the showing of a film. After being witness to a dispute between my father and elder brother a similar incident in the *Human Story* soon brought tears to my eyes and the painful look in Robert Taylor's eyes after seeing Irene Dunn struck down by a passing car in *The Magnificent Obsession* almost made me cry out. Even at the age of 18 or 19, Margaret O'brien's heartbreaking cry in *Journey for Margaret* almost got the better of me. As for films frightening me, only one scene ever really frightened me. Near the end of the fairly recent film *The Uninvited* the doors of the room suddenly burst wide open with a crash of incidental music. For a full two minutes after it I was held in fear wondering what was going to happen. In general though, it is only when watching a film which reminds me of something that happened to me in real life that I find it difficult to control my emotions.

I think I can safely say that the only effect films have had on my life lies in the fact that I am very keen on dramatic acting. I used to think when looking at British films that Britain needed more actors. That was when I was about 16. So I joined a small drama club. I got along very well until I had to change my work at the age of 18. Now the nearest I've got to the stage or screen is to work in a cinema as an operator. Some people may have expected me to stop going to the cinema for entertainment on my type of work, but instead I go a great deal more. *Dangerous Moonlight* was the film which changed or should I say added something to the list of my hobbies. My first hearing of *Warsaw Concerto* caused my to take music more seriously. Since then I should say that music has played a very important part in my life. Naturally, films including classical music have been among the films which I enjoyed most. However only one film really fully satisfied me in this respect. I refer to *A Song to Remember* which combined a really sensible drama with very good music.

Love, Love, Love. Is love, as made in films really like love in real life. It sometimes frightens me to think that I may have to go through what film characters do in order to secure myself a girl. Some of my married friends assure me that I will but I prefer to wait until it happens before I believe it.

So, there is my life, as connected with films and I must say it has been a very pleasant life. Films never caused me to want anything which I couldn't get by leading a normal life. The average film in my opinion is not as some people claim improper education for the younger generation. Young people go to the cinema for entertainment and not education, at least I do. Film Producers please note.

To the Film industry as a whole I like to say Thank You.

NO. 45

AGE: 18   FATHERS' OCCUPATION
SEX: F.   IN GOVERNMENT OFFICE
OCCUPATION: IN GOVERNMENT OFFICE
NATIONALITY: BRITISH

As a regular reader of *Picturegoer* and quite an ardent cinema fan, I felt extremely interested in this competition that gives scope to express one's feelings as regards films. My father and I both work in Government offices in London, the life of which I find rather monotonous, and were it not for the cinema and the pleasure it affords, I should miss a valuable outlet for my feelings. I am of English nationality and of female sex, and in my eighteen years of age have known numerous sensations and thoughts from the cinema world.

Until reaching the age of fourteen, I seldom visited the cinema but formed quite definite ideas on the films that I liked and understood. Films showing wild animals usually frightened me and I did not believe my mother's assurances that 'it was only a film'. At the age of eight or nine my favourite films were the Fred-Astaire-Ginger Rogers musicals. The rythmn of the dancing of these two stars quite captivated me and I longed to dance as they did. My parents sent me to a convent school for girls at the age of eleven and I forgot the cinema in the interests of school studies. When about thirteen years of age I saw the film of *The Adventures of Robin Hood* and from that day became a keen admirer of the cinema. The colour and picturesque scenery and last but not least, Errol Flynn, the leading man, enthralled me and I became addicted to the fashionable craze of collecting film star pictures. For a whole year I thought, talked and dreamed films and Errol Flynn became my screen idol. His good looks, handsome physique and most of all his moustache all helped to make me feel as if I was in love. However when the war broke out. I found that my idol had feet of clay and would not join the army, Thus ended my infatuation and I never liked the man since, and do not regard him as an actor.

I now began to enjoy all types of films and to realise the value of good and sincere acting. English history always interested me and historical films were not amiss to my taste. The film of *Marie Antoinette* impressed me very much and I would make drawings of the lovely gowns worn by Norma. Shearer in the chief part. Thus commenced my interest in drawing and designing. I began to form ideas of criticism and films did not exercise any power over me for a few years. It seemed as if my 'movie mad' period was over.

During my last year at school the film of *Arabian Nights* was generally released and as a result I desired to travel to Eastern countries. The glamour and colour in the film worked upon my imagination. However, in this case I did *not* fall in love with the leading man, Jon Hall, I am glad to say! Films of action and adventure in the East were now to my taste, because I thought that Oriental life was so romantic. This sensation still remains with me as a result of seeing such films as *The Four Feathers* and *The Desert Song*. The cold, grey climate of the British Isles compares unfavourably with the beautiful sunshine and colour shown on the screen. At times I have been most miserable when these wanderlust periods set in with a vengeance.

Being a member of the feminine sex I naturally admire the lovely clothes worn by the stars. My first hair style model was Olivia de Havilland and I dressed my hair in accordance with her own mode.

I never imitated clothes or shoes although I often, (and still do) longed for fur coats, evening gowns etc.

Films of the lives of famous men always made me long to invent or discover as they did. *The Adventures of Marco Polo* was such an example. More recently I saw the film of *A Song to Remember*, and now, am very fond of Chopin's music, and am interested in his romantic life story.

Up to date my feelings are quite normal towards films, although I criticise as I see fit. I admire quite a few actors and actresses of all nationality and now give examples. The late Leslie Howard greatly impressed me with his sincere acting and now I have a preference for the work of Laurence Olivier and Sidney Greenstreet. I do not think any actresses compare with Bette Davis or Vivien Leigh. I admit that when the heroes of the screen made love in a way that no ordinary man would do, I feel an excited sensation as if I were the heroine in the film, although this passes off quite quickly.

The actor, Dennis Morgan, in view of his good looks, delightful tenor voice and no mean acting ability, usually affects me in this manner.

In conclusion, I may say that I have benefited from the cinema educationally. Films have lent a great deal to my imagination, and I admire the great companies and producers that help to form the world industry. Thus is described my motion picture autobiography in its various stages.

Document No. 46 is contributed by one of the few writers who are not 'ardent' filmgoers. Her regular attendance at a serial performance did not begin until the age of ten. A gap of three years did not 'bother' her, and when attendance was resumed, the cinema was never an all-embracing interest. While strong impressions, mainly of horror, are recorded, the writer recounts her experiences with unusual detachment:' I do not think films affect my life a great deal. Determined and confident, I have my plans for life and no film influence can change them'. No. 46, on the other hand, whose attendance also began at the age of ten, writes 'indeed my life is well wrapped up in the cinema and I sincerely hope it won't be long before I can have a go at entering the industry myself'.

NO. 46

AGE: 21	PARENTS' OCCUPATION:
SEX: F.	FATHER—CIVIL SERVANT
OCCUPATION: NEWSPAPER REPORTER	MOTHER—HOUSEWIFE
NATIONALITY: BRITISH	

It is no easy task to trace my history as a film-goer because in the first place I have never looked upon myself as an ardent film-goer.

A film rarely impresses me. If it does, the impression does not stay with me long—unless the film is extrodinarily good—and the next day I am inclined to think 'Bah!'

As a child, seeing films was not a regular entertainment. I went so little, that when I did, it was considered a great treat, a treat which did not come about until I had plucked up courage to ask either of my parents for admission money.

However, when I was about 10 and went to live at . . . where my grandmother resided, life was so changed for me that I became a regular film fan, and followed the weekly serial at the local 'bug hutch', as the cinema was called, due to its age.

My grandmother, an ardent serial fan, went to the pictures on every pension evening (Friday). She enjoyed taking me and my young cousin for company. The three of us became well-known to the commissioner, box-office girl and usherettes.

At this particular stage, I liked cow-boy and Indians films, as well as gangster films and those in which people mysteriously disappeared or went flying off to the moon in weird contraptions.

They affected my boy-cousin and myself in our play. If we saw a Red Indian film we plagued our most generous uncle for money to buy bows and arrows.

If we saw a gangster film we used to turn the old sofa into a barge and pretend we were sailing down a river with stolen property aboard. Now and again and would 'fight' the cushions, and throw them 'overbroad'!

Speed way films affected us in such a way that my cousin—whom I called Bill. He called me George—would sit at the top of the sloping garden path, and roll about half a dozen balls down to me, at the same time giving a running commentary, similar to the ones heard on the films. Each ball represented a car. If one rolled into the bed of wallflowers, well, the 'car' had skidded, overturned and was on fire!

When I was moved away from my grandmother, it meant no more films for me. No more, in fact, for three years. Oddly enough, it did not bother me.

As a senior schoolgirl I started going to the films again, not because they attracted me, but because I wished to pass away a few hours.

Films were just something to watch, and that was all. I formed very few opinions, took little interest in the stars, male or female, or in their costumes.

A musical would never inspire me to hum the 'hit-tunes' and I was always cynical towards my form mates who used to discuss their film heros, and speak of the love films as if they themselves were in paradise at the mere thought of it.

At about the age of 15 I cultivated an interest in murder films, not that I was sadistically minded but that I prided myself in being able to solve the mysteries before the end of the film. And I usually did. In the end I went to so many that I became a plot critic and formed the opinion that Hollywood—in those days I never thought of a British film—was not capable of producing anything to make the brain work.

I sat in my 9d. seat and literally watched with eyes like an eagle for faults.

Horror films were beginning to flood the market at this period, but they left me cold. It seemed that I could not get a thrill out of any film, and I was disgusted.

Now older, I persuaded my mother to take me to these 'horror' films—still under 16 I had to be taken by an adult—but in my mind had imagined them far more horrible than they really were, that when I saw the actual film, I was disappointed.

Bela Lugosi and Boris Karloff in the worst of their make-ups repeatedly failed to make me duck my head beneath the sheets at night.

Yet I was frightened when I least expected to be. It was the film, *The Face Behind the Mask* which Mother—a keen reader of murder stories—invited me to see with her. I was 16.

Peter Lorre, in the film, plunged headfirst into a raging fire. Later, the audience saw his head and face completely smothered in bandages. Then came the scene where they were removed by the doctor.

All the mirrors in the surgery were covered. This made me think . . .

Lorre sat with his back to the audience. A nurse came into the surgery, faced him, and gave a horrific scream.

By this time I was all keyed up, and dreading to see his face. I covered my face with my hands but curiousity overcame my fear, and I began to spread my fingers out and peep through the space.

Lorre tore down a mirror covering and looked at himself. His reflection was seen by the audience. It was a ghastly sight. I saw only half of the shot.

A few minutes after I turned to my mother and said 'Wished I had seen it all now', and all that evening asked her to describe what I had missed.

But it did frighten me. It was the first and only film, so far, which has scared me. For days I was afraid to meet people in the dark in case their faces were disfigured. Sometimes, even now, the old fear comes back.

The experience played havoc with me during the first fire raids on this country. When ever incendiaries were falling, and we had them pretty badly around our way, I would think of Lorre's face in the film, and anxiously hope that if our house was set alight, no injury by fire would be caused to my face.

I did not take a wide interest in films, film stars and their lives until I was about 20, although in my later teens I went regularly, sometimes twice a week with the boy-friends. That was because I preferred sitting in a cinema than strolling the streets.

I had no particular taste in films then, except that once I remember chosing a film merely because the boy-friend said I had eyes just like the leading lady!

This may imply that I aim at patterning myself according to the film stars. That is not so and has never been. I do not copy their hair or dress styles, the way they talk or their behavier.

But I must confess that occassionally I watch their eyes and see how they use them I am told that my eyes are my greatest asset. Therefore I make a point of seeing how I can use them to advantage.

I have never had a film hero, and am not likely to have one. I prefer to 'go wakey' over something more concrete and nearer at hand than a film star.

Nothing infuriates me more than to hear my girl-friends go into raptures over certain male film stars. To me they are just ordinary men earning a living, and that's that. A rather cold and uninspiring opinion, I know, but film heros definitely leave me like an ice-berg.

As I grew older and with personal experience, I naturally became more interested in love films; not the sloppy cheap sentimental type which Hollywood often turns out, but the rare and welcome sincere film which has a great story of strong love to tell—films like *Now Voyager*, *Random Harvest* and *Back street* as well as others which I cannot remember at this time.

Certain love films do make me more receptive to love making. Often my emotions are aroused, particularly by the war time romances on the screen which can so easily be applied to members of the audience.

Often they make me sad, and I am depressed for the rest of the evening, wondering if my man will be killed in action or maimed as the one in the film.

But they are not lasting impressions. In the morning I have forgotten all about it.

Films have never influenced my ambitions. My desires to become a newspaper reporter, to travel and to sing could have been no greater had I not seen journalistic films, travel films and films starring Deanna Durbin, Jeannette MacDonald and and Grace Morre.

I began training for journalitm sometime before I saw any film depicting that life, which anyway, are all bunk on the screen! I had travelled, too, before travel films had time to impress me, and I have always been musically inclined.

The films I most yearn for now are those full of rich music which is the strongest type of film to arouse my emotions. Classical music can make me either gay or sad.

I thoroughly enjoy films like *A Song to Remember* featuring the life of Chopin I confess that I sat through this particularly film twice, a thing I rarely do, and then it was only to hear the music. I loathed the speaking parts.

On the whole, I do not think films affect my life a great deal.

Determined and confident, I have my plans for life and no film influence can change them.

Moreover, films are not my choice of entertainment, and I only patronize them when there is no competition from the ballet and opera theatres and sport.

Yet when I do go, I expect to see something true to life which will give food for thought.

NO. 47

AGE: 21   FATHER'S OCCUPATION:
SEX: M.   BACON CURER
OCCUPATION: CLERK
NATIONALITY: BRITISH

I shall always remember my first important visit to the cinema. The Local Gaumont was being opened by the Mayor and many other important townsfolk yet out of that impressive ceremony way back at the beginning of the thirties, the only part that stands out vividly to me today was the film. It was a musical starring Jack Buchanan and entitled *Goodnight Vienna*.

Why this particular incident should have aroused my first profound interest in the cinema remains a mystery, yet I am convinced that before that date, the thought of 'Going to the flicks' never meant much to me.

I was of course quite young at the time—about 10 years of age. For some years, I simply doted on musicals and the thought of seeing another Astaire-Rogers extravaganza provided plenty of excitement for little me. I found myself wanting to tapdance, although I was careful not to disclose any of these ambitions to my parents. Sometimes I wonder whether 'careful' was the word. The back-yard shows my pals and I used to put on were always received with wild enthusiasm. I might add that as the price for admission consisted of 3 'conkers' or (when such things were out of season) perhaps 2 pen-nibs, audiences did jolly well under the circumstances.

My enthusiasm for musicals continued for quite a while until I reached the age when more serious aspects of films began to make themselves felt. It all started with my seeing Bette Davies in *Dark Victory*. Never shall I forget her terrific performance in this film. It stands out as one of the most enthralling episodes in my movie experience. That really started the ball rolling and from that day to this I have been an ardent dramatic fan. In fact, I am hoping to study drama upon my demobilisation. I love great acting, for the emotional benefit I myself get out of it is greatly satisfying. That is why I am such an admirer of Bette Davis, Ingrid Bergman and Paul Muni.

As for films influencing my daily life, until I discovered that drama was my ideal, I must admit that my life was not unduly affected. I enjoyed helping to stage our so-called concerts with my neighbours and that was all. Today however, it is a different story. I discover that if I should miss a dramatic film that I had been bent on seeing, nothing would stop me until I cought up with it at last.

Films have made me want to visit the U.S.A. in rather an unusual way. By reading rather a lot of authentic literature on that country I have realised now hopelessly incompetent a large precentage of films have been in portraying life in the U.S.A. I have come to believe in the books I have read and the fact that they do not tie up with what I have seen on the screen, has made me even more eager to go there and see for myself. I am referring to modern life in the States of course.

Since my joining the Forces in 1942 , I have also become interested in the technical side of films not with the interest of a technician but artistically. I can now appreciate photography and lighting and I realise that the cinema is most definitely an art. That is why I uphold Orson Well's work and get annoyed when such masterpieces as *Citizen Kane* and *The Magnificent Ambersons* get snuffed at by the general public.

To-day I am an ardent film fan making sure I read all the reviews of the films as they reach the West End. I even keep a record of the date of arrival of each film and any other particulars that I think are worth recording.

Yes, indeed my life is well wrapped in the cinema and I sincerely hope it won't be long before I can have a go at entering the industry myself. I shall always be grateful to Miss Davis for revealing an ambition that had previously slept within me.

Nine of the remaining documents fall within the period of what is called 'secondary' education. It is most striking that so few of our contributors record their permanent habit of film-going as starting on or after the age which is chosen for a break in schooling. The great majority had formed their habit before reaching adolescence. The writer of No. 48 had, indeed, been to the cinema when about seven, and has a faint recollection of horror-impressions. But her visits were few and far between until she started at a High School. No. 49 took an interest in a children's club at 11, and is the only one of our contributors who took any active part in actual organization, serving on the committee and helping to choose the pictures. She now goes four times a week and regards this attendance 'as a habit, but a very nice one'.

NO. 48

AGE: 18 YEARS 1 MONTH	FATHER'S OCCUPATION
SEX: F.	MACHINE TOOL FITTER
OCCUPATION: CLERK-TYPIST	MOTHER'S OCCUPATION:
NATIONALITY: BRITISH	FLY DRESSER

Recollections of my first film are extremely vague. I was about 7 years old at the time, and my mother took me to see an 'A' film. I faintly recall a scene where a coffin lid slowly rose and a shadowy figure emerged. But it was the Walt Disney *Silly Symphonies* that attracted me most at that early age, though I always possessed a faint horror of films dealing with the wonders of the medical world. On the whole, I knew very little of films, for my visits to the cinema were few and far between.

When I started High School, however, my interest grew, and like most girls of that age, I nursed a very secret ambition to one day become a film star. My school friends and I often tried to dress our hair after the fashion of our respective film favourites, though with little success. More than once I used descriptions from films in my English compositions, and can now confess to learning more from historical films than from my history book!

I saw my most frightening film when I was 16; it was called the *Case of Dr. RX*. I remember when the Doctor imprisoned his victim on the operating table, while in a cell not far away was a huge gorilla. His fiendish plan was to interchange their brains, and he pushed the table just within the reach of the ape, who thrust out a hairy arm and slowly drew it towards him . . . Being alone when I saw this film, I clung to the arms of my seat in terror. I sometimes shed a few tears over a film, especially so in the film *Jane Eyre*, and similar films dealing with hardships of children or animals. When witnessing a favourite star in a love scene, I muse how wonderful it would be to be in the arms of one such as he, comparing him ruefully with a local boy friend.

Dresses, shoes, hats and handbags were always a source of joy to me, and I have often left a cinema deciding that my next seasons outfit would be like that of the star in the film I had just seen. The film *Lady in the Dark* was the source of my ambition to become the editress of a fashion magazine, and other films too, have presented me with momentary yearnings to become everything from a secretary to a waitress. In fact, if the Gods had been kind, yours truly would have the figure of Marie McDonald, the face of Hedy Lamarr, the voice of Kathryn Grayson, the feet of Eleanor Powell and possessed of the talent of Greer Garson.

NO. 49

AGE: 21	FATHER'S OCCUPATION:
SEX: F.	HAIRDRESSER (ENGLISH)
OCCUPATION:	MOTHER'S OCCUPATION:
SHORTHAND TYPIST SECRETARY	HOUSEWIFE (IRISH)

The first time I took interest in films, was at the age of 11 when I joined the Gaumont British Kiddies Club. I remember we always had cowboy pictures (serials) shown each week on Saturday afternoons. They were of great excitement to me, and my eight year old sister, who used to accompany me. The cowboy pictures as we called them, led us to play cowboys and Indians in the garden with other children. This was of course after school hours. For horses we used thick poles about 5 feet long with a piece of string tied at the top end for reins.

Later at the age of about 13, I was asked to join the committee of the kiddies club. The committee consisted of boys and girls representing different schools and colleges, and between us we decided which pictures we thought best to show at the cinema. Cowboy & Indian pictures were the most popular to them and to me, especially when the star was either the late Buck Jones or Tom Mix. They both had wonderful white horses to add to the attraction. In return for our work in the committee we were allowed to go each week in the evening and see an adult show, even if it was an 'A' certificate. No addmission fee to pay either. This made me feel quite grown-up and very proud of myself.

Deanna Durbin was my favorite star when I was 14 years old, and I have seen all her films. I was greatly influenced by her, and used to try and memorise the songs she sang in her pictures during the performance in the cinema. The way she sang them was how I tried to, but without success. My sister was more successful here.

When I was 15, I managed to get to see a 'H' certificate picture called *The Vampire Bat*, which was the most frightening film I have ever seen. It was about a woman who lived on human blood which she sucked from the neck of people asleep in there beds at night. I think what made me terrified was the scene in which she looked through the window into a girls bedroom watching her chance to get in, (during this suspense, I gripped and tore a bit of stuffing out of my seat) I also remember how white looking her face was with a sort of black tinge to it, and her hair was black and down to the waist in length. This vision at the window remained in my memory all the way home afterwards. I could not even speak to the girl I went with very much as she also was shaken. That night I never slept at all. I imagined I saw her looking in at my bedroom window, and I remember screaming which brought my mother hurrying in to see what the matter was. She found me in a cold sweat. I told her about seeing the face at the window just like I did in the film. She said 'all pictures are not real but just imagination, and that there was no such thing as a woman vampire. A Vampire was a sort of bird that lived hundreds of years ago in foreign countries'. Anyway it took me some time to get over it. I shiver now when I think of it.

At 17 I was very interested in great love stories. Tyrone Power was my idol and I saw his pictures three and four times. I think I must have fallen in love with him as I spoke quite a lot about him to my sister and friends until they got sick of me talking about him. I like his manner in acting, love making, his courage and daring. When he kisses his leading lady a funny thrill runs up my spine to the heart. Sometimes in dreams which seem very real, I imagine he is kissing me. This may sound ridiculous but it is quite true and is the way I feel. Tyrone Power to me is a very good swordsman which seems to suit his personality. I have seen everyone of his pictures to his last (*Crash Dive*) before he joined the marines. I miss seeing him on the screen very much and hope to see him again in the very near future. I envy his lovely wife Annabella, but I like her she is very charming and is a very good actress.

Films I think have made me more receptive to love making, sometimes I feel like kissing a stranger, but have never done this. I have always gone to the cinema with girl friends or my sisters.

My ambition through films is to be a secretary to a star. Of course it would have to be a star who I admired, and enjoyed his or her acting. I have longed to see America as the screen showes it, but I know it is just a dream not to come true.

Between 19 and my present age I go very often to the pictures (Four times a week to be exact) I am told it is not good for me, and I suppose it has grown to be a habit, but a very nice one. I could not stop away from the pictures for three nights running unless I was ill. I do get very dissatisfied with my way of life and neighbourhood. After seeing marvellous places like New York, Hollywood, California, Cuba, Washington, (I could go on for ever) on the screen, especially in technicolour, it makes me very miserable and unhappy sitting in my stuffy little office all day with nobody to talk to but myself (which I don't) and to go home to a house that should have been knocked down five years ago, although it is better than living in the funny wooden houses they are producing these days. Of what I have seen of them on the screen, I am really disgusted. They are more like huts than anything else.

I wanted to become a nurse when I saw the *Dr. Gillespie* series. I thought it would be wonderful to be a nurse and still think so. In the *Dr. Gillespie* series I fell in love again with Dr. Red Adams (Van Johnson), who I think has climbed to the top of the screen lovers ladder already. I even wrote to him telling him how much I enjoy his acting in the series, and for his performances in *A Guy Named Joe*, *Two Girls and a Sailor*, *The White Cliffs of Dover*, in which he only got a very small part. I asked him to send me a signed photograph which I received, and a very nice one it is. Now I am waiting patiently for his next picture to come through.

In the picture *A Guy Named Joe*, Irene Dunn's performance as a ferry pilot made me long to be one too. Although I was frightened for her when she kidnapped a bomber and flew to a munitions objective and drop her bombs on the target, which was supposed to have been Van Johnsons mission. I thought it was a great and inspiring picture.

Well I think this is all and hope it will be understood, and not misjudged.

The writers of two documents, Nos. 50 and 51, did not become interested in films until the age of 13. Both have been considerably influenced, particularly No. 51, who writes, 'My whole life has completely changed since I took to the films. I am easily irritated and upset, and have very little interest in my work'.

NO. 50

AGE: 24   FATHER'S OCCUPATION:
SEX: M.   WOOD CUTTING
OCCUPATION: DISCHARGED MEDICALLY   MACHINIST
    UNFIT FORCES BUT CANNOT RETURN   MOTHER'S OCCUPATION:
    OLD TRADE JOINER   HOUSEWIFE
NATIONALITY: BRITISH (PROBABLY)

I think I first became interested in films by hearing accounts of the current films at the local cinema from my school pals. My pals and I from the age of twelve or thirteen (when I first started to visit cinemas) made a regular weekly date for the cinema. I thought all films good especially Westerns, 'Slapstick' and Gangsters. At the age of sixteen I lost interest in Slapstick which only bored me. At eighteen the same happened with Westerns. I still like Gangster films. I prefer drama now and such films as *The Murder in Thornton Square* and *Dark Victory* I enjoy immensely. I also like comedies of the subtle type, Ray Milland in *French Without Tears* is a perfect example.

Films influenced my play considerably. Arguments developed amongst my pals and I on who should be Buck Jones and who should play the much maligned Indian, and I always thought gum-chewing made me look tough.

I have always wanted to visit the Hawaiin Islands, and see if the native girls are really as beautiful as the screen depicts. New York too had an attraction that fascinated me, but now I'd rather visit London. Hawaii still attracts. My screen idol—Ingrid Bergman is the only female star that's ever attracted me in my film going life. I think that if only I could meet a girl like her I'd find the one and only. She is so different from the cheapness of Betty Grable, Betty Hutton, etc. If its possible to fall in love with a screen star, I have.

When I was twelve a film trailer frightened me so much that I daren't go to bed at night without first looking in the bedroom cupboard and under the bed. The scene showed several policemen closing in on a cupboard, when they were a few feet away the cupboard door slowly opened and a ghost slowly drifted out. I still shudder.

Yes, films did at one time make me more receptive to love-making, because I thought an imitation of Gable or Power would delight the girl friend. Whether it did or not I cant say as my imitation probably had no resemblance. I soon realised though that imitations are cheap and naturalness is the only course. In fact I think the love interest in films is all very artificial and cheap. Technicolour musicals are the most boring films, with nine times out of ten no story, in fact nothing but hideously painted lips.

NO. 51

AGE: 16½   FATHER'S OCCUPATION:
SEX: M.   BUTCHER
OCCUPATION: SHORTHAND-TYPIST
NATIONALITY: BRITISH

When I was thirteen years old, and attending Elementary School, I was rather shy. One of my friends suggested I go to the films more oftener to broaden my outlook on life. This I did and now I go as often as 5 times a week. I just don't go to the films for the sake of going, I go because I want to learn and enjoy that which I like and take a great interest in.

At first I liked only Roy Rogers and Gene Autry films. I really got a thrill out of them at that time. However, on attaining the age of 14, I took a sudden switch-over, and went on to Thrillers and Musicals of which I took a very keen interest and studied them very thoroughly.

I have become so interested in films, that my ordinary life has now completely changed. For instance, before going to the films I would go as often as 6 times a week to the Young Mens Christian Association (I joined at the age of 14), each Sunday I went cycling with my pals, and occasionally went for walks. This has all stopped with a terrific Halt. No longer do I go 6 times a week to the club, or each Sunday go cycling and walking. Sunday evening means pictures to me.

I must admit that I have never been scared of a scene from any film. Though, I admit I do find it hard to conceal my emotions. As for instance in the film *My Friend Flika*, where Flika was lying in the water dying, Roddy McDowall lay with him in his pyjamas faithful to the last. At this point of the film I did shed a tear. However at the end of the film when Flika recovers and everybody's happy, at this point I really cried.

As for imitating from films, I certainly have done that. When I speak now, I speak so as each word I say can be understood without someone having to say to me 'pardon'. When I dress, I put my tie inside my shirt, a thing which I never done before. I take great pains over the parting of my hair which is now becoming rather curly.

Many times I have fallen for the stars of the films, some of those whom I greatly admire are Greer Garson, Gloria Jean, Ingrid Bergman, Ronald Colman, Walter Pidgeon, Humphrey Bogart, and Basil Rathbone.

Films have made me more receptive to love making, though I am sorry to say is of very little use to me as I am very shy towards where girls are concerned.

When I was young I was never taken to the pictures by anyone.

I have two ambitions which I hope one day will come true, the first is to go to America, which in my opinion is the greatest place on the map of the world. Where everybody is classed as one, which (if you don't mind my saying so), is not a policy generally carried out by all of the English people at the present day. Secondly I hope to become a Vocalist of great renown with some popular American band. I hope in future years my name will be a name quoted by every individual, who can enjoy a free world from the scars of War and enjoy the greatest thing of all called piece.

My whole life has completely changed since I took to the films. I am easily irritated and upset, and have very little interest in my work.

Well Sir, these are all true facts that I have written here. I am not saying them because I hope to win a prize, but I say them because it is the honest way I feel at the present time, and the way I will feel from this time onwards. Your paper is a great paper.

When this competition is finished, and should I win or not, would you please be good enough to send me this sheet back, as I would like to keep it as a mamento for future years.

I would also like to mention that I am now running a club for the American Film star called Gus Schilling of Universal Pictures. That I think will tell you how much I admire the stars. I think you can understand running a club is no easy job. With a magazine to publish every month of all the latest events of the stars etc.

Good Luck to You and Your Paper.

Three documents, Nos. 52, 53 and 54, fall into the fourteen-year-old age-group, and one, No. 56, records the experience of a young man who visited a cinema for the first time at the age of 16. The writer of No. 52, a woman of 47, holds a view that one might have expected to have been more clearly demonstrated by our documents: '. . . this report . . . may prove that a person who reached early adolescence *before* seeing any films is less likely to be influenced by the cinema, since other forms of recreation had already established themselves'. Her view would not appear to be supported by our document No. 51, though the few documents in this collection of contributions from people who began attendance at the cinema after the age of 11 may in itself be a proof of her contention. On the other hand, we should not forget her significant sentence: 'I may add that I was never allowed to go to the cinema without other members of the family, nor did I ever want to do so. My affection for my parents and *the complete happiness I always found at home* may have accounted for this; the cinema was never an "escape", for I had nothing to escape from'. No. 54 visited films as a little girl but did not become interested until the age of 14. No. 55 also went as a child, but records no interest until 14. No. 56 first saw a film at 16, but at 21 now goes 'about five or six times a week'.

NO. 52

AGE: 47   FATHER'S OCCUPATION:
SEX: F.   SOLICITOR'S CLERK
OCCUPATION: MOTHER'S OCCUPATION:
  HOUSEWIFE AND FICTION-WRITER   HOME DUTIES
NATIONALITY: BRITISH

I have seen the development of films from the beginning. My very
first visit to a cinema was in 1912 or thereabouts, when I was taken
by older members of my family to see such films as *Queen Elizabeth*
with Sarah Bernhardt and *The Crusades*. My father had been deaf
since boyhood, so this form of entirely visual entertainment made a
special appeal to him. Being then a schoolgirl in my early teens, I,
not unnaturally, was inclined to be a hero-worshipper, and chiefly
enjoyed those films which starred a romantic and attractive male
actor. Comedy—then almost entirely restricted to slapstick—appealed in a lesser degree, particularly Charlie Chaplin's films, which
developed in me an appreciation of what might be described as the
finer shades of humour.

My brother—two years older than myself—and I had for some time
read with delight a weekly series of tales, known as *The Buffalo Bill
library*, and it was this liking for tales of the Wild West which made
me specially partial, during the next few years, to the 'Broncho Billy'
type of picture.

Being already past childhood when I saw my first film, I cannot
remember that the cinema influenced my play-hours at all. It was
just another amusement, neither more nor less attractive than reading or any other diversion. I may add that I was never allowed to go
to the cinema without other members of the family, nor did I ever
want to do so. My affection for my parents and the complete happiness I always found at home may have accounted for this; the cinema
was never an 'escape', for I had nothing to escape from, it was simply
one form of entertainment for leisure hours, and by no means the
chief one.

I cannot recollect ever being frightened by a film, perhaps because
my parents did not take me to any film which was in any way
horrible or macabre.

After my mother's death in 1915, my sister and I went regularly to
the cinema with my father every Saturday afternoon. We found
special pleasure in the excellent comedy-dramas then showing—
Constance Talmadge's films, and those starring James Kirkwood and
Tom Moore, and, among English players, Henry Edwards, Chrissie
White and Alma Taylor. I saw *Under Two Flags*, starring James
Kirkwood and Priscilla Dean, no less than 7 times, and *Way Down
East* six!

My appreciation of films during the following years was largely
dependent on personalities. I always preferred an indifferent film in
which a favourite star appeared to a finer picture featuring someone

Tyrone Power in *The Razor's Edge*. "At 17 I was very interested in great love stories. Tyrone Power was my idol and I saw his pictures three and four times. I think I must have fallen in love with him as I spoke quite a lot about him to my sister and friends until they got sick of me talking about him. I like his manner in acting, love making, his courage and daring. When he kisses his leading lady a funny thrill runs up my spine to the heart. Sometimes in dreams which seem very real, I imagine he is kissing me." (see Document No. 49)

Errol Flynn in *Never Say Goodbye.* "For a whole year I thought, talked and dreamed films and Errol Flynn became my screen idol. His good looks, handsome physique and most of all his moustache all helped to make me feel as if I was in love." (see Document No. 45)

who did not appeal to me—and this prejudice still sways me considerably, though I realise it is not one to boast about!

With regard to the emotions raised by films, I rarely find myself moved, either to laughter, tears or enthusiasm, by the scenes which appeal to the majority. This is not from any snobbish patronage, or desire to be 'different', but purely a personal idiosyncrasy. Subtlety, restraint, the power of small things or incidents to show emotion,—these touch me.

I don't think I have ever felt inclined to imitate anyone on the films, either in mannerism or looks. Neither have I ever 'fallen in love' with a screen actor, though I have had unreasoning 'crushes' on a few film stars, not always of the male sex. And I cannot honestly say that films have made me 'more receptive to love-making'. Being naturally of a sentimental disposition, films have only made me realise—rather sadly—how nice it would be if real life lovers behaved as the romantic film ones do!

Temptations? Well, I must admit I have sometimes envied the beautiful ladies their gowns or their coiffures, but certainly not to such an extent as to constitute a temptation. Nor have films ever made me wish to leave home, nor caused me to be dissatisfied with my way of life or my home town. I think I have always realised, quite clearly, that films *are* just films, and that the exotic, glamorous kind of life some of them depict is not to be found anywhere in reality.

Neither have they given me any vocational ambitions. But this may be because my own interest lies in the creation of imaginary places, characters and situations, through the medium of story-writing.

To sum up—the cinema has always been to me a form of entertainment, a mental diversion, either by the stimulation of interest in uncommon or admirable characters, or by simple relaxation and recreation. My personal preference is for stories which depend on the development and interplay of character for their appeal, and, in the lighter class, those pictures which combine real-life situations with amusing, neat dialogue, or else out-and-out 'foolish' films, like Laurel and Hardy's short comedies.

I am afraid this 'report' on my reactions will be of little value or use, but it may prove that a person who reached early adolescence *before* seeing any films is less likely to be influenced by the cinema, since other forms of recreation had already established themselves in my life.

I should like also to stress the fact that happiness at home and a certain amount of parental guidance and control keep filmgoing and one's interest in the cinema in a right perspective to the rest of one's work and play.

NO. 53

AGE: 20   FATHER'S OCCUPATION:
SEX: F.   FOREMAN STONE-
OCCUPATION: MASON
   HOSIERY MACHINIST   MOTHER'S OCCUPATION:
NATIONALITY: BRITISH   WARPER

I first became interested in films when I was about 14 yrs. of age. Musical films always interest me most if it has a romance in it. I like a romance in a film. I still like musicals the best now.

I used to go to the cinema with my mother at least twice a week since getting older I go as many as three, four and even five times a week.

Films never did interfere with my play.

I was frightened by a film once the title of which I cant remember. It took place in a hospital. There was a man stood on the stairs you could just see the shadow of a raised hand clasping a knife ready to kill. There was also a scene where a stretcher containing a man moved along the corridors from one ward to another by itself. I was scared to go to bed that night.

Yes I find it hard to control my emotions aroused by a film.

I dont think I have imitated anything from a film unless Ive done anything and havent noticed whether Ive copied it from a film.

Yes I have fallen in love with my screen idol. He is a newcomer to films his name is Gene Kelly. I first fell in love with him when I seen him in *For Me and My Gal* which I seen four times and could see it again and again. I saw *Cover Girl* five times. I have a picture of Gene Kelly sent direct from M.G.M., Hollywood. I also have pictures of other film stars to whom I wrote to in America. But I really fell for Gene when he had that love scene with Judy Garland in *For Me and My Gal*. The scene where they had that long kiss which made Judy Garland clench her fists (until her knuckles shown white I suppose). Ill never forget that.

Yes, films have made me more receptive to love making. Especially after seeing a love scene in film if either Gene Kelly Spencer Tracy or Van Johnson takes part in it.

Well my ambitions and temptations due to films is to be a film star like Judy Garland I would like to be like her and to be able to sing like her.

Yes after seeing *Christmas Holiday*, starring Gene Kelly and Deanna Durbin. The part they played I dont think suited either of them. After seeing that film I felt very dissatisfied with my way of living and my neighbourhood.

Ive often thought Id like to travel and go to America with their modern ways and everything. Yes Ive wanted to leave home.

No films didnt give me ambitions to be a nurse etc.! But I would like to be a film star. I like American films better than English films. I think I have said now how I feel about films and its all true.

NO. 54

AGE: 16	FATHER'S OCCUPATION:
SEX: F.	BUILDER
OCCUPATION: ASSISTANT LIBRARIAN	MOTHER'S OCCUPATION:
NATIONALITY: BRITISH	HOUSEWIFE

I first became interested in films when I left school at the age of 14 years. I gave up most of the games I was so fond of. Such as Netball and shinty. I took up a position in a small library to begin with and I have succeeded to better myself within the last month.

At first I used to like a Detective film, but I soon grew tired and un-interested in them. A musical, 'did something to me', and as soon as I had seen one I felt lively. That was up to my 15th year. This last year has been wonderful in my film world. I visit the cinema not less than twice every week, and I have found myself keeping a record of every Picture I've seen since this year 1945 began.

I like a film to laugh and cry about, such as *Love Story* starring Stewart Granger. *The Seventh Cross* with Spencer Tracy and Signe Hasso, *Days of Glory* with Gregory Peck. *The Climax* with Susanna Foster and Turan Bey, and *Old Aquaintance* with Bette Davis and *30 Seconds Over Tokyo* with Van Johnson.

As a very little girl I used to visit the cinema with my youngest brother who is five years my senior. We used to play scenes from gangster films, until we grew tired. Even now we still take a great interest in discussing our dislikes and likes together. My friends and I used to have concerts but no one took an interest to organise us properly.

I saw Sonjy Henie many times and each time, I used to come home, put on my roller skates, and skate until I had my hearts con-tent. I can not say I have been frightened by any Picture, but I find the love scenes holding my attention and longing to have a boy friend after the style of Gregory Peck or Van Johnson.

I hate girls who giggle and I often find myself immitating the Haughty laughter of Bette Davis.

I once fell in love with Alan Ladd only to find that he was married and has a child and possibly children by now.

If I go out with a boy it sometimes gets on my nerves because he does not say nice things as Robert Taylor probably would. When Ive seen a Susanna Foster film I feel like singing just like her. I have often wanted to be away from home in one of the services, such as being a nurse, but I am too young.

In other words, 'I'm just an in-between'.

When I look at my friends I often feel bored especially the girls; their favourite conversation is about their new hat or dress.

I have always wanted to have my voice trained and be a singer like Deanna Durbin or Susanna Foster.

I shall probably end up in the same old town, but I don't want to really.

NO. 55

AGE: 22   FATHER: DECEASED
SEX: F.   MOTHER'S OCCUPATION:
OCCUPATION: USHERETTE   HOUSEWIFE
NATIONALITY: BRITISH

I first became interested in films when I saw Nelson Eddy, in *Naughty Marietta*, I was fourteen at the time.

The films I liked at first were musicals and I still do. There are times when I enjoy a drama, and times when I enjoy a comedy, it all depends.

My Mother used to take me as a child but not very often, once every month to be exact.

Films did not affect my play or my activities, because as I have informed you I did not go much until I reached the age of fourteen. I was very frightened at one film I saw which was called *Charlie Chan in Egypt*, the part which frightened me most was where the Hero was shot and the Uncle was left to look after him, but he happened to be the murderer, and he was just about to stick a knife in the wound, when the police arrived.

I do find that films affect my emotions at times when I happen to see sad films at which I find I shed a tear. To the next question I answer nothing, because I find I dont take any notice of their dresses or their manners.

Yes I have most certainly fallen in love with a screen actor and singer, Nelson Eddy, because I just love great singers. I never let love scenes on the films affect me at all, because at times they over-do it.

My ambition is to be a singer, I have always longed to go to Switzerland. I have always been satisfied with my way of living, but if I had the chance to travel I would most certainly do so.

I have said before I long to be a singer so I think that answer applies to this last question.

NO. 56

AGE: 21   FATHER'S OCCUPATION:
SEX: M.   MINER
OCCUPATION: MINER
NATIONALITY: BRITISH

I never had a chance to go to the films when I was a child, you see I was in the hospital nearly five years with a T.B. spine, but I am pleased to say I came out cured, and am now fit and healthy and over 12 stone. The very first film I saw was *Gold is Where You Find it*, starring George Brent and Olivia De Havilland, I was about 16 and I knew from then on that going to the pictures was going to take up most of my own time, and I now go about five or six times a week. You know many of my friends use to tell me that when I got older I would lose interest and not bother with them, but instead of loseing interest I am seeing more and more. Here is an example for you, in

1942 I saw 306 films, in 1943 I saw 382, and in 1944 I reached the grand total of 430, I hope I can beat that total in 1945. You see I know exacte number of films I see each year for I put them all down in a book which I call Film Book, I put down the title of the film, the name the stars in it and the name of the company that produced it, then at the end of the year I make notes on the films which I thought where good. I have never been frightened or got emotional over any film, but one scene got me a little excited and has stuck in my mind, it was from the film, *The Big Shot*, the scene was where Humprey Bogart and Irene Manning where trying to escape in a car and were being chased by the police, over the icey roads. I like any kind of film, Drama, Comedy or Musical if there is a storey to it. When I first started the pictures I had a crush on Alice Faye, but that has past, and they are all now on the same footing. I don't mind the love scenes as long as there's not to much of it. All the ambition I have is to meet the people of whom little is said, the Camera man, Recording director, Musical director, etc., etc.

P.S. The two films I think the best I have ever seen are, *The Song of Bernadette* which I think is the most dramatic film screened, the other is *Judas Was a Woman*, the only french film I have seen which I thought was magnificent. Runners up were *San Francisco*, *Random Harvest*, and *Laura*.

The next document, No. 57, falls into a category of its own. The writer visited the cinema once a week 'from an early age'; yet he is the only one of our contributors who records a break in cinema attendance covering 'several years' from the age of fourteen. He is the only contributor who shows any real appreci- ation of the film as an art-form, and who has seen any consider- able number of the screen 'classics' from different countries.

NO. 57

AGE: 36   FATHER'S OCCUPATION:
SEX: M.   COMMERCIAL
OCCUPATION: TRANSPORT MANAGER   TRAVELLER
NATIONALITY: BRITISH

From an early age I remember being taken by my mother and father to a local cinema every Thursday evening. Most of the films I saw in those days have faded into oblivion, but I still recall laughing very much at Max Linder's *Trip to America*, and being very thrilled by *Ride on a Runaway Express*. Maybe this latter exhibited the first glimmerings of an interest in technique and the moving camera.

However, it remained in abeyance for many years, for when I reached the age of about fourteen, and joined a tennis club, I ceased to take much interest in films. Even in those days, I must have been critically minded, and became tired of the eternal sameness and lack of originality of the majority of films. For several years tennis occupied most of my spare time and only very occasionally did I enter a cinema, attracted by something or other,—maybe a star, maybe publicity, (at this date I can recall no important reason), and the result was to keep me in an apathetic attitude to films.

After going to work, I began dropping into films occasionally on the way home from the City. And then something happened. I discovered that there was a way of discriminating between films and that was to find out who directed them. I don't know how I first got hold of this idea, but it has been my guiding star ever since.

The first film I remember seeing that showed me the possibilities of technique in the film was Asquith's *Shooting Stars*, which, although actually directed by A. V. Bramble was mainly interesting because of his script.

About this time I discovered the periodical *Close Up*, which, highfaluting and precious as much of its writing was, did give me an entirely new angle on films, and made me long to be able to see the films mentioned therein. A few of these, mainly German films, did succeed in getting into cinemas, but it has always been one of my greatest regrets that the film *The Love of Jeanne Ney*, greatly eulogised in that magazine, I missed when it was generally released round the Gaumont circuit, owing to its being very stupidly renamed *Lusts of the Flesh*, and my not recognising it in that guise.

It was shortly after this that a little 'flee-pit' in a back street amongst some of the worst slums in . . . started a programme of 'screen classics'. 'Talkies' had arrived at most cinemas by this time, but the manager was only interested in showing the best of the silents. To this little back-street slum cinema, with wooden forms, came people from all over London to programmes of films never seen before or since. The double feature programme changed twice a week and every film shown was of interest to connoiseurs. During the two or three months this season lasted, we saw *Mother, Storm Over Asia, The End of St. Petersburg, Turksib, Earth, The Student of Prague, Warning Shadows, Berlin, La Passion de Jeanne D'Arc, Les Neauveux Messieurs* and many other films of a like nature, some of which thrilled me immensely, especially *Turksib, Mother* and *The Student of Prague*.

Always at these shows I made a point of speaking to the manager afterwards to see what treasures he had in store for us. On one of these occasions, I met a girl who was also discussing films with him, and she was reading Paul Rotha's *The Film Till Now*. This book had only just been published and was difficult to get hold of, and when I expressed my desire to read it, she took my name and address, and eventually wrote to me and lent me the book.

This book which gives a historical survey of silent film, together with Elmer Rice's *A Voyage to Purilia*, which I read shortly afterwards, and which is a brilliant satire on films, bringing in every cliché ever used in films, practically finished my education in cinema. Never again could I be fobbed off with the inferior, the shoddy, the meretricious, the hackneyed story, the inevitable coincidence.

And what since? It has all been rather in the nature of an anti-climax. I had seen the pick of the finest films almost all together, and what masterpieces I have seen since have been spread out over the years, and with the complete submerging of the silent film in the swamp of the talkies, silent films have been seen less and less, except at occasional film societies' showings or sub-standard versions given by enthusiastic amateurs. And for all the brilliance of some talking films, the complete unity and artistry of the silent films has never been recaptured. The Avenue Pavilion and the Forum continued the good work of the back-street . . . cinema, and to-day, the number of cinemas has increased but the quality of the films has, alas, very considerably depreciated.

Turksib, which, to this day, is still my number 1 film, and which I have seen 19 times (a film, in my opinion,—unlike that of most people who are only interested in seeing a film once, because then they 'know it'—when it is good enough, should be treated like a symphony, something to experience numerous times, and each time providing new delight) first showed me the scope of the film. Here was a film without actors, and with human beings dwarfed by the magnitude of the theme of the building of a railroad. This interest in the documentary movement, has increased with the years. Here, away from the studios and the aping of the theatre, is the true medium for the film, and until producers realise this, and the public appreciate that the film, like no other medium, can 'present the world to the world', as one of the commentators of the ridiculously inadequate news-reels is for-ever telling us, until then the full scope of the film will not be utilised. We have seen a trend in the right direction in many of the magnificent British documentaries and fictional films with a documentary approach, dealing with the War. Let us hope they will appreciate the great power of the film for 'winning the Peace'.

My interest in films has made me wish to make films myself, but except for a little amateur work, I have never succeeded in getting 'into' films, although I have hopes at the moment of entering a small documentary group. In the meantime, I have maintained my interest, by writing occasional articles for various papers, and am at the moment engaged on a history of British Films.

Three documents remain. They have been separated from the rest, regardless of age-grouping, because none of the writers has enjoyed a normal home life. Two were brought up by widowed mothers, the third was reared in quite exceptional circumstances. In the case of the last document, No. 60, these circumstances are so exceptional that the experience there recorded, while of first importance to the sociologist, cannot be classed with that of any other writer who has contributed.

NO. 58

AGE: 19½
SEX: F.

In answer to your request for more personal, cinematic information, here are my own experiences:—

I am English, aged 19½, well educated, & have travelled abroad quite considerably. I have read extensively, covering a multitude of subjects; and as regards personal appearance—well, that's sufficiently superior to an old boot! My father, who was in the R.A.F died when I was very young. My mother trained as a masseuse in the Great War, & since my father's death she has devoted her life to looking after my sister & I.

I was taken to the movies, as a child, by my mother, and grandmother, to see animal pictures, travelogus and Silly Symphonies. I did not enjoy it. The rather stuffy atmosphere gave me very bad headaches. (This was also due, in part, to having bad eyesight, from which I do not suffer now.) When this was discovered, I was not taken any more, & I didn't mind in the least. I can only recollect one of these early films—*S.O.S.—Iceberg*, which I hav since discovered starred Rod la Rocque. For years I did not see any films at all, but in 1938, when I was 13, a friend took me, half against my will, to see *The Housemaster*. I found that I not only thoroughly enjoyed the film, but that I did not suffer from a bad headache afterwards, which had been my chief dread. So the next week I thought I would like to go again by myself, & I went, to see *Frou-Frou*. I knew nothing about the film, of course, nor about the star in it, but the title captured my imagination. I remember finding Louise Rainer irritating. In a short while, I was visiting the movies quite often, with no parental opposition, & very soon I had 'favourite stars'. The next step, of course, was that I wanted pictures of these stars, so I started taking *Picture Show*. Not content with the slow rate at which my collection was growing, I soon started taking *Picture Goer, Film Pictorial*, and *Film Weekly* every week, out of pocket-money given to me by an indulgent granny, who would keep me with any hobby. New ideas (to me) followed thick & fast—& very soon I was buying American film books (which I infinitely preferred, & still do, to British ones) & had a number of pen-friends, all over the world, with whom to exchange film pictures.

I got an album, & stuck my best pictures in it. This filled up, & I got another—and another,—etc.

The movies had become my most absorbing topic. I had so assiduously read so many film books, that I had begun to be something of a theoretic expert on the subject, & people appealed to me when they required cinematic information.

I never go to a movie for the sake of going, I only go if there is one that I wish to see, & only wish to see those with my *favourite stars* in. I go for the stars, not the story. My taste in films is fairly wide, & has scarcely varied at all during the years I have been picture-going. I like technicolor musicals, with Hayworth, Grable, Miranda, Faye, etc. jungle 'hokum' stories, with my *favourite* star, Dorothy Lamour; Sonja Henie's skating films, and Maria Montez à la pantomime films; I like Spencer Tracy's strong drama films & the wonderful acting ability of Ingrid Bergman, Margaret Sullavan, & Katherine Hepburn. My favourite film of all is *Gone With the Wind*, which I have seen three times,—& I also like comedies, especially those with Bob Hope in. And I *do* like Frank Sinatra—I don't swoon(!), but nevertheless I think he's wonderful,—'he's got a certain something' that the others haven't got!

Now to answer the questions you gave as guidance.

Films definitely have had & will have a very powerful influence in my life. From an early age I have been imbued with an intense admiration for America, and most things American. The films I have seen have increased this. Whilst at school, which I left when I was 16, I used as many American slang phrases as I could, & put up with being laughed at by my school companions—who were as most English schoolgirls are, just content to follow each other, & ready to make fun of any original ideas, being quite content to stay in their own familiar little rut. Nowadays everyone uses American slang, but when I did it five years ago, it was quite a brave thing to do.

I make a considerable amount of my own clothes, & have taken or adopted, many patterns from clothes worn by various stars, & have been complimented on the results.

I have not consciously adopted any mannerisms, but I have been gifted with a good voice, & friends have said that I have several of Bing Crosby's vocal & facial, expressions, when I croon, & this is possibly, because I have made a close study of him. I have inherited acting ability, so all my energies are devoted to earning myself enough money, in an office job which I loathe, to take myself to America, enter a good training school to polish up my crooning & dancing, and then go to the Pasadena Training School to improve my histrionic ability, & then one day—is it too much to hope?—to get on to the screen myself. This is the biggest ambition that the movies have given me, & I *know* the field is crowded, & I know the way is hard, but I mean to try. That is why I must earn some money first, so that my family at home need not worry about the possibility of my starving!

Films have increased my desire to travel. I have covered miles in France & the British Isles, but amongst the places I intend to visit, if I possibly can, which have interested me through having seen them on the screen are: Swan Valley, Cuba, Havana, Argentina, all the Southern States of America, Canada, Hawaii, Norway, & Switzerland. Yes, emotions aroused by films *are* hard to control. Scenes such as the Phantom had in *Phantom of the Opera;* Walter Hudd's moon madness scenes in *Black Limelight*, the hypnotism scenes in *Dark Tower*, the scenes of the club-footed man in *Mata Han.*(?) etc, etc, stand out in my memory as frightening. I never see 'cooked up' horror films such as *Frankenstein*, & I try to avoid creepy secondary films.

Did I ever fall in love with my screen idol—I'll say! Most impressionable kids do. At 14 I thought Mickey Rooney perfect, At 15 I was crazy about Robert Taylor, and at 16, Clark Gable was tops, I still like him, & friends often wonder how I can like Gable & Sinatra so much when they so totally different. But I do.

I don't think films have made me more receptive to love-making—maybe 'soft lights and sweet music', but not films,—but they certainly have taught me how to handle men—how to adapt my own personality to please different men, & how to hold their interest, once gained. In no other branch of entertainment—stage, radio, books,—is the code of censorship so rigid, & through this, the movies have taught me that it *is* possible to have any amount of real fun, without becoming 'easy' with the opposite sex.

This motion picture autobiography reminds me of a story. A man went to buy a second-hand typewriter, and the shop assistant sold him one which had belonged to Mussollini. He explained that it was a very good machine, but that it had one small fault—the letter 'I' had been broken, through overuse!

However, as you did ask for intimate personal experiences, I hope that what I have written may be of some use to you.

NO. 59

AGE: 27   MOTHERS' OCCUPATION:
SEX: F.   HOUSEKEEPER (WIDOWED)
OCCUPATION: BUS CONDUCTOR
NATIONALITY: BRITISH

My widowed mother became a cinema pianist for a while in a third rate cinema and as there was no one with whom to leave me at home I had to accompany her daily, this introduced me to the cinema at the early age of four.

Of the pictures and players of that time, 1922, I can recall nothing but I can recollect (possibly because the incident has been recalled so often by my mother) that one day I threw myself down on my bed, stabbed myself with a bread-knife and with gurgles and groans died a most realistic and horrifying death.

This was apparently the sequel to many thrilling adventures. Such as falling from high buildings comprised of chairs and being hanged with a skipping rope. Anyway the knife episode was too much for mother who rushed me to school next day and pleaded with the 'head mistress' to accept me as a pupil in spite of my youth. The 'bread-knife' incident was recounted and I was taken in hand by the Education Authorities.

My first authentic memory of an actual 'film' is of a Harold Lloyd comedy, but the only scene that stands out in the memory is one where he sways miraculously on the ledge of a high building. (It

horrified me, and significently there never has been to this day a
comedy scene of this type that has raised the desired laugh with me.
People falling or nearly falling leave me tense).

I vividly recall the *Tarzan* serial of this period. I was probably
about 'nine' years old and a regular 'once-a-weeker'. A girl friend
and her brother were my regular companions at this time but their
keenness never rivalled mine. I think we paid 'fourpence' at 'eleven
oc' on Saturday mornings, but soon after this the cinema closed
down and we were driven to a better class theatre where we were
forced to pay sixpence.

It was here that at the age of about ten I saw two films that left
a lasting impression on my memory. In the *Covered Wagon* a scene
where a banjo is played beside the wagons out on the prairie has
left rather more of an impression of sadness than a clear-cut memory.

Similarly a film which I have only recently identified as *Guilty*
translated from Emile Zola's *Therese Raquin*, has left a very definite
impression. The scene pregnant with sordid atmosphere is where the
guilty couple blame each other for the murder of the woman's
husband, whilst the mute paralyzed mother of the dead man sits
helpless in an invalid chair.

I still remember the ugly atmosphere, the frightened wrangling
of the pair, the helpless, venemous hatred in the old woman's eyes.
I hate the memory of it but it is a scene which has so firmly imprinted
itself on my mind that I know I shall never succeed in eradicating it.

Closer memories are of *The Three Musketeers*. I became an ardent
admirer of Douglas Fairbanks. I know I liked Mary Pickford too,
but for the life of me I can remember nothing about her.

Follies of 1929 possibly the first talkie musical, Ginger Rogers and
Guy Kibbe, I began to appreciate 'wise-cracks' and to rely less on
action for interest. Musicals became my favourite screen fare.

At the age of sixteen I was going alone to the cinema as often as
three and four times in a week and each visit was a fresh 'thrill'. I
would queue for hours. Beautiful women—beautiful clothes—
glamour—music—perfection. The story didn't metter, if the heroine
was beautiful she could double-cross the hero to her hearts content,
the man didn't matter, beauty gave her the right to be unscrupulous.

My dealings with the opposite sex were much on the same lines
(not that I thought I was beautiful), young men were fools, all right
for companions in sport, cycling, swimming etc: but no souls! No
conversation! No appreciation of beauty!

The exquisite dancing of Jessie Mathews started a scap-book craze,
I became her most ardent fan. I wrote poems about her, I prayed
for her. I followed her to garden parties, civic receptions, grand
openings, flower shows. I haunted her house for months skirting the
grounds and desiring no more than the sight of her or the sound of
her voice.

Depricatory or critical remarks to my 'idol' had me 'redfaced'
and 'up in arms' in her defense. I was 'ribbed' unmercifully by all

who knew of my crush but pictures and clippings were usually produced as 'balm' by my tormenters.

At seventeen or eighteen a persistent desire to be a character actress had me re-enacting scenes from films I had seen. I would play two or three parts, I reflect that my memory must have been truly amazing and my confidence and dramatic ability I now believe would have been worthy of training.

I really think my keenness for films fostered my desire to 'do things'. People travelled, rode horses, had cars, clothes, careers and homes such as none of my acquaintances had. But those things did exist, and I had as much right to them as the next.—I decided to marry for money!

I refused to let my feelings become involved. I still considered young men to be soulless. When the 'money marriage' presented itself I hadn't the moral courage to accept it. There was a man included in the bargain to be with—to live with—to look at—to talk to day after day. You didn't just 'marry money' you didn't even just 'marry a man'. You took a husband!—I came to earth!!

At twenty-seven I still like good pictures, musicals need too much padding and I now prefer a good ballet or opera, I am a regular theatre goer.

In my films I appreciate anything that is well done, story, dialogue, direction or individual portrayal. I am a keen critic and would have liked to be associated with film production. But, had I any say in such matters I would never use the old comedy gag of falling over a cliff or slipping off a window-ledge thirty stories up.

That, in my opinion is strictly drama!

NO. 60

Dear Sir,

I am answering your request for motion-picture autobiographies. I had meant to reply to your first request but owing to lack of time and conditions then, I was unable to, finding in a subsequent issue of *Picturegoer* that you had already acknowledged contributions. I am rather late with this, but with the magazine taking a considerable time to reach me, I am writing at the first opportunity.

First of all, my age is 25, and with regard to the other necessities you ask for, I have been in the Royal Army Medical Corps for almost five years. I have, however, done little medical work, to which I am not adaptable, and for about the past year have worked in the 'unit' post-office, which work I enjoy. I have no set occupation, nor in 'civvy street', sorry, before joining the army. Then I was an errand-boy, in a general food stores in South-West London, where I was born. My father's occupation was a mechanic and racing-car driver, to the best of my knowledge. My mother had no occupation that I know of. Both were British.

I am an ardent film-fan, in fact a film-fan friend of mine calls me a film-fanatic. I have never come across anyone who is as ardently interested and educated in films as an entertainment as myself. You ask for truth and frankness about intimate personal experiences. I will try to give them to you. I first remember film-going at the age of nine in 1929 when 'talkies' were coming into their own. I remember seeing a few 'silents', but cannot remember any names. The first film I can remember the name of was also the first 'talkie' I saw, Show-Boat. The second, Noah's Ark. I went alone to these films as I remember I invariably did. I can remember nothing of either film. I was living in Croydon at the time, and I remember a third-rate cinema close handy to home, I visited often. This catered more for the juvenile, with a monopoly of Westerns. In common with other children, they were my favourites, with such stars as Tom Mix, Tim McCoy, Buck Jones, etc. I also liked comedies of the Slim Summerville type. I don't believe I particularly enjoyed Show-Boat or Noah's Ark, except from a boy's stand-point, of action or inane comedy, and only went from the current curiosity of seeing a 'talkie'. I also remember seeing The Terror, which I have an idea was photographed in green and, I believe, frightened me as it was meant to do. (I have since read it was a terrible film in itself!) I went once or twice a week, parents permitting, from the ages of nine to eleven, but the only other films I can remember during that period were Sunny Side Up, (with Charles Farrell and Janet Gaynor, I later found out) and, I believe, Titanic. The former film first inured me to musicals. I remember leaving the cinema with an odd feeling of sentimental pleasure, at peace with the world, and sorry that it was over. Titanic fascinated me, and I can still picture the horrible confusion after the iceberg had been hit, or vice versa.

I cannot remember seeing any Charlie Chaplin films during this period, but was very disappointed that I could not see City Lights, which I never have. I seem to remember a Conrad Nagel film for some reason, in which he, or another character, committed suicide by jumping off a roof. (I have a horror of looking over a high parapet). One other film I remember the name of during this period, was a Western with Tim Mc.Coy, I believe, called, Beyond The Blue Sierra. Allied to this film I also remember the well-known piece, William Tell, as background music during an inevitable chase. This piece fascinated me, and whenever I hear it, I think of this film, invariably. During this period, I liked these particular films, but only from a boy's point of view. I only knew by name the Western stars and Charlie Chaplin. I also felt very hard-done-by if I could not make a regular visit to the pictures, and preferred going on my own.

My next stage was between the ages of 11 and 13. During this period I was living in Watford. I remember seeing Scarface, I Am A Fugitive From A Chain Gang and King Kong, but can remember little or nothing about them, exclusive of the fact that I have seen them all again since. About this time, the 'A' certificate was inaugurated, but I remember I saw these films on my own, despite that, and quite clearly remember getting someone to take me in to see *King Kong*, and during the pervormance having quite a job to convince an usher I was over 14! I believe I enjoyed these films, mainly seeing them at other boys' recommendations, of fascinating horror and spectacle.

I took my first girl to the pictures at this stage, rather annoyed that her brother insisted on coming! The film was *Sign of the Cross*, seen again since. I didn't like this film at all, one scene standing out in which an arrow is seen to pierce a man's body and appear at the other side. This nauseated me. (I remember watching for this scene, when I saw the film again some seven years later, and hardly noticing it also enjoying the film, and the players' acting.) *F.P.I.* is another film I remember. You will notice all these films are of the sensational type, which no doubt appeal at that age. I still liked Westerns and serials had come to my notice, though I never seemed to follow one through, missing many episodes. Films were still a boyish appreciation, and I knew no further star's name.

At 13, I returned to London, and Wheeler and Woolsey became favourites of mine in *So This Is Africa*. (They were film favourites of mine until Woolsey's death in 1937 or thereabouts, which quite upset me. I believe I could still enjoy their films if re-issued. Their bent was crazy comedy, and I liked them better than Laurel and Hardy.) About this time, the film *42nd Street* was released, and I remember standing outside a cinema where it was showing, and feeling very down hearted that I could not go in, due to lack of finances. It was early evening, in the winter, and gay lights lit up the cinema, big placards announced the 'greatest spectacle of all time', etc., etc. Large queues were waiting, and altogether I felt a sense of frustration. I went to children's matinees still, and liked crazy comedies, Charlie Chase, etc., and the usual Westerns, also horror films, such as the 'haunted house' vehicle. I still went on my own, and once or twice a week where possible. I remember selling at a second-hand bookstall, a bunch of '2d. bloods' to get 4d. to see a film I cannot remember. (My people were in a bad way financially.)

Perhaps I ought to explain something here. At the age of nine, I was boarded out with strangers due to estrangement between my parents. (You ask for no restraint.) From 9 to 11, my first stage, I was with these people. From 11 to 14, I was living with my mother and stepfather. I was an only child of my parents. My mother and stepfather had a baby girl. I felt left out in the cold. I made my own amusements. I worked in a newspaper shop as a 'paper-boy' from 11 to 13, and often went to the pictures through free passes due to placards displayed outside. On moving to London, I was regarded as an imposition, and 'packed off out' when in the way. At 14, I left school, and of a Friday night, went to the pictures regularly, on my own.

About this time, I saw the first film which ever really 'moved' me.

It was called *20 Million Sweethearts*, starring Pat O'Brien, Dick Powell and Ginger Rogers. I had never felt as I did, after seeing this film. It was a queer feeling of sentiment, exuberation and serenity, and yet disappointment at realising it was only a film, and not reality. It was, and is, really hard to explain. The film was an unpretentious musical, and yet I class it as outstanding. The story was simple, yet I found it very human. Boy-meets-girl, boy-loses-girl, then re-united by a match-maker. The thread of the story was at a radio station, comedy was predominant, and songs pleasant. One stood out, and I have an idea this song caused me to feel the way I did. It is still my favourite song, 'I'll String Along With YOU', a fast favourite of the day. The feeling was much more acute than the few years ago after seeing *Sunny Side Up*, but similar. I seemed to be 'walking on air', as the saying is. This film, therefore, endeared me to musicals, which have been my favourite ever since. The stars in this film, and even the other players, have been favourites of mine ever since, too. They were the first 'names' I knew outside Westerns stars and the other comedians mentioned. I count this film as the beginning of appreciation of human, logical story films, and becoming a film-fan in the true sense. I don't think I have ever recaptured that feeling of exhilaration to the extent I felt it after this film. (It is rather strange to note that the three stars in this film, are still stars to-day.)

This film then, changed my outlook on films. I still liked Westerns, and had managed to see a serial right through for its twelve episodes at a third-rate cinema where I had seen the epoch-making film of mine. I was quite jubilant at seeing this serial right through, a scientific mystery melodrama called *The Vanishing Shadow*, which I can remember very well, and even the tune of the background music played before and after each episode, a somewhat 'exciting' theme. Seeing this serial consecutive weeks at the same cinema, often meant seeing feature films, which I did not fancy. I did not like romances, or sophisticated comedies and the like. Action films, such as Westerns, murder mysteries, and comedies of the ingenuous type I liked. I remember missing night-school to see *The Man Who Knew Too Much*, which I thoroughly enjoyed. This was the first double-feature programme I can remember the names of, the other film being, *Mrs. Wiggs of the Cabbage Patch*.

Before reaching the age of 15, I was sent to a boys' home through my parents, where I stayed for 18 months. Here, amongst other chaps my own age, I relied on the films, as we all did as a sole means of entertainment, also because it was within the means of our skimpy pocket-money. We went out to work during the day, I was still an office-boy, which job I had had since leaving school, and arranged by my said parents. Week-ends then, were our only chance to indulge. Saturday, we would see two shows, Sunday evening one. Quite often, we saw a filmshow through twice on a Saturday. My range of films was growing, but I still disliked 'love' themes.

The James Cagney—Pat O'Brien comedy melodramas became firm favourites of mine, and I also made a point of seeing their individual films. Now, not always the title attracted me, but the stars. *Top-Hat*, I made a point of seeing, and the Ginger Rogers— Fred Astaire combination, also became a favourite. (O'Brien and Rogers being already favourites as mentioned.) I began to find there were many more films I wanted to see than I was able, so I picked out the more attractive from my point of view. This led me to making a list of the cinemas in a certain radius, numbering about twenty, and listing their films of a week for Saturday visits, and the one-day change for Sunday. This I did through placards. The other chaps in the 'home', relied on me for 'what's-on', and usually relied on my judgement which I found they usually appreciated.

At this 'home', I abandoned my previous procedure of going alone to the pictures, and always went with a pal or pals, from one to a whole 'gang' of us. This did not detract from my enjoyment of films: most of us through circumstances alone, were film-fans: and we had great enjoyment afterwards discussing scenes in films, and films as a whole.

I made no distinction with cinemas. The cheapest seats at most cinemas varied from matinee prices of 4d. at the 'bug-houses', to 1/- at the de-luxe ones. I went to see the film and not the cinema; comfort was a secondary consideration. If a film I wanted to see was on at a 'bug-house', and not elsewhere, I went to see it. I also took note of both films on at a cinema and went to one that had two films on I wanted to see, when possible. The habit of going to one particular cinema every week no matter what was on, as some casual film-fans do, did not appeal to my policy. So, I and my pals, visited a wide range of cinemas, say, within a 2d. 'bus or tram ride. (The 'home', by the way, was in South-West London.) So, one week, we might go to the Trocadero, the next, to Gattis'! It was surprising how cheap a time we could have, and enjoyable, with a visit to the cinema, fares, and a snack at a café—the fares eliminated if a local cinema. I certainly enjoyed my small world of entertainment, and again, I had to make my own. But I was happy, and that was, perhaps, all that mattered. On Bank Holidays, etc., we used to get a 1(- for the day, and sandwiches. These times we often saw a programme through twice, even three times. Finances would not allow two or three separate visits, and there was little else to do, minus a 'passport'! I remember the Easter of 1936, going to four different shows on the four days. I had worked out the programme for each day, and how much it would cost, and saved accordingly. Three of my pals likewise.

At this Easter, I made the 'acquaintance' of my favourite film-star of all time. His name was Ross Alexander, and the film *Shipmates Forever*, starring my old favourite, Dick Powell and another favourite accrued while at the home, Ruby Keeler. The film was a musical, with a heavy sentimental flavour, which is not too appreciated by

most filmgoers, I believe; in Britian, that is. But I liked these sentimental films, and still do. I class this film as outstanding from my
point of view, The title-song is also a standing favourite of mine.
As in *20 Million Sweethearts*, I believe the song helped to make my
great enjoyment of the film. In subsequent films I saw, with Ross
Alexander, he became, as I say, my favourite film-star. His death,
early in 1937, came as a great blow, so soon after classing him as
my top favourite. I felt as if I had lost a dear friend, and thought
it was a cruel trick of fate for, of all stars, my particular favourite
to die. He was a light comedian, with a personality all his own,
and with more dramatic roles, was fast becoming a star in his own
right, having starred in numerous second features. Of these I classed,
Boulder Dam, as his best, mainly, perhaps because it was a sentimental
story of the rehabilitation by a 'good' woman and kindness of a bad
character, a type of film I did and still do enjoy.

You will see, therefore, that I was deeply moved by a sentimental
film. Another instance, of this, I recall, seen during this period, was
the film, *Tough Guy* with Jackie Cooper, an unpretentious film from
critics' standards, but I, again, classed as outstanding. This film
had as the second 'star', an Alsation after the style of *Rim-Tin-Tin*,
whose films I had always wanted to see after only dimly remembering one. This film *Tough Guy*, was essentially a 'gangster' film,
popular to their extreme at that time, I believe. It also brought to
my notice Joseph Calleia, who played a 'gang-leader' whose heart
is softened by Jackie Cooper's love for his dog (Rin-Tin-Tin, jr.,
I believe). As a homeless boy, Cooper persists in following Calleia,
who had taken pity on him and his dog, and Calleia finds his 'gang'
do not take kindly to it. After many 'touching' scenes it is climaxed
by an aspirant to Calleia's throne intending to bump him off,
attacked by the dog at the critical moment. He shoots it; Calleia
incensed to fury by the act fires at his henchman, who fires back.
Both are mortally wounded. I found Cooper's tearful outburst on
finding his dog shot and Calleia dying almost too much for my
pent-up emotions. I honestly confess I was in tears. Whether the
heavy sentiment 'played-up' in this film is acting or not I maintain
that a film which arouses the emotions to such an extent (I am sure
I was not the only one in tears, by any means) has a quality I have
found lacking in many so-called 'human' films, praised by the
critics. Undoubtedly, the Americans are more sentimental than the
British, and unfortunately, these type of films do not always seem to
be appreciated by the staid Britisher. (Perhaps I ought to mention
that *20 Million Sweethearts*, was on the 'sentimental side', as was the
song mentioned from it). Many films from that time have brought
tears to my eyes, and still do. If a film does this, one must have
'lived' the story, and therefore enjoyed it.

I have mentioned I enjoy sentimental themes and songs, and
during this period I came to know the typical Hawaiian music,
which also left me in a similar frame of mind. The film was *Flirtation*

Walk, with again my first favourite as a film-star, Dick Powell, and a perfect cast from my point of view, with such favourites of mine as Ruby Keeler, Pat O'Brien and Ross Alexander. (Ruby Keeler became my favourite female star.) Since this film I have always made a point of seeing a film with a Hawaiian setting.

For some strange reason, at this time, I thoroughly disliked Bing Crosby. I had many an argument with the other chaps who admired him. I always rating Dick Powell way above his class! I realise I was rather irrational as I had never seen a film of his, and argued all he did was Boo-boo-boo, etc.! However, after leaving the home, a pal recommended me to see *Waikiki Wedding*, of his, betting me 2/- I'd like Crosby. I must admit I had to pay the bet and was glad to, I really enjoyed him, and the film, especially as it had a Hawaiian setting. I not only found he did more than 'boo-boo-boo', but was a very good comedian. Since then I've been a staunch admirer of Crosby.

I bought my first film-magazine in 1936. Ginger Rogers' life-story was the reason, Since then I have always followed film-news, reviews, criticisms, etc., through film magazines.

So, this period when I was 15 and 16, made me an out-and-out film-fan. Musicals my favourite, with comedies next, crazy or sophisticated, 'tough' films, such as 'gangster' themes, 'horror', and mystery. And any film that had a sentimental strain. I *dis*-liked historical, romantic, and 'straight' films, Greta Garbo and Charles Boyer were particular dislikes. (It is rather strange to note that I still have no particular liking for them, and after seeing Boyer during the 1935-6 period in *Shanghai*, which bored me stiff, though I remember the name, I never saw him until a month or two ago in two films the same week! I'm still not impressed.) I knew many comedians' names then from Eddie Cantor to the 'small-part' players. I noticed that the vast majority of my favourite films and stars were Warner Bros. studios so I have always regarded them as my favourite studio. Though 'pin-ups' belong to this era, I remember I had one or two pinned-up in my locker at the 'home', of my favourites!

I disliked British films, except comedies. They were always so 'lifeless', which is still the main trouble these days.

I used to buy the 'Boys Cinema', magazine, which carried stories of films. I remember reading *Boulder Dam*, and thinking what a smashing film it would make and as mentioned, I was not disappointed. I believe I still have this particular issue at home.

I left the 'home' soon after my 16th birthday, and went into lodging. I had got another job, in a shop, and reckoned I was able to look after myself. For four years I did so, until being called-up, though my wages during this time were far from luxurious. But I was able to indulge in my favourite pastime, and that was all that mattered to me. My visits during these four years exceeded an average of every other day in most years. I lived a secluded lonely life outwardly and at times I realised it, but my love of films, and the enjoyment they gave me, quite compensated for my more depressing thoughts of the small world I lived in. I was unsociable, I know, but I attribute this to a shy and embarrassed nature. And somehow, the films had built a conception of life, which life itself, tended to contradict, my ideals made through films, not being realised in true life. But, instead of making me disbelieve in and dislike film-life, it made me bitter towards real life.

Films taught all the things I should like to associate with life. Crime does not pay, the wrong-doer getting his just deserts; kindness pays; love-thy-neighbour; plumping for the 'small' man, 'flaying' the rich; making the best of life; 'true' love wins in marriage; decency; the mild and honest man triumphing over the immoral, unscrupulous one; all the ideals worthy of life, which we would all like to see, or would we? at least, one would presume so. It is oft-remarked that films should be more like life. If they were, people would be disgusted to 'see' how they lived and would protest strongly; in fact, of course, such a film would never get past the censor. So, I maintain, as that course is impossible, that, as has also been said, that life should be more like the films. I try to live my life as films would have us believe, and they have helped me to get a great deal out of life, though it is 'tough' going.

During that four years, I can honestly say that but for the films, and my enjoyment of them as a pastime, and ideals associated with them, I would have found life unbearable. Many people would say that it was a means to an end, and only forced by circumstances, or, perhaps, I was just 'short-sighted', and mentally lazy, or just childish. Be that as it may, life tends to make people hypocritical, and truth avoided.

In that period, I saw many films which impressed and moved me deeply. This stage also made me appreciate the 'serious' film, with a message. The prime example was *Mr. Deeds Goes to Town*. I did not fancy this film when first released and it was only after a friend told me how good it was that I went to see it at a smaller cinema, rather reluctantly. I found, after queueing well over an hour, and the film some way through, that it would be useless to wait. But this convinced me that it must be an unusually good film, and so when I next saw it advertised, I eagerly went; and sat through it twice! Since then, every chance I had, I saw the film again. Though, classed as a comedy, its dramatic portent and message predominated. (I recently had the good fortune to see the film again, and being on leave, went the following day as well.) Since then I have always made a point of seeing Frank Capra's films.

I also came to appreciate acting during this period, such as in the above film, and also *Fury*, which brought me another favourite with Spencer Tracy, also Sylvia Sidney, and Bette Davis after *Dark Victory*. *Fury* perfectly blended horror with simple sentiment. I'll never forget the scene when the mob is marching on the jail. It still gives me goose-pimples as I think of it. The background music was blended perfectly with the action. Rising to a crescendo, it stops dead as the mob stops uncertainly outside the jail, confronted by the nervous but grim jailers. After brief exhanges of words, a tomato is thrown by someone in the crowd, landing a bull's eye on the sheriff, Edward Ellis. This is the signal for action and the mob goes mad. Spencer Tracy trying to sooth his nerves by speaking to his little Scotch terrier, which comes to him in his hour of need. And Sylvia Sidney arriving at the point of exhaustion to see Tracy's face framed in a cell of the burning jail. The reality of the film was almost horrifying, and credit was due to Fritz Lang the director, as well as the stars. An outstanding film, *You Only Live Once*, by the same director, likewise made me appreciate the tragic film. The climax was almost overwhelming, with Henry Fonda, an escaped 'murderer' wrongly convicted, and Sylvia Sidney, in sight of freedom by being about to cross a state line, are killed by the police. The tragedy was heightened by the fact, that Sylvia Sidney is shot short of the 'line', and Henry Fonda carrying her 'across' the line, realises she is dead, and is himself shot, though figuratively on 'safe' ground.

Many films of the tragic and sentimental type left a deep impression on me. Others I call more readily to mind are Spencer Tracy's *Boys Town* and *Captains Courageous*, and *Winterset*.

But though I enjoyed these, films of the opposite type were equally as well enjoyed. The funniest film I have ever seen is *Bringing Up Baby* with Cary Grant and Katharine Hepburn. (Joe E. Brown's *6-Day Bike Rider* a close second.) This was in the vogue of crazy comedies and was supposed to be the crazy comedy to end all crazy comedies. I had not liked Grant or Hepburn before classing them as the romantic type but this and other crazy comedies changed my opinion of many former 'not-fancied' stars. Eddie Cantor's *Strike Me Pink*, was another great comedy, I thought.

On the musical side, Alice Faye became a top favourite after *Wake Up and Live*, of the decent, reserved girl type, and starting a new cycle with the 'nervous, meek hero' type, as portrayed by Jack Haley. The Ritz Bros. were a brand-new musical comedy type, and became great favourites. I didn't like the Marx Bros. until seeing, *A Day at the Races*. That changed my opinion.

The juvenile era was now coming into its own, with Mickey Rooney, Judy Garland, and Deanna Durbin. The first film I saw in each star's case, made them top favourites, where they still remain in my estimation, though I liked them best as juveniles, Mickey Rooney's first Andy Hardy film *You're Only Young Once*, left me with a similar feeling to *20 Million Sweethearts*, a few years earlier. I was very thoughtful on leaving the cinema. Perhaps it could best be described as a sense of frustration at my own inabilities to enjoy life as in the 'film-family' life. Probably because they had been denied to me. '*Love Finds Andy Hardy*, the third one of the series left its mark even more. I saw it on Xmas Eve, and the film's story was laid round Xmas. I was feeling very lonely at the time, I remember, and the film made me realise it all the more. The 'humanity' of the film was almost overwhelming, I found, and Judy Garland as the 'girl-next-door' in the film, perfectly personified the sort of girl I would like to have as the 'girl-next-door'. I think I'd be right in confessing I fell in love with her. A previous film of hers, *Listen Darling*, had likewise impressed me, as did subsequent films. Mickey Rooney and Judy Garland, then, typified life as I would like to see it. Judy Garland's feeling, sincerity, friendliness and innocence as she portrayed them, impressed and moved me deeply. Rooney's personality could not be denied.

Deanna Durbin had a similar quality to Judy Garland, but different in that she was more refined. She introduced me to operatic singing, which I thoroughly enjoyed. Her first films were something new in entertainment.

Another type of film I particularly enjoyed was started with *The Shop Around the Corner*, with James Stewart and Margaret Sullavan, a simple romance, played with beautiful charm and sentiment by the two stars as shy lovers, also bringing to notice Felix Bressart, as a lovable, kind old matchmaker. James Stewart's shy awkwardness appealed to me, first noticed in *Born To Dance*, a musical with Eleanor Powell, I particularly enjoyed, leaving me with that feeling of wistful satisfaction.

Another unusual type of film I thoroughly enjoyed was *Five Came Back*, no top-stars, but a terrific drama of twelve people who crash in a 'plane on an uncharted cannibal isle.

This then gives you the idea how my tastes changed. Westerns were entirely forgotten, except the large-scale ones, with well-known stars. *Stagecoach* for example, which was on a par with *Five Came Back*, in a different setting, made great by the acting of the individual players, and not the 'stars'. I now enjoyed romantic dramas, straight dramas, and serious films, in fact most films, but historical films were still taboo (I never did like history at school!), and the heavy 'mushy' films, such as Greta Garbo's. Romantic and crazy comedies were much to my liking, now. But I should point out that the stars and individual players nearly always decided what films I would see, and only when the critics praised a film unanimously would I go and see it, if I didn't fancy it, or 'star-value' was small. I followed all reviews, criticisms, etc. in daily papers, and so forth. And though I saw at least six films a week (I still made weekly lists of films up to nearly 40 cinemas. Visits were made through a process of elimination), I missed many I wanted to see, as I saw re-issues, and visited many films numerous times. The majority of those I have listed I have seen two, three or more times. Quite a few run into double figures. The film I have seen most times is Eddie Cantor's *The Kid From Spain*, approximately at my last estimation, 14 times. This film fascinated me, with Eddie Cantor's comedy, wisecracks and songs. This film, also leaves me with that feeling of sentimental satisfaction. During this four-year period I started making a list of films I saw, with stars, opinion, and data, which to this day I still keep up.

After joining the army at the age of 20, I found my film-going considerably curtailed, but took every opportunity of going, and found I looked forward to it more than ever, with a monotonous, hum-drum existence, being told what to do, and when to do it, after my previous independence. On leaves, I went almost every day, and here changed my policy of going locally, usually going to see the latest film up the West End, but, of course, picking them out, still. I had found, years earlier, that I never fancied going to the pictures, just for the sake of going. I would never see a film I didn't fancy, even if it meant doing nothing. So, often during my first army years, with only one cinema perhaps, within reach, I would not bother to go for that reason. I was often really depressed when I couldn't get to see, through being on duty or confined to barracks, a film which I wanted to see. My tastes remained the same.

After coming overseas two and a half years ago, film-going was almost non-existent for a time, until I was transferred from active duties to a base job. Here cinema-going was rather different. Mobile cinemas, very primitive, sitting on forms, or perhaps on the grass in the open-air. One film I saw over two years ago, through an American show, was *Arsenic and Old Lace*, which wasn't released until this year in Britain. In North Africa, films seen in French cinemas, had French sub-titles, but of course, the dialogue remained the same as spoken, so films could still be appreciated. I remember in a small North African village, mooning about aimlessly, when somebody said there's a film-show down the road. The village had no cinema, and eventually we found it was being shown in a small hall. Chaps were coming out disgustedly. 'Can't hear a darn thing', they said. 'It's lousy', and so forth. I asked one the name of the film. 'Oh, I don't know, Cary Grant's in it I think. Keeps breaking down. Sound's useless'. Another chap said 'Somebody goes to town; it's called'. No good, though. 'What', I said, 'Is it *Mr. Deeds Goes To Town*?' 'Yeah, that's it'. I wasted no more time! The film's presentation was awful, the sound garbled, lighting dim, and it kept breaking down. But, I never expected to be seeing this favourite film of mine, in a makeshift hall in a small cock-eayed village in North Africa. I enjoyed seeing the film as much as I had ever done, and when the strange show was over, I was completely at peace with the world, experiencing that strange sentimental satisfaction I always felt on complete enjoyment of a film. Wistfully, I trudged back to reality. The many poignant scenes in this film always affect my 'waterworks', and this time had been no exception.

So, for the two and a half years I have been overseas, my attitude towards films is much the same as it has been in the past ten years. I still like the type of film I liked then, and realise how big a part films have played not only in my enjoyment of life, but in life itself.

You ask about mannerisms influenced by films. I suppose the majority of filmgoers have adopted and taken for granted the American slang which is commonly heard everywhere. I am no exception. Otherwise, I don't think I have adopted and taken on any particular mannerisms, or mode of dress. Mine is more the mental aspect. Though, I like to indulge in imitating particular comedians in lighter moments, reminiscences, or explanations of a film. As for love-making, with my shy temperament, I have had little experience (I am not married), but would probably adopt James Stewart's attitude for instance and looking upon it as not to be abused. I have often felt, and wished, I could have the good fortune, as portrayed on the screen, with regard to life and love. I have often yearned to travel, but now I have had the chance, I am not so sure. But seeing the world through the eyes of the army is not like travelling unattached.

Summing it all up, I am left in a confusion of indecision. *Life in reality*, and life on the films *are unfortunately, not allied*. Perhaps I take the films too seriously. Perhaps my emotions are too easily moved. Escape to, or through, a world of make-believe. People, and life, on the silver screen is too artificial, too good, it is said. Maybe it is people and life that make it artificial. Anyway, it is nice to think that life could be like the films if people did imitate the 'characters', instead of just envying or ridiculing them. Yes, I am thankful I can appreciate films, and the messages and morals they try to present, admirably and indifferently. I wonder why films are the most popular entertainment of the modern age, as they are reputed to be. The argument that they are within everyone's 'pocket', may be an answer. Certainly, not because they are novel; they are some forty or fifty years old as an invention. I think the main reason is that it offers more variety than any other entertainment. One can relax and be taken to any part of the globe, can 'live' with the characters, and many emotions come into play. And all by the simple process of moving pictures. A truly marvellous achievement.

In closing, I will say I trust you find this of some interest, and excuse the length. This then is my film auto-biography, and an interpretation, which has helped me to see how incomplete and hypocritical life really is, and realise how complete and true it could be, through the medium of enjoyment and education. All power to the film-industry, and may the more serious-minded keep up the good work.

P.S. Perhaps I'm crazy, but then this is a crazy world.

3. An Appreciation

What conclusions can we draw from these documents? Selected as they are from a much larger number of documents obtained by means of a competition, can they be accepted as any guide to the effect of the cinema on the development of our contemporary society?

Only 5 per cent of the documents came from the Greater London area, the rest being drawn from over a very wide field, as were those published in *Sociology of Film*.

40 per cent of all the contributors are under 20 years old, 38.3 per cent between 20 and 25, 8.3 per cent between 25 and 30, 10 per cent between 30 and 40, and 3.3 per cent over 40. The younger age groups provide the more ardent filmgoers, but it is important to realize that the reactions recorded in the older groups are not essentially different: 'I still go very often to the pictures', says the writer of one of our Documents, 'I like to go on my own and get carried away by the acting, especially when it is an actor you have a little warm spot for, for I'm sure youngsters aren't the only ones who go because they like the ways and actions and little mannerisms of their favourite actors.' Nor do family responsibilities substantially transform the film experience, as is shown by the documents contributed by the 13.3 per cent of our contributors who are married. Married people may be less inclined or may have less time than single people to enter competitions of this kind; they may visit the cinema less frequently; but on the whole it appears that their reactions to films are not greatly different from those of single people.

It is with these reactions that we are primarily concerned. We do not claim that our 60 documents give a clear guide to the percentage of filmgoers amongst different sections of the population. Such an analysis is given in detail in Appendix 1[12]. The majority of our documents are contributed by clerks and other 'black-coated' workers, and only 10 per cent by members of the proletarian working class. This may be due to reluctance to put their experience down on paper. It is not due to the fact that this class does not go to the cinema, as is clear from Appendix I.

What we do claim is that our documents reveal the extraordinary influence exerted by the cinema on filmgoers. The bulk of the contributors went first to the cinema during childhood, and formed a *habit* of attendance at an early age. 44 per cent of the children of school age in the sample examined by the Social Survey investigators went to the cinema once a week or more often (see Table 19, Appendix I). 79 per cent of those between

[12] *The Cinema Audience*, An Inquiry made by the Wartime Social Survey for the Ministry of Information by Louis Moss and Kathleen Box.   New Series No. 37.b. June-July, 1943.

14 and 17 years of age went once a week or more often. In the lower income groups, 47 per cent of the children went once a week or more often (Table 21, Appendix I). The habit revealed in our documents is shown by the Social Survey Report to be a habit widespread amongst children and adolescents, and, to a lesser extent, amongst adults. Are the effects of this habit good or bad, as revealed in the stories told by our contributors?

The most important point conveyed by the documents is the high percentage of the horror, fright and nightmare experiences. Almost two-thirds or 66 per cent of all the writers give more or less detailed descriptions of shock experience. We are inclined to believe that this figure may be of representative significance in the numerical or quantitative sense, even while allowing for the fact that only certain kinds of cinemagoers are prepared to recount their experiences. The following digest shows that these horror experiences are not confined to one group of the contributors, but in fact run right through the whole series of documents.

DIGEST I

No.	Sex	Profession	Age	Region	Single or Married	Horror, Terror, Nightmare
1[13]	M.	Errand-boy	25	London	s.	yes
2	M.	Clerk	22	no addr. given	s.	yes
3	F.	Weaver	22	Wallasey	s.	yes
4	F.	?	19	Lancs.	s.	yes
5	F.	Hosiery Mach.	20	Leicester	s.	yes
6	F.	Usherette	22	Worcester	s.	yes
7	F.	Schoolgirl	15	Ealing	s.	yes
8	F.	Typist	17	Glasgow	s.	yes
9	M.	Cinema Oper.	20	Durham	s.	hardly
10	M.	Transport Mgr.	36	London	?	no
11	M.	Joiner	24	Herts.	s.	yes
12	M.	Shop Assistant	23	York	s.	hardly
13	M.	Crane Driver	20	Essex	s.	yes
14	F.	?	18	Surrey	s.	yes
15	F.	Housekeeper with Mother	16	Northants	s.	hardly
16	F.	Clerk	18	Lancaster	s.	no
17	F.	Apprentice	16	Surrey	s.	yes
18	F.	Student Nurse	19	Berks.	s.	no inform.

[13] In order to safeguard the anonymity of our contributors the numbers 1—60 in this Digest are not *identical* with the numbering of the Documents.

DIGEST I—*Continued*

No.	Sex	Profession	Age	Region	Single or Married	Horror, Terror, Nightmare
19	M.	Clerk	21	?	s.	no
20	F.	Factory Worker	20	Cumberland	s.	yes
21	M.	Inspector of Castings	39	?	m.	no
22	F.	Housewife	30	Birmingham	m.	yes
23	M.	Schoolboy	15	Birmingham	s.	yes
24	M.	Miner	21	Derbyshire	s.	no
25	F.	Housewife	37	Ramsgate	m.	no
26	F.	Clerk	18	Middlesex	s.	yes
27	F.	Clerk	19	Birmingham	s.	yes
28	F.	Bus Conductress	27	Middlesex	s.	yes
29	F.	Housewife	26	Essex	m.	no
30	F.	Clerk	30	Birmingham	s.	yes
31	M.	Clerk	21	Yorks.	s.	yes
32	F.	Chem. Assistant	21	Leicester	s.	yes
33	M.	Bank Clerk	21	?	s.	no
34	F.	Housewife	43	Coventry	m.	yes
35	F.	Housewife	22	Kent	m.	yes
36	M.	Schoolboy	15	Somerset	s.	yes
37	F.	Typist	18	Kent	s.	yes
38	F.	Ass. Librarian	18	Northumberland	s.	no
39	F.	Bank Clerk	18	Fulham, S.W.	s.	yes
40	M.	Schoolboy	12	Bristol	s.	no
41	F.	Clerk Inland Rev.	20	Lincoln	s.	yes
42	M.	Schoolboy	15	Nr. Birmingham	s.	yes
43	M.	Soldier	20	?	s.	no
44	F.	?	19	Reading	s.	hardly
45	F.	Inland Rev.	17	?	s.	yes
46	F.	Medical Student	22	Perthshire	s.	yes
47	F.	Laboratory Asst.	23	Mercastle o Tyne	m.	yes
48	F.	News P. Reporter	21	London	s.	yes
49	M.	Typist	16	Northumberland	s.	no
50	F.	Typist	18	Worcester	s.	yes
51	F.	WAAF	25	Middlesbrough	s.	no
52	F.	Typist	17	Oxon.	s.	yes
53	F.	Typist	21	Leeds	s.	yes
54	F.	Housewife	47	?	m.	no
55	F.	Clerk	16	Devon	s.	yes
56	F.	Typist	19	?	s.	yes
57	F.	Secretary	39	?	s.	yes
58	F.	Typist	23	Staffs.	s.	no
59	F.	Clerk	22	Middlesex	s.	no
60	F.	Typist	27	Bucks.	m.	yes

Many of the horror, terror or fright examples deserve the closest study (see for instance documents 24, 46, 26). These experiences are of such intensity and persistence that they must raise the question whether the mental health of the community is not seriously endangered by their uncontrolled continuance. We have pleaded in *Sociology of Film* for a State censorship of films for this very reason and we do not intend to re-open the debate here.

We prefer to give a more exact psychological appreciation of the fright, terror, etc. phenomenon. It is obvious that a certain dose of thrill and fright is a basic requirement of human nature.

Play with shock has been described as one of the basic phenomena of early childhood[14]. We ourselves have observed a child of three years whom her doctor let fall playfully from the top of a sofa on to the seat. The child, not yet master of language, screamed with delight and fright: 'Don't do it again', meaning *do* it again. Naturally the play was continued for some time. This case is a fine example of what William Stern has termed *Angstlust*.

Angst is what Goethe described as an *Urphaenomen*. Kierkegaard[15] and the existentialist philosophers who followed him have reflected on the philosophical significance of the experience. (Rilke in his *Aufzeichnungen des Malte Laurids Brigge* has given a most remarkable description of a child's *Angst* experience. Rilke had read his Kierkegaard[16].)

We do not propose to discuss the origin of the fright etc. phenomenon (the term *Angst* is quite untranslatable), it suffices to say that *Angst*, in French perhaps *angoisse*, is a universal human experience shared by children and adults alike[17]. To quote Karl Groos; 'There are people who are quite fearless in danger, but yet are terrified with regard to the horror of the unknown (*unheimlich*)[18].

Play, play with shock, the love of adventure, thrill, excitement, suspense, are indispensable elements of human nature. There can be no objection that films should to a certain extent

[14] Cf. Karl Groos, *Das Seelenleben des Kindes*, Berlin 1921, p.277.

[15] Cf. Sören Kierkegaard, *Le Concept d'Angoisse*, Paris, 1935. (With an important introduction by Jean Wahl).

[16] Cf. Rilke, *Die Aufzeichnungen des Malte Laurids Brigge*, vol. I, Leipsic, 1920, pp. 132 sqq. See also, Heidegger, *Sein und Zeit*, vol. I, Halle, 1927, pp 184 sqq., and André Gide, *Si le grain ne meurt*, Paris s.a., pp. 134 sqq.

[17] Thouless suggests anxiety as English equivalent for *Angst*. Cf. his *General and Social Psychology*, London, 1943, p. 155. We doubt whether the English term suggests the full implications of the German term.

[18] Cf. *op. cit.*, p. 284. See also Stern, *Psychologie der frühen Kindheit*, Leipsic, 1927, pp. 448 sqq.

appeal to those instincts or emotional attitudes. But it is an immense problem to what extent the degree of suspense, thrill etc. is healthy or when it becomes harmful. We believe our documents may provide material to solve this problem.

Nor is this problem a new one. It may perhaps be opportune to remind the reader that Aristotle has raised it in his *Politics* (1341b, 1342a). Though he speaks of music in these pages, his argument can and perhaps should be applied to the social function of the contemporary cinema, for Aristotle discusses the principles which ought to guide the Athenian legislator of the 4th century B.C., as we attempt to suggest principles for the legislator of the modern mass state:

'Songs are divided by some philosophers whose notions we approve of, into moral, practical and that which fills the mind with enthusiasm: they also allot to each of these a particular kind of harmony which naturally corresponds therewith: and we say that music should not be applied to one purpose only, but many; both for instruction and purifying (*katharsis*) the soul (now I use the word purifying at present without any explanation, but shall speak more at large of it in my *Poetics*[19]); and, in

---

[19] It is well known that the famous passage in Chapter VI of the *Poetics* does unfortunately not fulfil Aristotle's promise. For a discussion of the *katharsis* problem we refer the reader to: J. Bernays: *Zwei Abhandlungen über die aristotelische Theorie des Dramas*, Berlin, 1880, E. Zeller: *Die Philosophie der Griechen: Aristoteles und die alten Peripatetiker*, Berlin, 1879, pp. 770 sqq. We quote the decisive passage for the benefit of those readers who may have difficulties in obtaining this classic work from a Library: 'Die Katharsis wird seiner (Aristotle's) Darstellung nach allerdings durch Erregung der Affekte herbeigeführt, sie ist eine homöopathische Heilung der Affekte; aber nicht von *jeder beliebigen* (our italics) Erregung der Affekte erwartet Aristoteles diese Wirkung, sondern *nur von ihrer kunstmässigen Erregung* (our italics), und als kunstmässig gilt ihm, wie dies aus seinen Aeusserungen über die Tragödie deutlich hervorgeht, nicht diejenige, welche die stärkste Gemütsbewegung in uns hervorbringt, sondern diejenige, welche sie auf die rechtmässige Weise hervorbringt. Käme es bei der künstlerischen Katharsis nach der Ansicht des Aristoteles nur darauf an, dass gewisse Affekte erregt werden, und nicht wesenlich zugleich auch die Art, wie und die Mittel, wodurch sie errgt werden, so hätte er den Masstab für die Beurteilung der Kunstwerke nicht aus ihrem Inhalt und seiner sachlich richtigen Behandlung, sondern einzig und allein aus ihrer Wirkung auf die Zuschauer entnehmen müssen, wovon er doch weit entfernt ist.' Cf. also Ingram Bywater, *Aristotle and the Art of Poetry*, Oxford, 1909, W. D. Ross, *Aristotle*, London, 1937. See also Th. Gomperz.*Griechische Denker*, Vol. 3, Leipsic, 1909, p. 317. Gomperz appears to accept Zeller's interpretation of the famous passage: 'Die Pflege der Musik soll jedoch nicht ausschliesslich diesem, im Sinne des Aristoteles höchsten Zwecke dienen. Ihm reihen sich vielmehr drei Nebenzwecke an: die Anregung zu unmittelbarem Handeln, die Sache der '*praktischen*' Musik; die *Unterhaltung* oder Erholung und endlich die *Katharsis*, d.h. die Befreiung des Gemütes oder die Entladung von Affekten . . . Es ist nicht viel anders, als wenn wir neben der edlen und gehaltreichen *Oper* auch den banaleren unter den *Operetten*, mit Einschluss freilich der in inhaltlosen 'Koloraturen' sich ergehenden Bravouropern eine selbständige, wenngleich untergeordnete Stellung zuerkennen.'

the third place, as an agreeable manner of spending the time and a relaxation from the uneasiness of the mind. It is evident that all harmonies are to be used; but not for all purposes; but the most moral in education: but to please the ear, when others play, the most active and enthusiastic; for that passion which is to be found very strong in some souls is to be met with also in all; but the difference in different persons consists in its being in a less or greater degree, as pity, fear, and enthusiasm also; which latter is so powerful in some as to overpower the soul: and yet we see those persons, by the application of sacred songs to soothe their mind, rendered as sedate and composed as if they had employed the art of the physician: and this must happen to the compassionate, the fearful, and all those who are subdued by their passions: nay, all persons, as far as they are affected with those passions, admit of the same cure and are restored to tranquillity with pleasure. *In the same manner, all songs which have the power of purifying the soul afford a harmless pleasure to man.* (Our italics). Such, therefore, should be the harmony and such the music which those who contend with each other in the theatre should exhibit: but as the audience is composed of two sorts of people, the free and the well-instructed, the rude and the low workers and hired servants and a long collection of the like, there must be some music and some spectacles to please and soothe them; for as their minds are, as it were, perverted from their natural habits, so also is there an unnatural harmony and overcharged music which is accommodated to their taste; but what is according to nature gives pleasure to everyone, therefore those, who are to contend upon the theatre should be allowed to use this species of music[20].'

The Greek philosopher was as we have seen a great realist. The society for which he wrote and which he interpreted, accepted 'overcharged music' only for the lower ranks of the social organism. The slaves stood outside the Athenian democracy, but their masters took them when they were well behaved to the theatre.

Yet one would misunderstand Aristotle entirely, if one were to forget that he required 'overcharged music' to be 'purifying' and 'affording a harmless pleasure to man'.

Our contemporary cinema disintegrates society by the increasing application of such plots and techniques which assume the function of Aristotle's 'overcharged music' *without* purification. Aristotle, while he clearly states the perennial norm of art,

---

[20] I have used the translations of the *Everyman* edition, but not without consulting the Greek text.

compromises with regard to the less educated masses, but he has never pleaded for indiscriminate mass stimuli. Only the late Roman Empire resorted to this; we know with what results.

We believe it is possible to study the psychological mechanisms of suspense, thrill, fright and similar phenomena in relation to their social effects. Once these phenomena are properly studied, it might be possible to say where, in principle, their use by the visual medium of the cinema may have a destructive or positive result.

Perhaps we should insert here as an illustration of Aristotle's meaning a note, taken from our film diary. We saw recently in a small repertory cinema in London two films in a two-feature programme: the first film was a technicolor American musical: *Dixie* with Bing Crosby as leading actor, an amiable example of what Aristotle may have meant by 'overcharged music', yet the film is pleasant to the soul, even to somebody who may prefer Mozart to Bing Crosby. The second feature was *Seawolf* with E. G. Robinson as the chief actor. In this film no respite was given: sinking ships, murders, mental torture—altogether an atmosphere of gloom and despair prevailed. Our mood of delight and relaxation had completely vanished, our nerves were tense. One left the cinema fatigued, without relief.

The shock and terror experience must be related to the phenomenon of *participation mystique* (Cf. *Sociology of Film*). 'I have been attracted', writes a schoolboy of 15½ years, 'to the cinema now for nearly 10 years. I have always been fascinated by the phenomenon of moving pictures. If I find the film I am watching is exceptionally good, I forget that what I am watching is really a string of transparent photographs and I *join* (our italics) in the situations with the characters. The film, to my eyes, takes a third dimension.' (See document 12). This wonderful description explains why people fall in love with screen stars, by no means adolescents only as our documents show. 'At 17 I was very interested', writes a 21 year old contributor, 'in great love stories. Tyrone Power was my idol and I saw his pictures three or four times. I think I must have fallen in love with him . . . When he kisses his leading lady a funny thrill runs up my spine to the heart. Sometimes in dreams which seem very real, I imagine he is kissing me.' (Document 49). Lovers, even partners for life are chosen according to film experiences. (See Document 5). Films become a social reality.

Our documents show also how early our writers have started becoming regular, ardent and passionate filmgoers. A 21 year old miner hopes to reach in 1945 the annual figure of 430 film

attendances! Nor should it be overlooked that many of the
shock and terror experiences date back to those early and
earliest years.

At present the average boy or girl starts his or her film visits
at the age of four or five. At first perhaps they prefer Mickey
Mouse, Serials, Westerns, at the age of 10 or 11 in the case of
girls the colourful musical begins to hold their fascination,
whereas the boy of the same age may prefer the thriller or
murder picture. Many girls prefer these also. At a later age—
perhaps in the case of town children at 13—the first signs of
discrimination appear.

Film tastes depend *entirely* on education, education in the
widest sense. Heritage, family background, friends, and type and
quality of school shape the early film taste. In addition of course,
apart from the educational standards, the social status of the
cinemagoer is important for a correct assessment of film preferences.

With regard to all these problems our documents make more
detailed research imperative, though it appears possible for the
attentive reader to relate a curve of a changing film taste to the
equally changing curve of the life pattern.

No document is perhaps more significant in this respect than
No. 60. Here, in the absence of more normal forces, films appear
as a dominating 'educational' influence on a contemporary
human life. The author of this remarkable piece of self-analysis
is indeed movie-made. Yet it is fair to say that the value patterns to which he adheres and which he defines with superb
clarity are perhaps the ideal fulfilment of the Hollywood film
kitchen. They are the value patterns of the Hays Code-*pur sang:*
' . . . the films had built a conception of life, which life itself,
tended to contradict, my ideals made through films, not being
realized in true life. But instead of making me disbelieve in and
dislike film-life, it made me bitter towards real life. Films
taught all the things I should like to associate with life. Crime
does not pay, the wrong-doer getting his just deserts; kindness
pays; love-thy-neighbour; plumping for the "small" man
"flaying" the rich; making the best of life; "true" love wins in
marriage; decency; the mild and honest man triumphing over
the immoral, unscrupulous one; all the ideals worthy of life,
which we would all like to see, or would we? At least, one would
presume so. It is oft-remarked that films should be more like
life. If they were, people would be disgusted to "see" how they
lived and would protest strongly; in fact, of course, such a film
would never get past the censor. So, I maintain, as that course is

impossible, that, as has also been said, that life should be more like the films. I try to live my life as films would have us believe, and they have helped me to get a great deal out of life, though it is "tough" going.'

One might well ponder over these sentences and put them into the context of European ethical reflection. (But it would require a whole book to trace the process of how our value patterns have become increasingly empty and meaningless. Perhaps, one day, I shall write this book). It is a long and depressive journey from Aristotle's *Nicomachean Ethics* to this document, but it may well be that our young author—he is 25—who so sincerely strives to formulate his *Weltanschauung* is not less representative for our contemporary moral conception of life than the great Greek philosopher was for his age.

Reading further in this moving *confession de foi*, we meet the doubt of indecision. Should Film be like Life? 'Summing it all up, I am left in a confusion of indecision. *Life in reality*, and life on the films *are unfortunately, not allied.* Perhaps I take the films too seriously. Perhaps my emotions are too easily moved. Escape to, or through, a world of make-believe. People, and life, on the silver screen is too artificial, too good, it is said. Maybe it is people and life that make it artificial. Anyway, it is nice to think that life could be like the films if people did imitate the "Characters", instead of just envying and ridiculing them.'

Indeed: Life should be like Film. The solution of our author is certainly logical and serious.

Generally speaking however, only one document in 60 shows a complete serenity of mind (Document 28). The authoress is 19 years and has the gifts of a fine writer: 'I deplore the fact', she writes, 'that ninety-nine per cent of every film issued can be typed. Thus it became my ambition to pick out the other one per cent of films to see—the film that did not fall into a definite category.' On this note we may conclude this short appreciation of our documents.

III. A STUDY IN FILM PREFERENCES

... if democratic government is less favourable than another to some of the finer parts of human nature, it has also great and noble elements; and that perhaps, after all, it is the will of God to shed a lesser grade of happiness on the totality of mankind, not to combine a greater share of it on a smaller number, or to raise the few to the verge of perfection. I have undertaken to demonstrate to them that, whatever their opinion on this point may be, it is too late to deliberate, that society is advancing and dragging them along with itself towards equality of conditions; that the sole remaining alternative lies between evils henceforth inevitable; that the question is not whether aristocracy or democracy can be maintained, but whether we are to live under a democratic society, devoid indeed of poetry and greatness, but at least orderly and moral, or under a democratic society, lawless and depraved, abandoned to the frenzy of revolution, or subjected to a yoke heavier than any of those which have crushed mankind since the fall of the Roman Empire.

ALEXIS DE TOCQUEVILLE

(Quoted from *Prophet of the Mass Age. A study of Alexis de Tocqueville*, by J. P. Mayer, p. 42 sq.).

1. INTRODUCTORY

THE DOCUMENTS WHICH FOLLOW were again obtained through the *Picturegoer* by way of a competition.

In spite of the considerable and puzzling variations in film tastes the first two competitions[21] appeared to indicate, we felt it was essential to attempt a more distinct isolation of this most tricky phenomenon of the film experience.

The question we asked was as follows:

YOUR HELP REQUIRED AGAIN

Our University Lecturer, who has received much valuable assistance from our readers, again offers three prizes of £2 2s. 0d., £1 1s. 0d. and 10s. 6d. for the best answers to a simple question.

[21] With regard to the first competition see: *Sociology of Film*, chapter IX, with regard to the second one see chapter II of the present volume.

He wants to know the films you like and dislike and wants you to give reasons for your likes and dislikes.

Naturally it is your own personal opinions he wants about your film preferences and not those of any critic you have read or of any friend.

Write frankly and sincerely and, in addition to your name and address, give your profession, age, sex, profession of father and mother, and nationality.

We received about 150 answers of which we print a selection of 50. This time we say: selection, not instalment. The documents were selected from only one point of view: we tried to obtain the largest amount of variation. When we had selected the first 50 contributions, we felt the other documents were mainly repetitive, though we admit that from the point of view of the social scientist we would have preferred to print them all. But again reasons of space made this impossible.

There are also repetitive features amongst the first 50, but these appear relevant for the phenomenon of film preferences. We shall refer to some of these repetitions in our interpretation.

We give now a statistical digest of the printed contributions which again show a considerably wide area distribution. At the time this investigation was under way, there was reason to assume that *Picturegoer* reached about one million readers. The documents represent naturally only the most 'reflective' type of film fan, but we do not think that the notion we get of film preferences is unduly over-rationalised or over-systematized, though it cannot be taken as a sample in the sense of numerical statistics.

It may perhaps be possible to formulate, on the basis of our material, such questions which will in future enable us to bridge the gap between our more qualitative approach and a strictly statistical one. For the present, however, we do not think that the reaction structure of our cinema going millions is fundamentally different.

The following digest gives a 'statistical' illustration of some relevant points with regard to our documents:

DIGEST II

No.	Sex	Profession	Age	Region
1A[22]	M.	Bank Official	52	Portsmouth
2A	F.	Cinema Operator	?	Hants.
3A	F.	Clerk	16	Leeds
4A	F.	Dramatic Art and Music ..	18	Perth
5A	F.	Clerk	28	Warwickshire

No.	Sex	Profession	Age	Region
6A	F.	Civil Servant	24	Cheshire
7A	F.	Housewife	48	Cardiff
8A	M.	Student	19	North Ireland
9A	F.	Capstan Operator	19	Manchester
10A	M.	Sorting Letters	23	Northampton
11A	M.	Employee L.M.S.	18	Scotland
12A	M.	Draughtsman	25	Kent
13A	F.	Schoolgirl	15	Birmingham
14A	F.	Student Nurse	19	Jersey
15A	M.	Bricklayer	64	Durham
16A	F.	Machine Operator	24	Surrey
17A	F.	Housekeeper	46	Birmingham
18A	M.	Art Student	21	Firl
19A	F.	Just left school	17	Plymouth
20A	M.	Private Secretary	36	London
21A	M.	Schoolboy	14	Durham
22A	F.	Radio Assembler	23	Lancs.
23A	F.	Clerk and Typist	20	Bristol
24A	F.	Typist	34	Cambridge
25A	F.	Legal line	58	Harrow
26A	F.	Schoolgirl	14	Lancs.
27A	F.	Clerk	16	Liverpool
28A	F.	G.P.O. employee	18	Middlesex
29A	F.	Schoolgirl	14	Ayrshire
30A	F.	Schoolgirl	12	Bath
31A	F.	Textile Worker	18	Yorkshire
32A	F.	Student	17	Lancs.
33A	F.	Typist	19	Middlesex
34A	F.	Printing Machine Operator	19	Warwickshire
35A	F.	Private Clerk	16	Yorkshire
36A	F.	Shop Assistant	17	Woverhampton
37A	M.	No information	17	Nottingham
38A	F.	Telephone Operator	25	Leicester
39A	F.	Typist	24	Warwickshire
40A	M.	Farming	25	Worcester
41A	F.	Schoolgirl	12	Somerset
42A	F.	Typist	20	London
43A	F.	Typist	20	Scotland
44A	M.	G.P.O.	22	Middlesex
45A	F.	Housewife	23	Monmouth
46A	F.	Typist	23	Staffs.
47A	F.	Typist	24	London, S.E.
48A	M.	Sergeant	26	London, S.E.
49A	F.	Housewife	30	Staffs.
50A	M.	Journalist	48	Manchester

[22] Again the numbers 1A—50A are *not* identical with the numbering of the Documents which follow.

The female element among the contributors is in the majority: 36 against 14 males. The age group distribution is as follows:

Under 20 (23) 46 per cent; between 20 and 25 (13) 26 per cent; between 25 and 30 (5) 10 per cent; between 30 and 40 (3) 6 per cent; over 40 (5) 10 per cent; and no information (1) 2 per cent.

The class structure of the contributors proves again the prevalence of the black-coated workers. We would prefer the term *Mittelschichten*. The professional classes are represented by only one contributor. The members of the upper class may not be readers of the *Picturegoer*. If they are, they do not take part in competitions of this kind.

We tried to include in our digest a short characterization or typification of the film preference attitude of each contributor, but we were unable to do so. It would have given a simplified picture of the problem.

The documents which now follow, are naturally unedited. We were interested primarily in two questions: 'In what state is the present mass taste in regard to films?' and 'Is the film industry right when it says: "We provide the entertainment the public wants?"'.' Our interpretation of the following documents in the light of these two questions is given later. At this stage, it may be convenient for our readers to examine the state of public taste amongst different sections of the population, classified according to age, as indeed, are our films under the existing system.

2. DOCUMENTS

We begin with a document which cannot be fitted accurately into any age category, since the writer has not stated her age. Nor are the views she expresses typical of the majority of entries. This document therefore stands alone.

NO. 1 A

AGE: —	FATHER'S OCCUPATION:
SEX: F.	BAKERY EMPLOYEE
OCCUPATION: CINEMA OPERATOR	MOTHER'S OCCUPATION:
NATIONALITY: BRITISH	—

I have been a filmgoer ever since I was about fourteen, but only since just before the war have I become critical of the entertainment offered by the various companies.

I have great dislike for films which distort and alter historical facts. *Lady Hamilton* was an outstanding example of this. Films of the classics which have been altered also infuriate me although I do not mind so much in modern novels which are not so well known. I dislike extremely the noisy, typically American type of musical which has no story, and therefore no real reason for existing at all. I also hate films which are just plain stupid, and a re-make which is not announced as such.

First and foremost I like a film with a story, with true-to-life characters who act as normal people would. I like a film with action in it, especially of the type usually provided by Humphrey Bogart, and a really *good* Western. I like certain actors because they *are* actors. Their looks come a poor second; for example, James Mason, Michael Redgrave, John Mills, or Van Heflin are ones I like; and Errol Flynn and Robert Taylor are the type I dislike. I like films of the English countryside because they are usually quieter and more restful than most American films. Only sometimes they are *too* restful and drag a bit. I like a film with good music provided it is introduced naturally and logically and not grafted on anywhere the director thinks it should be with no regard for the story. Occasionally I like to see a film of the 'fantasy' type like *Thunder Rock* or *Halfway House*. You don't have to really believe in them to enjoy them. I also like a leavening of the type of humour in which Abbott and Costello are experts; although I don't like all exponents of knockabout comedy. For instance, I cannot stand Laurel and Hardy. In varying degrees I like all the films of Bob Hope. His style is unique, although several other actors strive to reach his level. His apparently spontaneous repartee always appeals to my sense of humour.

I do not like a film which starts out as a farce and then tries to be serious drama. *Government Girl* is a good example of this. A film should always keep to one style, or at least to styles that harmonise successfully.

I hope these views are not too incoherent, as my likes and dislikes seem to have become mixed up a bit, in spite of my efforts to keep them separate.

I have tried to give my views honestly and frankly, and I think I have succeeded.

The youngest contributor is a schoolgirl of twelve, whose views do perhaps accord with her age. It is a pity that her style of writing should appear to cast doubt on her sincerity, and, therefore, on the value of the document.

NO. 2A

AGE: 12
SEX: F.
OCCUPATION: SCHOOLGIRL
NATIONALITY: BRITISH

FATHER'S OCCUPATION:
R.A.F. (PREVIOUSLY
MANAGER OF — CO.)
MOTHER'S OCCUPATION:
HOUSEWIFE,
PREVIOUSLY CLERK

Since I saw *Frenchman's Creek*, *Since You Went Away*, *Mrs. Parkington* and *Music for Millions*, I really have more faith in Joan Fontaine,

Claudette Colbert, the exceptional acting ability and charm of Greer Garson, and the childlike simplicity of the sweet budding young actress, Margaret O'Brien.

Sometimes I ask myself why I liked those films when my heart really lies in Musical Comedy. Well, all of the films I have mentioned so far are quite likely to have happened to somebody and out of those four the most fantastic is *Frenchman's Creek*, and that is not quite in the Arabian Nights fantasies. Besides I have no doubt that Arturo de Cordova will succeed Spencer Tracy as a heart stealer, and Margaret O'Brien can tell me that one does not have to be a Shirley Temple to acquire fame as a child star; that Claudette Colbert has developed into a sincere actress with a flair for 'straight' acting, and I have no cause to doubt where Greer Garson's talent lies.

I knew all the aforesaid films, would be successes because of their distinctive directors and producers. Most of those films come under drama and I suggest that before making Shakespeare's plays into films, less fantastic plays and stories should be adapted for the screen.

Films I detest are films about the music halls in the gay old nineties in which nearly every scene shows coarse music hall artists 'walking out' on their harassed, buttonless-waistcoated, shirt sleeves-up producer. Frankly, I think those days are to be ashamed of, and it's waste of film to make such repulsive films.

I went miles out of my way to see Frank Sinatra in *Step Lively* and I don't believe a more ridiculous, rubbishy and nonsencical picture could be made. The dialogue, in plain slang, was absolute trash and Frank Sinatra went down in my estimation, more than I felt possible. Another film to grumble about was *Penthouse Rhythm*,—a bit too fantastic in the modern world and a little bit too creative.

Being a very great admirer of Bing Crosby I welcome any film of his; musical or drama. His greatest—*Going My Way* cannot be bettered and in my estimation no other film ever made could possibly equal it. The acting, humour and above all, Bing's crooning were superb.

I am also a very great admirer of Deanna Durbin and, not particular as I may seem, I'd go to see any film of hers because even if Deanna sings blues or *Ave Maria* in a film she would never differ. That warm infectious personality and sweet voice could never be spoilt—I'm sure.

I want to see less films like *The Moon is Down, Step Lively, Penthouse Rhythm, Cinderella Swings it, Sweet Rosie O'Grady, Give Me the Moon* and more films like the first four I mentioned besides, *Madame Curie, Tonight and Every Night, Keep Your Powder Dry, This is the Life, Little Nellie Kelly, Thirty Seconds Over Tokyo* and more Sherlock Holmes films. Moreover I ask British film producers to come off their high horse and try to get more like Hollywood. I'll give Gainsborough credit for a very enjoyable film *I'll Be Your Sweetheart*. More films please containing the following, Bing Crosby, Greer Garson, Deanna Durbin, Joan Fontaine (in a role similar to the one she played in *Frenchman's Creek*), Margaret O'Brien, Van Johnson, Jennifer Jones,

Ingrid Bergman, Claudette Colbert, Robert Walk and I think Joan Leslie should be given a chance, and not be allowed to wither away.

Please spend the money and film stars on the really good films and decent ones, not on cheap musicals from the old music-hall dump.

The three fourteen-year-olds, two girls and a boy, show surprisingly little variation. The boy shows a catholicity of taste which echoes some of the documents in the first series, but it is notable that the strong impressions of horror recorded in the first series have either ceased to affect the three school-children whose contributions follow, or have never affected them to the same extent as the writers of the earlier documents.

NO. 3A

AGE: 14   FATHER'S OCCUPATION:
SEX: F.   OWNER OF SHOE-SHOP
OCCUPATION: SCHOOL-GIRL   MOTHER'S OCCUPATION:
NATIONALITY: SCOTTISH   —

I don't know whether my tastes are peculiar, like a lot of other people's, or just silly, or whether I am too young to enter for this competition but I can simply try.

I like good musicals, good drama and 'thrillers', really interesting and eerie. I dislike films which either hand a thin thread of story onto numerous songs and dances, or those silly comedy films, such as the Abbot and Costello series, or those comedy 'shorts' which are utterly senseless, without story or reason. I also dislike most crime 'shorts'; I dislike intensely crime and murder films which are a mixture of stupid policemen blundering about, and silly blondes on incredibly high heels. That's the bare outline of my likes and dislikes.

By a good musical, I mean films like *Tonight and Every Night*, the *Road to Morocco, Singapore, Zanzibar* series, and those films dealing with the lives and music of great composers such as Chopin, Handel, etc. Here I refer to the lovely *A Song to Remember, The Great Mr. Handel*, I thoroughly enjoyed all these films; of course, I have a decided weakness for the *Road* films, and am allergic to Bing Crosby. That may prejudice me in favour of the *Road* series. I am not at all fond of really 'highbrow' music, yet I certainly liked *A Song to Remember* very much indeed. As an example of the type of musical I do *not* like I'd say *Pin-up Girl, Sweet Rosie O'Grady, Incendiary Blonde*. Some of the songs were passably good but the story spoilt the film, it was hopelessly weak, and at times tailed off altogether, while everyone in the film apparently forgot that there was more to acting a part in a film than singing, dancing and giving an undoubtably pleasant display of legs.

Now to drama. I'll say unashamedly that I won't hear anything against Bette Davies. I consider her acting alone makes a film superb. I thoroughly enjoy every film in which she stars. I saw a pitiful attempt at drama by Deanna Durbin in *Christmas Holiday*. I could say a lot on the subject of Miss Durbin but that's not the purpose of this answer. I'll merely say she's a flop. *Since You Went Away*, I enjoyed reasonably well, though the pathos was much too emphasised. You ask for reasons why you like and dislike a film; well, if I really enjoy a film I just feel satisfied with that film, I feel happy, because I was sure I understood it, and it had held my attention throughout. When I don't enjoy a film, I'm almost cross, and disgusted, because I considered it, to be frank, rubbish! That I had fidgetted often, and longed for the end. Maybe those are not the reasons you want, though.

As to thrillers, well, I think the best thriller I ever saw was *The Uninvited*. It really thrilled me, and I never stirred once in my seat, from the moment it began till the finish, except for occasional gasps and starts at 'creepy' bits. I really like that type of film, it had a good story, it was well acted, or as I thought, the 'atmosphere' was convincing. A film such as *Laura*, I also like. I love detective films which keep you guessing right to the end.

Oh, I forgot to say I also dislike violently 'sloppy' films, such as *Love Story*, *Madonna of the Seven Moons*. The British film industry must be far gone when it has to turn out such rubbishy muck as that! Of course, again, I can't stand Stewart Granger, and this also may prejudice me against his films. I'm not very clear, am I? Still, I'm trying hard! To get on to may next dislike. Abbot and Costello and Laurel and Hardy bore me to tears. I can see nothing at all funny in their stupid tumbling about, and absurd predicaments. Yet I can get a really good laugh out of Bob Hope's or Jack Benny's cracks. It's not a question of looks, I'd certainly award none of them the prize for beauty, but Bob Hope seems really amusing, to me. Those apparently side-splitting shorts, I sit through (when I see them) with a very bored expression, while around me boys and girls, and sometimes adults, laugh heartily. I don't know if anyone shares my opinions or not. I think I've told you what you asked now. I *think* so; my reply may be very unsatisfactory. I've just told you honestly my likes and dislikes. I can't do any more.

NO. 4A

AGE: 14

SEX: F.

OCCUPATION: SCHOOLGIRL.

NATIONALITY: BRITISH

FATHER'S OCCUPATION: ELECTRICAL ENGINEER

MOTHER'S OCCUPATION: SHOPKEEPER (ELECTRICAL)

One of the films I like very much, is *Keys of the Kingdom*. The chief reason why I liked this film is because we do not get many religious films and it is a change from the 'Modern musicals'. It is well acted and praise goes to Gregory Peck as it is the first film in which he has taken the leading part. It is full of adventure and it is interesting the way the story is told and showing the star growing up from childhood.

Song of Russia is another film I like; chiefly for its music. It is lovely to sit and listen to good music like Tchaikovsky's. The acting and the story was quite good and it is always nice to have a pretty girl and a handsome man in this kind of film.

I like *Since You Went Away*, because it is the life of an ordinary family. I like it because the stars all show a different kind of character. I also like this film because it is a war picture in the home and not in the battlefield. It is acted well and the theme song goes with it splendidly. I like *For Whom the Bell Tolls* chiefly for the colour and the scenery, and Ingrid Bergman was very pretty and brought out the 'Maria' hair style. The acting was very good but I think the scenery and the colour were the best part of the film. I like *Murder in Thornton Square*, because it has nothing to do with the war. The dresses were beautiful and this film brought the new star Angela Lansburg to the 'Front line'. Charles Boyer's voice was as fascinating as ever and again Ingrid Bergman played her part extremely well. The film was well acted and an improvement on *Gaslight*. Now coming to the British film *Madonna of the Seven Moons*. Of course this was a big hit and I liked it because it had two stars in it who have risen to fame recently. It is well acted and the only fault I find with it is the way they spoke. You would hardly expect to hear the educated London dialect in the slums of Florence, but still that wasn't the actor's fault.

Blithe Spirit was very entertaining. The setting was good and Rex Harrison played his part well and Margaret Rutherford brought in most of the comedy. I liked the story, because the whole matter was treated lightly, and I think it is one of Noel Coward's best.

Dis-Likes:—

I did not like *Hollywood Canteen*, because there were too many stars in it and no good acting. When there are a lot of stars appearing in it and only for a short time, you can hardly expect good acting and a real story.

The Affairs of Susan was another film I was not too keen on. Chiefly because Joan Fontaine doesn't seem to suit that part. On the whole, I think she suits the part she played in *The Constant Nymph* and *Jane Eyre* better.

Two British films I disliked were *Waterloo Road* and *Great Day*. There was no real story to the former, which seemed to be quarrels all the time, and I think Stewart Granger should either play a villainous part as in *Madonna of the Seven Moons*, or a happy sentimentalist as in *Love Story* but not an 'in between'.

As for *Great Day*, there was not much story or acting in it, and in the end, when the Great Day came, you didn't even see Mrs. Roosevelt, which was a dissappointment because this part was supposed to be the climax of the film. Another reason why I didn't like it, was because it didn't show what happened to any of the family in the end,—you are still left wondering how Eric Portman got off, and whether Sheila Sim did marry the farmer or not.

NO. 5A

AGE: 14 YEARS 6 MONTHS
SEX: M.
OCCUPATION: SCHOOLBOY
NATIONALITY: BRITISH

FATHER'S OCCUPATION:
COMMERCIAL
TRAVELLER
MOTHER'S OCCUPATION:
HOUSEWIFE

In reply to the article featured in August 18th's *Picturegoer*, I am writing a letter to you which will illustrate the films I like and dislike. I must be a very easy going person because there are much more films I like than I dislike, or maybe it is that majority of the films I see are good. I am an ardent film fan, and I have every *Picturegoer* since May 1st 1942. In the next few lines I will try to convey to you my taste in films.

The Films I Like

Dramas

All the 'Bette Davis' films, because her studios realise she is a grand actress, so they give her good stories, which she carries out exquisitely e.g. *The Little Foxes, The Letter, Marked Woman* etc. These conditions also apply to Greer Garson and Walter Pidgeon, e.g. *Blossoms in the Dust, Madame Curie* etc. British Studios also apply to this method in such good stars as James Mason, Stewart Granger, John Mills, Margaret Lockwood, Patricia Roc, Phylis Calvert, Tom Walls, Rosamund John, etc. who have made such memoriable films as *The Man in Grey, We Dive at Dawn, Love Story, The Way to the Stars* etc.

Westerns

The only Westerns I like are when the stars are either James Cagney or Gary Cooper because they put so much life into their parts, e.g. *The Plainsman, The Oklahoma Kid* and *The Westerner.*

Spy Dramas

I like a good Spy Drama and Warner Bros. seem to have turned out some very good ones, E.g. *Casablanca, Conspirators.* English Studios also made a true drama with *The Man From Morocco.*

Gangsters

A good gangster film is always very acceptable to me. The men best at this sort of thing being Edward G. Robinson, Loyd Nolan, Humphry Bogart, and James Cagney and George Raft. These men dynamited films like *Unholy Partners, Big Shot, Jonny Appolo* and *Angels With Dirty Faces* and *Broadway* which I enjoyed imensly.

Horror Macabre and Hokum Thrillers

I enjoy most of these, and I also enjoy the actors who make such films as *Frankenstein, Dracula, Phantom of the Opera, Mumy, Wof Man* and *Mad Doctor of Market Street* complete successes. The men I refer to are Boris Karlof, Bela Lugosi, Claude Rains, Tom Chany Jnr. and Snr. and Lionel Atwill.

Stage Successes

These are really just plays photographed, but being there is no theatre in my town . . . I enjoy such films like *Arsenic and Old Lace, Blithe Spirit, Love on the Dole* and *The Little Foxes* very much.

Tarzan Films

These with Jonny Weismuller are always first rate entertainment for me because being an animal lover animals are so naturally brought to the screen together with exiting jungle adventures.

Animal Films

All animals in films I greatly enjoy, being an animal lover. The Best of these being *Flika, Lassie* and *The Sergent Mike.*

Series

Some series are good. The ones I like best are 'The Andy Hardy Films', *Henry Aldwich* and *Four Daughters* which brings me to

Family Films

These I adore. The best being *Four Daughters, Adam Had Four Sons, Sunday Dinner for a Soldier* and the *Sullivans.*

Classical Films (Musicals)

Being a lover of good music I have enjoyed immensely *Music for Millions, Song of Russia, Thousands Cheer, Phantom of the Opera* and *The Climax* and *The Great Waltz.*

Comedys

Of these I enjoy all the 'Abbot and Costello', 'Bob Hope' and Jimmy Durante and Laurel and Hardy and Alan Carney and Wally Brown. The best of these being *We're in the Army Now, The Big Noise, Chumps at Oxford, Jitterbugs, A Haunting We Will Go, Who Done it, Lost in a Harem* and *Rookies in Burma, Here Come the Waves* and *The Eve of Saint Mark, The Major and the Minor, The Bride Came C.O.D., They Got Me Covered, She Got Her Man* and *Show Business* turned out to be very amusing films.

Entertainment

For good entertainment I enjoy seeing a good old Maria Montey-John Hall-Sabu-extravaganza. I know the critics do not aprove of them, but I do they are so light and enjoyable, and although they have little or no story whatever I enjoy seeing them, because they drive your blues away. The ones I enjoyed most were *Cobra Woman, Gypsy Wildcat, Ali Baba* and *Arabian Nights.*

South Sea Island Films

The technicolour, and music and romance of these films I find delightful so you will not be surprised to find I enjoyed films like *Rainbow Island, Her Jungle Love, Beyond the Blue Horizon, Aloma of the Seven Seas, Hurricane* and *Typhoon.*

Stars in Films

Some stars always give a good performance and sometimes a dull film can be made vastly entertaining for me through the work of Eve Arden, Barbara Stanwyck, Van Heflin, Claude Rains, Joan Fontaine, Claire Trevor, Jack Olay, Ray Milland, Bette Davis, Loyd Nolan, and James Cagney.

Musicals

I am a great lover of musicals. I therefore enjoy nearly everyone but recently I have been dissapointed by two films *Greenwich Village* and *Something for the Boys*. I think they are the only films (Musicals) I have not enjoyed. My favourite musical stars are Carmen Miranda, Alice Faye, Betty Grable, Rita Hayworth, Harry James, June Allyson, Kathine Grayson, Gloria De Haren, Margaret O'Brien and Dorothy Lamour. My favourite musical couples are: Judy Garland and Micky Roony, Nelson Eddy and Jeanette MacDonald, Fred Astaire and Ginger Rogers, Donald O'Conner and Peggy Ryan, who always make a musical very enjoyable for me. My favourite Musicals are: *Here Come the Waves, Hello Frisco Hello, Lilian Russell, Patrick the Great, The Merry Monohons, Chip of the Old Block, Irish Eyes Are Smiling, Bathing Beauty, Two Girls and a Sailor, Music for Millions, Coney Island, Song of the Islands, Dixie, Bowry to Broadway, Song of the Open Road, Show Business, Moon Over Miami, Alexanders Ragtime Band, Thank Your Lucky Stars, Cover Girl.*

Murders

I enjoy a good novel murder, the ones that I have enjoyed most being the *Thin Man, Sherlock Holmes* and *Falcon* series. Recently I have enjoyed three extremely good murders. These were *Laura, Double Indemnity* and *Phantom Lady, The Suspect* being a close runner up also *The Woman in the Window.*

Best Sellers

These are generally adopted well to the screen. Some good examples being *For Whom the Bell Tolls, Gone With the Wind* and *Hatters Castle* and *The Citadal*. Some poorer examples being *The Constant Nymph* and *To Have and Have Not* and *Fanny by Gaslight.*

Adventures

Errol Flyn seems to be best at this sort of thing and I have greatly enjoyed *Robin Hood, Dodge City, Northern Pursuit, Uncertain Glory* and *Edge of Darkness*. Douglas Fairbanks Snr. and Jnr. and Tyrone Power are also very good at this.

Biographys

I greatly enjoy a good biography. Two of the best recently being Chopin *A Song to Remember* and *The Adventures of Mark Twain* which were superbibly acted by Conel Wilde and Frederick March.

Films I Have Disliked

Most of these have been second features, which I think should be abolished, they are so poor.

The East Side Kids series because their morals are bad.

The Blondie series because they are plain stupid and too crazy to laugh at.

Jonny Mack Brown westerns because the story is the same over and over again.

Anne Miller musicals because they have no story or sense whatsoever.

George Formby, Arthur Asky, Happidrome comedys because they somehow do not catch on the screen.

Silly Bedroom Farces and Slapstick affairs such as *Three's a Family, Up in Mabel's Room, The Beautiful Cheat* and *The Doughgirls* and *Kismet.*

Grim war dramas because they are too realistic and you can see them every time you go to the cinema on the newsreel e.g. *Purple Heart, Story of Dr. Wassal, Gualdalcanal Diary,* all of which were very good films, but not to my mind good entertainment.

Two schoolgirls of fifteen appear to have very different impressions. The first, No. 6a, clearly is a frequent visitor to the cinema and dislikes principally 'straight' films. No. 7a writes an extraordinary document, in which a small number of 'straight' films are commented upon favourably and at length, but which ends up with one solitary sentence devoted to the type of film she likes *best*—the 'American song and dance film, and . . . Betty Grable's films most of all'.

NO. 6A

AGE: 15
SEX: F.
OCCUPATION: SCHOOLGIRL
NATIONALITY: BRITISH

FATHER'S OCCUPATION: ACCOUNTANT
MOTHER'S OCCUPATION: HOUSEWIFE

I'm afraid I have rather a wide range of likes and dislikes especially likes, but as you asked for them here goes.

I like musicals especially those in technicolour, I like them better still if they have dancing in them (e.g. *Cover Girl* and *Tonight and Everynight*). I like them because they make you feel light-hearted and I may add, ambitious. You can settle down to them after a hard days work without having to remember a very intricate plot.

I also like films in which classical music is featured (e.g. *Song of Russia, Music for Millions, A Song to Remember*) and which have a good, but light story running through them.

I like light love stories of all sorts, especially if they have a bit of the war in them. I liked *Dragon Seed* because it was so simple, not all glamour (glamour is all right in the right place). It made me feel as though it was really happening instead of having the feeling that it

was only a film after all and could not possibly happen in real life.
And then I like adventure films of sea land and air, esp. about the
air. *Winged Victory* I thought was very good and *Thirty Seconds Over
Tokyo* impressed me very much, I suppose there was some glamour
in it, but it did not strike me as being there. It seemed to be so simple,
just routine as anyone would come up against. *The Black Swan* I liked
because of the adventure, and because of the romance which was not
too piled on. I liked *In Our Time* because it was exciting and different,
and because, this I must add, the acting was superb.

I don't like dull films. To take one example—*None But The Lonely
Heart*. This film was all in the dark it was very morbid. Anyone who
felt rather fed up and went to see this film would feel twenty times
worse. The weather never changed in the film—any American seeing
this film would think that the sun never shined in London.

And then in this film, as in others, there were Americans trying to
imitate the English and I must say, very badly. Half the dialogue
was in Yankee twang and half in what was supposed to be a Cockney
Accent, though I for one would not have recognised it if I had not
known the story to be taking place in London.

Another great dislike of mine is funny films, such as are made by
Laurel and Hardy, the three stooges, Flanagan & Allen, etc. The
Blondie and Henry films I think are a scream, but when it comes to
ridiculous antics performed by grown men I think it is absolutely
unnecessary.

I don't like sloppy, piled on love stories, though we rarely get
these now.

Perhaps if I add a list of likes and dislikes it will help.

Likes
*Desert Song. Can't Help Singing. Keys of the Kingdom. This is the Army.
A Song to Remember. A Place of One's Own. Meet Me in St. Louis. Dragon
Seed. Love Story. Fanny by Gaslight. Music for Millions. Madonna of the
Seven Moons. In Our Time. Song of Russia. East Side of Heaven. Dixie.
Thirty Seconds Over Tokyo. Flight Lieutenant. Winged Victory. Since You
Went Away.*

Dislikes
*None But the Lonely Heart. Arsenic and Old Lace. Storm Over Lisbon. The
Magnificent Ambersons. Mrs. Parkington. Rose of Tralee. Between Two
Worlds.*

So you see my number of likes, greatly outnumber my dislikes.

NO. 7A

AGE: 15 YEARS 3 WEEKS   FATHER'S OCCUPATION:
SEX: F.   SCHOOLMASTER
OCCUPATION: SCHOOLGIRL   MOTHER'S OCCUPATION:
NATIONALITY: BRITISH   HOUSEWIFE

I liked *A Place of One's Own* very much ideed. It was an original
story and well acted by James Mason, Margaret Lockwood and
Barbara Mullen.

As I rather like James Mason as a dashing young man, I had my doubts at first as to whether I should like him as an elderly, retired, Yorkshire draper, but when I saw him as such, I liked him tremendously. He was such a kindly old gentleman and was quite willing to please everybody—so long as he was not put out too much himself.

Barbara Mullen made a very sweet little woman who had no children, but longed for someone to love and care for.

I thought Margaret Lockwood filled this part very well and made a very charming young companion.

I think, though, that the police found the mysterious doctor rather too quickly, and if he was dead when he arrived at the house he need not have rung the bell and waited to be let in. I think he could have walked straight in and have been found going up the stairs. The master of the house would have thought that the maid had let him in, and the maid thought the master or mistress had done so.

Blithe Spirit was another film which I enjoyed seeing. It was extremely well done and was very funny indeed. I thought Margaret Rutherford gave a superb performance as the eccentric old Medium. The part of Elvira was very well done, especially when she was so absolutely bored with the comical antics of the old Medium who was trying to get her back again. Elvira's Americanisms, I thought, made her seem funnier than ever among the English people and the typically English surroundings. This film is one of the best I have ever seen.

This Happy Breed was quite good, though I did not like it nearly so well as the others. It was so ordinary and so natural that it seemed a little odd. It was well acted, but at times it was so painfully slow, that I could have got up and screamed.

Way to the Stars was another good film which I enjoyed very much. I think John Mills played his part very well, (he is one of our finest actors), but he always looks either worried to death or else greatly relieved over something. Rosamund John was ideal for the part of 'Toddy', and played it very well. Douglas Montgomery was very good as Johnny, but I do not see why he had to die at the end. It seemed entirely unnecessary and did not help the plot at all.

Another film which I saw recently was *Czarina* with Tallulah Bankhead, William Eythe and Anne Baxter. The film was very fine and the costumes were gorgeous, but some of the language was modern American slang, which I am sure they did not use. Tallulah Bankhead was just the right actress for the part and her acting was fine, but at times her speech was so slangy it was hard to believe she was supposed to be a Czarina. Otherwise this was a good film.

Tarzan films I do not care for. I don't like all the fighting and killing, the wild beasts and all the horrible jungle creatures which are always ready to kill someone. The one thing I do like in these films is Cheeta, the chimpanze. I think he is a wonderful little creature and can always be relied on for an amusing scene.

The type of film I like best is the American song and dance film, and I like Betty Grable's films most of all.

Three sixteen-year-old girls, all out at work, contribute documents which contrast most strikingly with some of those in our first series. Here are no escapists losing themselves in the films they see, but three writers who continue the strain of realism notable in Nos. 2a, 4a, 6a and 7a. No. 8a prefers British to American films because they are 'more real', went twice to see *Millions Like Us*, and dislikes shooting and the taming of wild horses and jazz bands—'Some folks would sooner have that kind of music, but I would rather have just plain ordinary music played on a brass band in the local park'. No. 9a likes two films which 'told the story of a very ordinary group of people' and contrasts English films with American films which 'are so realistic in parts that certain members of the audience will apply the most fantastic incidents into their own lives. They then imagine themselves all sorts of characters in fiction.' There is more than a breath of morality in the contributions of these young writers. No. 5a, it will be remembered, could stomach *Dracula* but dislike the East Side Kids 'because their morals are bad'. No. 9a rejects heroines 'who are almost always the type of woman seen pacing either Piccadilly in London or Lime Street in Liverpool'. No. 10a is an even more devoted adherent of realism than the other young writers, and is one of the few contributors who mention documentaries.

NO. 8A

AGE: 16   FATHER'S OCCUPATION :
SEX: F.   UNSKILLED PAINTER
OCCUPATION: PRODUCTION CLERK   MOTHER'S OCCUPATION :
NATIONALITY: BRITISH   HOUSEWIFE

This subject interests me immensley for I am a very keen reader of the *Picturegoer* and I visit the picture houses regularly.

The films I like best are the musical ones, not the Jazzy type as the American night club chorus girls. But the ones where you see a good story and sensible music and singing. I have one favourite star which in my opinion is always the top in these sort of films, she is Deanna Durbin. Although of my early age, when she was discovered my family have always took me to see her films. And so I have seen all her films up to the present date. I always enjoy her pictures although she is not as popular now as she was in her younger days. Their is one film I shall always remember her in, because I like it the best, it is *First Love*, I think she sang beautifully in this picture. Other pictures I enjoyed seen her in are *That Certain Age*, *It's a Date*, *Nice Girl* and *Hers to Mould*. Her latest picture *Can't Help Singing* has just been to

... and I was sorry to see she was a blonde in it. Since then she has made another picture called *Lady on a Train* it seems that it's going to be like *Christmas Holiday* but I shan't mind for I liked it.

Then comes other musical ones like *The Climax* where Susanna Foster sang her way to stardom and Boris Karloff supplied the mystery parts. The later re-issue of *The Desert Song* where Dennis Morgan and Irene Manning sang charmingly together. Any film which contains songs I like.

I also like serious music which is featured in films. I thoroughly enjoyed *A Song to Remember* where Paul Muni gave a splendid performance of Professor Ebner and Cornel Wilde was good as the great composer Chopin. The life story of Handel was also very good, and an excellent title for the film was *The Great Mr. Handel*. I also enjoyed *Dangerous Moonlight* where the Warsaw Concerto was played beautifully.

My next choice after musical films is Dramatic films. I would sooner have the British ones not American. I think the British pictures are more real to one who is British. I have three favourite stars in British pictures they are Phyliss Calvert, Patricia Roc and Margaret Lockwood, these three in my opinion can come up to any Hollywood film star either for looks or acting. I first liked Phyliss Calvert when I saw her in *The Man in Grey* which made James Mason a very popular star. *Fanny By Gaslight* was just as good although they banned it in America. But the best film I have ever seen her in is *Madonna of the Seven Moons* this was a marvellos film, and the acting of Phyllis Calvert and Patricia Roc was great.

Millions Like Us was a typical English Picture where Patricia Roc was just a home girl who stayed at home to look after her father, and was so upset because she had to go and work in a factory. And leave her father all alone. But she fell in love with Gordon Jackson a very shy air gunner in the R.A.F. She married him but was soon left a war widow. Pictures like these are something what happens everyday to some-one. In this picture Eric Portman made a good foreman in the factory. Anne Crawford was the gay and giddy type who thought she could put Eric Portman where she wanted him. I went to see this picture twice because I liked it so much.

Margaret Lockwood gives us a wonderful performance in *Love Story* where she was a pianist suffering through heart trouble and not much longer to live but this didn't prevent her from falling in love with Stewart Granger a discharged airman who was slowly going blind. It was a very interesting story, because neither of them knew about each others illness till rather late in the picture. The 'Cornish Rhapsody' played in this film was wonderfully played on the piano (I do not know who played it, but Margaret Lockwood did the finger work very well.)

Those are the films I like, and now for the films I don't like.

There does not seem to be many pictures that I really dislike, becuase when I see the actors or actress in a film, and I like them I go and see the picture and then I know weather I like it or not. I could tell you quite a few like that. But you want to know what I really dislike.

Well the jazzy pictures seem to be the ones. Where someone is blowing a trumpet and making such a racket, folks are listen so intently on the screen, and I'm bored to death with it. Betty Grable seem to be the film star I cannot bear, and I think her pictures are awful, I have only seen one of them but that was enough. I don't like pictures with more than one band in. Because I think these pictures have no story to them or at least not much. Such films like *Stage Door Canteen* and *Hollywood Canteen* I did really enjoy, their songs that were songs and were well sung but the rest—I just hate to tell you what I thought when some of the bands started playing what *they* called dance music. Some folk would sooner have that kind of music, but I would rather have just plain ordinary music played on a brass band in the local park.

Besides the jazzy pictures that I don't like I have another kind that I cannot stand they are cowboy pictures of course, not many comes nowadays but when I was small quite a few was shown. Of course I like Roy Rodgers when he starts singing. But when they start shooting and taming wild horses. Thats where I go out. I think those are the films I dislike I hope I have given you the reasons you prefer.

NO. 9A

AGE: 16

SEX: F.

OCCUPATION: CLERK

NATIONALITY: BRITISH

FATHER'S OCCUPATION: SHIPPING CLERK

MOTHER'S OCCUPATION: STAFF NURSE

I like best a film which tells a story. Preferably a story with a happy ending. As much as possible I like to live the story with its heroine, without the necessity of using a large amount of imagination.

Usually I dislike films about war, or propaganda films of any discription. However, I enjoyed very much the films, *The Seventh Cross*, featuring Signe Hasso and Spencer Tracy, and *Dragon Seed*, starring Katherine Hepburn. In both these films the leading actors were ably supported by the remainder of the cast. Both films told the story of a very ordinary group of people. They were not dazzingly good or outragiously bad folk. They managed to strike a happy medium. They were not dare-devil in their courage. They portrayed plain, humanity. The lines:—

'Courage isn't a dazzling light,
That flashes and passes away from sight,
It's a slow, unwavering, ingrained trait
With the patience to work and the strength to wait.'

might have been written for characters of the type shown in these films. They were folk who disliked rotteness in any shape or form, so that when they came up against it, they fought it. Quietly, unassumingly but effectively.

In contrast to these was the more recent *Tomorrow the World* with Skippy Homeir. In my estimation this film was an insult to adult intelligence. Why the critics praised such a film is beyond my imagination. Skippy played the part of a twelve year old Hitler-youth. His performance was superb. This boy was a liar, thief and even murderer. But, one was expected to believe that his character was made so because he was under the influence of a certain political party, whilst normally, he was a healthy, honest, respectable boy. Added to this there was a scene which made me smile! We were shown a scene in which the head-mistress of Skippy's future school was interviewing him, in her study. On being questioned about his studies in Germany the youth reeled off a number of advanced subjects (I can't recall what they were) which a man in his 'twenties' might study in England. Later, when taking his leave of the head-mistress, the boy was informed that he would join his cousin's grade.

Then we were shown a form-room scene. Did you notice what was written on the black-board? I did. It was the metric system. In a later form-room scene the board showed that the students were learning division sums of a simple nature. In both cases the Arithmetic was a grade which I was taught when I was eight years old. What this twelve year old Hitler youth learned from such a lesson after the education he had received in Germany is beyond me.

This is only one film but there are many similarly stupid ones made.

I enjoyed *Music for Millions*, *The Sullivans*, and *And Now Tomorrow* for their entertainment value only. I hope more films of this type will be made.

I dislike intensely films like *Frenchman's Creek* and *Coney Island*. These heroines are almost always the type of woman seen pacing either Piccadilly in London or Lime Street in Liverpool. I imagine these films please only the unintelligent. I may be wrong!

I like such films as *Wilson* and *Keys of the Kingdom* because they blend entertainment with education to a certain extent. I believe it is a good method of acquainting the public with great men and good literature. It is only since such books as *Henry V*, *Rebecca*, *Pygmalion* and *Jane Eyre* were filmed that the majority of people are learning to discriminate a good story and a trashy one.

I have tried to give a concise reason for liking or disliking certain films through the medium of examples. Most of the examples are films made in America, featuring American actors and portraying American life. Now British films.

I go to see all British films with the exception of those made by George Formby. I have seen two of his films and they will last my lifetime!

I think English films are 100 per cent. entertainment. Whilst in the cinema every incident might have happened to any member of the audience, each happening is so realistic. Once outside the cinema one can return to grim reality and realize that the film was a fairy-tale. A great many American films are so realistic in parts that certain members of the audience will apply the most fantastic incidents into their own lives. They then imagine themselves all sorts of characters in fiction. One has only to stand in any London tube to see the number of girls who imagine themselves a second Veronica Lake or Ginger Rogers or even Lauren Bacall! Possibly Hollywood trades on this susceptibility but I doubt if much is really gained from it.

Two films I shall never forget are *In Which We Serve* and *The Way Ahead*. The glimpses of home life were suptly real without any decoration. Also each character was a true soldier in his own line of warfare. They even managed to convey that 'They also serve, who only stand and wait'.

It is a pity that so few British films are made and that so many British film stars are under contract to American film studios.

NO. 10A

AGE: 16

SEX: F.

OCCUPATION: JUNIOR ASSISTANT IN ACCOUNTS OFFICE

NATIONALITY: BRITISH

FATHER'S OCCUPATION: LITHOGRAPHER

MOTHER'S OCCUPATION: —

As I am very interested in acting I am what people call a 'regular filmgoer'. I like comparing British and American films because I am one of the many filmgoers who have great confidence in the success of British Studios and the films which they produce.

I have been very annoyed at the way in which British films have been treated in America—even our great films such as *The Way Ahead* and many others. Some people may argue that the American way of life is so different from ours that they do not understand our films— then, why do we accept their films and acknowledge the good ones— in spite of the difference in our ways of life. No, that is no excuse! Both American and British audiences should want to see each others way of life and so there would be greater understanding between the two countries.

But I certainly do not think that some of the American musicals which are shown in this country, help to promote better understanding. I dislike the Betty Grable musicals that seem to rely on legs, scanty clothes and beautiful girls for their popularity. I admit that these kind of films are good entertainment value for a certain type of filmgoer but, in my opinion only about ten per cent of the stars in these films have any acting ability. But I do not finish here because I realize that this ten per cent of the 'musical stars' often have great acting ability besides their art of singing or dancing. Ginger Rogers and Rita Hayworth are, to me, two of these outstanding personalities—they can act as well as dance and so their films are very enjoyable. I do wish though that American producers would use their discrimination about putting certain stars in certain films. If a man or woman is a very popular singer, dancer or skater, why try to make them into actors? I know that we like to see these people on the screen but surely men and women with greater acting could be left to do the acting. A scene could be woven into the story in which the hero or heroine could go to see Sonja Henie or hear Frank Sinatra and we, also, could enjoy watching them without cringing at their acting. They could be their natural selves and feel happy in the knowledge that they are capable of doing their scenes.

I feel that another fault of American films is to try and glamourize America and her people too much. They try to show you America through rose-coloured spectacles and many people fall for this but I feel that this is wrong. By all means let us see the American way of life and their houses but let us also see the poorer classes conditions and not just the mansions and hotels. When I am watching some of these films it is very hard for me to enjoy them properly because I am continually thinking—'This cannot be true!' and 'That couldn't possibly happen!'

By this time I will have given the impression that I am prejudiced against American films but this is not the case. It is true that I appreciate and can understand British films better—understand—surely that is the root of the matter. British producers and script-writers give us stories that can be believed and they appreciate the cinema audiences' sense of values and intelligence. But, in saying this I do not mean that our studios have no failures—most certainly not. One kind of film that I dislike is the reproduction of the old Music Halls and life at that time. If we have to be given the Music Halls and the life-stories of the stars in that period let us be given them as they were. In most of these films the Music Hall is generally modernized to suit the modern cinema audiences. After all, Music Hall is an entertainment on its own and I do not think that it should be reproduced in this way.

My next remark is a complaint rather than a dislike and it applies to every country that produces films. Why are we given films that have been based on famous books only to find that often the story has been altered beyond recognition. Have the producers no feelings for the authors and the public? We read of a film coming—based on a book that we have thoroughly enjoyed—perhaps our favourite book —only to find, when the film eventually arrives, that we hardly recognize it! I think that this is unforgivable!

I am thankful though that I can thank America for one exception of what I have just said. The acting and production of *Jane Eyre*—my favourite book—was wonderful. I was very grateful that the story was left as Charlotte Bronte wrote it. Oh, and another instance is *David Copperfield*. My memories of this film, which I saw a long time ago, helped me greatly, when studying the book for School Certificate.

And now, I come to the films that I enjoy most of all. I think that first in my list would come the life-stories of great men and women—

if they are not altered to suit the actors or directors. Several examples come to my mind as I think of this kind of film. The foremost is I think—*Wilson*—not only because it is the most recent film that I have seen but because America has given us a true life story of this great man and also, a great actor—Alexander Knox—has been given a wonderful chance to show his ability. Although this film contained a great deal of propaganda we British can understand how proud America must feel to have had a man like Wilson for their President. I am certain that this film will promote greater understanding between America and Britain and it has shown us, the younger generation, that men had ideals of a World Peace long before we were born and it is up to us to try and win that peace. This sort of film leaves me with an unexpressable feeling—a kind of 'good' feeling—a feeling that a great man relied on us, the future generation, to carry on his fight and to win it.

Britain has also given us such films as *Victoria the Great* and *The Younger Mr. Pitt* which make the History Books seem much more interesting and alive. I have often seen a film of a certain person's life and then found a book on that subject and thoroughly enjoyed that book which might otherwise have been very uninteresting—just because, in my minds eye, as I am reading, I have a picture of that person and the surroundings in which they lived.

But, also, just as I like reading novels I like to see films that I know are not true stories of any persons life. I particularly enjoy a strongly dramatic film, which could possibly refer to any person in the world. In these films the essential points are a good story and brilliant acting and we do not always get this but in many cases we do. I think of *Dark Victory* with Bette Davis' wonderful acting, and *The Man in Grey* and, more recently, *They Were Sisters* and *Since You Went Away*. In mentioning these four films I notice that both America and Britain are producing some good dramatic films.

Since You Went Away was exceptional for its variety of moods and atmospheres. After a very sad scene—in which I cried a lot—and rather enjoyed it—came a funny scene or a love scene—which relieved the tension very well. This is good construction—it prepares the audience for the next sad scene—if there is one. I like the love stories in any film to turn out right in the end but if it has been good acting and an interesting story I do not mind if it ends sadly. I dislike films that end happily when I know that really it wouldn't have done in real life. Although *Since You Went Away* was an exceptionally good American film I think that Britain, on the whole, produces better dramatic films.

With such stars as James Mason, Margaret Lockwood, Stewart Granger and Phillys Calvert we have the necessary resources. British producers seem to be particularly good in period films and, at this time in the history of British films, it would be a great pity if America gained the advantage of these stars. Britain must do everything in its power to attract these stars to remain here.

Next on my list of films that I enjoy comes my one weakness— films with my favourite stars in them. Naturally I do my utmost to try and see all their films. This is not very hard as I have only two favourite stars, Joan Fontaine and Eric Portman. I liked Joan Fontaine best in *Jane Eyre*—although she could not rely on looking glamorous she showed how great an actress she is. She can take the part of a girl of fifteen—in *The Constant Nymph*—and yet she can play with equal success, a part like Dona St. Columb, in *Frenchman's Creek*,—that, to me, is great acting. Eric Portman is, I think, one of Britain's greatest actors. His acting is so sincere and natural that one never seems to realize that he is only acting a part.

As I am a pianist and a great lover of music I like to see as many films that include piano playing and classical music as possible. These films are, I think, essential to the music loving public. As tours of famous orchestras are very few and far between it is a great advantage to see and hear them on the screen. I remember two films of this kind which were excellent. The greatest was *Battle for Music*—the story of the struggle of the London Philharmonic Orchestra at the beginning of the War. This film, besides the beauty of the music, and the thrill of seeing the famous conductors, gave me a greater interest in the orchestra itself. A recent film, *A Song to Remember*, gave the life story of Chopin and again, in addition to the beautiful piano-playing it gave me a greater interest in playing Chopins music. I have a great hope that some day very soon British studios will give us films that will be just as good as seeing 'Prom' Concerts in the Albert Hall. It would be a great opportunity to people like myself, who long to see these famous orchestras and conductors but who are only able to listen to them on the wireless.

Next on my list come the great semi-documentary films such as *In Which We Serve* and *The Way Ahead*, in which British studios have been so successful. These films, besides being so interesting to us, will be very valuable in the years to come. They show the true British spirit in the years of war and the type of man against whom we were fighting. I certainly think that these films ought to be preserved for use in future years.

Last, but not least on my list of films that I enjoy are films of life in other countries. I am eagerly awaiting the time when Germany and France begin to produce their own films once again. If these films are well produced it will be much more interesting to see the life in these countries through films, rather than by reading books about them. As it is one of my ambitions to travel and see other countries I enjoy these kind of films very much.

And here ends my list of likes and dislikes in films. I would just like to say that I read all that I can about films and also listen to critics views on them. But I never rely on their advice; some critics often go a little too far. I understand that people who do not read film magazines need some guidance but every person has different tastes and should be allowed to form their own opinions rather than be prejudiced about certain films because they have heard a certain critics views on them. I admit though, that critics can be very helpful—sometimes!

The appreciation of 'realism' is apparent again in Nos. 11a and 12a. Like most of the younger writers, these seventeen-year-olds cite films with a good story as their favourites. The 'modulated colours' of *Henry V* are noted with appreciation, documentaries appear again, while the Betty Grable type of film is regarded as sickening 'because it is so false'. *Tarzan* and 'westerns' are again rejected. No. 11a hopes that 'producers in the future will concentrate more on a good story and script and will shelve their all technicoloured dynamic stupendous productions' and condemns *Mrs Miniver* as 'America's prize misinterpretation of the English home'. Nos. 13a and 14a, a girl and a boy of seventeen, are different from their two contemporaries. The girl, a shop-assistant, chooses adventure romances as her favourites 'because they are romantic, thrilling and very enjoyable'; the boy, who is much closer to the contributors to our first series of documents in this book, likes good lavish musicals which 'make you forget your worries for a couple of hours'. This age-group is not nearly so all-embracing in its tastes as the younger writers. British 'music-hall' films are again condemned, and a 'purely coarse film, *Christmas Holiday*'. The repetition of praise for films including 'good' music is most striking.

NO. 11A

AGE: 17
SEX: F.
OCCUPATION: JUST LEFT SCHOOL,
   PLANS FOR BEING CONTINUITY
   GIRL ON FILMS
NATIONALITY: BRITISH

FATHER'S OCCUPATION:
SOLICITOR
MOTHER'S OCCUPATION :
—

I think the best way is to select the films that I have liked and give my reasons for their appealing to me.
In the first section, *Pride and Prejudice, When Ladies Meet, Dear Octopus, The Prime Minister, Kipps*. These are not war films and have nothing at all to do with war, they vary considerably in plot and I must say that the lighter appeals to me most, that is *Dear Octopus*. It was well acted and produced to the nth degree, and that is usually the case with British films. It had a good plot, I am a great admirer of Dodie Smith's writing so no doubt this added a lot to my pleasure. With *Pride and Prejudice* and *When Ladies Meet*, the acting of Greer Garson, and in the former Laurence Olivier made one ignore any

imperfectudes overseen by the Hollywood Studios. *The Prime Minister* had a great life as a plot, that of Disraeli, John Gielgud and Diana Wynyard headed a strong cast of British actors. With *Kipps* the simplicity of the chief characters endeared me to it and again there were no blemishes neither on the production nor the acting.

Henry V. I must put in a class of its own, never has such a film been made and I do not think it ever will be made by an American studio. The whole idea of commencing in the Globe Theatre and then widening out into the glorious battle of Agincourt was unique. The acting was of the very first class, and although Laurence Olivier was wonderful, Esmond Knight, Robert Newton and etc. were little behind him. The laurels of such a fine production must be bestowed upon Laurence Olivier. A thing which might have spoiled the film for me was the technicolor I was terrified it would blare out as it has always done before, but the modulated colors enhanced the beauty of the Irish (French) hills.

Now for the last but stupendous class, that of films serious or otherwise to do with the war.

The First of the Few, Gentle Sex, In Which We Serve and *The Way Ahead* were fine films, the latter two of which I could see over and over again; chiefly because I think them more polished than the former, also, a great point for me, I liked the actors more.

The Demi Paradise, Millions Like Us, English Without Tears, 2000 *Women, This Happy Breed, Love Story,* I like, mostly for the reason that stars that I liked were in them, Margaret Lockwood, Penelope-Dudly-Ward, Patricia Roc, Phyllis Calvert, Anne Crawford, Celia Johnson, Laurence Olivier, Michael Wilding, James Mc. Kechnic. However it is not only the stars that make a film, Greer Garson and Joan Fontaine are excellent but in every film that I have seen them in there has been some flaw which has jarred me, or the general acting has not been up to their standard. America is inclined to say 'We have a wonderful star, why waste having any more good acting and bothering about finishing the film off—he (or she) will get us our money'. (That at any rate is the way I think they see film industry.)

I left out a film in the first group which I feel needs some mentioning *The Divorce of Lady X* made in 1937 I think this film is typical of those at this time (in Britain) Laurence Olivier, Ralph Richardson, Merle Oberon etc. were all excellent. Although there has been little said about this film I think it ranks with the best-sellers of pre-1937 period.

It is difficult to choose any documentary that I have liked best, I have liked every one that I have seen. *The Battle of Russia* deserves mentioning because it is the longest one that I have ever seen and is really up to the mark continuously.

I have seen a number of foreign films but those which I liked best were *La Marseilleise* (French) and *The Song of Russia* (Russian) both were authentic in their own sphere and carried me away.

Now for the films that I dislike, I can't very well give their titles because I know what I dislike and keep away from them—any American film with either Frank Sinatra or Betty Grable and their like. Any murder. The American film of the Betty Grable type makes me feel really sick chiefly beoause it is so false. Ginger Rogers on the other hand I quite enjoy because she 'looks' nice and *can* act. Murders I dislike because I loathe anything 'creepy' the same with ghost-stories. As for Westerns I wouldn't go near a cinema with one in, so ridiculous people rushing after each other popping guns and throwing cardboard chairs at each other. *Tarzan* and other jungle stories I steer clear from for the reason that again they are so false with colors that make my every nerve want to scream.

Well that is about all and I hope that I have been of some assistance in your research.

NO 12A

AGE: 17   FATHERS' OCCUPATION:
SEX: F.   GLASS MERCHANT
OCCUPATION:
STUDENT INTENDING TO ENTER LIVERPOOL UNIVERSITY
NATIONALITY: BRITISH

As I am interested in the theatre it is only natural that my cinema tastes should be influenced by this. I am not going to bring up the eternal question of cinema versus stage but will merely say that although each medium has its own merits and subjects especially suited to each sphere there are many good plays which can, and have been, turned into films.

I do appreciate a good stage play successfully adapted for the screen. I think Noel Coward's plays are an obvious example. *This Happy Breed* which I enjoyed on the stage, acted by the author, made an equally amusing film with the added attraction of technicolour—more recently too there is *Blithe Spirit*.

It is only just lately that we have seen Shakespeare successfully served up as a palatable and an exceedingly colourful if not dainty dish for cinema audiences to masticate. I refer to Laurence Olivier's production of *Henry V*—a vitally interesting experiment which opens up new hopes for those longing to see Shakespeare appreciated by the masses.

Besides liking adaptions from the stage, to my mind many of the best films in recent years have been those of classics, novels and best sellers. *Wuthering Heights* I consider one of the most outstanding of these. For this film conjured up anew the farouche atmosphere of the bleak Yorkshire moors. Here I must mention background or incidental music, which, when used to its full advantages can be of tremendous importance to the artistry of the film, and can give great pleasure to the audience.

In the case of *Wuthering Heights* the music I believe was written for the film. The music from *Laura* has been popularized—and the *Warsaw Concerto* made the film *Dangerous Moonlight*. *The Great Lie* brought Tchaikovsky's First Pianoforte Concerto to the ears of more people. All these films I liked immensely. But to return to the adaption of the novel, *Pride and Prejudice* was a graceful and artistic film of Jane Austen's classic. In this film the acting of all the characters—both the principle and supporting cast was of the highest order. I think good acting is just as essential on the screen as in the theatre, and am not one of those people who, happily for them, can thrill at a hero registering latent passion by the jerk of an eyebrow whilst the heroine, reclining seductively on a satined divan, gives a flutter of the false eyelashes for encompament. My powers of endurance are positively strained to breaking point when next the audience is treated to a long series of close-ups during which they can almost hear the lovers' hearts palpitating in strict ballroom tempo. I begin to squirm uncomfortably in my seat when the heroine displays her unconditional surrender. All this to the music of tender throbbing guitars—in glorious technicolour—in fact a super colossal production which has a few luscious curves thrown in.

I do not object to the Romance and Glamour if the dancing is good and the musical numbers original and well directed. A case in point if *Cover Girl*.

My pet aversion is the sickly sentimentality of the Oh so prudishly patriotic film. *Mrs Miniver* is the classic example of this—also being America's prize misinterpretation of the English home—in which the ordinary man was raised to the splendour of the aristocracy. The brilliant photography of the rescue at Dunkirk is unforgettable —a most moving spectacle in an otherwise 'phoney' production.

The English film *A Canterbury Tale*—is notable too for its shots of scenic beauty—these I liked very much—and especially those of the cathedral interior.

Since You Went Away like *Mrs. Miniver* had an inspiring theme— this time the homefront—but could it not have been presented in a better way?—With less tea-jerking. The housewife's life has not been all milk and honey but there is surely no need to depress them still further—and to take two hours or so to do it!

Joyfully it seems not too optimistic to hope that the advent of peace will put 'finis' to the exploits of certain heroes who spend their time frollicking through occupied Europe, smashing spy rings, outwitting the entire Gestapo and winning Olga Petrovska, the beautiful spy, as a reward for gallantry.

It is to be hoped that producers in the future will concentrate more on a good story and script and will shelve their all technicoloured dynamic stupendous productions. English films should succeed in foreign markets if they continue to produce films like *In Which We Serve*, *This Happy Breed*—*The Man in Grey*, *Madonna of the seven Moons* and *Demie-Paradise*—all in my opinion first-rate entertainment.

NO, 13A

AGE: 17   PARENTS' OCCUPATION:
SEX: F.   FATHER—ELECTRICIAN
OCCUPATION: SHOP-ASSISTANT   MOTHER:—HOUSEWIFE
NATIONALITY: BRITISH

I read in the *Picturegoer*, of your wanting help on films. Having allways wanted to voice my oppinion, I think this a heaven sent opportunity, so here goes.

Murders will be at the top of my dislikes, I positively loath them. The reason is that once you have seen one, you have seen the lot. All, with few exceptions, are based on two theories, Jealousy and Robbery. Being a girl is another reason, but frankly I find these films dull and uninteresting. If it wasn't for the background music, they would be flat.

War and Revolutionary films come next. The first I recall seeing was, *Hitlers Madman* with John Carradine as Hydrick, it turned me off them all. I just don't like them, they show deliberate killing and most of them are propaganda. Here I make two exceptions, first Documentary films such as *Target for Tonight*, *The Memphis Belle* and *The Fighting Lady* I find these very interesting, and as there is only one commentator you can concentrate better. The second exception are The Gaumont British, Universal and Pathe Gazette News reels. We know these are filmed on the battlefields, but we don't know where the others have been filmed, more than probable they dont know what a battlefield looks like.

Jazz and Swing films are my last dislike, and I do hate these. I can't find a bad word to describe them, they play the same monotonous and tuneless music (row) over and over again. I don't think they are nice to listen to at all.

Now for my likes :—

Adventure Romances will allways be my favourites, I like them because they are romantic, thrilling and very enjoyable. Since seeing *The Black Swan* and *Frenchmans Creek*, I love them all the more, and being in Technicolor adds more to the fascination. Of course the acting of the Stars has a lot to do with it. In the latter film, Joan Fontain's portrayal of the neglected wife and mother was sincerely and beautifully done. Also very good were, Arturo de Cordova, Basil Rathbone and Cecil Kellaway. I do hope there will be more of this type.

Romances come second with me, just ordinary ones like *Pride and Prejudice* and *Love Story*. The reason I liked *Love Story* was because it was sincere, the scenery lovely (filmed in Cornwall) and the music perfect. It also helped to admire Margaret Lockwoods performance of a good girl, as much as I like her bad girl parts.

In my oppinion British Romances are more noteable than American ones. I am not saying Hollywood hasn't made any good ones, because they have. Look at M.G.M., Garson—Pidgeon films, they are a great success, so successful that Greer Garson has won the Gold Medal award three times.

Musical films come next, such as *Cover Girl* and *The Great Waltz*. We could do with more of these. Here my reason is that they are pure entertainment, nothing more, and the music is *not* jazz. The latter film being the life and music of Johann Strauss. I really enjoyed this film especially the music. Thats mainly my reason for liking it, but there was a good biography of Strauss behing it. Here again I hope there will be more of these, especially my favourite composer, Tchaikovsky.

Comedies, are my last likes. Abbott and Costello being the best. I have seen all their films, and I wouldnt have missed them. My reason, well they keep you laughing or smiling all the way through their films. You come out of the cinema much more happier than when you went in. I know I do. I think their best was *Hold That Ghost*, and can truthfully say my sides ached for hours after I had seen it. As there havn't been any in town for some time, I am looking foreward to their next lot of films.

NO. 14A

AGE: 17
SEX: M.
OCCUPATION: ——
NATIONALITY: BRITISH

PARENTS' OCCUPATION:
FATHER—MANAGER OF A FOOTBALL
CLUB
MOTHER—HOUSEWIFE (W.V.S.)

In answer to your article in *Picturegoer* which I have had fortnightly throughout the war, I have decided to try for the 'reply' to your most interesting 'question'.

First of all I must say that I am a thorough 'film fan' and see an average of 260 films a year. My range of likes and dislikes in films is very wide. I will endevour to explain these to you. Although the war is now over I must say I have enjoyed immensly all the 'war' films Warner Bros. have turned out. Examples of these are *The Mask of Dimetrious*; *The Conspirators*; *Hotel Berlin* (an excellent film), *To Have and Have Not* and *Passage to Marseilles*. These pictures are definate. They give you something to think about. I also like a good lavish musical. They make you forget your worries for a couple of hours. Examples *Hollywood Canteen*, *Something For the Boys*; *Tonight and Every Night*; *Cover Girl*; *Bathing Beauty*. These films put one in a good humour. Otherwise a good comedy is always acceptable such as: *Without Love*, *Here Come the Co-eds*, *Arsenic and Old Lace* (a brilliant example). I don't mind a love story or a thriller now and again. For the former *Love Story*, *The Very Thought of You*, *Under The Clock*, *Now Voyager*. And the latter *The Unseen*, *A Place of Ones Own*, *Dark Waters*, *The Murder in Thornton Square*. A film that strongly appealed to me was *Laura*. This had a little of everything, as did *Keys of the Kingdom*. I think these can best be described as films that *appeal* to you, as do *Experiment Perilous* and *The Woman in the Window*.

For an example of 'different' films we have:—*Since you went Away* or *The Constant Nymph* or *Guest in the House* or *Strangers in the Night*. Mind you *Madonna of the Seven Moons* and *They were Sisters* were typical examples of films with good solid foundations; a background to work upon. The best 'sea' films I ever saw were *Action in the North Atlantic*, *Lifeboat* and *Western Approaches*.

The type of film I do not like (In other words my 'Dislikes') are: *None but the Lonely Heart*, I like good acting and can appreciate it when I see it but not morbidity in its worst degree. The same with *Mrs. Parkington*. This just went on and on, as did *Champagne Charlie*. Another bitter disappointment was *Casanova Brown* which was just plain silly and stupid. For an actor like Gary Cooper can surely do better than that. The same applies to *Knicker-Bocker Holiday*. It was not up to the mark. *Kismet* was an utter bore. For a purely *coarse* film *Christmas Holiday* took the cake. I can't see why producers and Directors, carry on with films they know wont appeal to their public. Everybody to their own taste I know, but surely give us some taste!!! No, for grand entertainment: *Wilson*, *Frenchmans Creek*, *The Enchanted Cottage*, *An American Romance* and *The Climax* every time.

The 18-year-old group begins to move away from the objective approach noticed in the preceding documents. It is true that No. 15a looks for 'something that might happen in real life', while No. 16a praises British films for their 'atmosphere of realness', but an echo of the earlier series is noticeable in the statement 'The only reason I would go to a musical would be to study the actresses' hair styles and dress'. No. 17a is so much addicted to Mr Granger that she cries on returning home after having seen one of his films, while No. 18a, who has been a movie fan since he was five, writes 'I like going to the movies because I like glamour'. It is not unexpected that he should write so much in terms of the 'stars'.

NO. 15A

AGE: 18
SEX: F.
OCCUPATION: G.P.O. EMPLOYEE
NATIONALITY: BRITISH

PARENTS' OCCUPATION:
FATHER—SOLDIER
MOTHER—HOUSEWIFE

When I go to the cinema, I go to be entertained, and having seen the film I like to feel convinced, and satisfied with my entertainment. I enjoy quite a few types of films but in nine cases out of ten the draw is the star in the film. The sort of film I like best has plenty of outdoor scenes, and children. Always, I look for a sense of freedom in a film, something refreshing, something that really might happen in real life. Children too, seem to be the embodiment of freedom and happiness. One of the most refreshing, charming, film I have ever seen was *Sunday Dinner for a Soldier*. Here the children, the elder sister, the grandfather, the animals, the houseboat all seemed so real, and their experiences might happen to anybody. For that reason too I enjoyed *National Velvet* and the beautiful refreshing scenes shot by the sea.

On the more serious side I like a good film taken from a novel whether modern or old but to convince me the acting must be at a very high standard. Here, the stars attract me, Bette Davis, Ida Lupino, Joan Fontaine, Ingrid Bergmann; and as I watch them I think how wonderful it must be and how satisfying to them to be able to act like that. What an achievement to really be able to convince the audience that you are happy, sad, indifferent, cruel, etc. I like a film of a serious nature to have an unhappy ending although I can never remember crying in a cinema if the hero or heroine died.

Then too, I like a film in which one scene stands out above all others so that I remember it for a long time afterwards, such as King Henry wooing the French Princess in *Henry V*, the duel scene in *The Life and Death of Colonel Blimp*, of Agnes Morrcheat's performance in *The Magnificent Ambersons*. I find great pleasure in thinking back over them.

I like a comedy but it must be very clever and fast and funny so that I can laugh all the time. It must also have a great many surprises in it. I like some films with classical music running through them. Especially I enjoyed *Song of Russia* because of Tchaikowsky's beautiful music. I think that his music is more beautiful than any other composer's.

Lastly I like travel films because I can learn something from them about other countries. Although I should like to travel all over the world, I shall never be able to, and through seeing films about other lands, this makes up a little for not being able to go, (but only a very little I'm afraid).

The films I dislike most are modern musicals and also the 'gay nineties' type. The acting is generally very bad, the plot is repeated again and again, and after a day I have forgotten all about the film. The only reason I would go to a musical would be to study the actresses' hair styles and dress. Very sentimental films tend to depress and even sicken me. The players never win my sympathy in the slightest.

I do not like American films with scenes set in England because they are always inaccurate. England looks in these films Hollywood would like her to look. This annoys me very much.

I do not like seeing films taken from novels I have read as they are nearly always chopped about beyond recognition and if I was the unfortunate authoress of a book that had been hacked about I should feel like weeping with shame when I saw my book filmed.

I do not like crime films, thrillers, or murders, as I find myself imagining all sorts of horrible things when I am alone in the house or walking in the dark at night for a time after I have seen them.

Lastly, I am hoping that I shall never see a war film or an 'underground army' type of film as long as I live. I want to forget all about war and try to help peace in this poor old world of ours for ever.

NO. 16A

AGE: 18
SEX: F.
OCCUPATION: TEXTILE WORKER
NATIONALITY: BRITISH

PARENTS' OCCUPATION:
FATHER—BOOT AND SHOE REPAIRER
MOTHER—TEXTILE WORKER BEFORE MARRIAGE

You ask for personal likes and dislikes in films, and reasons for such. Here's mine:—

I like period films of both the musical and straight types—particularly *Jane Eyre*, *Pride and Prejudice*, *Barrets of Wimpole Street*, *Wuthering Heights* and *Gone With the Wind*, of the straight type. I think I like period pictures because there are usually the best actors and actresses in them, and so almost always good, also the dress gives them, in my opinion, a 'certain something' that modern dress simply cannot.

The same goes practically for old-time musicals, with the exception that what is lost in the acting and story the music makes up for. Yes, I certainly like old fashioned films. British musicals are coming into their own, *Champagne Charlie* compares favourably with any musical Hollywood has produced yet. Another old-time British musical which I enjoyed, but didn't get much mention was *Variety Jubilee*. To me it was far more like what I think an old-time musical ought be, than say *Coney Island*, and the story a dozen times better. I don't think I shall be disapointed with *I'll be your Sweetheart* and *Waltz Time* either.

I do not like Eastern and tropical films, most of them at least, *Tarzan* may be a possible exception, although I wouldn't go out of my way to see *them*. Such films as *Rainbow Island*, *Sudan*, *Kismet*, *Cobra Woman* and *The Thief of Bagdad* are to me just ridiculous, and an insult to our intelligence, but of course that's just my opinion.

I have a great liking for some of the recent British pictures. *Maddonna of the Seven Moons*, *Man in Grey*, *Fanny by Gaslight* and *Love Story* all have received public acclaim, but I've seen *Halfway-House*, *My Ain Folk*, *Kiss the Bride Good-bye*, *Give me the Stars*, *Waterloo Road* and *Twilight Hour*. These films are unpretentious, but they have an atmosphere of realness of England and English life, that Americans cannot get. I think these ought to have more 'fuss' made of them, for at almost everyone of these I've seen, only half of the cinema has been occupied and all deserved a much better audience.

Why, when a good film is made, must another be made on similar lines, and always poor in comparison? Take a film like *Phantom of the Opera* there was a film which, although improbable, could be

(Above) from *A Tree Grows in Brooklyn* and (below) from *Mrs. Miniver*.
Examples of American film 'realism'.

From *The Overlanders.* Swimming the cattle across the Roper River (above)
Daphne Campbell rounding up the stampeding cattle (below).

believed, because of its acting. Then take *The Climax*, such a film I never wish to see again, as if any girl would stand for such treatment as Susanna Forster was supposed to stand for in that film. I know I shouldn't.

It's like a lazy child copying from a hard worker, and then spoiling it.

I like a good comedy, recent ones have been *Up in Arms, See Here! Private Hargrove, Princess and the Pirates* and *San Diego! I love You,—* such comedies as these really take you out ot yourself. All these vary but bring one thing—grand entertainment!

Love stories of which there are numerous good ones I pick out *White Cliffs of Dover, Lady Hamilton* and *Random Harvest* and *Love Story* as the ones I remember best, they are real, not over showy, but films of the sort which are always a success, in that they bring a tear to the eye. I like these sort of pictures but only when, as in these examples, they are so well acted that they are always believed.

Three good British pictures I don't want to forget, are *The Gentle Sex, The Way Ahead* and *This Happy Breed*. The stories and acting in these, has made them unique.

I don't like popular plays, musical comedies, and books, which are turned to films and spoilt. They are either mutilated beyond recognition, or acted badly. *Arsenic and Old Lace* is one of these. After seeing the play, and enjoying it immensly, I looked forward to seeing the film version. But what a disappointment! Instead of the old ladies being 'dotty', Cary Grant made it appear, by his acting alone, that he was more crazy than they, although he was supposed to be the only sane one of the family. Also the story had been altered, and bits added. Why? The play was a success in England and America, and would have been ten times better on the screen had it been left in its original state or had another actor in the main role. The *Desert Song* is another example, and almost always the change is for the worse. I for one wish it stopped. I'm waiting now for the British screen version of *Pink String and Sealing Wax* and I hope it sticks at least a little to the play.

I like films that have most of the action on the sea *Mutiny on the Bounty, China Seas, Reap the Wild Wind, Cargo of Innocents* and *Captain Blood*. They have more adventure and thrills than stories taken on land, and bring a real thrill.

I'm tired of modern musicals with an embarrassing story which makes me want to curl up inside, such films are *Step Lively, Springtime in the Rockies, This is the Army*. The music is enough in itself to entertain, but is spoilt by the poor story. Others are *Best Foot forward* and *Bathing Beauty*.

I like the *Road* films. They provide comedy that is on its own, and I'm looking forward to *Road to Utopia* the latest of the series. Bing Crosby and Bob Hope are the perfect comedy pair.

As a rule I don't like religious films, but *Going My Way* is an exception. The simple character study by Barry Fitzgerald certainly deserved the 'Oscar' it received. And who else but Bing could have portrayed Father O'Malley to such perfection? I should like to see more films like this one, but I hope they won't be poor imitations.

Murders! I don't exactely thrive on these, but a really good murder film never goes amiss with me. I liked *Laura* I think the best of the latest thrillers, because it was unusual. It kept me guessing right up to the end. *The Lodger* I liked because I didn't have to bother wondering who the murderer was, I just had to wonder who the next victim would be. *The Cat and the Canary* combined comedy and thrills to perfection and I certainly enjoyed it, even though it did give me the creeps.

I like films where children have featured parts, such as *Music for the Millions, Journey for Margaret* and *Jane Eyre.* They bring both laughter and tears and hardly ever fail to please. Especially I like films where children and animals are featured together. *My friend Flicka* and *Lassie Come Home* are excellent examples. I don't wish for anything better than these charming films.

Some of the skating pictures I have enjoyed, particularly *Lady, let's Dance* probably because there was more variety in it than in most of this type. I think the skating sequences are too long especially Sonja Henie's films, they tend to become boring after a while.

I don't mind a really good documentary film, as long as propoganda doesn't hit you in the eye all the time. *Western Approaches, Memphis Belle* and *The Fighting Lady* give a true picture of what the fighting forces have had to put up with, and I think its only right we should see a bit of it.

I do not like Preston Sturges films, *The Miracle of Morgan's Creek* was absolutely disgusting, and not in the least funny. *Hail the conquering Hero* is another, whatever entertainment value they have must be beyond me.

The *Thin Man* series—how pleased I was to see that a new one of these had been released.—After having had poor imitations of these for so long, what a relief to see a real one again. Such a detective as Nick Charles as played by William Powell is unrivelled on the stage or screen.

I think every one is tired of underground war films, I certainly am, for however good they may be, they have a similarity that is bound to spoil them, such a one as *Seventh Cross.* Although credit was due to it, for it was excellently acted, you'd seen the invariable chase by Gestapo so often before, that the whole thing seemed familiar, and therefore not entertainment in the form which I like.

Another thing I don't like are the ridiculous 'shorts', such as Edgar Kennedy and *Three Stooges.* Why must an otherwise good programme be spoilt by such as they. They are just too silly to laugh at.

I like Western films, good ones that is, such as *The 'Cisco Kid* and *Jesse James at Bay* to go back a bit. Roy Roger's western musical comedies are very pleasing, and I like them because they are a change from the usual musicals, both in dress, story and music. The straight westerns like the two I mentioned are good entertainment because they hold you, and make you feel you are part of the story with them.

Outdoor films such as *Home in Indiana* and *Tawny Pipit*. These have a freshness that makes me enjoy them. The scenery too is almost always one of the main attractions to me in these films.

I don't think Flanagan and Allen and George Formby films are made enough of. They compare more than favourably with the Abbot and Costello films, as they have more than good comedy,— They can sing pleasing and 'catchy' tunes. And the stories they are in are every bit as good as Abbot and Costello ones. I should like to see more of them and have them more advertised.

Well, I think I've got all my likes and dislikes off my chest, hoping they are of some use to you.

NO. 17A

AGE: 18   FATHER: BANK AGENT
SEX: F.   MOTHER: HOUSEWIFE
OCCUPATION: TAKING UP DRAMATIC ART AND MUSIC
NATIONALITY: BRITISH

I have always found that I do not enjoy a film unless it has a definite story such as you read in a book. When you read a novel you have a picture of the story in your mind. Many films have a weak story, American ones especially. You sit and yawn while some theatre proprieter whose show is not paying, picks up a blonde from the gutter and turns her into a glamour girl overnight, and the company is saved from ruin. All the while a jazz band and drummer, are doing their best either to deafen you, or make you insane. But that is not meant for a slight against Frank Sinatra or Bing Crosby.

The type of film I enjoy most, is that which has a romantic story. If my favourite film star is acting in it, better still. I am very much influenced as to who the actors are. I must confess if I was given the choice of going to a film which was supposed to be very good, or to go to a film with a doubtful story, I would go to the latter if my favourite actor was in it. I can give you an instance of this. I had no idea of what the story of *Madonna of the Seven Moons* would be like, I went to see Stewart Granger alone. Actually I enjoyed the story tremendously, and I was glad that lovely Phylis Calvert was the heroine. But put say Charles Boyer whom I abhor in Stewart Granger's part and I would have felt sick during the love scenes. But when Stewart Granger is kissing the heroine (in any film he has been in), I experience a real thrill. Afterwards however when I come down to earth again, and go home, I feel so terribly lonely. It seems silly, but I cry. If only that could happen to you, something inside me seems to say. I do wish I could find an explanation to that feeling. I try to satisfy if by day dreaming, but it only seems to encourage the lonely sensation. I am an 'only' and just one of my school friends lives in . . . , so perhaps if I knew more people I would have less time to dream.

I like religious films, such as *The Song of Barnadette*. The latter touched me greatly, and it seems strange that I should enjoy a hot blooded love story every bit as well, though in a different way I suppose.

In some ways I enjoy a ghost story, but seeing it filmed, plays havoc with my nerves. After seeing such films as *The Univited, The Unseen, Dead of Night* and such like, I scarcely sleep a wink. I positively hate horror films, I have never had a great liking for screen comedians. I cannot stand Laurel and Hardy for example, though I enjoy George Formby's performances.

I used to be fond of Western and gangster pictures, but I have tired of them. They all seem to run along the same theme. I enjoy a good murder, provided there are no ghosts and it is not too hair raising.

Pictures including good music interest me such as *Song of Russia* and *A Song to Remember*. I like some modern music, the Cornish Rhapsody and the Warsaw Concerto for example.

Technicolour films about animals such as *Son of Flicka* and *Lassie Come Home* I find quite enjoyable, but what honestly thrills me is an interesting intriguing story with a strong love affair. *For Whom the Bell Tolls* is a good example.

On reading this over, I am somewhat disappointed. I have strong likes and dislikes, and I cannot express on paper the wild thrilled feeling that runs through me during a film I am enjoying terrifically, especially during love scenes.

NO. 18A

AGE: 18
SEX: M.
OCCUPATION: EMPLOYEE OF L.M.S. RAILWAY CO.
NATIONALITY: SCOTTISH

I like going to the movies because I like glamour. I wish to be sincere so I will tell you now that I prefer American films to British. The average British film in my opinion is dull, uninteresting lacking the glamour witch is essential to a film. I enjoy musicals like *Meet Me in St. Louis, Cover Girl, Two Girls and a Sailor*. Dramatic films such as *Mrs. Parkington, Now Voyager, Song of Bernadette*, thrillers like *Laura, Dark Waters, Guest In The House*. These are the type of films I like to see. I have been a movie fan since I was five years old. I still enjoy the glorious company of Judy Garland, Bette Davis, Greer Garson, Clark Gable, Rita Hayworth, Ingrid Bergman, Orson Welles, and many of Hollywood's stars to whom I say 'Thanks' for years of fine entertainment.

The same stress on acting and on sincerity, with high praise for British films, runs through the next age-group (six documents). There are references to a 'thinking picture', to 'good, sensible and substantial' German films, to films which 'deal with problem', and to the realism of such films as *The Way to the Stars* and *Waterloo Road*. Even No. 24a, who likes 'musicals' because they 'cheer you up and stop you from feeling so fed up', speaks of 'films that are worth seeing because they nearly always have a good story and the situations that happen in them could happen in any home'.

NO. 19A

AGE: 19   FATHER: EX. ARMY CAPTAIN
SEX: F.   MOTHER: HOUSEWIFE
OCCUPATION: SHORTHAND TYPIST
NATIONALITY: BRITISH

I will deal with the films I like first. I definitely like *The Way to the Stars*. This film was a 'thinking picture' down to earth, dealing with individuals and always in a subtle way 'hitting the nail on the head'. The acting was very good, the scenes well set and the continuity was also very good.

I enjoyed *Frenchman's Creek* immensely. Joan Fontaine was very beautiful and she certainly showed she could act well. The supporting players were very good too—a film whose supporting players act indifferently is doomed from the start. This was a 'meaty' film, with lovely costumes, and beautiful settings.

Madonna of the Seven Moons was another film I shall not forget. Miss Phyllis Calvert acted extremely well as did Miss Jean Kent, and a host of 'bit' players. Here again the continuity was well maintained. The Italian back streets and houses were just as I imagine them to be. Alan Haines, as the young English diplomat, was the only blot on the landscape. I am very fond of *good* stories which deal with the supernatural.

Blithe Spirit was a film I could see many times and still laugh in the same places. Noel Coward is a brilliant writer, and this together with superb acting by all the major characters, good photography and the marvellous make-up of Miss Kay Hammond as the ghostly Elvira, all contributed to make a very good film.

Since you went away is the last on my list of likes (although there are myriads more). This film was well directed, well presented and well acted, with the exception of Miss Shirley Temple who always seemed to either be in the way or to have forgotten how to act. It was a charmingly sentimental film.

Now for my dislikes. It is a long time since I've seen such an awful film as *The very thought of You* starring Dennis Morgan and Eleanor Parker. Hays Office which passed this awful slop should be ashamed of itself. It makes me more than a little disgusted that characters in a film of this calibre are allowed to slobber and sob for an hour or more when one can't even say 'damn' in a war film (something wrong somewhere!).

I was very disappointed with Gary Cooper and Teresa Wright in *Casanover Brown*. How extremely impossible was the burning down of his in-laws' home. No! the actors in this film definitely deserved better material.

I was very disappointed with *I love a soldier* too. Sonny Tufts looks all right on the screen until he opens his mouth and tries to act. I am no 'school-marm'; but really, the story! Paulette Goddard deliberately went out on her own (with the best intentions, of course!) to pick up strange soldiers and give them a good time for one evening—huh!!! The story seemed to have made itself up as it went along.

On this dismal note I have come to the end of my praises and condemnations.

I apologise for putting the word 'Miss' in front of some actresses' names and not before others—this is entirely unintentional—I am never quite sure when one *does* put 'Miss' or 'Mister' before players' names and when one does not.

NO. 20A

AGE: 19   FATHER: BAKER
SEX: F.   MOTHER: HOUSEWIFE
OCCUPATION: PRINT MACHINE OPERATOR
NATIONALITY: BRITISH

Now you have all the particulars required here are my views on films.

The films I seem to enjoy most are those with either a bit of everything in or one that is dead serious such as *Jane Eyre*. I say the above mentioned film twice and I could easily sit through another show. I liked that particular film because the director seemed to get everything just right, every scene had its equal amount of sorrow, pity and dry humour. The acting of the two children, and Joan Fontaine and Orson Welles was brilliant and they all seemed the right people for the part.

Another film I liked very much and once more saw twice was, *When Irish Eyes are Smiling*. Its just the opposite from the last film I mentioned but it was really enjoyable. Monty Woolley made the film seem witty, Dick Hayes gave out well with his singing and June Haver supplied plenty of the glamour needed for its colourful background. The story was reasonable and not drawn out too much.

The films I dislike are cowboy films. As soon as you see one of the gangsters getting away on his horse you know that the hero will go after him and either lasso him or have a good fight; whenever that part of the film comes round I feel like walking out.

Another film I dislike are the usual smart detective films such as *The Saint*. They make the lives of crooks as glamourous as possible and whenever theres a fight the Saint always comes out on top by either pulling a knive out of his sock or pulling a gun from his sleeve. At the end of the film they hardly ever give a full explaination of why, where and how the crime was comitted so that if any one in the audience is a little slow at grasping the full details of the film they are just as wise at the end of it as they were at the beginning.

NO. 21A

AGE: 19   FATHER: INSURANCE AGENT
SEX: F.   (EX-PROFESSIONAL CONJURER)
OCCUPATION: MOTHER: HOUSEWIFE
 COMING TO ENGLAND FOR NURSING
NATIONALITY: BRITISH

Talk about frank and sincere opinions, I have been in the German Occupation for 5 years and have seen a great number of German films in that time. My goodness, talk of good, sensible, and substantial films, there's nothing to beat them (and you know it.). All these Bacalls', De Carlos, and Grables, Ugh!!! Give me a great old favourite; or, if it is necessary, discover someone who can *act*: say: from a flapper, to a grey haired (attaboy! Anna Neagle). Someone who can play sophisticated and 'pas tres ordinaire' parts.

Of course not necessarily the short, skinny, heroine, opposite the tall, broad, and bronzed hero, which is noticeable to me, after 5 years of isolation from British and American films.

What about Ronald Colman in *The Prisoner of Zenda*, *Lost Horizon*, and *The Tale of Two Cities*, Greta Garbo in *Anna Christie*, *Marie Walewska* and *Camille*? What about such films as, *The Drum*, *Tovarich*, *The Good Earth*, *The Garden of Allah* etc.? That's what you call good films. Old; too true, but satisfying. Not like these modern *To Have and Have not*, *Diamond Horse-Shoe*, *The Enchanted Cottage*, (not bad), and as for these everlasting war films,—let us forget—.

As for thin legs, (Betty Grable should be sued, for not having enough visible means of support), false hair, and orange vivid red, and almost peuce lips in the 'Glorious' technicolour, Well!!!

Please give us something worth seeing, not that my 5/- or 6/- makes much difference to you, but people are fed-up with, 'leg-shows, crooning, jazz,' etc.

Why not produce more films like, *Waltz Time*, *Thunderhead*, *Son of Flicka* and *The Affairs of Susan*? (I saw the German version of the latter in 1941—*Margaretta 3*).

NO. 22A

AGE: 19   FATHER: OVERLOOKER IN FACTORY
SEX: M.   MOTHER: HOUSEWIFE
OCCUPATION: STUDENT
NATIONALITY: BRITISH

I have a special taste in films. Let me mention a few I have enjoyed immensely and perhaps you will get an idea of my favourite type: *Millions Like Us* (Gordon Jackson, Pat Roc); *Tawny Pipit* (Ros. John, Bernard Miles); *Demi-Paradise* (L. Olivier); *Once upon a time* (C. Grant); *Kipps* (P. Calvert). Four of these films are British. They have one thing in common. That is: sincerity. *They each deal with a problem.* What is more, they are essentially British. There is nothing I dislike more than an imitation of Hollywood in British films: imitation in dialogue, accent, and action. And I sincerely dislike showing-off in films. This is a fault of many British productions, such as *Love Story, Madonna of the seven moons* and *2000 Women.* All these three had for me many pleasant aspects, especially the music in *Love Story.* But they struck me as being unreal and artificial. Personally, Stewart Granger gives me a sort of pain every time I see him, especially every time he opens his mouth. His voice is far from pleasing. He acts well enough. But he is a 'show-off'. At least he appears to be. He reminds me of Errol Flynn. But Flynn has one redeeming 'quality': he tempts me to laugh every time he is being heroic or making love. In *2000 Women* there was too much 'showing off'. Here I felt there was too much search after realism. Perhaps I shouldn't say that. I mean that the search was made in the wrong way and defeated its object. Some of the 'realistic' jokes were embarrassing and unnecessary. The women were somehow not convincing. The aim of it was too obvious. I imagined the whole time that the object was to show Hollywood that our women aren't what too many Americans imagine our women to be: bashful and restrained and 'sophisticated'. True enough the women here were neither bashful nor restrained, but the film went too far. Renee Houston walked around with a badly done up face and washed-out expression, Phyllis Calvert kept up her hard-boiled and hard-voiced role. Patricia Roc looked demure and brave. Jean Kent vamped. This is all very well. I presume that the hurriedly done up faces etc. was part of the search for realism. The plan didn't seem to me to come off. The film was unreal, fantastic and not British.

Now take *Millions Like Us.* Here was not perfection, I admit. But here was sincerity, pathos and charm. Here were real, every-day people. Here was a very appealing and moving, natural love theme. Here was English humour. In *Tawny Pipit* the humour was delightful, the setting charming, the story simple but delicious (perhaps 'simple *and* delicious' is better). And Bernard Miles gave a real pleasant country-vicar performance as a country vicar.

I think *The Demi-Paradise* was one of the best films I've ever seen. The acting of Laurence Olivier was superb. Sincerity is this film's keynote. The theme was Anglo-Soviet relations, and the differences between the two countries were supremely well brought out. Here was plain speaking and plenty of things to think about, presented in an entertaining and non-dictatorial manner.

Once upon a time I found delightful, sympathetic, original and light hearted. The fairy-story atmosphere was present all the time, but at the same time the human touch was not lost. The little boy was very enjoyable to watch, with his boyish love for his caterpillar, and his boyish trust in his hero.

Of course I enjoyed *In which we serve* and *This happy breed* a lot—particularly the latter. The photography in both was truly beautiful, the acting sincere and moving. My favourite stars in these films were John Mills, giving a very life-like and happy performance as the sailor, and Celia Johnson, who was superb in the latter film. But still in these two pictures I felt here was something foreign to my nature. Perhaps I missed the sweet, homely, open-air atmosphere of *Tawny Pipit*. Perhaps these Noel Coward films were too sleek and sophisticated for my liking.

Perhaps the worst film I ever saw was *Shanghai Gesture* with Gene Tierney and Victor Mature. The atmosphere here was well conveyed, but the acting was mostly trash. Gene Tierney, I felt, needed a good slap in the face. So did Victor Mature—to get rid of that smug expression of his. Perhaps it is Victor Mature whom Mr. Granger resembles, more than Gene Tierney.

But I *could* stand Gene Tierney in *Heaven can Wait* with Don Amede. This film pleased me a lot with its rich humour and satire and delicious nonsense. I like especially Rita Hayworth and Deanna Durbin. (Though it is fair to say that my favourite Deanna Durbin is the one who appeared in *Christmas Holiday*). Perhaps my favourite musical to date is *Little Nelly Kelly* with Judy Garland, with its gay lilting Irish tunes and happy cordiality. But then it is such a long time since I saw this film, and my idea of screen-craft has changed since then. But I remember enjoying this hearty picture, I'm waiting patiently for *Waltz Time* to come to . . .

I also like a really good thriller. Especially did I enjoy *Double Indemnity* with Barbara Stanwyck. But then who can withstand the subtle charm and voice of Miss Stanwyck. And she can act. Another type of thriller was the Charles Boyer film *Flesh and Fantasy*, of which I heartily approved. The suspense in the tight-rope walking scenes was killing. The acting throughout was on a high level. I love the 'light-hearted' love making of Charles boyer—especially did I like him in *Appointment for Love* which was truly and refreshingly witty.

I think I detest all Errol Flynn pictures. His heroics and his grin make me rather mad—or *made* me rather mad, for now I never visit his performances.

I cannot finish without saying a word about Vivien Leigh's films. Especially did I admire her in *Lady Hamilton* and in *Waterloo Bridge*, while her superb performance in *Gone with the Wind* I found wholly satisfying. The last film, by the way, I admired, but it was too much at one go for me. Two other actresses deserve words too. They are Ida Lupino and Betty Davis. I always see their films if I get the chance. I liked Miss Lupino best, I think, in *The Light of Heart* with Monty Woolley. Her acting was very moving. I cannot decide which Betty Davis film I admire most. Her versatility is wholly surprising and delightful. Perhaps I remember her most in her wicked roles . . .

In *Jezabel* and in *The Little Foxes*. Betty Davis makes me feel strangely uncomfortable sometimes when watching her. Especially did I feel this in *Now, Voyager*—particularly at the beginning when she was so awkward herself. But then after the change, I felt alright again. Perhaps Miss Davis has more 'hold' over me than any other screen performer!

But how very far we have got from the charming unassuming atmowphere of *Tawny Pipit* and the delightful performances of Mr. and Mrs. Tawny Pipit, especially that of Mrs. Tawny Pipit!

NO. 23A

The following paragraphs contain my likes and dislikes among British and American films.

I start with *The Way to the Stars*, as it is, in my opinion the best film ever shown. It has everything in the way of pathos and humour, judged by British standards. There is a great abundance of understatement, that quality which is British, and British only. Compare parts of this with *Since you went away*. In the latter film the the three principals spent almost the entire film disolving into tears, which was boring in the extreme, and lost its pathos by continual repetition. In *The Way to the Stars* the very lack of 'Slush' made a lump in your throat, which was enhanced by the fact that after making you feel how terrible it all was, you were suddenly switched over to a scene of uproarious fun, or at any rate to something that made you laugh—in- instead of cry. The Americans were as we see them, but they were so delightful that you really liked them. What about Johnny Hollis who fell for Toddy—but never kissed her. What about Peter who proposed to Iris in such a delightfully unique manner. These people made you feel good, you lived with them, thought with them, felt as they felt, and in fact for two hours you were not you sitting in the one-and-ninepennies, but were living in that film. That is why I thought it was the finest film I had seen.

Before this film, however, there are many I have enjoyed, such as *Waterloo Road, Goodbye Mr Chips*, and other past glories of the British screne. *Waterloo Road* had most of the things a film should have. Here was a family you knew existed, here was a soldier whose troubles were the same troubles as soldiers you knew, here was a 'Ted Purvis', just like the one you had met. The whole film was so natural that once more you lived with the film characters, laughed and sympathised with them and you went out of the cinema immensely cheered by the fact that the soldier had fought a great fight, and won, and that the rotter had really got his deserts.

Let us consider some of Noel Cowards' successes, namely, *In Which We Serve, This Happy Breed* and *Blithe Sprit*. The last two were photographed in technicolour. There were a joy to see for this fact alone, for British technicolour is streets ahead of the American. In these two films the colours blended so perfectly in every way that it made you want to see them through twice just for the colour alone. There were no blinding and dazzling conglomerations of colours here, no ultra tanned specimens of man and women-hood, no red, yellow, or mauve and green stripes to insult your colour sensitivity, here was the beautiful house, the sunlit lawns, not too green, but just right to bring back a terrific nostalgia for the country. *Blithe Spirit*, not advertised as hysterically funny, made me nearly sick with laughter, the dialogue was impeachable, or course, the cast was chosen admirably, and it was filmed magnificently. I have seen many films described as 'one long laugh from beginning to end' or similar descriptions, and have sat through it hardly smiling. Bob Hope makes me want to walk out. *This Happy Breed* with the same witty dialogue made you feel you had met that family. The aunt who had 'turns', the harassed mother, the 'boy next door', once more you shared with them their happiness and sorrow, just as you did in *In Which We Serve*. Here you were proud of the British Navy, no other country could feel as the British felt over this film, it was not one long weep, or one long view of fights, blood and death, but it had a little to sober you, a little to cheer you, it gave you a glimpse of the families, the men and their home lives, it made you feel strong and proud, and what could one ask for more than that?

Many novels have been adapted with varying success. *Fanny by Gaslight* made a good picture. Well balanced between Love and Hate, the sordid, and grand, the beautiful and the ugly, it provided you with excitement, and had such a tender love story that you could forgive their running away to Paris to live together. *They were sisters* provided the same type of entertainment, once more kindness, love and generosity showed up, but balanced the cruelty and hate. There was a strong story, a cast well chosen and a quality of acting worthy of the highest praise.

Fairly recently I saw *Something for the Boys*, it was practically devoid of a story, it dazzled you with clashing colours, and was altogether too fantastic. This film seemed typical of the American 'Musicals'. I like a good story, human actors and actresses, not just big eyes, big lips, and miles of legs. *Since you went away* was badly lit, to my mind, and just one big slush from beginning to end. Some while ago I saw Joel McCrea as an airman and Claudette Colbert as 'Peggy', I cannot recall the title, but it appalled me. Here was a horrible show of emotion. Compare the airman's words as he dived to his death, with those of Johnny Hollis in *The Way to the Stars*. Peggy was photographed giving a speech to American housewives, they photograph her fainting. The publicity given to the whole thing was disgusting, and only shows more strongly the difference of the British and American approach to grief. *The Enchanted Cottage* was a good story spoilt by the blindman. That too was badly lit. Britain may not have *Stars* according to Americans, but we have actors and actresses who can 'wipe the floor' with many Americans.

I enjoyed *Going My Way* because I like Bing, and because that film had a humour and sincerity, and an understanding unusual in

American films. I liked *A Song to Remember* despite the glaring technicolour and the awful misrepresentation of Madam George Sand.
Cornel Wilde was good as Chopin and lent reality to his portrayal
because he was a newcomer. The music made up for most of the
errors, because with such moving music you were lost in the glory of
it. There have been older American pictures I have enjoyed, but it
is the British pictures that have stuck in my memory, and impressed
me with their characters, whether loveable or otherwise.

NO. 24A

AGE: 19   FATHER'S OCCUPATION:
SEX: F.   ELECTRIC WELDER
OCCUPATION: AT PRESENT CAPSTON   MOTHER:
   OPERATOR   DECEASED
(REAL OCCUPATION: DRESSMAKER)
NATIONALITY: BRITISH

I read in this weeks *Picturegoer* which I received today about your
wanting personal opinions on films so I thought Id try.

The films I prefer are musicals and murder mysterys also the films
about ordinary families like *This Happy Breed* for instance. Those are
the films that are worth seeing because they nearly always have a
good story and the situations that happen in them could happen in
any home. Not like some of the films you see.

I like mysterys with a good story to it. Like *Laura* or *The Suspect*.
The reason I like mysterys is because it gives you a chance to use
your brains, and fancy yourself as an amater detective.

Then musicals are the type of films that cheer you up and stop you
from feeling so fed up. At least thats the effect they have on me. I
always like to see a song and dance film when Im down in the dumps.

The films I don't like are these misunderstanding type. You know,
boy meets girl, fall in love, fall out and then get together again. Anything like that bores me stiff, because you know darn well, everything
will be okay in the end, but the film takes a long time to make it right.

Then again, I don't care for the comedy shorts like Andy Clyde
and The Three Stooges. I think they behave crazy, bashing one
another around. I can't see anything funny in those shorts. You see
Im the type that likes a film with action and a good story. Not the
type that seems to have been slung together any old how.

Anyway, I think thats all there is to write about so Ill not bore
you any longer.

Two writers of twenty, both women, again ask for good stories
and good acting. No. 25a likes to 'live in the picture for a few
hours', but she does not appear to continue to do so after leaving
the cinema. No. 26a looks forward to second features, particularly to travel talks. Both condemn the 'glamourizing' of Hollywood.

NO. 25A

AGE: 20
SEX: F.
OCCUPATION:
STOCK CLERK AND TYPIST
NATIONALITY: BRITISH

FATHER'S OCCUPATION:
DRIVER
MOTHER'S OCCUPATION:
HOUSEWIFE

Having read the last issue of *Picturegoer* I decided that I would try and express my feelings about films.

First of all films which I do not like:—

I just cannot get any enjoyment from the overcrowded star films such as *Star Bangled Banner* and *Hollywood Canteen*. I, for one, go to a film show to see decent acting. It does not worry me whether the actor or actress is famous or unknown. Credit should always be given where it is due. Therefore, these pictures with a cast of numerous stars, to my mind are just so much wasted film. No one star is given a chance to act and the whole thing resolves itself into a hopeless muddle with no story to follow and nothing of much interest at all.

Other types of films which to me are senseless, is the overflow of musicals filmed in Glorious Technicolour which have been circulating during the war years. Surely technicolour could be used for much better purposes than as a pretty background for a star who has a voice but couldn't act if she tried, or for some beautiful yound lady who drifts about the screen for an hour or so looking as charming as possible. Also, why a star such as Don Ameche or Robert Young should have to act as stooge to some pretty lady in these nauseating films, is beyond my comprehension. If we must have musical films why not some more on the style of *A Song to Remember* or films starring those two grand singing stars Nelson Eddy and Jeanette Macdonald.

Now for films I like:—

I do like to see a film with a good story running through it. Most of the pictures which I have thoroughly enjoyed have been books or novels which have been filmed. Having read a good book and knowing the characters, it is, to me, interesting to watch the film and see if the star's portrayal of the various people is anything like the author intended they should be. It is like seeing all the people I have read about, and loved, come to life and invariably I forget the present day world and simply live in the picture for a few hours. That is what I call enjoyment and relaxation. I love a film that has to be followed closely. That is why these silly musicals bore me to tears.

I do really enjoy coloured films and I think that Technicolour can really make beautiful films that will be remembered for many years to come when it is used in films like *Gone With the Wind*, *Frenchman's Creek*, *North West Mounted Police* and *Henry V*. I would much rather sit through these films again, or new ones like them, with their colours and superb acting, than go within yards of a cinema showing some crazy comedy or musical.

I enjoy listening to any good singing star, as I am very fond of music, but why give actors like Allen Jones and Dennis Morgan, whose voices, I think, easily rival Nelson Eddy's such poor films to star in. True, they have both been in a few good films but the majority of their pictures have been very weak.

Just to sum up, I would like to see more really good musical films giving people who really have superb voices, a chance to star, and plenty of films with good stories and opportunities for the many outstanding and talented actors and actresses of today. Also less lavish musicals and third rate stories which, I imagine, must exasperate any intelligent film fan.

NO. 26A

AGE: 20   FATHER'S OCCUPATION:
SEX: F.   POLICE CONSTABLE
OCCUPATION: SHORTHAND-TYPIST   MOTHER'S OCCUPATION:
NATIONALITY: BRITISH   HOUSEWIFE

I have not the time to be a habitual picturegoer, so when I get the chance to spend a few hours in the cinema, naturally I choose the film I wish to see. I often think that I have more enjoyment this way than if I were to visit a picture-house two or three times in a week.

My animosity against the cinema is not strong—I know what I like and on the whole I am satisfied. Starting with the main feature, I like a good story—that is essential and I like the producer to stick to the story, that is if he is making an adaption from a book. I really can't see any reason for side-tracking into scenes alien from the general text. I can think on one film—*Madame Curie*—one I looked forward to seeing because I was familiar with her life story and thought it juicy material for the film world to knawe. I saw *Madame Curie*, or rather I saw Greer Garson, a dashing glamourised, good actress making me believe that she had known poverty! The film should have been called *The Love Story of Pierre Curie and Marie Sklodovska*—not *Madame Curie*. I wanted to see her when she was old, her work during the Great World War No. 1—they did not have to employ battle scenes for that part of her life, it could have been portrayed in a field hospital —and it would have given colour (not technicolour) to that part of her life. What I did see of the ageing *Madame Curie* was a perfect Hollywood make-up addressing a hall of eager students, a perfect Hollywood ending. If the war had not been on, would it not have been a good experiment to make this film with an international film unit. I like a good scientific picture, but they are not good box office unless they are garlanded with Hollywood roses, and this seems to prevent a producer taking a chance. What excellent material these cautious men are missing, but what chances they are giving lesser known independent companies.

I like continental films in their original state, not remakes by our own studios. I like these films because they are sincere no matter how absurd the plot may be or trivial the dialogue. There is good honest down-to-earth work put into these films and I like to applaud their efforts.

I have enjoyed a few good adaptions from best-sellers, one in particular—*Rebecca*. More than once I have spent an evening in a cinema showing this film, in preference to a third rate at another hall. In my opinion this film was a 'first', almost perfect in acting, dialogue and scenery and the music, I must not miss out an important part of the film. They kept to the book as near as they could and I passed over the adaptions necessary—in this case they helped the film.

Two films of a serious nature, that seems to be my taste. Comedy? Has to be a very good picture before I can let myself go. Irene Dunne's pictures seem to be the answer, here I can see wit performed in a sophisticated manner, laughable fun as she canters through not always improbable situations. As for the other comediens on the screen, I snap my fingers at them, but that is just my taste.

I never did like war films and I still don't like anything with the slightest flavour of war. My reason? I have no wish to relive the past in a cinema.

I come to the second features, usually what I look forward to. My first choice is James A. Fitzpatrick's Traveltalks. I bow to this man, and I thank him for his work which I am sure he enjoys thoroughly for bringing his country to my eyes. How often has one of his films superseded a highly coloured main feature. Another second feature series—*Crime Does Not Pay*. We don't get enough of them and surely crime is just as rampant here as in the States. Couldn't Scotland Yard co-operate with the English studios and start a series over here. Then on very rare occasions when I am lucky enough to see one, I enjoy the little cameos on medical research where silent acting predominates and the narrator in plain American explains the subject. Westerns I don't dislike, but feel indifference towards them. The Stooges—a man threesome enjoyed by the children, but not by me. The Marx Brothers I do like, but I can count on one hand the times I have seen them!

Only once have I seen an experimental film made in America. It was badly made and the story was piecey, but there was enthusiasm oozing through the lens of the camera. *The Seventh Victim* was the title—I have yet to find out who the second victim was. This film was trying to break away from the usual run of mysteries, to bring its art to the man in the street and if they failed, it was through no fault of trying. Taking all defects into consideration, I admired the work put into it and the acting of the unknown young actors and actresses who had been given a chance to show what they could do. That chance means a great deal when you are striking out for yourself.

On the whole, I don't care where a film is made whether it is in China or over here, so long as it conveys to me that here is good material and here is a good film. What I would like is an international studio producing films of the world in general and isn't

there a saying about two heads being better than one, but in this
case, it would be much more.

The next two documents are extremely interesting in their
different ways. Both show considerable critical faculty and the
second an interest in films as such, as distinct from the private
lives of 'stars' etc. It should be noted that the second writer says
that reading was his main recreation as a child.

NO. 27A

AGE: 21
SEX: M.
OCCUPATION: ART STUDENT
NATIONALITY: IRISH

FATHER'S OCCUPATION:
HARPIST
MOTHER'S OCCUPATION:
—

Before I start to state my tastes in films I would like to say that
there are one or two things in general that I like to see in any film.

I, personally, go to the films for enjoyment and relaxation not for
education or the development of my critical faculties. Nevertheless I
unconsciously notice good art direction, colour control and photography, and where any one of these are lacking it irritates and upsets
my enjoyment of the film.

The cinema screen aims at realism and colour naturally helps this
effect besides adding extra charm and beauty. For this reason I
prefer Technicolour films.

So much for the Technical side, now lets take a few films. We'll
start with two musicals. One I liked and one I didn't.

The first, *Bathing Beauty*, I liked. Why? Well first of all the colour
and photography were superb this alone being worth the price of
admission. Secondly it had the semblance of a story. (So few musicals
have. The producers seem to think that once they use 'glorious
technicolor' all they need is a dance-band and some bare legs.) The
music was well handled and varied, the water-ballet beautiful and
the bumour excellent.

I might add here that I like humour in any film—even drama.
Indeed in the case of drama it acts as an excellent foil to the more
serious moments.

The second musical I have chosen I did not like. *Meet Me in St.
Louis* with Judy Garland. I found it very artificial. Judy Garland was
made up very artificially and the story was also very artificial.

In *Bathing Beauty* the story may have been far fetched but it did not
appear artificial. *Meet Me in St. Louis* was more like a stage play. The
characters did not seem real. I enjoyed the tunes.

We in Ireland have only just started to get war films. Personally I
am a little tired of them already. There is a dreadful sameness about
people being blown up. One battle to me appears much the same as
another. Of course these are exceptions. I liked *The Story of Dr.*

From the Film *Dead of Night*. An example of 'refined' British film horror.

Barbara Stanwyck in *Double Indemnity*. "I also like a really good thriller. Especially did I enjoy *Double Indemnity* with Barbara Stanwyck. But then who can withstand the subtle charm and voice of Miss Stanwyck." (see Document No. 22A)

Wassell, For Whom the Bell Tolls and *The Way Ahead*. The humour in *The Way Ahead*, the fact that *For Whom the Bell Tolls* dealt with the romance of two people, with the war only as a background and the fact that I like 'doctor' pictures may account for my liking these. (Apropos of Doctors, I'm very fond of the *Dr. Gillespie* series.)

Perhaps the American propaganda connected with and running through their pictures has been the greatest irritation to me. They just load it on. *This is the Army* reeked with it. This also was one of the musicals which lacked a story if not a moral. *Mrs. Minniver*, a different type of war film, I liked. It was so natural. I personally found Mr. and Mrs. Minniver very like Monsieur and Madame Curie. Perhaps they were meant to be.

Pictures like *Little Foxes* and *Old Acquaintances* leave me cold. I felt that both of these films (and all pictures on that type) would have been far more suitable for the stage. They were to static for the screen.

As regards to books and plays adapted for the screen. I think that where a film is much advertised beforehand as having been taken from a certain book or play that the film should run as closely as possible to that book or play. This is not always observed. Admitting that certain changes are necessary (cutting down dialogue to the minimum etc.) that does not excuse flagrant and unnecessary changes such as letting one of the leading characters live on the screen when his death scene occupies a whole chapter in the book.

History is very much abused at times.

I must admit that I do wince at some of the biographical films which are made. *Billy the Kid* and Chopin to name two extremes. Chopin's music in a *Song to Remember* was charming of course.

Westerns are seemingly produced to a standard set of regulations and must never vary therefrom. As a support to the 'big' picture I find them enjoyable enough.

A superior type of western made fairly recently was *Tall in the Saddle* with John Wayne. It has a better story than the average western and the acting was on a higher lever.

I should like to see more of this type. *Stagecoach* was another good western made several years ago and there have been few in between that have reached the same level as these two mentioned.

A newcomer (I think), Miss Audrey Long, showed considerable promise in *Tall in the Saddle* and I should like to see more of her. (How about a picture of her in *Picturegoer*.)

The Roy Rogers series are more musical than western. Most of them are pleasant enough but nothing to write home about.

I like a good comedy. Not so much the Abbot and Costello type so much as *The Major and the Minor* or *Libelled Lady*.

In conclusion I have found it rather hard to answer your simple question as I do not know the reason it was asked. I have tried to give my reasons for liking and disliking films in general rather than give a long list of particular films.

No. 28A

AGE: 22   SEX: M.

OCCUPATION: JACK OF ALL TRADES. ER-
RAND BOY TO CLERK, UNDERGROUND
PIT WORKER TO ORGANISER, AT PRE-
SENT WORKING IN G.P.O. EX-SERVICE

NATIONALITY: BRITISH

FATHER'S OCCUPATION:
LABOURER

MOTHER'S OCCUPATION:
DOMESTIC SERVANT

Although the above details are all that is asked for I feel that it would be an asset if I gave a few more which might be of interest and help.

Money was never plentiful in our household and as a result film going was a considered a luxury and only on rare occasions were any of our family able to visit the cimema, about once a year and then the film was usually a musical. I can only remember seeing; *Love Parade*, a Marie Dressler film, *Top Hat* and *Follow the Fleet*. Plus a few cowboy films now and then. Reading was my main recreation until I left school . . .

Things altered when I left school for I then began to earn a wage and had enough pocket money to enable me to vist the cinema when I wished. The result—I went whenever I had a sixpence to gain admission, I saw any and every film; I would think nothing of spending nine hours in a cinema (or rather three different ones). To me there were only two types of films, the good and the very good. I joined the Army when I was seventeen and this brought to a close this particular phase of filmgoing.

Nevertheless, although I have been very active in local public life since my return from the forces nothing has been allowed to stand in the way of my film going and three times a week would be a fair average. My girl friend is only eighteen years of age and to a large extent judges a good or a bad film according to the facial attributes of the male stars. I have never seen the performers as individuals but only as characters in a particular film, I am not interested in the dirt and dope concerning a stars private life I am only interested in their performance.

Possibly this might show what I mean. My girl states that she is really interested in films and expect that she considers taking a film book each week and writing fan letters to be a practical sign of her interest. (It was whilst reading her film book that I learnt of your request) I recently bought two copies of the book *Film* by Roger Manvell, if her copy ever gets opened it will surprise me.

I realise the power of the film and the part that it plays in our life but I must be too lazy to do anything about it. I like reading Charles Kingsley but it is easier to read Edgar Wallace.

I will give the films that I have liked exactly as they come to me, the films that I dislike are few.

Firstly the only two films that I would take the trouble to see again and again (and have repeatedly seen) *Fantasia*. *Bathing Beauty*. Red Skelton, Basil Rathbone-Esther Williams.

The Way to the Stars. The Way Ahead. The Edge of the World. Major Barbara. The Man Who Could Work Miracles. South Riding. Cover Girl. All Films dealing with the Barbary Coast. *A Night at the Opera. Maytime. The Enchanted Cottage. Mrs. Miniver. Blossoms in the Dust. Kings Row. A Day at the Races. My Buddy.* The First three of the *Blondie* series. *The Magic Bullet. The Great Waltz.* (Ruined by Luise Rainers' performance.) *Waterloo Road. I Met a Murderer. Dead Men Tell No Tales. Random Harvest. Rebecca. The Story of Irene and Vernon Castle. I'll Walk Beside You. Thousands Cheer. Robin Hood. The Man in Grey. They Were Sisters. I'll Be Your Sweetheart. How Green Was My Valley. Revelry With Beverly. Gods Country and the Woman. Natasha. We from Kronstadt. Lenin in October. St. Martin's Lane. Dark Victory. Now Voyager. Sweethearts. 29 Acacia Avenue. Meet John Doe. Mr. Deeds Goes to Town. Love Affair. The Constant Nymph.*
Dislike.
Blondie films. *Hardy* films. *Fifth Chair.* Both funny but so unreal. *Arsenic and Old Lace. Pygmalion.* I like Shaw but disliked film.

I can never rember the films that I really dislike because I just forget them, the films mentioned above had some good points and therefore still remain fresh in my mind.

Two of the 23-year-old category are most carefully and analytically written. The writer of document No. 29a is a young housewife who wants films to reproduce life only if they include 'touches of humour or grand drama or the sinister twist'. She has a leaning towards 'mystical' films, even 'impossible' films, but on the whole her approach is summed up in her words 'I like films about the sort of people I know, or even films about people like me, but I do not like to see everyday things happening to them'. The suggestion of fantasy is not, apparently, carried into the film-world itself, and here again, as in No. 30a, we find a demand for a good story, in which the characters or the film as a whole are not made subservient to the glamour of a 'star'. The same stress on realism appears in No. 30a, and in No. 32a.

NO. 29A

AGE: 23½   FATHER'S OCCUPATION:
SEX: F.   RAILWAY WORKER
OCCUPATION: HOUSEWIFE   MOTHER: DAUGHTER OF
NATIONALITY: BRITISH   A FAIRLY WELL-TO-DO
                                FARMER

I have been tempted to answer your film questions before, but have always finished up by thinking, 'Ohm I can't be bothered—anyway, I never win contests,' but this time I really mean to have a go at it! And now for my film likes and dislikes.
I like intelligent films; and I don't mean high-brow, eductational

204 BRITISH CINEMAS AND THEIR AUDIENCES

features, or lengthy, argumentative dramas, but just authentic or sensible films with characters in whom I can believe. This is important; I must be able to believe in the people, even if the things that happen to them are unbelievable. I like comedies in which the people are real people who say witty things, and have incredibly funny things happening to them—e.g. Bob Hope pictures, and sophisticated comedies; I hate slap-stick of the Olsen and Johnson tradition. I saw *Hell's A-popping*, and though I laughed once or twice, I left the cinema feeling rather ashamed of myself, and disgusted because I'd wasted 2/3d on such idiotic nonsense. I've given their films a wide berth since. On the other hand, I like Ginger Rogers comedies, because the amusement is in the witty and appropriate sayings, or the creditable tho' exaggerated incidents. I like musicals that are 'natural'. I dislike lavishly staged musicals, where one brilliant cavalcade of wildly whirling chorines succedes another, paining the eyes and confusing the senses. I think that *Rose Marie* and *Maytime* were the two most beautiful musicals that have ever been produced. I prefer Betty Grable and Alice Faye in costume musicals, where there is some pretence of a story, rather than in the lavishly staged extravaganzas that I mentioned.

To be more serious, I like Bette Davies dramas, because she makes every character she plays, a believable one. I find that I like most best-seller productions, so long as the film sticks to the story, but does not make the characters too verbose or dull. One can have too much reality—e.g. *The Grapes of Wrath*—I thought it was an unusual film, brilliantly acted, but it was not entertainment. It was the sort of thing that happens to many of us, without the touches of humour or grand drama or sinister twist that would make it entertainment. One *lives* that sort of thing, and does not go to the cinema to meet it again, but to get away from it. I do not like films that have all the stress laid on the actors or actresses (as opposed to the characters in the story) in which the story seems to have been built round or even on to, the famous actress starring in it, but I do want the characters to be at least as important as the story. Even a really strong story can suffer if the characters are subservient to the plot and never really develop into real people. I like films that give me something to think about, to discuss, criticize, argue about; and first among these (at the moment) come the mystic films, which seem to be enjoying a revival at this time.

To mention a few:—*Half-way House* (which I thoroughly enjoyed), *The Unseen*, and *A Place of One's Own*. My husband does not believe in them, but he still enjoys them. They are my first-favourites at the moment, tho' I expect one's enjoyment will diminish as more and more mystics film are turned out. I like detective films and thrillers—subject to the before-mentioned conditions—that the characters should be natural, and the film intelligently produced. Paradoxically, I love really impossible films—like the *Tarzan* stories. *Lost Horizon, The Wizard of Oz* (two completely different films), and

Heaven Can Wait are three of my 'remembered with pleasure' films.
I did not like *Citizen Kane*. I thought it confusing and dull. I
thought *Gone With the Wind* had all that a perfect film should have,
but was too long. Both my husband and myself like historical
romances, if not too far-fetched. That is, we enjoyed *Elizabeth and
Essex* and *Henry VIII* but disliked *The Black Swan*. We really enjoyed
Robin Hood because we had not expected it to be believable. I think
that is the main difference—we hate films that are supposed to be
authentic and are not intelligently presented, but enjoy films that
are frankly incredible, but good entertainment. My husband likes
cowboy films and gangster stories—I do, too, so long as there is a
really strong story, or at least, other entertainment in the way of
music or comedy. We both hate harrowing, sub-stuff—and, honestly,
immoral films. And in this respect, we don't mind American films
so much as British. When an American film opens with a shot of a
silk-stockinged leg, it somehow seems quite natural and commonplace, but when a British film does so (i.e. *They Were Sisters*) it is
merely embarrassing. Probably this is because, one can feel superior
so long as the film is not of one's own nationality, whereas if it is, one
feels slightly ashamed. Well, I think I've covered just about all my
likes and dislikes—oh, about 'shorts' I like shorts of the *Crime Does
Not Pay* series, and the *Sherlock Holmes* chronicles, but I hate short
musicals and comedies. They always seem so empty and uninteresting. Also, I prefer *good* British films to American ones, because they
always seem more natural, though a British film can be spoiled for
me by a too, too devastatingly superior accent from the chief actress
(the actors don't seem to offend so often in this way). To end with,
here is a list of the films I really have enjoyed (though it will be
rather incomplete, as I have not a very retentive memory):—British
films—*Henry VIII, Under the Greenwood Tree, The Ghost Goes West, In
Which We Serve, The Way Ahead, Half-way House, The Man in Grey,
Rebecca* (was that British?) *A Place of One's Own*, and *Night Train to
Munich*—and *They Were Sisters*. I didn't like *Fanny By Gaslight*, and
thoroughly agreed with the American ban on this film. American
films:—(At random) *Lost Horizon, A Song to Remember* (Merely for the
music), all the Nelson Eddy-Jeanette MacDonald musicals, *Four
Sons, The Little Foxes* and all the other Bette Davies films, *Suspicion,
Arsenic and Old Lace*, all the Bing Crosby films, because I like Bing
Crosby's voice, *Keys of the Kingdom, Reap the Wild Wind, Ladies in
Retirement*, and most of the big production comedy-thrillers—i.e.
Laura, Double Indemnity etc. I forgot *Goodbye Mr. Chips* when listing
the British films. I shall probably think of dozens of films I really
enjoyed after I have sent this, but I would like to put on record that
I once saw one film three times, and I can't remember the name.
Merle Oberon and George Brent were in it, and it was about a
murderer being taken by ship to America to be executed who gives
up his chance of freedom because he falls in love with a rich and
beautiful young lady who is suffering from an incurable and fatal

heart disease. I saw *Strange Cargo* starring Clark Gable and Joan Crawford twice. I like films about the sort of people I know, or even films about people like me, but I do not like to see everyday things happening to them. I like to see places I have never visited, incidents that I have never taken part in (and usually, ones that I would not like to take part in) and I like to enjoy—on the screen—experiences I have never been called upon to face in real life. That is probably why I prefer historical films, thrillers, sophisticated comedy, super-natural films, and all the 'frankly impossible' epics from *Tarzan* to *Dumbo*.

Well, I guess that is really all, and if I haven't won a prize, at least I hope I have helped a little in the search for data on the film lectures. Please excuse mistakes in typing; it is very late, and, having just finished scrubbing the floor, I am rather tired.

NO. 30A

AGE: 23   FATHER'S OCCUPATION:
SEX: M.   ROAD-SWEEPER
OCCUPATION: SORTING LETTERS (AFTER   MOTHER'S OCCUPATION :
    OVER 4 YRS. IN R.A.F.)   DECEASED
NATIONALITY: BRITISH

Broadly speaking, I suppose that of the number of films I have seen over the past five or six years, very few can be called to my mind as deserving a lode of brickbats.

Let it not be thought, however, that all the rest brought me applauding to my feet. Truth to tell, most of them are completely forgotten, yet they possess virtue even in oblivion. The inability of some of the most recent films I have seen to stir my memory must surely prove that they served a perfectly adequate purpose in giving me entertainment of a purely relaxative kind. If they were meant by their producers for nothing more, then, on the whole, those gentle-men have succeeded in their modest aim.

But this letter must do more than issue luke-warm praise to mediocrity: films outstanding for their positive goodness and nega-tive badness must be laid bare and examined.

When marshalling my ideas as to what films are good, I note with some surprise that I can easily let myself in for an accusation of chauvinistic bigotry, for the greater part of them are British.

Films like *This Happy Breed, Waterloo Road, The Way to the Stars* and *Great Day* always appeal very strongly to me. They provide no soul-tearing tragedy, their effect is exquisitely sentimental rather than heavily emotional. And I prefer sentimentality to emotionalism (unless one is quarried from Aberdeen granite, one has to incline towards one or the other). Furthermore, such films, whilst playing gently on the heart strings, play with a familiar hand. American films of a similar character cannot bring their meaning so close be-cause the settings are comparatively strange to me even though the circumstances are much the same.

Before I tuck my heart back up my sleeve, I must mention another favourable aspect of this British type of film. Consciously or unconsciously, a thin moral thread seems always to have been woven into the fabric, though, as far as I am concerned, the adedd value of their moral is comparative rather than actual. My point is that I am not expected to watch a Barrymorean cleric in the pulpit, snarling his pious exhortations at me. Denham moralizing is neatly put over, and I like it.

Other pictures which I can cheerfully remember are those which pretend to be nothing more than sheer clowning. The Marx Brothers spring most readily to my mind—theirs is humour in the strictest philological sense of the word: they are gloriously wet. They get down to the rock bottom of comedy which is, I submit, debunking.

The dignity of the harp could easily be upset by some buffoon tearing out its strings and getting tangled up in them, but could its pre-eminent status be more devastatingly shattered than by a seeming nit-wit playing it to perfection to an audience of packing cases and the other two brothers?

Professional respectability is caricured to a frazzle by Marx of the painted face. His choice of names always starts the ball rolling—I, Cleaver Needle, the Legal Eagel, Wolf. J. Flywheel, the detective, and so on. He reduces the awful facade of pride in wealth and office to the loping form of Groncho Marx and pads his hilarious way into the arms of the inevitable dowager.

This stuff is real comedy: in addition to the essential debunking, we have witty talk, the absurd situation, and the custard pie. What more could the laughter-seeker ask?

The Hope-Crosby combination takes second prize in comedy, but they are always careful not to hit below the belt. Nevertheless, quick-fire repartee is stimulating. I find that I have to keep my wits sharpened up to catch all the flashes from the rapiers, but I invariably walk out at the end of a H-C. film wondering how many laughs I missed.

Abbott and Costello and Jack Benny seem to give me twinges of retrospective amusement, but they are nine-tenths in the Forgotten Legion. One always knows what to expect from them: A and C invariably drag in a pourly disguised version of the old music-hall 'change for a fiver' routine; Benny's comedy gives me the impression that it has all been carefully rehearsed—it is too slick.

Still looking back, I discover that I have enjoyed other films not because of their overall quality, but because of extremely powerful acting in them. I used to think the term 'making a film,' as applied to an actor, another instance of Hollywood's pretentious verbiage, but now the truth of it is upon me. Orson Welles in *Jane Eyre* is the best example I can call to mind at the moment—although the part of Edward Rochester should have been secondary to that of Jane Eyre herself, the very great force of Welles' acting overwhelmed everything else. But difficult as it is not to appreciate and enjoy such mastery, I cannot on reflection say that *Jane Eyre* was a good film. Many others fall into line with this—they lose their balance by failing to bridle effectively outstanding acting ability. As vehicles for one actor they succeed, but as films they do not.

So much for my likes. I must now search my vocabulary for all its available abuse. And this will be thrown at the mealy mouthed self-righteous vanity of the profession as a whole. Why, oh why does it so aggresively thrust itself on the public as consisting of moral giants who, through hell-borne adversity, eventually come sweating to the stars? I am heartily sick of the winsome, warm-hearted, sweet-natured, modist, and—of course—pure young personification of American girl-hood who, armed with nothing but Faith and a gawky side-kick of a colleague, ultimately finds her tonsular genius realized on Old Broadway. Wealthy suitors (never seducers—only agents try that) offer her all the jewels west of stinking Suez, but no, the bleary-eyed Teutonic mother turns up at the last minute successfully pleading the cause of young Elmer next door who used to be studying engineering (pre 1941) but nowadays sports a Pair of Silver Wings.

Can anyone, after all these years, be taken in by such syrupy trash? Light musicals are all right, but surely Hollywood could find a better medium for them than the glorification of the private lives of its scions. Limbo also cries out for Irish mothers, Dead End Kids, handsome doctors, London fogs, fighting parsons, psychiatrists, graduation ceremonies, and—a loud cry this,—singing cowboys. They have had their time. The popularity of animal films has always escaped me. I do not suggest that horses and dogs suffer any kind of cruelty by being made to muzzle into the faces of Southern belles and snivelling boys, but it doesn't seem to be quite in the order of things. The theme is overworked anyway.

Also, never again let me see an outwardly normal man fire a Browning gun from the hip, even if he is fighting a lone battle against every weapon that came out of Osaka. I'm not saying it can't be done, but I had to endure no little humiliation when I remember that the Browning I sometimes had occasion to fire was mounted in a concrete base and then would almost leap out of my hand. Seriously speaking though, an incident like that ruined an excellent film.

But I have yet to mention the worst film I ever have seen. Its title: *Somewhere in Camp*. A British picture, too. Its plot might have been hatched from *Chick's Own*, the scenery was obviously canvas, the hero would have been hard-pressed to play the part of a shrouded corpse, and the humour was filthy. In its ninety minutes it exaggerated every bad feature of British made comedy.

To generalize again, the George Formby type of comedy makes me tremble when I think that it might somehow reach America. For bawdy innuendo it takes whatever cake is awarded for that sort of thing. Congreve might have been able to put it over two-hundred

and eighty years ago, but Formby can't do it today. A Purity Drive
is called for.

NO. 31A

AGE: 23   FATHER'S OCCUPATION:
SEX: F.   STOREKEEPER
OCCUPATION: SHORTHAND-TYPIST   MOTHER'S OCCUPATION:
NATIONALITY: BRITISH   HOUSEWIFE

In my view, likes and dislikes in the matter of films depend largely
upon one's temperament. However, I can do no better than to detail
numerically my own personal ideas as follows :—

DISLIKES

British films—but *not* British technicolour which I consider knocks
Hollywood out cold.

I hate, loathe and detest those dreadful slapstick 'comedies'
featuring the Ritz Bros., Three Stooges, Olsen & Johnson etc. In
fact I would love to be absolutely selfish and say that Hollywood
ought not to be allowed to screen such tripe. However, for the sake
of retaining the goodwill of the fans (?) of the above-mentioned
'funsters', I'll be big and say let them remain—maybe I can find
those black glasses I keep around for such emergencies.

Next in my list of film 'pet aversions' are Westerns—those rip-
roarin' rides across the plains (or wherever rip-roarin' rides do take
place) just give me a very bad pain in the neck, quite apart from
the fact that if I do happen to be dogged by bad-luck and the second
feature is a Western, I usually manage to sit in front of a child whose
blood pressure rises so high that he or she persists in standing up,
thumping me on the back (it has been known to be on the head too)
and yelling 'Go on cowboy', and all the other sweet nothings kids
usually yell at such times.

If Roy Rogers, Bill Boyd etc. found themselves in the place I
wished them in these moments, I guess they just would'nt be in
Hollywood.

Now let's talk about more pleasant things.

LIKES.

I hope my more cynical type of friends will never hear me say
this, but I love a very sad film with a bit of weeping now and again.
Silly is'nt it, but there it is—I revelled in *Song to Remember, Song of
Bernardette, Old Maid, Now Voyager, Great Lie*, etc. Maybe its the
touch of sentiment which even the most hard-boiled person must
contain in his or her makeup.

From this, it will be seen that my particular favourites are the
more serious type of films, especially those which include the least
inkling of music (this being one of my greatest weaknesses).

It is sometimes nice to go crazy with Bob Hope, Jack Benny,
Red Skelton (the ballet scene in *Bathing Beauty* was a peach), and it
is even fun to go utterly mad in fantasy with Walt Disney.

Some of the really charming 'short' films I have seen recently rank high in my 'likes'—*Animal Wonderland, Return of the Vikings, Student Nurse* etc. I would like to see more of these. I particularly enjoyed a 'short', featuring Arthur Askey in how and how not to sneeze.

Betty Grable, Rita Hayworth, Carman Miranda, musicals are also among my firm favourites. The more the merrier.

I trust the above, or at least some of it, will be found useful to you in your investigations.

NO. 32A

AGE: 23

SEX: F.

OCCUPATION: RADIO VALVE ASSEMBLER

NATIONALITY: BRITISH

FATHER: AIRCRAFT WORKER

MOTHER: HOUSEKEEPER

I must confess I am rather fussy about the kind of films I see. For instance, the so called musicals that Hollywood produces, hold no interest for me at all. Perhaps it is because I am a 'highbrow'. The film *A Hundred Men and a Girl* I enjoyed thoroughly. *The Great Lie, Song of Russia* and *A Song to Remember* are the type of films I could see over again. They seem to take me away from the ordinary world. 'Well any film does that', you could say, but I dont find it so.

A Betty Grable film, Alice Faye or Betty Hutton, and others of their kind just leave me cold, they seem so empty and futile. I just consider my time as wasted, and more often than not, there is absolutely no story at all in the film.

But on the other hand, I enjoy and roar with laughter at the antics of Abbot and Costello. *Hold that Ghost* was the first film I ever saw, with Abbot and Costello and it was in my opinion the best. Mickey Rooney is a very great favourite of mine. Also Donald O'Connor and his clever little partner Peggy Rynan. Mickey's films are a tonic to me, especially the last one I saw which was *A Yank at Eton,* Donald and Peggy are two clever young actors. Their dancing is good and the wise cracks really amusing. But just one fault I find with their type of film, I've noticed that classical music is made fun of and swing glorified. Now whilst appreciating good swing, I dont think this is quite fair.

Going on to the straight films, I much prefer those which have been taken from a well known book. To name a few, *Rebbeca, Frenchman's Creek, Jamaica Inn, How Green was my Valley, Key of the Kingdom* and many others I could name. All these films stand out in my mind. I can be sure before I go to see them that it will be worth-while. *The Way of all Flesh* with Akim Tamaloff taking the lead was a great picture. It was so much like everyday life, something that could have happened to anyone.

I am very fond of good 'thrillers'. But American thrillers always seem to me a little too fantastic. Whereas the few British ones I have seen have given me a real thrill of horror. Such as the *The Case of the Frightened Lady* so quietly sinister. But I have just recently seen

Murder in Thornton Square and I must say it was extremely good.

Liking outdoor life myself, naturally makes me fond of the outdoor type of film. I scarcely ever miss a good 'Western'. One of the reasons I like them so much. is to see some of the lovely scenery in America and Canada. I like the films that have been from Zane Grey's books, although they are too few. I enjoy very much historical films, but not very many seem to be made nowadays. War films seem to be having a long run, and I do not like them very much. One or two are outstanding to me, *Foreman went to France* and *The Way Ahead*, they were indeed good.

Films I do not like are the silly flimsy stories of divorce and falling in and out of love so easily. They give me a wrong impression of life especially in America.

Well, that is my humble opinion of the kind of films I like and dislike. I am not so fortunate as to live in a large town, therefore we do not get films very early after they are released.

The next four documents, all written by young women of 24, repeat the strain found in so many of this series of contributions —stories must be credible, and films based on historical episodes or on best-sellers should not wander too far from the facts or the book. No. 35a and No. 36a are both notable for their reaction to crime and horror: 'How I sigh for the old "horror" films! How I enjoyed the delicious shivers down my spine that *Dracula* produced!' And No. 36a classifies under 'likes', 'Thrillers and Mysteries: the tougher the better . . . Reasons:—Mystery and action hold the interest, Sex appeal of the tough and brutal hero'.

NO. 33A

AGE: 24

SEX: F.

OCCUPATION:

    TYPIST—ADMIRALTY

PARENTS' OCCUPATION:

    FATHER: L.C.C. CLERICAL OFFICER

    MOTHER: HOUSEWIFE

    NATIONALTY BOTH BRITISH

Having been for many years an ardent Film Fan, I decided to enter for your competition—it has long interested me, and although I find it difficult to remember all the films I have enjoyed thoroughly I have compiled the following which is a brief summary of the films which are, in my opinion, some of the best.

The War has brought about so many so called masterpieces which I have found boring and dull, but a few gems here and there stick in my memory for the depth of feeling and really brilliant acting which has been put into them. I call to mind Spencer Tracy's performance in the *Seventh Cross*, the film was interesting from the point of view of it taking place inside Germany, actually I suppose this would not come under the heading of a War film—but its in that category—I lived every moment of that film with Spencer Tracy,

his sincere portrayal of a 'good German' did much to help me understand more fully the problem of that country. For a real War film—
about REAL people—I enjoyed *The Sullivans*, it had everything this
film, pathos, humour, stark tradegy and the human touch, the
children's performances were some of the most natural I have ever
seen, the film seemed to touch everyone, it reminded me vividly of
a great friend of mine whose son was killed in this war—a tribute to
the ordinary men who helped to bring victory to our Nation. *Journey
for Margaret*, a wonderful performance by that talented child actress
Margaret O'Brien, I have seen children during the 'blitz looking
like she did, confused and alone and trying hard to understand the
mystery of life, each moment of Robert Young's performance was
a credit to the screen. *Casablanca*—with all its excitement and thrills,
its real action, the wonderful acting of Claude Rains, his supporting
performance was worthy of note, he was a Frenchman from the
saucy angle of his hat—to his smart leather boots, I admire this
actor very much. *Mrs. Miniver* was touching and very sentimental,
I liked it for its beauty, its thrills (have never felt so moved as when
I saw all those 'little' boats waiting to go to Dunkirk) and the restrained performance of Greer Garson—never bettered. *Since you
Went Away* maybe the War is not so real to America as to us here,
but this film seemed to me to show the ordinary American people,
it helped me to realise that they too were sharing the hardships,
partings and worries of a major War. Claudette Colbert's warmth
of feeling which went into the part of the Mother was a joy to watch,
Joseph Cotton's debonair charm was a thrill for all the ladies, and
I was delighted at the charming girl Shirley Temple has grown into
—a grand picture, I enjoyed every moment. *The Story of Dr. Wassell*
—a film to remember, a film of exceptional interest, notable for the
acting of Gary Cooper, who is always good, but especially suited
to a role of this type, and an extremely good performance from
Dennis O'Keefe, who proved, at least to me, that he really could act,
if only he were given the opportunity, I liked the performance of
Signe Hasso—a girl who I think will go far, she has talent and
beauty. While on the subject of War films, I must mention *The
Great Dictator*, which was such a clever farce, and helped us a lot
when things were looking bad—to laugh at the Dictators, I admired
greatly the performance of Charlie Chaplin, he is indeed a fine actor.

The run of psychological films has been of great interest to me, at
last the screen is 'growing up', I consider *Laura* a real treat, adult
entertainment at its best, with good performances from all the cast
and a haunting tune to make the film all the more interesting, *Guest
in the House*, another thriller of this type, very gripping and until
the last moment it had me guessing as to quite what was going to
happen, again all the cast were splendid, and it was grand to see
Ralph Bellamy back again on the screen. *The Picture of Dorian Grey*
an adaption of Oscar Wilde's famous novel, it was different rather
morbid perhaps but so unusual that I could'nt help liking it, I was

carried right away from the war, this is my idea of good escapist films. George Sanders, as usual, played his part to perfection—who else could have taken his place? This brings me to *The Moon and Sixpence* another of these cynical books which filmed so remarkably well, I heard little of this film from the critics, but personally I enjoyed it thoroughly, the dialogue was splendid, the cynicism of the main character showing to the full, I always enjoy a film where the dialogue is well written and well put over, this film was definitely an adult one, and it is hoped more of this nature will soon be forthcoming.

Musicals, as a whole, do not attract me, but I must say I enjoyed every moment of *Show Business*, the fun and humour of that film was the best I've seen for many a long day, the smart wisecracks, the top-whole performances of Joan Davies and Eddie Cantor, the songs were good, the dancing fine in fact a really good 'Blues-chaser', which I went and saw twice. *Holiday Inn*, is the best musical I have ever seen, but then the one and only Bing Crosby was in it, and he was allowed to really sing—and the numbers were excellent, the dancing of Fred Astaire, always a delight to watch, the charm of Marjorie Reynolds, in fact a charming, unassuming film which I could go on seeing and never be bored, in my opinion a really 'nice' film. The comedies such as *The Road to Singapore, Zanzibar and Morrocco*, notable for the expert clowning of Bing and Bob Hope, are always a treat for me, I enjoy them thoroughly, the jokes, the songs and above all the clever way in which the two main stars set out to have a really good time, thus making the audience enter into the spirit of the film.

How beautiful was *Rebecca*, I was pleased, when I saw the film, to see how like the book it was, so often I am disappointed in the filming of famous books which are altered beyond recognition almost, but *Rebecca* was marvelous, the cast seemed to have been picked straight out of the pages of the book, each one was just as I had imagined they would be, Joan Fontaine, a sensitive and very lovely actress, one of the best on the screen I think, was Daphne Du Maurier's heroine come to life, and Laurence Olivier her hero, a deeply moving and very wonderful film, with the supporting roles played excellently. Another deeply moving film was *The Sign of the Cross*—and another religious film *Going My Way*, proving that religion is not always 'straight laced', but is infinitely human and touching. Bing's performance won him the coverted Oscar—he deserved it if only because the part was so different from what he has always been on the films, Barry Fitzgerald's performance was delightful, I had to see this film twice, just to appreciate to the full the warmth and humour of the dialogue, the sweetness of the boys choir and the utter sincerity and naturalness of Bing. My mind thinks of many splendid films, *Gone with the Wind* a thrill for any Picturegoer, with Clark Gable acting as never before, and our own Vivian Leigh, proving to Hollywood that our stars CAN act— *San Fransisco*, with its magnificent photography, its wonderful acting,

The Count of Monte Cristo, with Robert Donat proving what a fine actor he is, and then going on to his superb *Mr. Chips*—a splendid part for a splendid actor. *For Whom the Bell Tolls*, which I enjoyed for the sheer beauty of Ingrid Bergman, and the wonderful scenery. *Dark Victory*—a sad lovely film, with Bette Davis playing the first sympathetic part I remember seeing her perform, notable too for the discretion and beauty of the dialogue, and the excellent direction. *Christmas in July* a little film, a film about us—the ordinary people—I imagine that what the hero in this film did, namely try and give as much happiness and joy as possible to his friends and family, is just what any of us ordinary folk would do, had we been fortunate enough to win a competition. *The Prisoner of Zenda* another book made into a film, and bringing to life all the romance of Anthony Hope's novel, Ronald Colman—an ideal hero, Madeline Carroll a beautiful Flavia—Douglas Fairbanks—a defiant villian, who I could'nt help liking in spite of himself, perfect for the part, as indeed all the cast were. *Claudia*—a charming portrait from Dorothy McGuire—*Jane Eyre*—a spirited example of Orsen Welles —a period film which I think everybody could enjoy. I remember well the quiet charm of *Little Women*—the excitement of *The Plainsman*—the tenderness of *The Three Comrades* all films which I have enjoyed to the full.

I must just mention *Snow White and the Seven Dwarfs*—which was a miracle of Walt Disney's art, a delightful film—a frightening film— a truly remarkable film—a credit to the great industry.

Now I come to British films, which have improved so much in the past few years. Such films as *First of the Few*—the *Way Ahead*—*49th Parallel* (what a loss to our Films is Leslie Howard—a magnificent actor) *Dangerous Moonlight* (lovely Warsaw Concerto), our own stars in our own films prooving that these at least can hold their own with the American standard. I remember how I enjoyed *We Dive at Dawn* —a splendid tribute to our men of the Submarines, with a truly great performance from John Mills, it had all the 'realness' of actual life, it made me think of people I knew, they were not actors, but any young sailor—suffering hardships and peril. *The Man in Grey* one of the best British—and some brilliant acting from James Mason, the perfect screen villian—and our own Shakespeare adapted for the screen—*Henry V*—the beginning, I hope of a series of Shakespeare plays brought to the screen, what a pleasure to hear our English language spoken correctly and in such beautiful tones. Lastly the two BEST British films ever made—*In which we Serve*, and *This Happy Breed*, such realism, such tradegy and humanity, these people were us, were our Fathers and Mothers after the last war, were our husbands and brothers in this war, the troubles and trials were what we have had to endure, the upsets and misunderstandings of every day, I thank Noel Coward for two films which will make film history, for bringing to the screen the best there is of human nature, and for making two films which can be considered truly great, and which will last for all time.

I come now to the best film I can remember seeing—*The Magnificent Ambersons*—never have I sat so entranced and so interested as I did whilst watching this film. To me it was life in all its splendour and drabness, the Orson Welles commentary thoroughout the film was a treat to listen to, Joseph Cotton's performance a gem, a welcome return to Delores Costello—a small but suitable part for Anne Baxter, a grand performance from Tim Holt, a young actor who I watch for and try to see as often as possible, and above all the superb performance of Agnes Moorhead, what a wonderfully sincere actress she is, Orson Welles certainly knows how to pick his people. I have never seen such acting, I don't think I ever will. I enjoyed the unusual shots, specially the close-up of the carriage in the snow, gradually fading until at last it was just a tiny picture in the corner of the screen, the splendour of the staircase, the unusual lighting, the softness of the shadows, a wonderful film, a typical Orsen Welles film, but a triumph of Motion Picture History. I have never enjoyed a film so much—or been so thrilled with any performance as I was with Agnes Moorhead, she deserved an Academy Award. I hope to see her for many years to come, always giving a perfect portrayal. The film was directed in the way that only Orsen Welles can, it was superb in its interest, its human appeal, its tenderness, its tradegy— it is a marvelous film in every respect.

It is more difficult for me to state my dislikes, there are so many ordinary films which I have forgotten all about, but which probably I did'nt like when I saw them, one film I can remember disliking intensely was *Something for the Boys*, it was so artificial and unreal, not even the most uncritical person could believe in it, I know it was supposed to be farcical—but why bother to make it, the colour was too glaring, the film slow and boring, in fact I would much rather not have seen it. *The Stars Look Down* a drab uninteresting film, which in spite of the big build up it received from the critics, I found hopelessly dull, I could see nothing to appeal to me at all, it was not even 'real', there was no depth and not much feeling, even the pit disaster scene failed to move me, I could'nt believe in the charecters, or in the plot, the film was so different to the book, and therefore failed to please me. Musicals of *Greenwich Village* type, where they take a perfectly good song like 'Whispering' and try to make it into a Symphony—what a disgrace to Symphonic Music, and how monotonous was the plot—I could tell almost before it started, how it was going to end, these so called escapist films bore me, I would rather see a good War film, providing it was really GOOD, than sit through a glaring, gaudy film of this description, they are just another musical, which failed to make a hit. *The Fifth Chair* another disappointment, and such a waste of stars—so called screamingly funny, and yet failing to make me laugh very much. Abbott and Costello film's bore me, I so dislike their slap-stick humour, the first film they made *Rookies* was good, I laughed a lot, but since then they have just repeated themselves, until now even their jokes are the same, only maybe told differently. *Till we Meet*

Again—not even impressive, so unnatural, and so obviously faked all the time, I've never seen such an obvious case of a *Hollywood Nun*, not very nice, I thought. The so called comedy *Here Come the Waves*, just another bore, glamourising the American W.A.V.E.S. who I am sure cannot all look like they did in that film. Sonny Tufts looking ridiculous—and Bing Crosby nowhere near as good as *Going My Way* standard—a disappointing film. On the whole I can usually find some small performance—or something about a film to make up for it being bad, and if I think I will really dislike a film, I usually give it a miss, so my comments on that side of your question are somewhat limited.

I trust I have given you a fair example of my taste in films, maybe they are good—or more likely I think—maybe they are bad, but they are mine. I must just say this, that I always enjoy a trip to the Cinema, and make it a practice to read as much about films, the lives of the stars and the hundred and one interesting points which make the film world so very fascinating to people like me.

NO. 34A

AGE: 24   PARENTS' OCCUPATION:
SEX: F.   MOTHER: HOUSEWIFE
OCCUPATION: STENOGRAPHER   FATHER: DEAD
NATIONALITY: BRITISH

MY MOVIE LIKES AND DISLIKES

Perhaps the quickest way is to deal with each branch of the film entertainment categorically, and then summarise the whole.

Firstly, MUSICALS

These I appreciate to the utmost, whether 'A' or 'B', with the usual exception of a negligable and often unnecessary story attachment. I would instance the Crosby-Hope and the old Rogers-Astaire shows as my favourite types, chiefly because the characters depicted were likeable and amusing, but not meant to be taken too seriously. Deanna Durbin will always attract me in spite of her many critics, simply because to me she remains the 'Peter Pan' of my teens and I can always trace the sweet ingénue of *Mad about Music* and other early films, however sophisticated she may try to be. Betty Grable, Lamour and Carmen Miranda have a certain 'brassiness' which has no appeal to me, being rather 'cheap' in my estimation. Here I have dealt chiefly with American films.

British musicals do not raise enough competition to really interest me and are usually of an irritating nature. Which seems such a pity, but is typical of the film industry in Britain as a whole.

Secondly, DRAMAS & THRILLERS

Here I can hand it to British producers and directors, they can convince me of horror, especially when it amounts to psychological

Miss Lauren Bacall. "Another new film that gave me pleasure was *To Have and to Have Not* — and I must admit that my pleasure was derived from the presence of Miss Lauren Bacall, she's terrific, she's disturbing and she can act. She is seductive but not voluptuous, alluring but not flashy, sophisticated but not haughty and I think she's the most startling thing to flit across the screen in years — if she had not been in the film I should not have been impressed, her personality literally radiates virility and a sort of slithery fascinating glamour." (see Document 38A)

From the Film *To Have and to Have Not*. Humphrey Bogart and Lauren Bacall.

stuff such as that from Alfred Hitchcock. The Americans seem to want us to be comfortable even in the most horrific situation, or whitewash the culprits, even where true stories are concerned.

Thirdly, COMEDY

This has an ever-changing public and policy, like my own, just according to current taste. Today we revert either to the extreme of slap-stick, e.g. Abbott & Costello, or romantic satire and wit, such as *Blithe Spirit* or the *Affairs of Susan*. Of the two types, I can laugh more heartily at the latter, but admit both need clever handling. and I do appreciate the best both can offer.

Fourthly, 'HUMAN' Stories

Of the various categories under this heading, I select the *Hardy Family*, *Flicka* and *Lassie* series as most interesting. I also like those small-town subjects, British or American, maybe because it gives me the chance to laugh at myself, see how even an 'ordinary' existence has its moments and how small some of our worries really are when viewed from a detached angle.

Fifthly, LOVE & ROMANCE

Here my choice depends on my mood and also my own personality.

Confessing to a certain passion in my nature, naturally I like love-scenes, but an over-dose or prolonged embraces embarrass me (and the rest of the audience, by Midlanders reactions!) I realise the film-age of passion which disappeared so suddenly as Ramon Navarro and Valentino and John Gilbert shows signs of returning to life, I hope, with more wit and sophistication. Boy-meets-girl romances are always refreshing to me; triangles bore me; Bette Davis' acting I admire, but continual self-sacrifice irritates me; and the mask-like new faces with which we have recently been inundated, with the possible exceptions of Van Johnson and Lauren Bacall, bewilder me.

SUMMARISING

Having been a movie-fan since the early age of eight, a star name means little to me but more the producer, musical director, or bit player who will cause me to choose my week's film. Here we get a Friday film that is maybe a year old in which case I can see both the good and bad and form my opinion, unprejudiced by critics, which is after all the only real box-office. I feel the latter find it difficult to be without personal prejudice, which is not their fault, and therefore although I read them regularly I am rarely influenced.

One prejudice I have, which I know is unfair, as one shouldn't have in the entertainment world, but that is advance boosting. British stars have so little, but still gain popularity, and I am afraid a 'different' voice, eyes, walk or hair-style, in my humble opinion, do not reserve the right to Stardom.

I can always say I've enjoyed Excitement in films; not murder or a love triangle or a psychological thrill individually, but each in part contributing to a thoroughly enjoyable film, much the same as a good book. Perhaps the influence of the early serials like *The Indians are Coming* and *Lloyd of the C.I.D.* have something to do with it. In those days there was such a surfeit of real 'Horrors' and 'Tragic Triangles' that I became oblivious to their effect, and now whenever my friends expect me to crawl under the seat with terror or weep buckets of sympathy into a lace square, without result, I'm classed as 'cold' which is rather amusing. For instance, *Since you Went Away*, though the acting was convincing enough I suppose.

With regard to Technicolor, I prefer pastel tints and have to hand it to Natalie Kalmus and her associates for outdoor scenes, which always excel the artificial glare of the musicals.

I prefer not to read about, or allow to influence me, the private lives of stars—after all, my employer does not expect me to let mine interfere with my work, even to get me a rise!

I object to the diversion from true facts in most Hollywood period dramas, but that is only in the cases where I know the actual facts— where I'm not aware of them, I don't really care. If the film is interesting enough to make me want to learn more of the actual circumstances I can always do that. I hand it to David O. Selznick for sticking to the book with *Gone with the Wind*.

I hope I have made my likes and dislikes clear to you, for what they are worth. Thank-you for enabling me to get them off my mind after all these years!

NO. 35A

AGE: 24   FATHER: ACCOUNTANT (ADMIRALTY)
SEX: F.   MOTHER: TELEPHONE OPERATOR
OCCUPATION: BOROUGHS'   MACHINE OPERATOR
NATIONALITY: BRITISH

First and foremost I dislike war-films. Probably I shall be called an 'escapist', but I like to go the pictures to get away from the world. One reads war in the papers, hears it on the radio, so surely that is enough. I like to feel that I am in a different world when I enter a cinema.

My second great dislike is the *Dead-End Kids*. I think they are most objectionable youths, with their pseudo-tough airs, and swaggering demeanour. I really believe that they have a bad effect on impressionable adolescents, and I have seen many imitation of them in the lads of my own town.

I like films of the type of *A Tree Grows in Brooklyn*. The people in this film were characters that one could believe in. They were real; the harassed, over-worked mother, the sensitive imaginative little girl, the happy-go-lucky father, with his Micawber-like optimism, and the gay lovable, warm-hearted 'Aunt Cissie'. This film showed how an imagination can make the most mediocre surroundings seem glamourous, and a lively fancy can rise above the drabness and sordidness of a hum-drum life. It was tenderly drawn and well-directed.

How I sigh for the old 'horror' films! How I enjoyed the delicious shivers down my spine that *Dracula* produced! When in my early teens, against my parents' advice, I saw *Dracula* and *Frankenstein* in the same programme, and I always remember the thrill of sitting in the cinema, and watching with a sort of fascinated horror, the nightmare events of these two pictures. Morbid as it no doubt is, I love weird films, with their scenes of misty church-yards, creaking doors, old dark passages, and gloomy grey halls. It is, I suppose, another form of escape, from the matter-of-fact every day life, to the world of fantasy, with its sombre half-tones. In this outlandish world flit vampires, were-wolves, mummies, ghots and monsters; and sheeted spectres forever open their tombs in the 'wee sma' 'oors'.

I also like films with a psychic trend, such as *A Place of One's Own*. Barbara Mullen gave a convincing performance of a woman who could look beyond the ordinary appearances of things, and who understood that there is 'more to a house than just bricks and mortar'. The atmosphere was well protrayed all the way through.

I enjoyed *A Song to Remember*. Overlooking one or two inaccuracies in the life of the composer, and several grating Americanisms in speech, the film was a treat for lovers of classical music. May we have more of this type of film.

Occasionally, I like a really crazy film, one of Abbott and Costello's, or a Will Hay film. The only objection to these films is, that the audience's shrieks of laughter are so loud that one misses about half of the dialogue. But this, I suppose is something that cannot be remedied, unless they held up the film for a few minutes till the shrieks subsided!

I do not care for films about American adolescents. They all seem to be jazz-crazy, and bug-mad, and the girls are boy-crazy, and the boys conceited, and possessing more money than sense.

I like a really good British picture, with a back-ground of delightful English country-side, like *Poison Pen*, *For You Alone*, and *Love Story*. It is a treat too, to hear the pleasing English voices of actors and actresses like Lesley Brook, Laurence Olivier and Margaret Lockwood.

In spite of my few dislikes, and prejudices, I am very grateful for the miracle of the cinema, where, for a small sum, I can enjoy classical music, drama, comedy, thrills, and the world of fantasy.

AGE: 24   FATHER: SOLICITOR
SEX: F.
OCCUPATION: TEMP. CIVIL SERVANT

NO. 36A
LIKES

Thrillers and Mysteries: the tougher the better, especially any of Lloyd Nolan's and Humphrey Bogart's. Reasons:—Mystery and action hold the interest, Sex appeal of the tough & brutal hero.

Crazy Comedy: especially the Marx Brother. This has the appeal of Lewis Carroll—probably relief from the tyranny of reason.

Social Comedy: Sophistication and a certain amount of wit. Vicarious pleasure in luxury, Satisfaction in imagining oneself looking like Rosalind Russell, and being made love to by Melvyn Douglas!

'Amiable' films: i.e. films of cheerful sentiment, not overdone (e.g. Deanna Durbin's early films). All Bing Crosby's. Films showing genuine American home life, (*Meet me in St. Louis*).—Pleasure in looking only on the bright side. The Durbin films belong to a fairytale world where everyone means well and the good are ultimately rewarded.

Westerns: Action.

Musicals: (if not too rowdy) especially Bing Crosby's, for reasons given above.—I have only liked these films since I began working long hours and feel like a 'tired business man'.

Cloak and Sword Dramas: Plenty of action and romance (in the Ruritanian sense).

I like all the above types of films partly because they hold the attention but are no strain on the brain. I also like films which are more difficult to classify, but which could be called 'intelligent'— films which are more interested in ideas, facts, realism (inner as well as outer) than in building up a star or disguising an antique plot by technical efficiency.

In this class are documentaries, first-rate British films like *The Way Ahead*, or exceptional films like *The Maltese Falcon* or *Stagecoach* where the treatment of an old theme, especially the photography, put them in a class apart.

My favourite among these films is the *French film*, which I enjoy for its acting, its wit, cynicism and realism and perhaps most of all the genuineness and passion of its love scenes. Contrasted with the American film, the French film is adult.

DISLIKES

American Romances: like *Mrs. Parkington* or *Frenchman's Creek*. Falsity and crudity of the emotion. Particularly hateful habit of falling into an embrace on two minutes' acquaintanceship, for no apparent reason.

American College films: Dislike of the American attitude towards sex, as shown in these films. Also dislike of the American attitude towards college education.

American Epics: Lack of action, crowds in themselves are boring. Dislike of the glorification of the American way of life.

American films of England and Europe: Crude and unintelligent films (e.g. *Summer Storm* which was laughable) made by people who fail to realise they don't understand their subject. Include here films which distort an historical character to make a star vehicle.

Three of the four twenty-five year old writers are men, but there is a singular unanimity in this group. 'Musicals' receive the usual shattering condemnation, and documentaries are again noticed. In No. 39a we find a second soldier whose whole approach to films has been radically altered by the breaking of the film-going habit.

NO. 37A

AGE: 25
SEX: M.
FATHER:
WHOLESALE PROVISIONS AND MINERAL WATER MANUFACTURER
MOTHER: HOUSEWIFE
OCCUPATION: ADMIRALTY
                ENGINEERING DRAUGHTSMAN
NATIONALITY: BRITISH

With reference to the relevant paragraph in the *Picturegoer*, my opinions on films are given below. I have been to the cinema regularly once a week for some twenty years, and I trust that my opinions resulting from this experience may be of some use.

A. Films I like:—

Normally, I can appreciate anything of any sort, as long as it is good of its kind; this applies to music etc. as well as films. However, there are some films which appeal to me more than others.

For comic films, the Marx brothers seem to be far above other artists, because their act includes real miming as well as very good humour and music. They are also sensible enough to include in their films other competent artists, such as singers etc. which produces a balanced film. Chaplin, I think formerly held their place, because of his miming and his portrayal of the inoffensive 'little' man.

For dramatic & melodramatic films, I prefer those with a real story, such as the biographical type like *Madam Curie* etc. and true to life stories like *Keys of the Kingdom, Random Harvest, How Green was my Valley* etc. Whilst welcoming the cinema as a form of escapism, I also admire good acting and drama, hence my statement above.

In this connection, when it comes to films concerning the ordinary working class and stories portraying scenes from real life, I don't think Hollywood can touch British films when the latter really try, e.g. *Colonel Blimp, This Happy Breed, The Way Ahead*, and *Waterloo Road*.

The last named film showed in uncompromising fashion a problem which has caused many heartaches; namely, the Service man who thinks his wife is unfaithful in his absence. The film treated the audience as adults and did not gloss over the sordid part of the situation or the unpleasant characters.

An American film on similar lines never shews the naked truth of life it must be clothed in sugary sentiment, buckets of tears, girls having babies, heroic mothers managing homes which need about 40 pounds a week to run etc. etc.

War films:—Here British films reign supreme. Rare as they are, they stand like giants beside the childish U.S. efforts e.g. *San Demetrio, London*; *The Way Ahead*; *Western Approaches,* and an excellent submarine film whose name I cannot recall, which featured John Mills and Eric Portman.

Their virtue in brief, seems peculiarly simple; namely, tell a plain, unvarnished tale from life, and leave it at that. I never remember being so gripped by a film as I was by the simple drama of the men in the lifeboat in *Western Approaches.* No tragic heroines with babies, tears galore, mock heroics, but an epic slice of life.

Musicals:—firstly theatrical musicals, which at the moment, seem the prerogative of Hollywood, but I think they are losing their grip. The best type seem to me to be those which not only present spectacle and colour with clever acts, but also have a story to tell. Films such as the original *Broadway Melody*; *The Great Ziegfeld*; *George M. Cohan*, make you realise what the great men of the theatre have done, as well as presenting good, light entertainment. Films including good music, like *Fantasia* and *Song to Remember* are as good as symphony concerts.

Murder and mystery films:—I like these again to treat the audience as having some slight intellect; good examples are *Double Indemnity*, *The Letter, Laura*. They only have one corpse, but present an intelligent and sensible story which holds the attention of the audience.

B. Films I don't like:—

Comic films which rely on pure slapstick and those films which the star(s) try to carry alone. Typical examples are Abbott and Costello and George Formby; these people usually occupy the screen for some 95% of the running time, using the same old gags and situations which date from the Ark. George Formby films follow a strict routine:—George is a goomph, George meets girl; George plays 'uke'; George beats villain; George gets girl. Intelligent use of this star, with good support would make all the difference in the world.

Dramatic films:—Here I have a big grudge against the U.S. for the idiotic pictures they show of England (or should I say Britain?). There are always fog, supposed Cockneys, Dukes and blue bloods with castles galore, and 'the stiff upper lip, you know'. I despair of ever seeing a normal, red-blooded British working man, home and decent weather in a U.S. film.

The *White Cliffs of Dover* was ruined by a false upper-class atmosphere.

Another detestable feature in many U.S. films, including musicals is the habit of glorifying a hero who is a *Smart Aleck.* That is, he makes money in peculiar ways, dresses flashily, is devoid of all manners, thinks it quite bright to force his way into a girl's bathroom or bedroom if she is changing etc. Such characters, cheap seducers and crooks, in plain words, do exist, but the idea that they are heroic characters or that they will reform for love of a good woman is sheer tripe. The effect of this film philosophy on the young is very questionable and undesirable in my opinion.

War films:—U.S. war films usually give me hysterics. I used to read tuppenny 'bloods' when very young, whose heroes were beginners compared with those in U.S. war films. They think nothing of capturing a whole division or sinking a fleet single handed.

The only U.S. war film I have seen which was actually clapped at the end (I only remember some 15 similar occasions all told in local cinemas) was the *Fighting Lady*. The reason for this seems obvious to me, it was an actual combat film taken by serving personnel; not a studio epic made by box-office grabbers who had never seen the battle line.

Musicals:—Unfortunately, Hollywood now seems to regard these as a mass-production job. One gets tired of seeing a series of acts thrown together without a story. If there is a story, it never varies:— Boy and girl struggling along, girl becomes famous; boy continues to struggle and worship from afar; girl links up with some impresario or other; girl turns back to first boy; curtain. Further, girl stars are now chosen from the obscurity which they deserve, and after much grooming, massage, and heaven knows what marvels of make-up and corsetry, emerge as another 'star' from the same old mould. The usually cannot act, sing, or dance; but by means of Technicolour, elaborate dress and undress, and much dazzling spectacle are called public favourites etc. Betty Grable, Vivien Blane, Constance Moore are typical examples. Troupers like Ginger Rogers put them to shame. Similar comparison applies to men; compare Fred Astaire and George Murphy with Victor Mature and John Peyne and other 'rising lights'.

Murder & Mystery films:—I dislike those with a corpse in every reel, secret panels and rooms, hooded fiends and other childish devices. Usually the villain is either perfectly obvious or else the plot is so complex that you end up wondering if you yourself did the horrors you have seen!

If you can forgive a diversion which indirectly concerns your enquiry, I should like to see the cinema used as an educational instrument as well as entertainment. Not only documentary films, or other academic features, but films with an educational slant could be shewn in schools. What more delightful way of learning could there be than seeing say *Henry V, Fantasia & Madam Curie* and learning respectively history, musical appreciation, and the story behind scientific facts? Those of us who have done any teaching or instructing know that a class will retain knowledge from a film or practical demonstration long after an abstract lecture is forgotten.

NO. 38A

AGE: 25   PARENTS' OCCUPATION:
SEX: M.   FATHER: FARMER
OCCUPATION: FARMING   MOTHER: HOSPITAL NURSE
NATIONALITY: ALL BRITISH

At your invitation in *Picturegoer* I would like to write about some of the films I have liked and disliked, and my reasons. First I will take the films I have liked.

The film that springs immediately to my mind is *The Picture of Dorian Gray*. When I went to see this film I knew I was in for a very free adaptation of Oscar Wilde's novel, so I was neither surprised or horrified at the complexes of Mr. Dorian Gray, but on the contrary, thrilled. I especially liked the scene when Dorian Gray murdered his artist friend in the top room of his house, the swinging lamp, in this scene, seemed to convey the whole ghastliness of the situation and made the audience feel what murder is like. . . .

. . . There were two old ladies in the row behind me, and when the film started one said to the other: 'Oh I do so like these old-fashioned films, there's always so much in them'.

As the film progressed and the pecularities of Dorian Gray were flashed across the screen the same old lady said: 'What a funny picture, I don't like it a bit'. To which her friend replied: 'It makes you think unpleasantly—I wish it would end'.

This was the opinion of the undescerning filmgoer, they did not understand the complex and therefore could not tolerate it. But to the educated filmgoer *The Picture of Dorian Gray* was something new and outstanding in screen art and will be long remembered.

Next comes *Frenchman's Creek*. What I liked about this picture was its boisterous swashbuckling atmosphere and the outrageous beauty of Joan Fontaine. It was all very romantic and marvellously gowned and had an extravagant air about it that added to its entertainment value.

I enjoyed a film called *Laura* mainly because of its dexterity of direction, originality of photography and for its first-class acting. The haunting title tune was a perfect match for the strangeness and unusualness of the film and was very largely responsible for the great ovation it received.

Now three British films—*Waterloo Road*, *Love Story* and *They Were Sisters*. These scored on their complete naturalness and by being thoroughly English. They were not as lavish as American Productions but they possessed a simplicity that drew a very large audience wherever they were shown. Other British films that have entertained me to the highest degree include *Madonna of the Seven Moons*, *A Canterbury Tale*, *Great Day*, *The Man in Grey* and *A Place of One's Own*.

I liked the picturization of the life of Chopin called a *Song to Remember*. I liked the acting of Cornel Wilde as Chopin—and how beautifully wan he looked. I also thought Merle Oberon was sufficiently panther-like as Madame George Sand. But of course the main attraction of this film was the music, which incidentally, was superbly played by Jose Iturbi.

Musical films of this type are always worth a visit if filmed by a company of repute. A few years ago we had *The Great Waltz* and recently *Waltz Time*—both films are worth a second visit for their music and romantic element.

A recent film I thought charming was *Under the Clock*. Its story was slight and unpretentious but the film had understanding and made one feel the emotions of the players—I mean it didn't seem at all wrong or unlikely that Judy Garland married a soldier after only a few hours acquaintance. In fact I for one got quite hectic when they got separated on the tube. I also liked the very close-ups of Judy Garland and Robert Walker when they realised they loved each other in the park. Personally I thought *Under the Clock* a gem in dialogue.

Another new film that gave me pleasure was *To Have and to Have Not*—and I must admit that my pleasure was derived from the presence of Miss Lauren Bacall, she's terrific, she's disturbing and she can act. She is seductive but not voluptuous, alluring but not flashy, sophisticated but not haughty and I think she's the most startling thing to flit across the screen in years—if she had not been in the film I should not have been impressed, her personality literally radiates virility and a sort of slithery fascinating glamour.

A Tree Grows in Brooklyn was the most real film I have ever seen, it did me good—it educated my heart a bit more. Little Miss Peggy Ann Garner's acting was a joy to watch and deserves an Oscar.

Of course there are screen classics that everyone can't help liking—these include: *Rebecca, Pride and Prejudice, Wuthering Heights, Gone With the Wind, David Copperfield, Little Women* (how wonderful Hepburn was in that). *Queen Christina*, and the *Barretts of Wimpole Street*.

Now a word about the films I have disliked. I saw one last week which I disliked intensely, it was called *Experiment Perilous* and starred Hedy Lamar, George Brent and Paul Lucas. The story was muddled and disjointed and somehow seemed 'fussy'. It was expensively staged and could have been good if the story had been interesting. Hedy Lamar looked as lovely as a dresden shepherdess—but what's the good of beauty without brains?

I am now going to utter the unforgiveable and say I did not like *Going My Way*. I found it slow monotonous and the egotistical acting of Barry Fitzgerald annoyed me intensely—and it doesn't suit Bing Crosby to be sentimental with Dead End Kids. Yes, *Going My Way* really bored me.

Of course I loathe 'Hot Rhythm' films where blatant jazz bands squawk distortedly—there's dozens of them—*Edie Was a Lady, Hot Rhythm*—nearly all Betty Grable films—*Tonight and Every Night* and *The Girls He Left Behind* to mention but a few. They are enough to give anyone a nervous break-down and definitely do cause dozens of headaches.

Then of course there is the second-rate occupied country films such as *Uncertain Glory* and *First Comes Courage*—they are not authentic and seem to delight in the grotesque and usually the photoghraphy is so dark that all one can see are shadows moving about upon a dark background.

I would like to close by accentuating the fact that I like my films realistic refreshing, beautiful to look at, artistically photographed, sensitively acted and delicately directed.

NO. 39A

Before the war I visited the cinema twice weekly, and shopped for my films. I was then twenty-one years old, and found the majority of films passable entertainment, rarely being bored.

Returning from the Middle East this year after a stay of nearly five years, I found that the old habit had gone. To-day I never see more than one show a week, sometimes only one a fortnight. I have the time, but the inclination is sadly lacking.

During my service abroad I was able to see a number of American and British wartime productions, but as the war years passed I found myself becoming more critical and selective, preferring to read a good novel rather than see a second-rate or 'average entertainment' film.

I thought that perhaps we in the Middle East were not getting the best films, but it seems now that nobody was, or is, getting the best in any appreciable quantity. Such films as *Citizen Kane*, *Major Barbara*, *Fantasia*, *The Gentle Sex*, reached the camp and civilian cinemas, but they do not represent average film entertainment.

The ration of bad to good was much higher amongst Hollywood films than it was with the products of British studios. All too few documentaries gladdened our hearts with their scenes of the British countryside and way of life. The cinema, as a whole, was wasting its time with the commonplace.

And it still seems so. Hitchcock, Welles, Pascal, Disney. Are these and one or two more the only men of originality and courage in the industry? Must we turn to plays and books for a reasonable standard of intelligence in entertainment? The commercial cinema has its moments, but they are still moments. The seeker after something different must go to the few small London West End Cinemas, specialising in films not confined to the exploitation of sex and sensation.

I may be accused of intellectual snobbery, but the fact remains that at an average super-cinema performance I am bored for seventy-five per cent of the time. And I am not prepared to go on paying one hundred per cent admission fee for twenty-five per cent entertainment.

Has the cinema changed since 1939, or have I?

The remedy rests with the public; but, judging from current box-office receipts, the public is satisfied.

AGE: 25
SEX: F.
OCCUPATION: TELEPHONE OPERATOR
NATIONALITY: BRITISH

FATHER'S OCCUPATION:
RAILWAY FOREMAN
MOTHER'S OCCUPATION:
OFFICE WORK

Films I like, well there are lots of films that I have liked enormously and looking back I find that they all vary greatly. But I also find that in most cases my favourite films have been British films or American made films with British stars. Therefore I definitely prefer a film in which I can listen to the perfect English diction which is so refreshing after the Yankee jarring effect. This however isn't all that I desire in a film. There must be a good story, I positively detest the musicals which are offered up very temptingly with glitter and sparkle but which contain practically no story at all or the usual 'local boy (or girl) makes good'. I also hate the bright dazzling Technicolor sequences which bedeck some of these films although I like colour when it is used discreetly. Films with an English background like the admirable *Waterloo Road* and *Love Story* (with its marvellous Cornish scenery) I'll always adore because I love our scenery more than any other I've ever seen and have never yet seen any American film which has portrayed it truly. Although of course I have my favourite stars I would not go to see them regardless of the film in which they are playing. Greer Garson for instance is my greatest favourite but I always read very carefully all about her films and if I do not think they are worthy of her great talents I avoid them. I like a good murder mystery but here again the story counts. Films like *Laura* and *Double Indemnity* were very much appreciated by me for their story value and great interest. Here I must say that America scores for there is no-one who can made a murder mystery like Hollywood. Films like *Blithe Spirit* I adore for the spirit of fantasy and great amusement derived from them is unique. Looking back I really think that the only films I definitely dislike are as I said Musicals with no story and too much dazzle (though I love music) and can always enjoy a film like *A Song to Remember* or *The Great Waltz*. Western films I detest and any films featuring crazy comedians. War films now I'm beginning to hate though some of them are so very admirable that I still go to see them when they are like *The Way Ahead* or *In Which We Serve*, both British films. Some films I go to see again merely to recapture the same joy and feeling of respect and admiration for a fine achievement. A film like the Gainsborough success *The Man in Grey* which had all the ingredients for a fine film merited a second visit as did the fine *Henry VIII*. I also detest the films which feature crooners though a marvellous singer like Rise Stevens is a delight to hear. I admire fine acting in any film but am sorry to see fine artists wasted in very inferior efforts and this is happening much too often. Well this is all I have to say. Please make no mistake, I admire most American films very much and realise always how far ahead they are in most things but still will plump for a good British film every time though I am afraid there are not nearly enough being made at the moment. And I still maintain the story counts every time.

The last contributor in the twenties (aged 28) reveals the very strong influence of the films she sees—'horror' films make her 'ill, mentally and physically', Charles Boyer makes her discontented with her boy-friends, she goes to the cinema to be 'entertained', not elevated or edified, and quite obviously wants to be taken out of herself.

NO. 41A

AGE: 28   FATHER'S OCCUPATION:
SEX: F.   PROFESSOR
OCCUPATION: CLERK   MOTHER'S OCCUPATION:
NATIONALITY: BRITISH   HOUSEWIFE

I must confess to being very pro-American in my choice of films— so often British productions are merely stage successes transferred to the screen. I detest the bedroom farce, with its 'high society' immorality of outlook, would far rather see the redoubtable Cagney, with his down to earth punches than the simpering effeminacy of the foppish 'gentleman' of so many of our own productions. My film must have a story, unless an extravagantly produced musical, which entertains the senses more than the intellect. I detest horror films that embrace the impossible, such as *Frankenstein* or *The Bat*, they make me ill, mentally and physically, and the utterly imaginative is only enjoyable to me when dealt with as in *I Married a Witch* with imagination and brilliance in direction. I adore American comedy and comedians, from Cantor to Kennedy, but *all* the British dialect comedians of the Formby school, leave me cold. Films of the Boyer type made me bored and discontented with my own boy-friends, but if they spoke and acted in the same way, I guess, as of too much caviare, I'd sicken. Bogart's films, virile as he himself, wake me up, quicken my repartee, sort of put me on my toes. The films of Colman, and the late Leslie Howard made me feel safe and happy in their company, and such as *The Lost Horizon* or *Smilin' Thro'* like listening to Chamber Music—O.K. Once in a while! I adored Olivier's *Henry V*. Why can't British films be always up to this standard. I have seen it four times already and shall see it again, more than once. Never have I ever wanted to see any other British film more than once—with the possible exception of Coward's *In Which We Serve*, and the like, which are not *all-time* entertainment. We have no Ann Millers, Astaires, Bill Robinsons or Eleanor Powells over here, so why do we try to make dancing musicals when we haven't the talent available. Far better to strike out for ourselves, make good films with scenarios especially written for the screen by brilliant authors. But do we? No! We get *A Little Bit of Fluff*, *Lady Windermere's Fan* (a rude American G.I. I know thought he was going to see a posterior of nobility—fan having *quite* another meaning over there!), *The Last of Mrs. Cheney*, etc., etc., all creaking with age and musty atmosphere. We *make* no stars, neither do we spend money on publicity to sell new names, but *established* stars—often too old to face the cruel camera— are put before us and then we are expected to be patriotic enough to favour the second-rate. Even the few French films made under all the difficulties they have had to encounter over there, have more genius and imagination than our own, and *Tonight and Every Night* the story of a *London* theatre during blitz days, was produced in America. Ah me, ah my!! I am aware that all this is a slight diversion from the question you ask, but I am writing it so that you may know, and understand, the psychology of a vast majority of average picture- goers. We like films that give us value for our money. I, personally, like the virile in entertainment, artists with personality and talent who *know* their job—be it Frederic March in *I Married a Witch*, *Fantasy*,—*Arsenic and Old Lace* with Cary Grants *comedy*—Cagney's *virility* in *Blood on the Sun*, Oliviers *drama diction* and *technique Henry V*, or the brilliance of *The Three Caballeros*—these at random. I want to see lovemaking and adventure such as I will never know, acting, dancing and singing par-excellence—clothes and decor beyond my means of attainment—I go to be *entertained* not to be preached at, edified, elevated or inspired to nobler things—neither do I go to be bored if I can avoid it! I detest sly innuendo of the cheeky chappie school, that makes me uncomfortable, and my escort blush (men *are* funny that way more often than women, you know). I'd rather see a film about a 'gunman's Moll' than one about an 'itsy bitsy' society doll who sobs all over the screen on losing her all, or the sordid story of illicit love and illegitimate birth. The gunmans Moll *does* stand up for herself, anyway. I don't like seeing poverty and distress on the screen, as in *Love on the Dole*—altho' I would do my utmost to allevi- ate it in real life. I visit News Theatres regularly, and would like to see travelogues confined to these alone, with two full length films on every cinema programme, we so rarely get our moneysworth in this respect. I love Disney cartoons, they are full of imaginative genius and beautifully produced. I detest the cruelty to animals that passes for humour on the screen in American films, and the vulgarity of their outlook toward cows and such. I hate films that try to preach a moral, talk of 'twerps' (I wonder if they know the *true* origin and application of this word?) show me poverty or suffering, the blind or maimed slum life or the other extreme the idle rich with their *prewar* sense of values. Bette Davies or Carmen Miranda—Robert Mont- gomery or Schnozzle Durante—Charles Boyer or Eddie Cantor— Garbo or Pop-eye—Noel Coward or Bob Hope—they're entertainers all, and I like to see them enact on the screen all the joyous, dra- matic, thrilling, lovely adventures I myself won't get out of life, whether I laugh or cry in the seeing, I am *entertained*, and grateful for it. Not for me poverty, disease, ugliness, sordid recrimination—that I can see in the world every day—and it definitely does not entertain me. Films have a great influence on the average picturegoer—more than the theatre ever had and—speaking for myself—my likes and dislikes are very marked.

Only three people in the thirty to forty age-group sent in documents. No. 43a is remarkable for its thoughtful approach and comments on films for children, and agrees with No.42a in disliking the portrayal of pert and precocious children on the screen. No. 44a repeats the moral streak which runs through so many of the documents.

NO. 42A

AGE: 34
SEX: F.
OCCUPATION: SHORTHAND TYPIST
NATIONALITY: BRITISH

FATHER'S OCCUPATION:
EX CAPTAIN REG.
ARMY (RETIRED)
MOTHER'S OCCUPATION:
HOUSEWIFE

Dislikes.

1. I dislike comedies about precocious or funny children who are always getting into scrapes, such as the *Henry Aldridge* series, or films about Jane Withers when she was younger.

I find it impossible to work up sympathy or laughter at such *unloveable* children. They just seem terribly precocious, interfering and too grown-up for words!

2. I am sick to death of lavish musicals: the novelty of the dancing and costumes has worn off: the tendency to use the third dimension: that is to invent any excuse to show scenes which could not possibly be put on one stage—or could follow one another so rapidly—all this I find irritating, and the plot is usually very weak or non-existant.

3. I dislike 'Thriller' films which are made completely without regard to logical sequences: just innumerable 'red herrings' across one's trail, so that in the end one is completely confused and can't care 'who dun it' or why!

4. I used to enjoy 'Society' comedies: what one would call the drawing room type of film, but during the war, the lavish rooms, horribly expensive clothes and jewels: the flippant behaviour seems in bad taste, and so unlike the world as it exists today.

5. I dislike war films now—we have had too many of them, and particularly the American type which sentimentalises too much and conveys the impression that the Yanks are the only ones with feelings viz. that recent film with Claudette Colbert, Jennifer Jones, and Shirley Temple. They were *so* gallant (all in a comfortable, un-bombed house, with cocktails and handy males) that I nearly howled with boredom.

6. One more dislike! English films with children. They are too stiff and well mannered, and make the film too stilted, such as *They Were Sisters* starring Phyllis Calvert.

Likes:—

1. I like intelligent 'Thrillers' of the Alfred Hitchcock type. I don't think I shall forget *The Lady Vanishes* in a hurry. The acting was superb: the suspense terrific, and nothing hackneyed about it.

2. I love period films, provided the Director knows what he is talking about and doesnt muddle them up—Americans are guilty of this sometimes.

3. I get a special 'kick' out of seeing my favourite classics filmed, especially nowadays when they adhere more carefully to the book: it brings such characters as 'Heathcliffe' in *Wuthering Heights* completely alive for me.

4. I loved *Our Gang* series about American children. What has happened to these?

5. I love coloured films from which you can tell the Technicolour man has a real sense of colour. I am an Artist by hobby and it is sheer joy to me to notice some of the blending and harmonies,—such as some of the El Greco touches in *Blood and Sand* and I shall never forget the dramatic appearance in *Wings of the Morning* of Annabelle coming downstairs into a room of subdued tones, (after one had got used to seeing her disguised in drab boy's clothes) clad in a burgundy evening gown.

6. I love the English films which have been made since the war; never before has English character, with its humour, pathos, stoicism, etc. been so perfectly portrayed with all the charm of the English countryside. When it is well made, give me an English film every time, particularly with lovely English voices; when it is badly made—there is *nothing* worse!

NO. 43A

It is always a great regret to me that being a 'grass widow' and tied to the house with two small children, I am able to go to the pictures much more rarely than I should like. But I read as much as I can about the current releases, just in case I do get an opportunity to see a film. I never go to the cinema for the sake of just 'going to the pictures'—it is always to see a film which I have either heard or read is good. Usually film criticisms by critics whose taste I know is nearest to my own—C. A. Lejeune for example.

I find it difficult to say the type of film I enjoy most, as I prefer my filmgoing diet to be as varied as possible—but I avoid the empty synthetic type of film—the 'second feature'—which to me has nothing in its favour, not even as pure entertainment. America is the chief sinner in turning out dozens of this type of film; they are utterly worthless and apart from being a sad waste of time, are an insult to anyone who makes any attempt at thinking for themselves. The main thing that I ask for is that a picture should be sincere, thoughtful and adult—and well photographed. I don't give a hang whether it is British or American, although when one of our pictures does ring the bell, it is more often a film which I think is getting pretty near to good cinema. They are usually less superficial and 'glossy' than the normal run of American films. But there certainly are exceptions, and our bad films are quite as bad as American efforts in the same category!

I wish that foreign films could be much more easily seen—they are a rare treat for anyone who doesn't live in London, or belong to a film club. I think they are as near to perfection as films have got so far. The last one I saw was a revival of *Katia* (during a visit to London) and I shall never forget it. The indescribable something—is it atmosphere—the perfect timing, the excellent photography, and above all the assumption that the audience was adult and thinking, and did not need to have everything explained twice over, and in words of three letters—it was a stimulating experience to see a film of that calibre. Although I do prefer a 'meaty' film, there are of course times when I want to be amused and distracted from worries and troubles, and then—avoiding musicals and leg shows like the plague —I go for sophisticated comedy, American or British. The type of film which one can enjoy as purely light entertainment—Rosalind Russell in some of her earlier pictures, or those of the *Thin Man* type.

Normally I go to see the acting of the stars in a film—chiefly because it is the best yardstick by which to judge the type and quality of the picture but I would not go to see favourite actors in a film I knew to be poor apart from their presence in the cast. But given a film without one single name I knew in it—and yet with an excellent report, be it British, American or foreign, I should have to see it.

I read a great deal, but when a book I am fond of has been filmed, I think more than twice before going to see it, because naturally enough, it is most unlikely that the actors will be anything like my cherished ideas of the characters—either in manner or appearance. *National Velvet* is in my eyes a sorry mistake—speaking from the stills and comments in the papers—and I could mention many more such unfortunate mutilations. To be fair I must admit that *Gone With the Wind* didn't have too many deviations—nor did *Rebecca*—but I really think they are two of the all too few exceptions. No, so long as producers will insist on filming books—I shall have to be strong minded and avoid them. (Of course, if I have not already read the book it is different—I read the book afterwards and enjoy its wider canvas and deeper meaning.)

As the mother of two children—the eldest nearly eight—I am wondering when I shall feel it will be good for them to visit the cinema—if at all. So far I have resisted the Disney films, excellent though they are. They seem to me to be too adult in manner and reasoning—and even horrific. I wish some brave film company would film some of the well loved and familiar childrens' stories—the simpler and happier ones—with live characters and without sophistication and permed and pert youngsters to mar them. Is it too much to ask? For purely educational purposes the screen has no equal both for children and adults, and I should like to see lots more educational films from biology to repairs round the house.

So in brief I enjoy any film which is thoughtful and sensitive, and sets out to achieve some purpose and succeeds, whether it is light entertainment or a film to ventilate some social or economic problem. I loathe anything which is empty and paltry—and the everlasting 'who-dun-it' type. (An exception to the last—the brilliant *Maltese Falcon*.)

I am a housewife and mother, thirty years of age, British, and my father was a civil servant, my mother a shorthand typist. And I am *not* a highbrow—but want to see a greater percentage of considerably more intelligent films of any type.

NO. 44A

AGE: 36
SEX: M.
OCCUPATION: PRIVATE SECRETARY
NATIONALITY: BRITISH

FATHER'S OCCUPATION: CLERK
MOTHER'S OCCUPATION: —

Films Liked:

Strong action films with bed-rock of meaty drama. Preferably hero who triumphs against adversity and gets the girl. Don't mind hero with silver spoon in mouth but prefer lowly beginnings.

Probably see myself reflected in lowly beginnings and see myself as I would *like* to be—masterful go-getter. Quite understandable since I am exactly the opposite.

Western films because they are so essentially *clean* and present no problems. Easy to understand—plain good versus evil—the scenery is redolent of fresh air and reminds me of countryside, of which I am keen lover.

Sentimental domestic dramas—make me feel at one with the characters—sympathise with their tiffs and rejoice when home happiness is assured.

Disney fantasies because of the lovely music, the absence of human frailties and their cleanliness also.

Comedies with slick dialogue, ingenious situations and hen-peck slant. Probably because I'm not hen-pecked and like to laugh at those who are.

Films disliked:—

Musicals. Story is sacrificed to introduce numbers and I am antagonized immediately. The noise distracts me and makes me think of big cities, which I detest. Too much leg and appeal to sex. No mystery about it and I think mystery is the source of woman's power.

Films with child stars. Children who are forward beyond their years nauseate me. I can't believe it natural and the celluloid stars become freaks to me. Simplicity of mind, natural shyness, and respect for elders—that's my idea of a child and I stick to it. I don't like films with bedroom scenes and any suggestion of smut. I become embarrassed both for myself and the audience.

Don't like films where a character is ridiculed upon a serious subject. Become embarrassed for *him* or *her* then.

I hate films where a star—man or woman—mouths a lot of high sounding talk about nobility of character, sanctity of motherhood etc. Cannot believe that ordinary people could bring themselves to talk in such a way and the unreality of it makes me squirm.

Hate back-ground music (coming from nowhere) for the same reason—unreality.

And finally I become prejudiced against stars whose private lives are not above board. Nothing to do with their art no doubt but I think of what they do—behing their masks of heroism and sacrifice—and it colours my impressions.

(Over 4 years sea-service might have strengthened some of my dislikes. The same might apply to other service-men. Suggest you repeat your experiment, in a year's time when we've all settled down again.)

Do the contributions of older writers show any great change in taste? I think not. It is remarkable that the only foreign contributor (No. 46a) is in general agreement with the bulk of our correspondents, except in his stressing of 'charm'. If these documents may be regarded as typical, they show none of the great changes in taste, in the later years, which are indicated in the years 14 to 25.

NO. 45A

AGE: 46   FATHER'S OCCUPATION:
SEX: F.   MERCHANT
OCCUPATION: HOUSEKEEPER   MOTHER'S OCCUPATION:
NATIONALITY: BRITISH   HOUSEWIFE

I base my first choice of film on those in which good acting is given a chance. Such films as *How Green Was My Valley, Madame Curie, The Man in Grey, None but the Lonely Heart, The Way Ahead, Now Voyager, Old Acquaintance* and *most* French films live in one's memory.

My second choice on the films which are a pleasure to the eyes and ear (shall I say escapist pictures), such as some of the technicoloured musicals, *Sweet Rosie O'Grady, Down Argentine Way, Kismet* and that charming pre-war effort in colour *Wings of the Morning.*

I like sophisticated comedy of the type of *The Women* and *Together Again* wich contain many witty wisecracks, but slapstick leaves me cold except in the case of Abbot and Costello as I find the latter unaccountably droll. Some stars, particularly the American actresses, will always draw me despite the type of film—others I would wish to avoid.

I hate college films, newspaper dramas, 'Dead End Kids', dance bands and their deified ladies and emasculated crooneys, the second-rate type of British film in which all the actors appear to be half-wits, impossible desert island romances and highly improbable horrific stories, tales of the Yukon, and deep sea fishing films and hackneyed westerns.

I like documentary and war films very much and Walt Disney I would never wish to miss.

Photography and continuity are important but should not intrude on the story so that one is unduly conscious of them.

NO. 46A

AGE: 48
SEX: F.
OCCUPATION: HOUSEWIFE

FATHER'S OCCUPATION:
SCHOOLMASTER
(FRENCH)
MOTHER'S OCCUPATION:
HOUSEWIFE (ENGLISH)

I think films with box office appeal are merely vulgar travesties of art.—'Box office appeal' boils down to 'sex appeal'.

The films I dislike are those which make a display of women, with little or no story, voluptious music and costume, more suited to Turkish mentality, than to the taste of cultured people. The beauty of woman in marble is good, in warm tints of undress merely gross. These are off my list for ever. I like pictures where life is shown as it really is, where human beings are natural, where the scenery does not come from a scenic artist's brush. French and Russian films touch the heights of artistry.

Once we reached up in *The White Hell of Pity Palu, Rain, The Pearl Divers, Henry V, Snow White and the Seven Dwarfs*. All Walt Disney's films are beauty, in that sense. Gertrude Laurence is my favourite, seldom seen! Glamour is another word for varnished vulgarity.

My favourite actor Claud Rains, he always is the character he portrays, a very great actor, my choice in front of the pretty pretty men like Errol Flynn etc.—James Mason also is an *actor*. I thought the *Tawny Pippet* lovely, because I love birds and the country. I hate Betty Grable and all her works. I like Alice Faye for the simple reason that she is essentially sweet, never blatant. Films which show murders and the hunt for the criminal are very poor going, also Sherlock Homes with his uncanny correctness, and Watson, oh boy, my nerves could not stand him, if I knew him in the flesh I'd murder him and give his friend another job.

So I like films which bear a slight resemblance to life, because we all know too well what life is like. Also I hate leg displays, because we all have legs and know what they're like.—There are fine books waiting to be filmed, Russian, French, English, translations from the Chinese also. I would raise the standard of all of it if I were Mr. Rank. Let us hope his films are not also rank. Thats all!

NO. 47A

As an extremely discriminating picturegoer I feel you might perhaps be interested in my views.

The films I choose (and my friends often seek my advice as to the films they should see) are films with a probably story, acted by people who can act and who have charm. In fact I think charm is what I look for most, which is probably why I never miss films featuring Ronald Colman, Charles Boyer, Irene Dunne, Gary Cooper, Ingrid Bergman, Joan Fontaine, Claudette Colbert and Margaret O'Brien. Danielle Darrieux in *Mayerling* (a film I've seen everytime it's come to Manchester, say 4 or 5 times) is another favourite.

I find English films singularly devoid of this elusive quality, however well acted. Perhaps because the American actors seem to have more unself-consciousness. All the Boyer-Dunne films I've seen so often as almost to know by heart and the most recent, *Together Again* is just as beautiful. People with charm like those two lose none of it by getting older, and the same applies to Ronald Colman in *Kismet*.

I'm not in a position to give a list of the films I dislike because I avoid their type like the plague—all Giant Musicals and most thrillers.

My nationality is Swiss, my age 48 and my profession that of Foreign Correspondent.

There was just one series of English films I went all over Manchester to see—produced, I believe, by a woman, in Kew Gardens. I forget their titles, excepting *Paws and Claws* and one about trees was particularly gorgeous; not only for their photography. The dialogue was superb, and quite the best I've ever found in a British film.

NO. 48A

AGE: 52   FATHER:
SEX: M.   M.A.(LOND.),
OCCUPATION: BANK OFFICIAL   RETIRED
NATIONALITY: BRITISH

In my opinion, entertainment, whether stage or film, should be instructive, or informative, or morally uplifting.

But a laugh is good for us all, and humour should be woven into this pattern of entertainment.

I take my films, not merely for the story, but for the colour, photography, direction and production.

By doing this, I maintain that I derive greater enjoyment from my film-going than the person who just goes for the story, or the stars. Films which were not popular successes, but which appealed to me greatly were *The Life of Mr. Handel*, *Wilson*, and *Henry V*.

The first-named film, I liked because of its delicate colour, and vision scenes; the second because of Alexander Knox's wonderful diction; and the last film because of the bold venture in filming Shakespeare.

Additionally, these films were instructive and informative, but were not of 'popular' appeal.

From the moral point of view, I liked *Without Love, They Were Sisters*, and *The Barretts of Wimpole Street*.

The first film intrigued me with Katherine Hepburn's natural and intelligent acting; the second film roused me with James Mason's realistic acting which really made one hate him, whilst the last film contained a brilliant characterization by Charles Laughton, and very fine Victorian atmosphere.

The *Abbott and Costello* type of film I just sit and laugh at (some times!), but I forget it as soon as I have seen it!

To me this type of film is so empty—I prefer a film which provides intelligent discussion, and thus remains in one's memory.

Travelogues and the News-reels particularly appeal to me—in these you have information and education *and* humour if properly presented by the narrator.

NO. 49A

AGE: 58   FATHER'S OCCUPATION:
SEX: F.   HAIRDRESSING
OCCUPATION: LEGAL LINE   MOTHER: (IRISH)

Likes and Dislikes:—

1. Generally, *all* films that show *good* acting.

2. Individually, any film with a tale, plot or background, that makes one think deeply i.e. *Grapes of Wrath, Thunder Rock, I'll be Seeing You, Enchanted Cottage*, etc.

I saw *The Stars Look Down* also *How Green Was My Valley* identical films, but what a different setting. The American one was ridiculous, in every sense, but, from comments I overheard much preferred to the English version.

3. The lighter type of British Life is very good to chase away worries, i.e. *Acacia Avenue, Never Take It To Heart*, but American humour is not so good.

The musicals. These must be *very* good to satisfy my taste. *A Song to Remember, Dangerous Moonlight, Waltz Time*. The Grable type I consider hash, there are quite a few of these, showing neither talent in singing, acting, nor setting, merely a frame for a pair of legs, or more nude body. (But everyone to their taste.)

The greatest fault I find in American films, is, using an actor/actress in one type of film, until one knows every action, movement or bat of an eyelid. This gets boring i.e. Garson, she has a peculiar lilt in her laugh, every picture it comes out again. Against that, is the individually of a woman like Miss Barrymore or B. Davis, but these are exceptions.

Trust this is something near the criticism you require; have been a film fan since 1906 (early films seen in Rouen).

The writer of our last document is 64, yet in essence his contribution does not differ from the general theme of most of the rest. Perhaps the most striking thing about his letter is his description of his mother.

NO. 50A

AGE: 64	FATHER'S OCCUPATION:
SEX: M.	BRICKLAYER
OCCUPATION: BRICKLAYER	MOTHER'S OCCUPATION:
NATIONALITY: BRITISH	HELPMATE TO FATHER

I am going to mention the titles of four films. First *The Common Touch*. I cannot remember ever enjoying a film so much as this as regards a film for what I call a working class audience. To me there were no special 'stars' all actors and actress's were of equal value, it was a very human, sensibly and elevating story, very well acted. The second picture or film is *Smiling Through* featuring Jeannette Mac-Donald and other 'stars'. As I sat watching and listening to this film story I seemed to be taking part in it myself, and each time I saw it (and I saw it many times) I enjoyed it more and more. The singing was superb, the acting was such that it made the story very real, the facial expressions of all taking part was very convincing although I saw it during war time, it made me forget war, and lifted my thoughts to higher levels, this was a clean, decent and elevating film, and time well spent seeing it and also well worth the money paid.

Sentimentally yes, upholding that most beautiful of all things Love, yes, and if these two things were to die out, I think this world, would be even a poorer place than it is to day. Love is ridiculed far too much in some pictures or films and on the 'stage' yes I know that I am old fashioned, but let us have more films like these two. And now from the sublime to the most ridiculous, I refer to two films, in which I got up out of my seat to leave the cinema, I was that disgusted, but I saw them through. First *The Miracle of Morgans Creek* a film that was anything but elevating, in fact, if the producer had been sitting with me, and had heard what some children were saying about it I think his face would have gone very red, a film that was of no use to the world, in fact not even a good moral film. The other film was *Cassonova Brown* perhaps, it was with seeing Gary Cooper in such stirring films before, and then to see him in a dud film such as this, another film that I think could have been done without. Yes let us have 'Decent' films like the first two I have mentioned. If anyone should have had an Oscar award, I think all the leading 'stars' in *Smiling Through* should have one each. As I am getting on in years, perhaps I shall never have the chance to travel, so I would like to see more travel films, which are a delight, and also good education. Films with Jazz and Swing bands I do not like, they are far too harsh.

3. AN INTERPRETATION

We now revert to the two questions which prompted our inquiry : (1) In what state is the present mass taste with regard to films? (2) Is the film industry right when it says: 'we provide the entertainment the public wants'?

Both questions are, we believe, firmly answered for the careful student of our documents. These answers are by no means encouraging in the light of a general diagnosis of our contemporary scene.

We take the second question first, because it is the easier one to answer. However depressing the standards of film taste may be, it is certain from the perusal of our documents that the British film exhibiters do *not* provide the entertainment the public wants. Almost the whole so-called second feature output is rejected by a majority of our contributors: the Betty Grable films, the Blondie films, the so-called comedies of the Three Stooges type, the cheap detective or murder films are unmistakeably disliked. Nor are the 'stupendous' American musicals liked by all.

These definite and sometimes even refreshingly abusive criticisms by our contributors are the more remarkable as most of them are not 'highbrows'. (Some who think they are highbrows suffer from lack of self-analysis). They are all ordinary average English, Scottish or Irish people. We quote for example a wonderful passage from document 37A: 'Murder and mystery films: I dislike those with a corpse in every reel, secret panels and rooms, hooded fiends and other childish devices. Usually the villain is either perfectly obvious or else the plot is so complex that you end up by wondering if you yourself did the horrors you have seen.' It seems obvious that the majority of our writers have a definitely different taste from the American film goer in Middle Town for whom Hollywood mainly caters.

There is unanimous agreement amongst our friends that films like *The Gentle Sex, The Way Ahead, Henry V, The Way to the Stars, This Happy Breed* speak their language, fulfil their wants, satisfy their fantasies and alleviate their frustrations.

All these films have what our contributors call 'a good story, action and good acting'. We quote again from a document which illustrates this point :

'I think English films are 100 per cent entertainment. Whilst in the cinema every incident might have happened to any member of the audience, each happening is so realistic. Once outside the cinema one can return to grim reality and realize that the film was a fairy-tale. A great many American films are so realistic in parts that certain members of the audience will apply the most fantastic incidents into their own lives. They then imagine themselves a second Veronica Lake or Ginger Rogers or even Lauren Bacall! Possibly Hollywood trades on this susceptibility but I doubt if much is really gained from it.'

'Two films I shall never forget are *In Which We Serve* and *The Way Ahead*. The glimpses of home life were subtly real without any decoration. Also each character was a true soldier in his own line of warfare. They even managed to convey that "They also serve, who only stand and wait".'

'It is a pity that so few British films are made and that so many British film stars are under contract to American film studios.'

The same girl writes: 'I dislike intensely films like *Frenchman's Creek* and *Coney Island*. These heroines are almost always the type of woman seen pacing either Piccadilly in London or Lime Street in Liverpool.' Do we have to express disagreement with this convincing representative of our younger generation?

It appears to us that a careful study of our documents may provide more significant norms and indications of what constitutes a spiritually healthy and 'good' film than any amount of box office statistics.

Naturally most of our contributors want to be entertained. They want to forget the dreariness of their lives, they significantly prefer *This Happy Breed* to *The Grapes of Wrath*. (See document 29A). They want a mythical, a heroic, yet naive 'realism' which goes together with escape. Our document 35A is here of particular interest:

'First and foremost I dislike War-films. Probably I shall be called an "escapist", but I like to go to the pictures to get away from the world. One reads war in the papers, hears it on the radio, so surely that is enough. I like to feel that I am in a different world when I enter a cinema.

'My second great dislike is the "Dead-End Kids". I think they are most objectionable youths, with their pseudo-tough airs, and swaggering demeanour. I really believe that they have a bad effect on impressionable adolescents, and I have seen many imitations of them in the lads of my own town.

'I like films of the type of *A Tree Grows in Brooklyn*. The people in this film were characters that one could believe in. They were real; the harassed, over-worked mother, the sensitive, imaginative little girl, the happy-go-lucky father, with his Micawber-like optimism, and the gay, lovable, warm-hearted "Aunt Cissie". This film showed how an imagination can make the

most mediocre surroundings seem glamorous, and a lively fancy
can rise above the drabness and sordidness of a hum-drum life.
It was tenderly drawn and well-directed.'
In films such as Mrs. *Minniver* and *The Best Years of Our Lives*
it is not difficult to understand the sociological reasons for their
success: it would appear that our contemporary masses see
their lives portrayed and interpreted as they experience them.
Happiness, enjoyment, and tragic disappointments, love, drink,
dance, a dose of religion, devotion for family and pets, naive
patriotism; with all this the masses identify themselves, in all
this they *participate*. Yet at the same time these films are not a
reflection of their own drab lives. For the style of living in *Mrs.*
Minniver and in *The Best Years of Our Lives* is *not* the average
middle-class standard. There are rich houses or well-furnished
flats, there are elegant cars, extravagant hats, for ever out of
reach for those millions who see themselves apparently portrayed. So it would appear that the film-maker pursues a
double aim: he subtly joins together sentimental self-interpre-
tation with the consoling comfort of a mythical escape into an
unfulfillable dream-world.

Yet there are those few who want films to be 'instructive, or
morally uplifting', but they are definitely in the minority.

Other 'Likes' which rank high are those of 'good', tense, but
not sordid drama. Here undoubtedly Hollywood comes into its
own. The film *Jane Eyre* for example is unanimously regarded as
a good film. Other perspectives are also significant: film as a
medium of visualizing literature and above all history: 'I like
such films as *Wilson* and *Keys of the Kingdom* because they blend
entertainment with education to a certain extent. I believe it is a
good method of acquainting the public with great men and good
literature. It is only since such books as *Henry V*, *Rebecca*, *Pygmalion* and *Jane Eyre* were filmed that the majority of people are
learning to discriminate a good story and a trashy one.' (Document 9A).

Yet history as portrayed in films is not always accepted un-
critically. Films like *Disraeli* or *Madame Curie* have been justifi-
ably criticized.

Nor should we forget that the musical needs of our contemporary masses are strong and that their likes and dislikes can be
fully illustrated by a detailed analysis of our material which is
not the purpose of this interpretation[23].

[23] We did not feel competent to undertake this task, but we should like to refer
our readers to the brilliant study by T. W. Adorno, *Ueber den Fetischcharakter in der
Musik und die Regression des Hörens*, *Zeitschrift für Sozialforschung*, VII, 3, Paris, 1938.

Another significant document is No. 15A. Its authoress is an 18 year old G.P.O. employee:

'When I go to the cinema, I go to be entertained, and having seen the film I like to feel convinced, and satisfied with my entertainment. I enjoy quite a few types of films but in nine cases out of ten the draw is the star in the film. The sort of film I like best has plenty of outdoor scenes, and children. Always, I look for a sense of freedom in a film, something refreshing, something that really might happen in real life. Children, too, seem to be the embodiment of freedom and happiness. One of the most refreshing, charming, films I have ever seen was *Sunday Dinner for a Soldier*. Here the children, the elder sister, the grandfather, the animals, the houseboat, all seemed so real, and their experiences might happen to anybody. For that reason too I enjoyed *National Velvet* and the beautiful refreshing scenes shot by the sea.'

'On the more serious side I like a good film taken from a novel whether modern or old but to convince me the acting must be at a very high standard. Here, the stars attract me, Bette Davis, Ida Lupino, Joan Fontaine, Ingrid Bergmann; and as I watch them I think how wonderful it must be and how satisfying to them to be able to act like that. What an achievement to really be able to convince the audience that you are happy, sad, indifferent, cruel, etc. I like a film of a serious nature to have an unhappy ending although I can never remember crying in a cinema if the hero or heroine died.'

Perhaps one is justified in drawing attention to the fact that the sense of freedom which our contributor experiences when seeing outdoor scenes and children in films may be explained by her class status. Shut in the office, she appears to satisfy her longing for fresh air by the fantasy fulfilment which films provide.

The same writer expresses her dislike of crime films, thrillers or murders which she shares with many others in these terms: 'I do not like crime films, thrillers, or murders as I find myself imagining all sorts of horrible things when I am alone in the house or walking in the dark at night for a time after I have seen them.' To the reader of Chapter II of the present volume this sentence can offer no surprise.

The star hero worship in the present documents is perhaps less striking than one might have expected from the documents of Chapter II. Our guidance-sheet in that chapter may have caused the overstress of the star phenomenon. Given good acting, the story, the plot is perhaps more decisive for a British audience. We are inclined to believe that the following tendencies, taken from document 23A may be representative: 'In *The*

Way to the Stars the very lack of "Slush" made a lump in your throat, which was enhanced by the fact that after making you feel how terrible it all was, you were suddenly switched over to a scene of uproarious fun, or at any rate to something that made you laugh—instead of cry. The Americans were as we see them, but they were so delightful that you really liked them. What about Johnny Hollis who fell for Toddy—but never kissed her. What about Peter who proposed to Iris in such a delightfully unique manner. These people made you feel good, you lived with them, thought with them, felt as they felt, and in fact for two hours you were not you sitting in the one-and-ninepennies, but were living in that film. This is why I thought it was the finest film I had seen.' What a striking example of *participation mystique* . . .

The documents show that most contributors have only seen American and British films. Those who have seen Russian, French or German films regret that they cannot see more of them. This, clearly, reflects on the commercial practice of the big exhibitor circuits whose managers alone must be blamed for the serious and potentially dangerous lack of internationalism in the film tastes of our contemporary masses.

We believe that the questions which were put at the beginning of this interpretation have been answered implicitly. One can say that in spite of the dictatorship in taste with all its serious repercussions on our value patterns, as it is exercised by the circuit monopolists, the hope of raising film taste is not entirely forlorn—yet.

The forefathers of British audiences once listened to Shakespeare. It was their response which made the Elizabethan theatre possible.

Our material—we must stress it again—defies any easy attempt at typification; either of a sociological or psychological nature. Of course there are affinities between class stratum and film preferences. (See for example document 15A). Moreover there are relations between temperamental structure and film taste (Document 42A), but we did not feel justified in drawing general conclusions in this respect. It is quite possible that further research might usefully start where we left off.[24]

[24] The main reason why I have refrained from such inviting vistas of further research was our primary *political* purpose of establishing the basic framework for a sound film policy. I cannot deny that I am in the first place a political sociologist. Nor did I think, judging from studies like Jung's *Psychological Types*, Spranger's *Lebensformen*, or Kretschmer's *Körperbau und Charakter*—I chose these works almost at random, that characterology and typological psychology in their present developmental stage could give me such help as I felt was required.

It is also true to say that many of our documents show little discrimination. They accept what is put before them, they do not select.

The ultimate choice between a further levelling down or a constructive use of those positive norms which lie open to everyone who has read our documents responsibly is a decision of cultural leadership which was a self-evident truth in the Athens of Euripides as in the Paris of Louis XIV.

A democratic State, fully aware of its task, requires a leading and responsible *élite* not only in the sphere of politics but also in the realm of culture.

IV. RETROSPECT

'*Le Cinéma*', writes André Malraux, '*est d'abord une industrie*'. Consequently the profit *motif* must primarily determine theme, the artistic and social purpose of films. If the artistic purpose is compatible or supposed to be compatible with business considerations, we may get an artistically conceived film, if not the 'hard business man' will always have the final say.

It was a long cry from the Nickel Odeon to our modern picture house palaces in which our modern masses are 'entertained', enjoying an apparent semi-comfort, and indentifying themselves with the luxuries and refinements of their screen idols which are for ever out of their reach.

Yet there is no doubt that a counter-movement has begun. Films can have *katharsis*. Recent films like *Brief Encounter*, *The Overlanders*, *Day of Wrath*, *Ivan the Terrible*, *Les Enfants du Paradis*, *The Last Chance*—incidentally all non-American films—cannot be explained as mere accidents. Their appearance reveals a tendency of the film medium towards art and the increasing concern with the interpretation of collective and individual value patterns.

The attentive reader of the foregoing pages must have realized that there exists a considerable percentage among the cinema-going millions which is waiting to enjoy intelligent and relieving comedy and purifying tragedy, a tragedy which is not morbid.

What proved possible in cultural policy in the case of the B.B.C. when this Corporation decided to introduce the Third Programme, deliberately appealing to an audience of perhaps one million out of perhaps another fifteen million who listen to transmissions from Music Halls, crime stories and quizzes, should be possible in the case of film.

Yet it is more than doubtful whether such a policy towards the deliberate raising of the cultural standard of films can be obtained as long as it is fundamentally a private business monopoly which by virtue of its financial weight dominates the international markets.

Here, if nowhere else, Marx' analysis of the capitalist structure during the phase which forms the transition period from a society of *laissez-faire* to a planned society appears to be fully justified.[25] The weight and strength of the film magnate becomes

---

[25] Cf. Marx, *Capital*, Everyman's Edition, vol. II, p. 844 sqq.

so powerful that he must dictate the standard of taste, and ultimately the outlook and tendencies of our contemporary civilization. Occasionally he will make concessions to make a film like *Henry V* or *Brief Encounter*, but he will not hesitate to exhibit together with these films the worst products of the Hollywood second feature output.

Originally, as the history of early liberalism proves, personalism and individualism were synonymous with capitalism. The unity of freedom of enterprise and freedom of culture characterize European capitalism from the English Revolution of 1689 to the beginning of the second half of the nineteenth century. Since then Liberalism is on the decline and the great critics of the democratic system—Tocqueville, Donoso Cortes, Jacob Burckhardt, Marx—were merely seeking how human freedom might be maintained within the inescapably growing net-work of modern capitalism, in which 'one capitalist lays a number of his fellow-capitalists low'.

Our contemporary film industrialism is only a typical illustration for a general feature of the Western mass society though it appears that the cultural bondage in which we live has received less attention than the analysis of the economic structure of our contemporary world.

Legislators and statesmen, who so rarely have the stature of a Franklin Roosevelt, take the cultural traditions of freedom for granted; they live and act in haste on an apparent capital which is already fully spent. Poets like Rilke escape into an esoteric world of their own and become isolated warners to a world which appears lost in emptiness. Churchleaders become administrators and pray words which have lost their meaning for our sufferings.

Neither escapism, nor traditionalism can be accepted as solutions to make the film medium into a responsible instrument of contemporary culture. We cannot isolate ourselves from the masses. We cannot all go into monasteries.

Films must become a deliberate concern of cultural leadership. Perhaps we should refer to an historical example in order to understand, how culture can become a legitimate field of social reconstruction.

When during the Restoration 'all by the King's example lived and loved', it was through the efforts of writers like Steele and Addison that new standards of taste and behaviour were established and ultimately accepted. The task which these men had set themselves was difficult and the difficulties they had to encounter were many. They are clearly reflected in the *Spectator* where we read in one of its fictitious letters:

'I am now between fifty and sixty, and had the honour to be well with the first men of taste and gallantry in the joyous reign of Charles II. As for yourself, Mr. Spectator, you seem with the utmost arrogance to undermine the very fundamentals upon which we conducted ourselves. It is monstrous to set up for a man of wit and yet deny that honour in a woman is any-thing but peevishness, that inclination is not the best rule of life, or virtue and vice anything else but health and disease. We had not more to do but to put a lady in a good humour, and all we could wish followed of course. Then, again, your tully and your discourses of another life are the very base of mirth and good humour. Pry' thee don't value thyself on thy reason at that exorbitant rate and the dignity of human nature; take my word for it, a setting dog has as good reason as any man in England.' (No. 158). In this passage Addison fictitiously criticizes his own secure position. His norm of womanhood, as we find it expressed in the *Spectator*, added grace, charity, re-finement to domestic life.

Yet social reality and stage presented quite a different picture. 'All the elements of an old and decaying form of society that tended to atheism, cynicism, and dissolute living, exhibited themselves . . . in naked shamelessness on the stage. The audi-ences in the theatres were equally devoid of good manners and good taste; they did not hesitate to interrupt the actors in the midsts of a serious play, while they loudly applauded their obscene allusions.'[26] It is against this background that the great work of Addison must be held.

Slowly, but with the firm hand of the master, Addison builds an ethical code which embraces the totality of man. It is a process of cultural education which brought the aristocratic values and behaviour standards of the Restoration period to its fall.

Perhaps we should give an example of Addison's educational practice. In an unforgettable contribution to the *Spectator* (No. 12), he discusses the subject of ghost stories. Joining the com-pany of his landlady's daughters, he 'heard several dreadful stories of ghosts as pale as ashes, that had stood at the feet of a bed, or walked over a church-yard by moon-light, and of others that had been conjured into the Red Sea, for disturbing people's rest, and drawing their curtains at midnight; with

[26] Cf. W. J. Courthope, *Addison*, London, 1884, p. 18. See also A. Beljame, *Le Public et les hommes de lettres en Angleterre au Dix-Huitieme Siecle*, 1660-1744, Second Edition, Paris, 1897. Leslie Stephen *English Literature and Society in the Eighteenth Century*, London, 1904; H. Taine, *Histoire de la Littérature Anglaise*, vol. III, Paris 1866.

many old women's fables of the like nature. As one spirit raised another, I observed that at the end of every story the whole company closed their ranks, and crowded about the fire: I took notice in particular of a little boy, who was so attentive to every story, that I am mistaken if he ventures to go to bed by himself this twelvemonth. Indeed they talked so long, that the imaginations of the whole assembly were manifestly crazed, and I am sure will be the worse for it as long as they live . . .'

Reading these lines, we think of the many horrors to which our children and adolescents are exposed, when they take thrilling delight in many films of today. 'Were I a father', writes Addison further, 'I should take a particular care to preserve my children from these little horrors of imagination, which they are apt to contract when they are young, and are not able to shake off when they are in years.'

Yet Addison is not at all a rationalist of the later Eighteenth Century type. In fact he is nearer to the integration of the two orders; the order of the heart and the order of the mind which Pascal had re-discovered in the Seventeenth Century.

'I look upon a sound imagination', Addison declares in the same essay, 'as the greatest blessing in life, next to a clear judgment and a good conscience.'

The *Spectator* was a formidable instrument in creating standards of taste and behaviour. The review was first printed in 3,000 copies, but it often reached editions up to 30,000. Thus a general culture was created. 'La culture générale', writes M. Beljame, perhaps the best expert on this epoch, 'qui s'est partout repandue a réuni toutes les classes de la société. Il n'est plus question de groupes divers de lecteurs, de Puritains et de Cavaliers, de la cour et de la Cité, de la capitale et de la province: les lecteurs sont maintenant toute l'Angleterre.'

But it was a bourgeois England which had won a victory. The problems of the cultural tastes and standards of a mass society became urgent when an industrial urban proletariate had come into being which, together with the new middle classes, demanded a new social integration. It is this integration which we have to perform here and now. There is a parallel sociocultural process going on which divides the Reading Public into an 'élite' which reads *The Times Lit. Suppt.*, T. S. Eliot and *The New Statesman* from those millions of readers who read the cheap detective stories or fiction. Much valuable material on these matters is to be found in Q. D. Leavis' important study *Fiction and the Reading Public*. My approach differs from Leavis' considerably. I do not share his contempt for the masses and I regard a cultural policy which stands only for the tastes of the '*élite*' (which in fact does not deserves the name) as dangerously unsocial. Western civilization can only remain healthy when a synthesis between cultural and mass standards can be brought about. In this sense democracy is still, despite the Education Act of 1944 and the Nationalization of the Coal Mines in 1947, a task, but not yet a fact.

Thus our contemporary mass civilization has to decide whether it strives merely for 'panem et circenses' or whether it intends to realize a culture in which individuals, personalities participate and share common tasks, common beliefs, common aims.

Perhaps the reader of this volume will agree with the author that it is still possible to make the film medium into an active and dynamic instrument of an all-round citizenship. Film in this volume as well as in our previous *Sociology of Film*, as we should like to remind the reader and particularly the critic, is taken here only as an example of making more explicit a possible and perhaps even necessary cultural policy for the modern 'democratic' mass state. Such a cultural policy is and indeed *must* be compatible with the freedom and spontaneity of the creative power which alone differentiates man from the robot. We must follow the example of Athens on the infinitely larger and perhaps more difficult scale of a mass society.

Culture does not grow like grass on the meadow, it requires a deliberate human effort. Cultural policy cannot be separated from social and economic policy. Both must be in line with each other.

It is therefore up to State and Society to decide which road we are to follow, and it is the citizen's task to see to it that this decision does not go wrong.

APPENDIX I.

Statistics of Cinema Attendance.

The following report speaks for itself. It is to our knowledge the most complete and detailed of its kind, ever undertaken in this country.

The economic, social, educational and age-group differences deserve the closest study, particularly in the light of Chapter II and III of the present book. We venture two points of criticism: in our view children's film attendances are probably considerably higher than the report indicates, considering the fact that mothers may not always know when and how often their children visit the cinema. (In this respect we refer the reader to Chapter VI of *Sociology of Film*). Moreover it is to be regretted that the report does not split up the attendance figures for the age groups 18—40, for only *then* would it be possible to have an adequate idea of the adolescent percentage of British film audiences. But even as the report stands, it indicates that children and adolescents make up *more* than ONE THIRD of our film audiences.

The Social Survey Inquiry contains no information as to what films our contemporary masses see. This is quite a serious lack in our knowledge and we hope that further inquiries may bridge this gap between a quantitative and qualitative appreciation of the film experience. Only by a synthesis of quantitative and qualitatative methods may we be able to devise the principles to be applied to regulating the mental and moral health of a democratic community.

J.P.M.

INTRODUCTION

In the course of an inquiry made by the Wartime Social Survey for the Ministry of Information into what sections of the civilian public could be reached by various publicity media, some questions were asked about cinema going habits. The cinema is an important publicity medium in war time and it is, therefore, desirable to know what sort of people go to the cinema and how often they go.

A sample of 5,639 people was interviewed. Men and women were selected in representative proportions from different regions and occupation groups, and they were asked simply how often they went to the cinema. Women who had children of elementary school age were asked how often their children went to the cinema. Details of the sample are given on page 273 sqq.

This inquiry should be regarded as only a first attempt to study cinema going habits. The data are subject to various limitations and these should be borne in mind in the interpretation of results.

(1) Only civilians were included in the sample and it is not known what proportion of cinema audiences are civilians and what proportion H.M. Forces.

(2) The inquiry was made in June—July 1943 and informants were asked only about their habits at that time. The actual question asked was: 'How often do you go to the cinema at this time of year?' In general, cinemas have smaller audiences in the summer than in the winter, and also there are variations from one year to another.

The results given in this report, therefore, can be taken as true for the summer months of 1943 only.

(3) People were asked about their habits in a general way, and in most cases their replies can be regarded only as approximations to the truth. Those who went to the cinema regularly one day in every week could give an accurate answer, but those who did not go at regular intervals had to say about how often they went on an average.

The average number of visits to the cinema per month, given in Section IV are, therefore, approximations, as are the figures (given in the same section) showing the proportion of cinema attendances accounted for by different people.

Possibly more precise results could have been obtained by asking people how many times they had been to the cinema in a recent specified period, but here again some approximation would be necessary on account of the unreliability of memory. However, it is possible to compare the habits of different groups of the population with one another.

In Section I the proportions of the sample and of different groups giving various replies are shown. Section II deals with those who went to the cinema once a week or more often. These may be described as 'cinema enthusiasts' and their composition is compared with the composition of the adult civilian population. Both of these sections are concerned only with adults.

In Section III the habits of children of elementary school age are shown, as described by their mothers.

Section IV sums up the results given in the previous sections and shows the composition of the civilian part of the average cinema audiences during the summer of 1943.

Summary of results

70% of adult civilians sometimes go to the cinema and 32% go once a week or more often (June—July 1943). Younger adults go to the cinema much more than older people, and children go rather more than do adults, but not as much as young wage-earners.

The lower economic groups and those with elementary education go to the cinema more than the higher economic groups and those with higher education.

Factory workers, clerical and distributive workers go rather more than other occupation groups. Managerial and professional workers, housewives and the retired and unoccupied go rather less.

Town dwellers go to the cinema more often than people living in the country, and women go rather more than men.

The cinema is able to reach large sections of the population which are less accessible by other publicity media. For instance, many of the groups with a high average cinema attendance, the younger age groups and the lower economic groups read newspapers less than do others. (See Wartime Social Survey report 'Newspapers and the Public'). On the other hand some smaller groups, the higher economic groups and those with higher education, read newspapers more but go to the cinema less.

In general it may be said that the larger groups of the popluation are relatively better represented in the cinema audience than they are in the publics reached by other visual publicity media such as newspapers and books.

I. FREQUENCY OF CINEMA GOING

Informants were asked, 'How often do you go to the cinema at this time of the year?' (June-July). An exact reply to the question was not, of course, possible in all cases but those who did not go regularly were able to say whether they went about once a fortnight or once a month, or whether they only went occasionally. Those who went to the cinema less than once a month were classified as occasional cinema-goers. The question was confined to 'this time of year' and the summer months, as habits vary somewhat according to the season. The summer months may be taken as the least popular period for the cinema, attendances being in general higher in the winter. There are, of course, variations from one year to another, and it should be noted that the results given in this report refer to the summer of 1943.

The percentages of the sample giving different replies are shown in Table 1.

TABLE 1

'How often do you go to the cinema at this time of year?'

	%	
More than twice a week .	4 ⎫	
Twice a week . . .	8 ⎬ 32%	
Once a week . . .	20 ⎭	
Once a fortnight . .	6 ⎫	
Once a month . . .	6 ⎬ 38%	
Occasionally . . .	26 ⎭	
Don't go now . . .	9 ⎫ 30%	
Never go . . .	21 ⎭	
SAMPLE . . .	5,639	

The cinema is thus an important form of recreation for one-third of the adult civilian population, who go once a week or more often.

A further 12% go to the cinema about once a month or once a fortnight, and 26% go less frequently.

30% do not go to the cinema during the summer months.

There are marked differences shown below in the habits of some groups in the population. Certain sections are, therefore, more open to the influence of cinema publicity than are others.

Analysis by Sex

There are, however, only small differences in the habits of men and women in this respect, as is shown by Table 2.

TABLE 2

'How often do you go to the cinema at this time of year?'

	Men %	Women %
More than twice a week .	4 ⎫	4 ⎫
Twice a week . . .	7 ⎬ 28	9 ⎬ 34
Once a week . . .	17 ⎭	21 ⎭
Once a fortnight . .	6 ⎫	6 ⎫
Once a month . . .	6 ⎬ 40	6 ⎬ 37
Occasionally . . .	28 ⎭	25 ⎭
Don't go now . . .	9 ⎫ 32	9 ⎫ 29
Never go . . .	23 ⎭	20 ⎭
SAMPLE . .	2,491	3,148

The proportion of women going once a week or more is slightly higher than the proportion of men.

Analysis by Age

There are very marked differences between different age groups.

TABLE 3

How often do you go to the cinema at this time of year?

	14-17 %	18-40 %	41-45 %	46-65 %	Over 65 %	All Groups %
More than twice a week .	20 ⎫	6 ⎫	1 ⎫	1 ⎫	— ⎫	4 ⎫
Twice a week .	23 ⎬ 79	12 ⎬ 43	6 ⎬ 27	3 ⎬ 17	1 ⎬ 5	8 ⎬ 32
Once a week .	36 ⎭	25 ⎭	20 ⎭	13 ⎭	4 ⎭	20 ⎭
Once a fortnight	6 ⎫	8 ⎫	6 ⎫	5 ⎫	2 ⎫	6 ⎫
Once a month .	5 ⎬ 18	7 ⎬ 39	6 ⎬ 46	5 ⎬ 41	2 ⎬ 26	6 ⎬ 38
Occasionally .	7 ⎭	24 ⎭	34 ⎭	31 ⎭	22 ⎭	26 ⎭
Don't go now .	1 ⎫ 2	8 ⎫ 18	9 ⎫ 27	10 ⎫ 41	9 ⎫ 69	9 ⎫ 30
Never go .	1 ⎭	10 ⎭	18 ⎭	31 ⎭	60 ⎭	21 ⎭
No information	1	—	—	—	—	—
SAMPLE[27]	304	2,368	714	1,692	454	5,639

Most remarkable is the very high proportion of children aged 14-17 who go to the cinema once a week and more often. 43% of this

[27] Discrepancies in sample figures here and elsewhere are due to some forms being unclassified in some respects. In Table 3 the sum of the sample figures for different age groups is less than the total sample figure because some forms were unclassified in respect of age.

group go to the cinema twice a week or more often and as many as one fifth go more than twice a week. It should be pointed out that children of this age who are still at school are excluded from the sample which is designed to represent the adult civilian population, an 'adult' being defined in this survey as a person who has left school. Thus this group consists of young workers, and it is clear from these results this group more than any other is open to the influence of cinema publicity.

The 18-40 group also show a higher then average proportion attending cinemas once a week or more often. This is a broad age group and it may be assumed from the general trend of the results that the younger members of this group go to cinemas considerably more than the older members.

Of those aged over 65 a high proportion, 69%, do not go to cinemas, and in the middle age groups the proportions going to the cinema only occasionally are higher.

The results of this analysis show that as a channel of publicity the cinema is likely to afford contact much more with younger than with older people.

The table below shows the proportions of men and women in different age groups who went to the cinema once a week and more, less than once a week, and not at all.

TABLE 4

'How often do you go to the cinema at this time of year?'

	Age:	14-17	18-40	41-45	46-65	Over 65
		%	%	%	%	%
Once a week or more	Men	76	38	24	15	5
	Women	81	45	28	19	5
Less than once a week	Men	21	43	48	40	26
	Women	15	36	43	42	25
Not at all	Men	2	19	27	43	69
	Women	2	18	28	38	70
SAMPLE	Men	151	841	378	897	193
	Women	153	1,527	336	795	261

About the same proportion of men as of women in the different age groups do not go to the cinema. Amongst those aged over 65 there are no statistically significant differences in the proportions of men and of women giving various replies. In the younger and middle age groups however, the proportion of women going to the cinema once a week or more is rather higher than the proportion of men, the latter more frequently going less than once a week.

Analysis by Marital Status

There is little difference in the habits of married and single people when age is taken into consideration. Comparison of married and widowed people with single people in the 18-45 age group shows a higher proportion of the single group visiting cinemas frequently, but it must be remembered that the average age of the single people in this group is likely to be very much lower than that of the married people, and if the habits of married and widowed people are compared with the habits of single people in the 46-65 age group no statistically significant differences are shown.

Table 5 shows the proportion of married and widowed people and of single people giving different answers in these two age groups and the proportions of all married and widowed people and all single people aged 18 or over giving different answers.

TABLE 5

'How often do you go to the cinema at this time of year?'

	Age 18-45 Married and Widowed %	Single %	Age 46-65 Married and Widowed %	Single %	Age 18 and over Married and Widowed %	Single %
Once a week or more	33	55	18	17	24	46
Less than once a week	43	34	40	41	40	35
Not at all	14	11	41	41	35	18
SAMPLE	2,164	918	1,521	171	4,097	1,144

In the 18-45 age group there is only a small difference between the proportions of married and of single people who do not go to the cinema. However, a considerably higher proportion of single people go once a week or more often.

It is clear from these figures that cinema publicity is likely to affect a greater proportion of the unmarried than of the married, chiefly because more of the former are in the younger age groups who go to cinemas more frequently.

Analysis by Economic Groups

Informants were classified in different economic groups according to the wage rate or salary of the chief wage-earner of their families. The lower group includes members of families in which the chief wage earner has a wage rate of £5 or less per week, and also members of families whose income is derived from state pensions or allowances. If the chief wage earner had a wage rate or salary of over £5 up to £10 informants were classified in the middle group, and if the salary or income was over £10, in the higher group. The lower group includes 75% of the population, the middle group 20% and the higher group 5%.

TABLE 6

'How often do you go to the cinema at this time of year?'

Economic Group	Lower %	Middle %	Higher %	All Groups %
More than twice a week .	5 ⎫	2 ⎫	1 ⎫	4
Twice a week . . .	9 ⎬ 35	6 ⎬ 25	3 ⎬ 19	8
Once a week . . .	21 ⎭	17 ⎭	15 ⎭	20
Once a fortnight . .	6 ⎫	7 ⎫	7 ⎫	6
Once a month . . .	5 ⎬ 34	8 ⎬ 50	6 ⎬ 53	6
Occasionally . . .	23 ⎭	35 ⎭	40 ⎭	26
Don't go now . . .	9 ⎫ 32	9 ⎫ 25	10 ⎫ 27	9
Never go . . .	23 ⎭	16 ⎭	17 ⎭	21
SAMPLE . . .	4,185	1,121	282	5,639

It is quite clear that in the lower economic group the proportion of frequent cinema goers is higher, and the middle group show a greater proportion than the higher group.

However, in the middle and higher groups the proportion of those who go less frequently is higher, and a smaller proportion of these groups than of the lower group do not go to the cinema at all.

In considering the very marked difference in the proportions that go to the cinema more than twice a week it should be remembered that the lower economic group includes a higher proportion of boys and girls aged from 14-17, and that of this age group as many as 20% went more than once a week. Boys and girls of this age in the higher and middle groups are more frequently at school still and are, therefore, excluded from the sample.

Analysis by Education

There are sharp differences between different education groups. Informants were classified according to the last place of education attended by them, elementary, secondary or technical school, university and other types of school. Figures are not given for the last of these groups as it includes a variety of different types.

About the same proportion of those with elementary education as of those who had been to secondary or technical schools went to the cinema once a week or more. Of those with university education a greater proportion went less frequently. The proportion not visiting cinemas is highest in the Elementary group.

Tables 6 and 7 show that substantial proportions of all economic groups and of people at all levels of education may be reached by cinema publicity. The differences observed between different groups in this respect are very much less than the difference between age groups.

TABLE 7

'How often do you go to the cinema at this time of year?'

	Elementary	Secondary or Technical	University
	%	%	%
More than twice a week	5 ⎫	3 ⎫	1 ⎫
Twice a week	9 ⎬33	6 ⎬31	1 ⎬14
Once a week	19 ⎭	22 ⎭	12 ⎭
Once a fortnight	5 ⎫	7 ⎫	10 ⎫
Once a month	5 ⎬33	7 ⎬46	12 ⎬68
Occasionally	23 ⎭	32 ⎭	46 ⎭
Don't go now	9 ⎫	8 ⎫	7 ⎫
Never go	24 ⎭33	13 ⎭21	11 ⎭18
No information	—	2	—
SAMPLE	3,728	1,472	139

Analysis by Occupation

In the table below replies have been grouped for greater clarity. The percentages of different occupation groups who go to the cinema once a week and more, less than once a week, and who do not go, are shown.

TABLE 8

'How often do you go to the cinema at this time of year?'

	Once a week or more	Less than once a week	Not at all	No information	Sample
	%	%	%	%	%
Housewives	25	39	36	—	1,732
Heavy manufacture	35	40	25	—	357
Light munitions mnfctr.	49	35	16	— ⎫	
Other light manufacture	42	34	23	— ⎬	1,051 [28]
Agriculture	13	27	58	2	217
Mining	36	37	27	—	156
Building & Transport	27	37	35	1	384
Clerical	40	48	10	1	467
Distributive	39	36	24	1	422
Miscellaneous	43	35	22	—	204
Managerial & Professional	22	59	19	—	324
Retired & Unoccupied	12	25	63	—	325
ALL GROUPS	32	38	30	—	5,639

[28] Sample figures for these two groups are bracketed because the proportion of munitions workers included in the whole sample is based on secret and confidential figures.

Relatively high proportions of workers in light manufacturing and in the clerical, distributive and miscellaneous groups go to the cinema once a week or more. Light munitions workers and clerical workers go more than other groups. Only small proportions in these groups do not go to cinemas.

Agricultural workers and the retired and unoccupied show the lowest proportions of frequent cinema goers. The latter group is composed largely of old people. 63% in this group and 58% of agricultural workers do not go to the cinema.

Of managerial and professional workers a high proportion go less than once a week. It will be remembered that the higher economic and education groups had a high proportion occasionally going to the cinema.

Of housewives a rather lower than average proportion go once a week or more often. Compared with other groups there is a high proportion of older people in this group, women in the younger age groups more often being wage-earners.

Amongst factory workers analysis was made of replies received from skilled, semi-skilled and unskilled workers.

Investigators asked the management or the welfare officer at the factories visited to grade the workers as skilled, semi-skilled or unskilled, and so the way in which workers were classified depends on the personal judgment of these people, and not on any recognised craft or trade union definition. This may account for the high proportion classified as 'skilled'. There are however, some marked differences between the different groups.

TABLE 9

' How often do you go to the cinema at this time of year? '

	Skilled	Semi-skilled	Un-skilled	All Factory workers
	%	%	%	%
More than twice a week	4 ⎫	11 ⎫	12 ⎫	7 ⎫
Twice a week	10 ⎬38	15 ⎬53	17 ⎬45	12 ⎬42
Once a week	24 ⎭	27 ⎭	16 ⎭	23 ⎭
Once a fortnight	7 ⎫	8 ⎫	4 ⎫	7 ⎫
Once a month	7 ⎬40	5 ⎬30	6 ⎬29	7 ⎬37
Occasionally	26 ⎭	17 ⎭	19 ⎭	23 ⎭
Don't go now	8 ⎫22	5 ⎫17	8 ⎫26	7 ⎫21
Never go	14 ⎭	12 ⎭	18 ⎭	14 ⎭
SAMPLE	796	418	180	1,408

The differences shown are no doubt related to the age composition of the different groups. It will be remembered that of young people aged from 14-17 markedly high proportions went to the cinema very frequently, and the majority of factory workers in this age group would either be just commencing work and therefore unskilled, or apprentices graded as semi-skilled. The semi-skilled group shows a very high proportion of workers going to the cinema once a week or more often, and of the unskilled very high proportions go more than once a week. Analysis of the age composition of these groups has not been made, but it is probable that the unskilled group is composed largely of very young workers and of labourers above military age. The skilled group on the other hand would be more mixed as regards the proportions in the middle and older groups but would not be likely to include many very young workers. Skilled workers go to the cinema rather less frequently than other factory workers. The results for this group approximate to the results given for distributive workers.

Analysis by Size of Town

Table 10 shows the proportions of people living in towns of different sizes and in rural areas who gave different replies. The replies have again been grouped as the differences may be seen more clearly in this way.

TABLE 10

' How often do you go to the cinema at this time of year? '

	Population of Town			
	Over 300,000	50,000- 300,000	Under 50,000	Rural Areas
	%	%	%	%
Once a week or more . .	37	38	30	15
Less than once a week .	38	39	39	35
Not at all . . .	25	23	30	49
No information . .	—	—	—	1
SAMPLE . . .	1,509	1,423	1,793	914

Half the people living in rural areas said they did not go to the cinema at this time of the year. It will be remembered that agricultural workers went less frequently than other occupation groups. Of those people in rural areas who do go to cinemas a relatively small proportion go as often as once a week. People living in small towns go to the cinema less frequently than those living in large and medium sized towns, but much more frequently than do people in rural areas.

These differences in habit are no doubt due in some measure to the distribution of cinemas in different types of district. For people living in rural areas a visit to the cinema means travelling to a town and there may not always be sufficient transport services. In a small town there are few cinemas and the choice of films is therefore limited. Nevertheless, as many as 30% in small towns go once a week or more often.

In considering the regional figures given below, these differences should be borne in mind, since the proportions of people living in the country and in small towns vary very much from one region to another.

Analysis by Region

TABLE 11

'How often do you go to the cinema at this time of year?'

	Once a week or more	Less than once a week	Not at all	No Information	Sample
	%	%	%	%	%
Scotland	33	35	30	2	600
North	44	30	26	—	335
North West	38	41	20	—	801
North East	29	39	31	1	501
N. Midlands	23	41	36	—	404
Midlands	37	38	25	—	524
Wales	26	36	38	—	339
E. Anglia	19	44	37	1	346
South	23	40	37	—	312
South West	21	32	46	—	380
South East	26	40	34	—	253
London	38	39	22	1	844
ALL GROUPS	32	38	30	—	5,639

East Anglia, the South, South West, South East and the North Midlands are all regions in which the bulk of the population lives in small towns or in the country.

The Northern region (Northumberland and Durham) shows a high proportion of frequent cinema goers and a somewhat low proportion going to cineams less often.

The results for London, the North West and the Midlands approximate to the results for those living in large and medium sized towns in the country as a whole. The North East shows a rather low proportion going to the cinema once a week or more considering the distribution of towns of different sizes and rural areas in this region.

In Scotland the proportions giving different replies are about average. In Wales the percentage of frequent cinema goers is somewhat low but it should be noted the sample is small.

On the whole it may be said that differences between regions are small when the distribution of the population in different types of district is taken into consideration. The only outstanding difference is that noted in the Northern region, and this is not particularly large.

II. WHO ARE THE CINEMA ENTHUSIASTS

The last section dealt with the frequency with which different sections of the adult civilian population visited cinemas. Members of the Forces were excluded from the inquiry and the habits of children will be dealt with later.

Those who went to the cinema once a week, or more often may be regarded as cinema enthusiasts, and these are more open to the influence of cinema publicity than are other civilians. It is worth while, therefore, to analyse the composition of this group and to compare it with the composition of the adult civilian population.

In the present section those who went to the cinema once a week or more are regarded as a group, and the proportions of this group having different characteristics, e.g. age, sex, occupation, are shown and compared with corresponding proportions of the whole sample.

Analysis by Sex

TABLE 12

	% cinema enthusiasts	% whole sample
Men . .	39	44
Women . .	61	56
SAMPLE .	1,771	5,639

Women are rather better represented in the enthusiastic group than are men, but the difference is not a very large one.

Analysis by Age

TABLE 13

Age	% cinema enthusiasts	% whole sample
14-17 . .	13	5
18-40 . .	57	42
41-45 . .	11	13
46-65 . .	17	30
Over 65 . .	1	8
Unclassified .	1	1
SAMPLE .	1,771	5,639

It is clear that the younger age groups are more fully represented amongst the enthusiasts than are the older. Of the enthusiastic group, 70% were aged under 41, but of the sample 47% are in this age group. It is thus mainly the younger groups that can be influenced by cinema publicity, and it would not be very profitable to publicize messages particularly intended for the older groups in this way.

Analysis by sex by age shows that both young men and young women are better represented amongst the enthusiasts than older men and women.

Analysis by Marital Status

TABLE 14

	% cinema enthusiasts	% whole sample
Married & Widowed	56	74
Single . . .	44	26
SAMPLE . .	1,771	5,639

It will be remembered that single people went to the cinema rather more frequently than married people and that this was related to the age composition of the married and single groups. More than half the enthusiastic group are married, but married people form about three-quarters of the population.

Analysis by Economic Group

TABLE 15

Economic Group	% cinema enthusiasts	% whole sample
Lower . .	80	74
Middle . .	15	20
Higher . .	3	5
Unclassified .	1	1
SAMPLE .	1,771	5,639

Amongst enthusiasts the lower economic groups are somewhat better represented than the higher. However, the difference is not very great and it should be remembered that in the middle and higher economic groups a greater proportion go to the cinema once a fortnight or less and a smaller proportion never go to the cinema than in the lower economic group.

Analysis by Occupation

In the table below the different occupations are grouped. The factory group includes workers in heavy and light industry, both munitions workers and others. 'Other Manual Work' includes agriculture, mining, building and transport and miscellaneous workers.

TABLE 16

	% cinema enthusiasts	% whole sample
Housewives . . .	24	31
Factory workers . . .	34	25
Other manual workers . .	16	17
Clerical, distributive . .	20	16
Managerial & Professional .	4	6
Retired & Unoccupied .	2	6
SAMPLE . . .	1,771	5,639

Factory workers and the clerical and distributive group account for 54% of the enthusiasts but only for 41% of the sample.

Housewives and the retired and unoccupied form only 26% of the enthusiasts but 37% of the whole sample. These groups are, therefore, somewhat under-represented. Managerial and professional workers are also somewhat under-represented.

Analysis by Size of Town

TABLE 17

	% cinema enthusiasts	% whole sample
Large town (over 300,000) .	32	27
Medium town (50,000-300,000)	30	25
Small town (under 50,000) .	30	32
Rural areas . . .	8	16
SAMPLE . . .	1,771	5,639

People living in large and medium sized towns are rather better represented amongst enthusiasts than people living in small towns, and those living in the country are under represented.

It was pointed out in the previous section that regional differences were related to the proportion of people living in towns of different sizes and in rural areas, which vary considerably from one region to another.

Analysis by Region

TABLE 18

	% cinema enthusiasts	% whole sample
Scotland ..	11	11
North	8	6
North West ..	17	14
North East ..	8	9
North Midlands..	5	7
Midlands ..	11	9
Wales ..	5	6
E. Anglia ..	4	6
South	4	6
South West ..	4	7
South East ..	4	4
London	18	15
SAMPLE:	1,771	5,639

In general those regions where large sections of the population live in the country and in small towns are somewhat under-represented.

The North West, London, the North and the Midlands together account for 54% of the enthusiasts, but only for 44% of the population.

Summing up this short section, it may be said that those enthusiasts who go to the cinema once a week or more, are drawn from all sections of the adult civilian population; but that certain sections are somewhat better represented among them than are others.

A relatively high proportion of enthusiasts are young people. In fact 70% of the enthusiasts are younger than 41. Women are represented in the group somewhat better than men. About a third of the enthusiasts are factory workers and about a fifth work in offices and shops.

The vast majority of them (92%) are towns-people. In the country the cinema is less important. They are scattered over all urban areas of Great Britain with no important regional differences.

It should be stressed that this section and the previous section deal only with the adult civilian population.

III. CHILDREN AND THE CINEMA

Amongst the married women interviewed in this sample were 759 mothers of children aged from five to fourteen. These were asked about the habits of their children. The question was 'How often do the children (aged five to fourteen) go to the cinema at this time of year?'

The 759 mothers had between them 1,182 children in the age group concerned, and where possible information was obtained about each child. No information was obtained about 169 (14%) of the children and results are based, therefore, on replies about 1,013 children only.

In the table below the proportions of children going to the cinema at different intervals of time are compared with the corresponding proportions of the whole sample of adults (see Table 1) and of the young people aged 14–17 included in the sample of adults (Table 3).

TABLE 19
Frequency of visits to cinema

	Children of school age %	Adults %	Those aged 14–17 %
More than twice a week	4 ⎫	4 ⎫	20 ⎫
Twice a week..	12 ⎬44	8 ⎬32	23 ⎬79
Once a week ..	28 ⎭	20 ⎭	36 ⎭
Once a fortnight	4 ⎫	6 ⎫	6 ⎫
Once a month	3 ⎬34	6 ⎬38	5 ⎬18
Occasionally ..	27 ⎭	26 ⎭	7 ⎭
Don't go now..	3 ⎫22	9 ⎫30	1 ⎫2
Never go	19 ⎭	21 ⎭	1 ⎭
SAMPLE:	1,013	5,639	304

A considerably higher proportion of children than of adults go to the cinema once a week or more often. However, the young people aged from 14–17 show a very much higher proportion going very frequently.

These results suggest that the cinema is an extremely popular recreation with the young, and although children go frequently when at school, as soon as they are earning money themselves, they go even more often.

Analysis by Economic Group

There are differences in the habits of children in different economic groups. In Table 20 results for the middle and higher economic groups are given together as the sample of children in the higher group is small.

TABLE 20

Frequency of children's visits to cinema

		Lower Economic Group %	Middle and Higher Economic Groups %
More than twice a week	..	4 ⎫	3 ⎫
Twice a week..	.. ..	12 ⎬ 47	9 ⎬ 31
Once a week ..	.. ..	31 ⎭	19 ⎭
Once a fortnight	.. ..	5 ⎫	4 ⎫
Once a month	.. ..	3 ⎬ 32	2 ⎬ 42
Occasionally ..	.. ..	24 ⎭	36 ⎭
Don't go now..	.. ..	3 ⎫ 20	1 ⎫ 27
Never go ..	.. ..	17 ⎭	26 ⎭
SAMPLE:		804	209

Children in the lower group go to the cinema more frequently. A substantial proportion in this group go once a week or more often.

In both the lower and the middle and higher income groups the children go to the cinema rather more frequently than do their elders.

TABLE 21

Frequency of children's visits to cinema

	Lower Economic Group		Middle and Higher Economic Group	
	Children %	Adults %	Children %	Adults %
Once a week or more ..	47	35	31	25
Less than once a week ..	32	34	42	51
Not at all	20	32	27	23
SAMPLE:	804	4,185	209	1,403

The difference between the results for adults and children is not so marked in the middle and higher economic groups and it should be noted that the sample of children in these groups is small. However, the difference is statistically significant. $X^2 = 6.38$. n = 2. P is less than .05 and there is thus evidence that the habits of children and adults in the higher and middle economic groups do differ. In the case of the lower economic group, the difference is quite clear.

Analysis by Mother's Education

There are some differences in cinema going between the children of women who went only to an elementary school and those who had further education.

TABLE 22

Frequency of children's visits to cinema

	Mother's education	
	Elementary %	Secondary or Technical %
More than twice a week..	5 ⎫	2 ⎫
Twice a week	13 ⎬ 50	6 ⎬ 28
Once a week	32 ⎭	20 ⎭
Once a fortnight ..	5 ⎫	4 ⎫
Once a month	2 ⎬ 29	1 ⎬ 45
Occasionally	22 ⎭	40 ⎭
Don't go now	3 ⎫ 21	—
Never go ..	17 ⎭	27
SAMPLE:	..756[29]	190[29]

The children of women with higher education went to the cinema less frequently. Half the children of women with elementary education only went once a week or more often.

There are no statistically significant differences between the results for children whose mothers had secondary education and for adults in this education group. Children of mothers with elementary education went to the cinema more frequently than adults with elementary education.

Analysis by Mother's Occupation

The mothers of 111 of the children went out to work and the mothers of the remaining 902 children were housewives only. Table 23 shows the results for these two groups of children.

TABLE 23

Frequency of children's visits to cinema

	Mother goes out out to work %	Mother does not go out to work %
More than twice a week ..	2 ⎫	5 ⎫
Twice a week	13 ⎬ 60	11 ⎬ 42
Once a week	45 ⎭	26 ⎭
Once a fortnight ..	4 ⎫	5 ⎫
Once a month	1 ⎬ 25	3 ⎬ 35
Occasionally	20 ⎭	27 ⎭
Don't go now	1 ⎫ 15	3 ⎫ 23
Never go ..	14 ⎭	20 ⎭
SAMPLE:	111	902

The sample of children with mothers at work is small, but the differences shown are nevertheless significant. The proportion of

[29] Sample figures do not check with the total because no analysis is made of replies for 67 children whose mothers went to other and various types of school. None of the mothers went to universities.

children with working mothers who go to the cinema once a week or
more often is considerably higher than the proportion of other
children who do so. It is, of course, possible that the children of
mothers who go out to work have an older average age, and this
might account for the difference.

The numbers of children in the sample in different regions are not
sufficient to permit a regional analysis of these results.

Summing up the results given in this section:

(1) Children go to the cinema rather more than adults but less
than young people aged 14–17.

(2) Children in families in the lower economic groups go rather
more than children from families in the higher economic
groups, and those whose mothers have only elementary
education rather more than those whose mothers have higher
education.

(3) The children of women who go out to work go to the cinema
more than do other children.

IV. THE CINEMA AUDIENCE

From the results given in Sections I and III it is possible to build
up a rough picture of the civilian cinema audience. These two
sections showed how often different groups of adults and children
visited cinemas, and from the figures given an approximate idea of
the average number of cinema attendances per month for each group
may be derived.

It will be remembered that some informants were classified as
going to the cinema 'occasionally' and others are going 'more than
twice a week'. It is not, therefore, possible to work out a precise
average but some indication may be obtained.

A further limitation of the data is that there is no information
about the habits of children aged over 14 who are still at school.
These were not included in the sample of adults, and mothers were
asked only about their children aged from 5–14. School children
aged over 14 however, form only a small section, between 1% and
2%, of the civilian population aged 5 and over. Their exclusion is,
therefore, not of great importance.

The average number of cinema attendances per month was cal-
culated as follows:

Frequency of Cinema attendance				Estimated number of attendances per month
Don't go to cinema ..	..	..	..	0
Occasionally ..	..	..	..	0.5
Once a month	..	..	..	1
Once a fortnight	..	..	..	2
Once a week ..	..	..	..	4
Twice a week..	..	..	..	8
More than twice a week	..	..		10

The averages given below must be regarded as only approximations to the actual averages, but they make it possible to compare the habits of different groups by means of a single measure.

It will be remembered that information was obtained from mothers of about 1,013 children. Where results are given for adults and children together the results for children have been weighted so that they are correctly represented in the whole sample of adults and children.

TABLE 24

Average Number of Cinema Attendances per Month

		Average
Adults	.. ..	.. 2.1
Children aged 5–14	.. ..	.. 2.7
Adults and children	.. ..	.. 2.2
Sex	Men	.. 1.9
	Women	.. 2.3
Age	14–17	.. 5.5
	18–40	.. 2.9
	41–45	.. 1.7
	46–65	.. 1.2
	Over 65	.. .4
Economic Group		
(Adults)	Lower	.. 2.3
	Middle	.. 1.8
	Higher	.. 1.3
Economic Group		
(Children)		
	Lower	.. 2.9
	Middle and Higher	.. 2.1
Education		
(Adults)	Elementary	.. 2.3
	Secondary or technical	.. 2.0
	University	.. 1.3
Occupation		
	Housewives	.. 1.6
	Heavy manufacture	.. 2.4
	Light munitions manufacture	.. 3.4
	Other light manufacture	.. 2.8
	Agriculture	.. 1.0
	Mining	.. 2.5
	Building and Transport	.. 2.0
	Clerical	.. 2.6
	Distributive	.. 2.8
	Miscellaneous	.. 2.8

Occupation   *Average*

   Managerial and professional 1.5
   Retired and unoccupied 9
   All factory workers 2.9
  [30] Other manual workers 2.0
   Clerical and distributive workers 2.7

Town Size
(Adults and Children)
   Large 2.7
   Medium 2.6
   Small 2.2
   Rural Areas 1.1

By calculating the total number of visits made to the cinema per month by each group, the composition of the civilian section of cinema audiences may be shown.

In the diagrams[31] below, the percentages of cinema attendances accounted for by different groups of the population are compared with the distribution of the population amongst these groups.

The diagrams on the right may be taken as representing 'the average civilian cinema audience' in the summer months of 1943.

TABLE 25

% Civilian Population aged 5 and over		% Civilian Cinema Attendances (June 1943)	
Men	37%	Men	32%
Women	47%	Women	48%
Children (5–14)	16%	Children (5–14)	20%

Children are well represented in the cinema audience and men somewhat under represented.

% Civilian Population aged 5 and over		% Civilian Cinema Attendances	
Age		Age	
5–14	16%	5–14	20%
14–17	5%	14–17	11%
18–40	36%	18–40	46%
41–45	11%	41–45	8%
Over 45	32%	Over 45	15%

Children from 5–17 account for nearly a third of cinema attendances but only for about a fifth of the population. Those aged over 45 account for a third of the population but only for 15% of cinema attendances. The 18–40 age group is well represented in the cinema audience.

  [30] Agriculture, Mining, Building and Transport, Miscellaneous.

  [31] The diagrams have been omitted, but the respective figures are given.

% Civilian Population Economic Group		% Civilian Cinema Attendances Economic Group	
Lower	75%	Lower	81%
Middle	20%	Middle	16%
Higher	5%	Higher	3%

The lower economic group is better represented in the cinema audience than are the higher groups.

% Civilian Population Town Size		% Civilian Cinema Attendances Town Size	
Large	27%	Large	32%
Medium	25%	Medium	28%
Small	32%	Small	31%
Rural	16%	Rural	9%

People from rural areas are under represented in the cinema audience, but people from all sizes of town are well represented.

% Civilian Population aged 5 and over Occupation		% Civilian Cinema Attendances Occupation	
Factory workers	21%	Factory workers	27%
Other manual workers	14%	Other manual workers	13%
Clerical and distributive	13%	Clerical and distributive	16%
Managerial and Professional	5%	Managerial and Professional	3%
Housewives	26%	Housewives	19%
Retired and Unoccupied	4%	Retired and Unoccupied	2%
Children (5–14)	16%	Children (5–14)	20%

Factory workers and clerical and distributive workers account for 43% of civilian cinema attendances but only for 34% of the population aged 5 and over. Housewives, the retired and unoccupied, and managerial and professional workers together account for 35% of the population but only for 24% of the cinema audience.

The above results may be summed up as follows:

Groups with higher cinema attendance	Groups with lower cinema attendance
Women	Men
The younger age groups and children	The older age groups
The lower economic groups	The higher economic groups
Those with elementary education	Those with higher education
Town dwellers	Country dwellers
Factory workers	Managerial and professional workers
Clerical and distributive workers	Housewives
	The retired and unoccupied

Comparisons with Other Publicity Media

It is of interest to compare the public reached by the cinema with the public reached by other kinds of publicity media. In Wartime Social Survey reports[32] 'Newspapers and the Public' and 'M.O.I. Publications' information is given about the extent to which different groups in the population read daily newspapers and other types of publication.

Where results show a trend, as for instance in analyses by age or economic groups, the direction of the trends shown for different types of publicity may be compared.

In Table 26 the average cinema attendances per month for different groups are compared with:

(*a*) The percentage who saw a morning newspaper 'yesterday'.

(*b*) The percentage saying they buy 'weekly or monthly magazines or papers about matters of public interest'.

(*c*) The percentage saying they buy 'small books (of the Penguin or Pelican type) about matters of public interest'.

TABLE 26

	Average Cinema attendances per month	% who saw a morning newspaper 'yesterday'	% buying magazines	% buying small books
Men	1.9 (2)	81 (1)	41	25 (1)
Women	2.3 (1)	67 (2)	40	17 (2)
Ages				
14–17	5.5 (1)	55 (5)	42 (3)	17 (4)
18–40	2.9 (2)	70 (3)	45 (1)	24 (2)
41–45	1.7 (3)	81 (1)	45 (1)	25 (1)
46–65	1.2 (4)	78 (2)	39 (4)	19 (3)
Over 65	.4 (5)	70 (3)	17 (5)	9 (5)
Economic Group				
Lower	2.3 (1)	69 (3)	36 (3)	15 (3)
Middle	1.8 (2)	86 (2)	51 (2)	34 (2)
Upper	1.3 (3)	92 (1)	62 (1)	49 (1)
Education				
Elementary ..	2.3 (1)	68 (3)	34 (3)	12 (3)
Secondary or Technical ..	2.0 (2)	82 (2)	55 (2)	37 (2)
University ..	1.3 (3)	87 (1)	59 (1)	68 (1)
Whole sample: ..	2.1	73	40	21

The figures in brackets show the rating

Sex

Newspapers and books show a contrary result to cinemas, the figures for men being higher than those for women. About the same proportion of both sexes buy magazines.

[32] New Series Nos. 37 and 37A.

Age

Younger people go to the cinema much more often than old people. With newspapers and books the figure for the middle age groups is highest, the young and the old seeing these less. In the case of magazines, as with cinemas, the figures for older people are lower, but the middle age groups buy magazines as much or rather more than the youngest group.

Economic Group and Education Group

The cinema figures are highest in the lower groups but a trend in the opposite direction is shown in the case of the other three publicity media.

From these comparisons it is clear that the cinema can be a valuable publicity medium in that cinema publicity is likely to reach particularly some of those groups in the population which are less open to the influence of other media, women, the younger age groups, the lower economic groups and those with elementary education.

The lower economic and education groups are numerically more important than the higher, and it may be said that cinemas reach a wider public than other media.

THE SAMPLE

The sample was designed to represent the adult civilian population, which was defined as all civilians aged fourteen or over with the exception of those still at school.

Representative quotas of men and women in different occupation groups were set for each of the twelve Civil Defence Regions, the number interviewed in each region being proportionate to its population.

A total of 5,639 people were interviewed. These were distributed as shown below.

(1) *Sex*

			%
Men ..	..	..	44
Women	..	..	56
Sample:	..	..	5,639

(2) *Age*

			Men	*Women*	*Total*
			%	%	%
14–17	..	..	6	5	5
18–40	..	..	34	49	42
41–45	..	..	15	11	13
46–65	..	..	36	25	30
Over 65	..	..	8	8	8
No information	..		—	1	1
Sample:	..	..	2,491	3,148	5,639

The age distribution of men is, of course, affected by the fact that large numbers in the middle age groups are in the Forces and are, therefore, excluded from the sample.

(3) *Economic Group*
Wage rate of chief
earner in family %
Up to £5   Lower   75
Over £5 up to £10. Middle   20
Over £10.   Upper   5
Sample: 5,639

(4) *Education*
Last school attended %
Elementary 66
Secondary or Technical 26
University 2
Other Type 2
No information 4
Sample: 5,639

(5) *Occupation*
Housewives 31
Heavy Manufacture 6
Light munitions manufacture ⎫
Other light manufacture   ⎬ 19
                      ⎭
Agriculture 4
Mining 3
Building and Transport 7
Clerical 8
Distributive 7
Miscellaneous 4
Managerial and Professional 6
Retired and Unoccupied 6
Sample: 5,639

(6) *Region* %
Scotland 11
North 6
North West 14
North East 9
North Midlands 7
Midlands 9
Wales 6
East Anglia..   6
South 6
South West 7
South East 4
London 15
Sample: 5,639

TOWNS IN WHICH INTERVIEWS WERE MADE

Scotland	North West	N. Midland	Wales	South West
Glasgow	Manchester	Nottingham	Cardiff	Bristol
Edinburgh	Liverpool	Leicester	Neath	Exeter
Aberdeen	Preston	Lincoln	Port Talbot	Launceston
Dumbarton	Accrington	Mansfield	Mountain	Taunton
Renfrew	Macclesfield	Lough-	Ash	Bideford
Coatbridge	Bolton	borough	Denbigh	Devizes
Galashiels	Wigan	Market	Llandidloas	
Banff	Salford	Rasen	Tredegar	Stroud
Perth	Rochdale			

Cupar (Fife)	Widnes	Midlands	East Anglia	South East
	Northwich	Birmingham	Ipswich	Maidstone
North	Bacup	Stoke-on-	Peter-	Rochester
Newcastle	Farnworth	Trent	borough	Uckfield
Gateshead		Wolver-	Stowmarket	Folkestone
Tynemouth	North East	hampton	Ely	Ashford
Darlington	Leeds	Dudley	Dereham	Redhill
Hartlepool	Sheffield	Burton-on-		
Spennymoor	Halifax	Trent	South	London
Chester-le-	Barnsley	Tamworth	Reading	Wimbledon
Street	Hull	Rugby	Southamp-	East Ham
Ashton-upon-	York	Redditch	ton	Fulham
Tyne	Goole	Evesham	Basingstoke	Walthamstow
	Pontefract		Alton	Tooting
			Aylesbury	Deptford
			Bicester	Kensington
				St. Pancras

APPENDIX II

On Roman Games

Do you ask me what you should regard as especially to be avoided?
I say, crowds; for as yet you cannot trust yourself to them with
safety, I shall admit my own weakness, at any rate; for I never bring
back home the same character that I took abroad with me. Something of that which I have forced to be calm within me is disturbed;
some of the foes that I have routed return again. Just as the sick
man, who has been weak for a long time, is in such a condition that
he cannot be taken out of the house without suffering a relapse,
so we ourselves are affected when our souls are recovering from a
lingering disease. To consort with the crowd is harmful; there is no
person who does not make some vice attractive to us, or stamp it
upon us, or taint us unconsciously therewith. Certainly, the greater
the mob with which we mingle, the greater the danger.

But nothing is so damaging to good character as the habit of
lounging at the games; for then it is that vice steals subtly upon one
through the avenue of pleasure. What do you think I mean? I mean
that I come home more greedy, more ambitious, more voluptuous,
and even more cruel and inhuman,—because I have been among
human beings. By chance I attended a mid-day exhibition, expecting some fun, wit, and relaxation,—an exhibition at which men's
eyes have respite from the slaughter of their fellow-men. But it was
quite the reverse. The previous combats were the essence of com-
passion; but now all the trifling is put aside and it is pure murder.
(During the luncheon interval condemned criminals were often
driven into the arena and compelled to fight, for the amusement of
those spectators who remained throughout the day.) The men have
no defensive armour. They are exposed to blows at all points, and
no one ever strikes in vain. Many persons prefer this programme to
the usual pairs and to the bouts 'by request'. Of course they do;
there is no helmet or shield to deflect the weapon. What is the need
of defensive armour or of skill? All these mean delaying death. In
the morning they throw men to the lions and the bears; at noon,
they throw them to the spectators. The spectators demand that the
slayer shall face the man who is to slay him in his turn; and they
always reserve the latest conqueror for another butchering. The outcome of every fight is death, and the means are fire and sword. This
sort of thing goes on while the arena is empty. You may retort: 'But
he was a highway robber; he killed a man!' And what of it? Granted
that, as a murderer he deserved this punishment, what crime have
you committed, poor fellow, that you should deserve to sit and see
this show? In the morning they cried 'Kill him! Lash him! Brand
him! Why does he meet the sword in so cowardly a way? Why does

he strike so feebly? Why doesn't he die game? Whip him to meet his wounds! Let them receive blow for blow, with chests bare and exposed to the stroke!' And when the games stop for the intermission. they announce; 'a little throatcutting in the meantime, so that there may still be something going on!'

Come now; do you (the remark is addressed to the brutalized spectators) not understand even this truth, that a bad example reacts on the agent? Thank the immortal gods that you are teaching cruelty to a person who cannot learn to be cruel. The young character, which cannot hold fast to righteousness, must be rescued from the mob; it is too easy to side with the majority. Even Socrates, Cato, and Laelius might have shaken in their moral strength by a crowd that was unlike them; so true it is that none of us, no matter how much he cultivates his abilities, can withstand the shock of faults that approach, as it were, with so great a retinue. Much harm is done by a single case of indulgence or greed; the familiar friend, if he be luxurious, weakens and softens us imperceptibly; the neighbour, if he is rich, rouses our covetousness; the companion, if he be slanderous, rubs off some of his rust upon us, even though we be spotless and sincere. What then do you think the effect will be on character, when the world at large assaults it! You must either imitate or loathe the world.

But both courses are to be avoided; you should not copy the bad, simply because they are many, nor should you hate the many, because they are unlike you. Withdraw into yourself as far as you can.

[33] From Seneca: *Ad Lucilium Epistulae Morales*, with an English Translation by R. M. Gummere, The Loeb Classical Library, vol. I, pp. 29 sqq. (With grateful acknowledgment to the Editors of the Loeb Classical Library and its publishers, Messrs. William Heinemann, London.)

BIBLIOGRAPHY

In addition to the books listed in the bibliographies attached to my *Sociology of Film* the following works might be usefully consulted by the reader :

GENERAL:

Dawson, Christopher, *Education and the Crisis of Christian Culture*, in *Lumen Vitæ*, Brussels, Vol. I, 1947.
Franks, Sir Oliver, *Central Planning and Control in War and Peace*, London, 1947.
Hayley, T. T. S., *The Anatomy of Lango Religion and Groups*, Cambridge, 1947.
Lévy-Bruhl, L., *La Morale et la Science des Moeurs*, Paris, 1937.
MacMurray, John, *Freedom in the Modern World*, London, 1932.
Marshall, T. H., *Sociology at the Crossroads*, London, 1947.
Proudhon, P. J., *Du Principe de l'Art et de sa Destination Sociale*, Nouvelle Edition, Paris, 1939.
Roth, Joseph, *Der Antichrist*, Amsterdam, 1934.
Spence, Lewis, *Myth and Ritual in Dance, Game and Rhyme*, London, 1947.
Tarde, G., *L'Opinion et La Foule*, Paris, 1904.
Weizsaecker, V. von, *Anonyma*, Bern, 1946.

HISTORY:

Bellen, E. C. van, *Les Origines du Mélodrame*, Utrecht, 1927.
Burke, Thomas, *The English Townsman*, London, 1946.
Ehrenberg, V., *Aspects of the Ancient World*, Oxford, 1946.
Eisler, R., *The Royal Art of Astrology*, London, 1946.
Huizinga, J., *Homo Ludens*, Basel, 1944.
Legouis and Cazamian, *History of English Literature*, London, 1945.
Mélèse, P., *Le Théatre et le Public à Paris sous Louis XIV*, Paris, 1934.
Nicoll, A., *A History of Late Nineteenth Century Drama*: 1850-1900, 2 vols., Cambridge, 1946.
Walbank, F. W., *The Decline of the Roman Empire in the West*, London, 1946.
Thomas, E., *Roman Life under the Cæsars*, London, 1899.

CINEMA AND FILMS:

Arts Inquiry, The, *The Factual Film*, Oxford, 1947.
Cohen-Séat, G., *Essai sur les Principes d'une Philosophie du Cinéma*, Paris, 1946.
Hardy, F., *Grierson on Documentary*, London, 1946.
Kracauer, S., *From Caligari to Hitler. A Psychological History of the German Film*, Princeton, 1947.
Malraux, André, *Esquisse d'une Psychologie du Cinéma*, in *Scènes Choisies*, Paris, 1946.
Mayer, J. P., *Film and the Child Mind*, in *New Statesman and Nation*, August 31, 1946.
Mayer, J. P., *Children and the Cinema*, in *The Highway*, November, 1946.
Mayer, J. P., *Towards a Constructive Film Policy*, in *The Highway*, October, 1947.
Moley, R., *The Hays Office*, New York, 1945.
Parliamentary Debates, November, 17th, 1946.
Rosten, L. C., *Hollywood. The Movie Colony. The Movie Makers*, New York, 1941.
Tyler, P., *The Hollywood Hallucination*, New York, 1944.

PSYCHOLOGY:

Blondel, Ch., *Introduction à la Psychologie Collective*, Paris, 1928.
Eysenck, H. J., *Dimensions of Personality*, London, 1947.
Fordham, M., *The Life of Childhood*, London, 1944.
Gesell, A., and Ilg, F. L., *The Child from Five to Ten*, London, 1946.
Kardiner, A., *The Psychological Frontiers of Society*, New York, 1945.

PSYCHOLOGY:

Lévy-Bruhl, L., *L'Ame Primitive*, Paris, 1927.
Lowy, S., *Psychological and Biological Foundations of Dream-Interpretation*, London, 1942.
Piaget, F., *La Formation du symbole chez l'enfaut*, Neuchâtel, 1945.
Selbie, W. B., *The Psychology of Religion*, Oxford, 1926.
Walter, E. J., *Psychologische Grundlagen der geschichtlichen und sozialen Entwicklung*, Zuerich, 1947.
Williams, Crawshay R., *The Comforts of Unreason*, London, 1947.
Young, K., *Personality and Problems of Adjustment*, London, 1947.

METHODS:

Cassirer, E., *Idee und Gestalt*, Berlin, 1924.
Eliot, T. S., *The Use of Poetry and the Use of Criticism*, London, 1933.
Gurvitch, Georges and Moore, W. E., *Twentieth Century Sociology*, New York, 1945.
Kaufmann, F., *Methodology of the Social Sciences*, Oxford, 1944.
Ogburn, W. F., and Nimkoff, M. F., *A Handbook of Sociology*, London, 1947.
Richards, I. A., *Principles of Literary Criticism*, London, 1930.
Weber, Max, *Gesammelte Aufsaetze zur Wissenschaftslehre*, Tuebigen, 1922.

INDEX

ASPECTS OF FILM

An Arno Press Collection

Adler, Mortimer J. **Art and Prudence.** 1937
Conant, Michael. **Anti-Trust in the Motion Picture Industry.** 1960
Croy, Homer. **How Motion Pictures Are Made.** 1918
Drinkwater, John. **The Life and Adventures of Carl Laemmle.** 1931
Hacker, Leonard. **Cinematic Design.** 1931
Hepworth, T[homas] C[raddock]. **The Book of the Lantern.** 1899
Johnston, Alva. **The Great Goldwyn.** 1937
Klingender, F.D. and Stuart Legg. **Money Behind the Screen.** 1937
Limbacher, James L. **Four Aspects of the Film.** 1969
Manvell, Roger, ed. **The Cinema 1950.** 1950
Manvell, Roger, ed. **The Cinema 1951.** 1951
Manvell, Roger, ed. **The Cinema 1952.** 1952
Marchant, James, ed. **The Cinema in Education.** 1925
Mayer, J.P. **British Cinemas and Their Audiences.** 1948
Sabaneev, Leonid. **Music for the Films.** 1935
Seabury, William Marston. **Motion Picture Problems.** 1929
Seldes, Gilbert. **The Movies Come from America.** 1937
U.S. House of Representatives, Committee on Education. **Motion Picture Commission: Hearings.** 1914
U.S. House of Representatives, Committee on Education. **Federal Motion Picture Commission: Hearings.** 1916
U.S. Senate, Temporary National Economic Committee. **Investigation of Concentration of Economic Power.** 1941
Weinberg, Herman G. **Josef von Sternberg.** 1967